D1271233

HANDBOOK OF 19TH CENTURY
NAVAL
WARFARE

SPENCER C. TUCKER

NAVAL INSTITUTE PRESS

First published in 2000 by Sutton Publishing Limited, Phoenix Mill, Thrupp, Stroud, Gloucestershire GL5 2BU

Published and distributed in the United States of America and Canada by the Naval Institute Press, 291 Wood Road, Annapolis, MD 21402-5034

Library of Congress Catalog Card Number: 00-103794

ISBN 1-557750-322-2

Manufactured in Great Britain.

CONTENTS

INTRODUCTION

The nineteenth century, and more properly the period 1793–1914, was one of great change in naval architecture, weapons, and warfare at sea. During this era wooden ships gave way to those of iron and steel construction, propulsion changed from sail to steam, and ordnance progressed from iron muzzle-loaders firing 8-inch, 68-pound solid shot to steel breech-loading guns hurling 16-inch shells weighing almost a ton. Submarines and mines came into general use. Automotive torpedoes were developed and naval aviation began; later in the century these two weapons would play decisive roles at sea. Simply put, the nineteenth century saw greater change in naval technology than any other comparable period in history.

In looking for chronological parameters for this book, it seemed logical to open with the Wars of the French Revolution and to end with the start of the First World War. This was the period of British naval mastery, when Britannia truly 'ruled the waves'. The book begins in 1793 with Great Britain taking the lead in the naval war against France to prevent that country from dominating the European continent; it ends in 1914, when Germany sought the same end. British dominance at sea, established during the Wars of the French Revolution and Napoléon, as a consequence of the 1805 Battle of Trafalgar, was not seriously challenged until the end of the nineteenth century, when Germany embarked on a major naval building programme. Despite this, the British had managed to keep well ahead, and by 1914 its fleet was by far the strongest in the world. By keeping the German High Seas Fleet in port and controlling the sea lanes for the Entente Powers, the Royal Navy played a crucial role in the Allied victory in the First World War.

This book concentrates on the evolution of the ships and their ordnance during 1793–1914. It is intended to be a useful introduction to the technological changes of the period as well as an overview of naval warfare. I treat the major naval battles and campaigns at sea to show how the changes in technology played out. I also discuss major policy decisions and motivations behind them, such as Germany's naval challenge to Britain beginning in the mid-1890s, the revival of US naval power at the end of the century, and the factors behind construction of important new ships such as the *Gloire*, *Dreadnought*, and *Holland*. I have also included discussion of some of the principal naval strategists, such as Alfred Thayer Mahan and Louis-Antoine-Richild Grivel. I hope there will be much here to interest both the specialist and general reader.

In investigating the ships I quickly discovered that there are many discrepancies in dimensions and characteristics of individual vessels. For the sake of uniformity, on British vessels at least, I have used statistics found in J.J. Colledge, *Ships of the Royal Navy*. Unless otherwise noted, length of vessels given are those between perpendiculars.

I appreciate the support of Jonathon Falconer of Sutton Publishing. I am grateful to my esteemed colleague Jeremy Black who was kind enough to suggest Sutton as a publisher and to the following colleagues who have both read the manuscript and made many helpful suggestions: Tyrone G. Martin, Eric Osborne, Eugene L. Rasor, Stanley Sandler, Joseph M. Thatcher, and Donald E. Worcester. Sarah Moore of Sutton Publishing, Editor for this book, has been a considerable help. I am also appreciative of financial assistance from the Virginia Military Institute to secure the illustrations, which have come from The US Navy Historical Center; The US Naval Institute; the National Maritime Museum, Greenwich; and the Imperial War Museum, London. As always, I am most grateful to my wife Beverly for her patient support of my long hours at the computer and for her insightful editorial comments.

CHAPTER 1

THE STATE OF NAVAL WARFARE AT THE END OF THE 18TH CENTURY

The beginning of the nineteenth century was the apogee of thousands of years of naval warfare under sail. The classic period of naval warfare, it is today still a source of great interest to writers and painters; for although the warships of this period were instruments of destruction, while under sail, they were objects of great beauty, and the men who manned them inspire us even today because they indeed had 'hearts of oak'.

STRATEGY

Although Alfred Thayer Mahan had yet to popularize the theory in written form, it was patently apparent to most early nineteenth-century statesmen that control of the seas meant world power. To Britain the *raison d'être* behind a strong navy was initially to protect the realm from foreign invasion. In the era before the airplane, so long as Great Britain

Frigate under sail. (*Royal Naval Museum, 1976/272*)

HMS *Victory*. (*Royal Naval Museum, 1956/90*)

controlled the sea approaches and the Channel she was immune from foreign attack.

But for Britain, control of the seas soon became part of a wider strategy. British political leaders saw the benefit that would flow from ready and secure access to foreign markets and raw materials; and control of these resources meant their denial to other powers. Great Britain, leader of the Industrial Revolution that began in the 1770s, used its navy during the Wars of the French Revolution and Napoléon to solidify its control of the worlds' markets. Britain's naval dominance was not seriously challenged until the end of the nineteenth century.

SHIPS

Warships of this period were floating wooden fortresses, propelled by wind and sails. They could have extraordinarily long service lives. HMS *Victory*, possibly the most famous warship in the world, was commissioned in 1765; Admiral Horatio Nelson's flagship in the 1805 Battle of Trafalgar, she was in active sea service for over half a century.[1]

At the end of the eighteenth century ship construction and ordnance had changed but little, although larger vessels were now heavily timbered to enable them to carry batteries of more than 100 heavy guns and to withstand the shock of their discharge. Complementing these were smaller specialized types.

The British did not always build the best ships. Many French and Spanish vessels were more strongly constructed and faster than their British counterparts, and some were more heavily armed. Such differences were trifling, however.[2] Britain's rivals at sea often failed to utilize their naval assets properly – the result of a lack of government commitment, poor leadership, and insufficient training and practice. In any case a vessel's speed was determined less by her design than by her condition and especially whether her hull was clean or fouled with barnacles.

Warships at the end of the eighteenth century were highly specialized. The smallest were gunboats; carrying a variety of rigs, these mounted only one or several guns. Next came cutters – single-masted, fore-and-aft rigged vessels – and brigs, two-masted, square-rigged ships. 'Sloop' was a general term applied to small warships capable of great range that carried their main battery guns on a single deck. This category of light warships might mount between 8 and 24 guns. Small vessels were used where a larger warship was not required, such as in carrying dispatches and escorting merchantmen. Large sloops could also be used to attack enemy commerce. These warships were comparable to twentieth-century frigates and destroyers. By the beginning of the nineteenth century, some sloops were over 100 feet in length and displaced 400–600 tons.

The workhorse of navies in the age of fighting sail was the frigate, comparable in its functions to the later cruiser. Fast and powerful, frigates scouted ahead of the main battle fleet in order to provide warning of the approach of enemy vessels. They also served on detached service and as commerce destroyers. France and the United States in particular embraced the destruction of enemy commerce, known by its French term *guerre de course*.

Frigates were square-rigged ships (each mast had cross yards), mounting their principal ordnance on a single covered gundeck. The open (spar) deck carried the lighter guns. Armament varied greatly, depending on ship size. Small frigates might carry 24–30 guns; the larger ones, 50–60.

Frigates grew in size over the years and, at the beginning of the eighteenth century, were up to 175 feet in length and up to 2,000 tons or more. American frigates of the War of 1812 period were the largest of their class in the world. The *Constitution* is 204 feet in length with a gundeck of 175 feet and extreme beam of 45 feet 2 inches; she displaces 2,200 tons. The *Constitution* mounted 24-pounder long guns as her main battery. The preferred armament for Royal Navy heavy frigates in the early nineteenth century was 18-pounders, for most British captains believed 24-pounders were too heavy for a frigate.[3]

During this period warships had grown both longer and wider in beam, to the maximum size their wooden frames could sustain without 'hogging', that is drooping at the ends. Improvements in rigging and sail system enhanced the manoeuvrability of the largest ships, and the introduction, beginning in the 1770s, of copper sheathing and bolts below the waterline slowed the build up of marine growth that hindered sailing qualities.[4]

The largest and most majestic vessels of the period of fighting sail were ships-of-the-line, or line-of-battle ships (a term that yielded to battleship), so known because with up to 30 inches of wooden planking protection they were capable of standing in the main battle line. These were three-masted, square (full) rigged vessels of two to four gundecks. Over 200 feet in length and 50 feet in beam, they carried crews of 600–800 men. By way of illustration, HMS *Victory* is 227 feet in overall length (186 feet on the gundeck), 52 feet in beam, displaces 3,500 tons, and was armed in 1805 with 104 guns (30 × 32-pounders, 28 × 24-pounders, 44 × 12-pounders, and 2 × 68-pounder carronades).[5]

The bigger the ship, the more expensive it was to build. Thus, in 1789 a British 100-gun ship cost £24 10s per ton, a 74 cost £20 4s, a 36, £14 7s, and a sloop only £12 3s. Contrarily, larger warships were less expensive to maintain per gun than smaller vessels.

Ships were 'rated' according to the number of guns they carried. Despite this rating system, armament varied widely from ship to ship, even among those of the same class. Individual captains had their own preferences and there were frequent changes in regulations.

Ships often carried more guns than their rate because captains generally wanted as much ordnance on their vessels as possible. This was prompted by the desire to be ready to meet an opponent with the maximum possible firepower. It was also a matter of prestige. But overloading a ship affected her sailing qualities and could actually damage a vessel by producing 'hogging,' and thus impede chances of her escaping pursuing ships.

By the time of the French Revolution the smallest ships-of-the-line carried 64 guns, although there were those who believed the smallest that could effectively stand in the line of battle was one rated at 74 guns. The largest first rate ships-of-the-line mounted 120 guns, although a few could carry more; but the workhorse ship-of-the-line at the end of the century was the 74. On the eve of the wars of the French Revolution three-quarters of French Navy ships-of-the-line were 74s, with the remainder being those rated at 80 guns, and the three deckers.[6]

At the turn of the century there was a trend toward larger ships-of-the-line. The world's only four-decker, the Spanish *Santísima Trinidad*, carried 136 guns. The largest ship in the Royal Navy at the end of 1793 was the French-built *Commerce de Marseilles*, a 120-gun behemoth taken during

the British siege of Toulon (August–December 1793).[7]

Most navies possessed ships-of-the-line, but the US Navy had none in active service until after the War of 1812. The *Independence*, launched in 1814, was the first American ship-of-the-line apart from the *America*, which was given to France on her completion in 1782. The *Pennsylvania*, laid down in 1822 and completed in 1837, was the largest US Navy sailing vessel and for a time the largest in the world. Originally designed for 136 guns, her initial armament was 16 × 8-inch shell guns and 104× 32-pounders.[8]

In addition to the smaller warships and ships-of-the-line there were also specialized

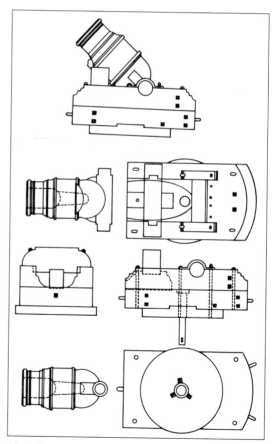

13-inch mortar and bed, drawing by William Clipson. (*Author's Collection*)

vessels. Among these was the bomb brig or bomb ketch, usually referred to simply as a 'bomb'. The French first employed such a vessel, known as the *gáliote à bombe*, at the end of the seventeenth century. This type was derived from the Dutch *galliot*, a short, beamy vessel and an ideal gun platform. Five such vessels took part in the 1682 shelling of Algiers, in which the land forts were destroyed and more than 700 people in them killed. This success at Algiers and another against Genoa two years later started a Mediterranean arms race when the British also built bomb vessels. The bomb vessel was about 100 tons burden and 60–70 feet long on deck. It drew only about 8–10 feet of water, which enabled it to manoeuvre close to shore. It was strongly built to enable it to withstand the shock of the discharge of its heavy mortars and was a fore-and-aft rigged vessel with a tall mainmast and smaller mizzenmast. Bomb vessels carried one or two mortars.[9]

Sailing warships were highly efficient and developed instruments of war. They were also self-contained communities designed to store supplies sufficient for their crews for months at sea in varying weather conditions without revictualling. Supplies included not only food, shot and shell, but any resources the crew might require, including spare cordage and spars sufficient to make most repairs at sea.

ORDNANCE

The largest warships were simply floating batteries designed to carry efficiently the greatest possible amount of ordnance to bring to bear at a particular location. Most ship guns of the period were long guns of the cannon type, a term dating to at least the thirteenth century and derived from the Latin *canna*, meaning 'reed' or 'tube'.[10] All heavy guns were muzzle-loaders. Breech-loaders had distinct advantages in that they could be worked by smaller numbers of men – they did not have to be hauled back into battery after firing – and they could be reloaded more quickly; but metallurgical techniques were not sufficiently developed for the close tolerances required to seal the escape of gases at the breech on the discharge of the gun, especially important with the development of more powerful, grained or corned, gunpowder. Some light guns known as swivels – essentially mankillers for short-range use and mounted in a ship's rail – used the breech-loading principle, but virtually all heavy guns at sea were muzzle-loaders.[11]

Bronze (comprised of ninety parts copper and ten parts tin) had been the favoured metal for cannon. It stood the shock of discharge better than iron, which tended to crack and explode rather than bulge. A gun exploding in the close confines below decks in a ship could have far greater consequences than a comparable event on land. It was also easier to cast, and, despite the fact that bronze was heavier than iron, bronze guns could be cast slimmer and therefore lighter. They could also be embellished with elaborate decoration, unlike guns of iron.

Bronze guns had the serious drawback of being up to three to four times more expensive than iron. Weight was not the factor on board ship that it was for field guns which had to be transported by teams of horses over land, so lower costs ultimately won out. Almost all heavy muzzle-loading warship guns came to be cast of iron.[12]

Britain was a long-time leader in the casting of iron guns, and Royal Navy ordnance was carefully proofed. In 1787 Thomas Blomefield introduced a new pattern gun. Blomefield guns took into account the pressure from the burning of the cannon powder and had a stronger breech. An elliptical bottom to the bore also removed a

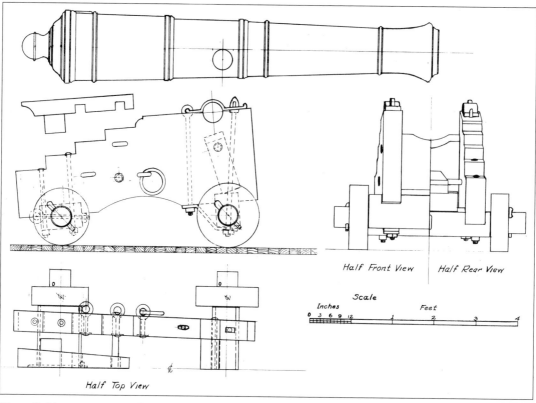

Blomefield pattern gun and carriage, drawing by Cary S. Tucker. (*Author's Collection*)

potential plane of weakness and lessened the possibility of a gun breaking apart during firing. Plainer and more functional in their exterior design, Blomefield guns were able to withstand the more powerful gunpowder produced from cylindrical charcoal. The Blomefield pattern gun also had a distinctive loop cast onto the piece for the reception of breeching. These guns were aboard ships of the Royal Navy in time for the Wars of the French Revolution and Napoléon.[13]

Guns were usually designated by the weight of their solid shot rather than the diameter of their bore. Thus an 18-pounder gun fired a ball weighing 18 lbs. The heavier the gun the more powder it could take and hence the longer the range and greater the velocity of its shot. Thus guns of the same size bore usually appeared in a variety of different classes. In the Royal and US navies these were by hundredweight or cwt (112 lbs). Thus a 56-cwt gun would weigh approximately 6,300 lbs.

Carriages for the guns remained largely unchanged over centuries. Although gunboats might have their main gun on a slide mount in the bow to be trained by turning the vessel, most shipboard guns were on 'truck' carriages, so-called for the four free-moving wheels known as trucks that allowed the gun when fired to recoil back against heavy ropes known as breeching. Once the gun was reloaded its crew hauled it back into battery by rope lines known as tackle, that ran through blocks to bolts on either side of the gunport. The cannon was supported on its carriage by lugs or pivots, known as trunnions, cast perpendicular to the axis of the bore.

6

Most shipboard heavy guns were mounted on carriages on the port and starboard sides of the ship (the broadside batteries). To aid in stabilizing the vessel, the heavier guns were on the lower or gundecks. Only a few long pieces, mounted on the top deck forward or in the stern and known as chase guns, could fire directly ahead or astern. They were sited to engage enemy vessels at long range.

On the gundecks, cannon pointed through the square gunports cut into the sides of the ship and, on the upper deck, through ports in the bulwarks. The bulwarks provided some protection for the gun crews, as did hammocks stored in the netting above. The lower gundecks, with their thick wooden walls, were relatively well protected.

In addition to cannon, the larger vessels carried small, short pieces known as howitzers in their fighting tops, to be utilized as anti-personnel weapons. Also in the latter category were swivel guns, mounted on the rails of smaller vessels. Howitzers and swivels were not counted as part of a ship's armament rating, however.

The table right is the Royal Navy gun establishment for 1792.[14] It illustrates representative armament for vessels during the French Revolution and Napoléonic Wars (all guns are of iron). As can be seen, there was increasing flexibility in the arming of warships. Whereas previously the 74-gun ship had been restricted to a single gun establishment, now there were three possible armament schemes for the rate. Flexibility was increased by the introduction of a new weapon, the carronade (discussed below). Another trend at the end of the eighteenth and early nineteenth centuries was toward standardization of armaments. Thus a ship might have 32-pounder guns on its lower deck but 12-pounders elsewhere. Standardization meant less confusion in the shot room and greater efficiency in battle.

Although guns had remained remarkably unchanged in type over time, there were several innovations. Cannon became smoother in their exterior finish, without the largely ornamental reinforcing rings and fillets. French designs in particular showed this new functional exterior. There was also increasing interest in developing

Rate	Armament
110	30 × 32-pdrs, 30 × 24-pdrs, 32 × 18-pdrs, 18 × 12-pdrs
100	28 × 42-pdrs, 28 × 24-pdrs, 44 × 12-pdrs
100	30 × 32-pdrs, 28 × 24-pdrs, 30 × 18-pdrs, 12 × 12-pdrs
100	30 × 42-pdrs, 28 × 24-pdrs, 42 × 12-pdrs
100	28 × 42-pdrs, 28 × 24-pdrs, 44 × 12-pdrs
98	28 × 32-pdrs, 30 × 18-pdrs, 40 × 12-pdrs
98	28 × 32-pdrs, 28 × 18-pdrs, 42 × 12-pdrs
98	28 × 32-pdrs, 60 × 18-pdrs, 10 × 12-pdrs
90	26 × 32-pdrs, 26 × 18-pdrs, 38 × 12-pdrs
80	30 × 32-pdrs, 32 × 24-pdrs, 18 × 9-pdrs
80	30 × 32-pdrs, 32 × 24-pdrs, 18 × 12-pdrs
74	28 × 32-pdrs, 30 × 24-pdrs, 16 × p-pdrs
74	28 × 32-pdrs, 28 × 18-pdrs, 18 × 9-pdrs
74	28 × 32-pdrs, 30 × 18-pdrs, 16 × 9-pdrs
64	26 × 24-pdrs, 26 × 18-pdrs, 12 × 9-pdrs
50	22 × 24-pdrs, 22 × 12-pdrs, 6 × 6-pdrs
50	42 × 12-pdrs, 8 × 6-pdrs
44	20 × 18-pdrs, 22 × 12-pdrs, 2 × 6-pdrs
40	28 × 18-pdrs, 12 × 9-pdrs
38	28 × 18-pdrs, 2 × 12-pdrs, 8 × 9-pdrs
36	26 × 18-pdrs, 2 × 12-pdrs, 8 × 9-pdrs
32	26 × 18-pdrs, 6 × 6-pdrs
32	26 × 12-pdrs, 6 × 6-pdrs
28	24 × 9-pdrs, 4 × 6-pdrs
24	22 × 9-pdrs, 2 × 6-pdrs
20	20 × 9-pdrs
Sloops	
18	16 × 6-pdrs
16	16 × 6-pdrs
14	14 × 6-pdrs

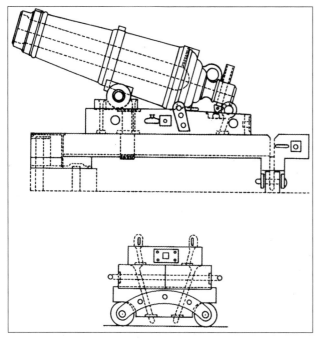

Carronade, drawing by William Clipson. (*Author's collection*)

forecastle. Savings in weight made it especially popular for smaller vessels, and in fact the carronade became the principal armament of brigs. Generally speaking it replaced the small 4- to 12-pounder long guns on board naval vessels. While in the smaller ships there was a shift to carronades, in the larger vessels the long gun remained in favour – although there, too, some carronades were included. At the turn of the nineteenth century the carronade had permeated throughout the Royal Navy: 74-gun ships generally carried the 32-pounder, frigates mounted an occasional 42-pounder, and bomb vessels had the 68-pounder.[16]

The French also employed the carronade, which they spelled, 'caronade.' The French Navy first adopted it in 1787 under the name of *obusiers de vaisseaux* (ship howitzers). The first French carronades were of bronze. Throughout the period through to 1856 the French Navy introduced new carronade models.[17]

The true carronade had no trunnions but was mounted on its bed by means of a bolt through a loop cast on the underside of the piece. All carronades were short, only about seven calibres (one calibre being the diameter of the bore) in length. Royal Navy carronades weighed about 50–60 lbs of metal for every pound of shot. US Navy carronades were closely patterned after those of the Royal Navy but were heavier, 60–70 lbs of metal for every pound of shot. This is in contrast to as much as 150–200 lbs of metal for every pound of shot in long guns.

The carronade used approximately one-third the powder charge of the long gun. Owing to its low muzzle velocity, windage could be sharply reduced. The carronade's ball moved at relatively slow velocity but produced a large irregular hole and considerable splintering.

shorter long guns. While these did not have the range of longer guns of the same calibre, this disadvantage was offset by their lighter weight, which meant smaller gun crews.

THE CARRONADE

The principal naval ordnance innovation at the end of the eighteenth century was the carronade.[15] Named for the Carron Company of Scotland, which produced the prototype in 1776, it was a short, light piece of large bore. The carronade appeared first in the Royal Navy at the beginning of the War of the American Revolution, was used more extensively in the wars of the French Revolution and Napoléon, and reached its greatest utilization in the War of 1812.

The lightness of the carronade enabled it to be employed where a heavier gun could not be supported, as on the poop or

While ideally suited for close actions, the carronade had its disadvantages. One was its excessive recoil; another was that, as it was so short, burning powder from it might ignite the ship's side or rigging. Its chief weakness, however, was its lack of range. Carronades were employed at point-blank, which meant about 450 yards for a 68-pounder and 230 yards for a 12-pounder. If the fighting was at long range, the carronade was a liability, as was revealed during the War of 1812.

By 1812 carronades had not only replaced smaller long guns but were also carried on the upper decks of frigates. Although most captains preferred the long gun for chase purposes and as a main armament, many smaller warships were armed exclusively with carronades. Thus during the War of 1812, in a battle fought at close-quarters, 32-pounder carronades on the USS *Wasp* inflicted heavy damage on HMS *Frolic*, also armed largely with carronades. The same was true in the victory won by the USS *Hornet* over HMS *Peacock*, another contest in which carronades were the principal armament.

The War of 1812 revealed its fatal weakness and heralded the end of the carronade. While a formidable weapon at close range, at longer range it was no match for long guns, even of smaller calibre. British carronade-armed vessels on Lakes Erie and Ontario were at a decided disadvantage when they confronted American warships, most of which were armed with more long guns.

Late in the war the tables were turned on the US Navy when its frigate *Essex*, armed almost exclusively with carronades, was defeated at long range by the British warships *Phoebe* and *Cherub*, both armed with long guns. This engagement considerably tarnished the reputation of the carronade and reinforced the conclusion that vessels should not be armed exclusively with them.

THE COLUMBIAD AND CONGREVE GUN

Among other new gun designs was the columbiad, the first American shell gun, produced during the War of 1812. It was a short, rather light weapon designed as an alternative to the carronade and usually designated as an 18-pounder. It may have been a rebored cannon. Lieutenant George Bomford (1750–1848), later head of the Army Ordnance Department, is generally credited with its invention. A chambered gun that combined certain features of the gun, howitzer and mortar, and fired either shot or shell, the columbiad was employed during the War of 1812 both in coastal defence and aboard some US Navy vessels, although its use onboard ship seems to have been limited largely to gunboats and a few larger vessels, all of them on the Great Lakes. A 50-pounder columbiad of about 7.4-inch smooth bore remains in the United States Military Academy collection at West Point. The columbiad is usually regarded as a transitional piece between the carronade and the later Paixhans gun. Some Americans later charged that Colonel Henri Paixhans of France simply expropriated Bomford's invention.

The British had the Congreve gun, designed by Sir William Congreve in 1814. It appeared in only one class: a 24-pounder, 7 feet 6 inches in length, weighing approximately 4,592 lbs. The Congreve gun's relatively smooth exterior form and single-curved breech may have influenced subsequent designs in England and the United States.

WAR ROCKETS

Another weapon employed at the beginning of the nineteenth century was the war rocket, actually the oldest of all explosively propelled projectiles. The Chinese had for centuries used rockets as anti-cavalry weapons, but it was their use in India by Tipu Sultan at the siege of Seringapatam in 1799 that gave Sir William Congreve the idea of improving on it. He made rockets weighing from two ounces – 'a species of self-moving musket balls' – to ones of over 300 lbs. In 1806 his rockets were successfully tested in an attack on the French port of Boulogne, and they were used with equal effectiveness in bombarding Copenhagen in 1807. They were also employed in the War of 1812, the 'rocket's red glare' providing inspiration for Francis Scott Key in writing the 'Star Spangled Banner.'

Continued experiments, however, failed to correct the rocket's problems of eccentricity in flight and instability. Because rockets often exploded prematurely, crews were reluctant to use them. Rockets also tended to deteriorate in storage. Their promise was not fulfilled until the Second World War.

ORDNANCE PRACTICE

Although navies experimented with the largest calibre guns, these proved too unwieldy, difficult to load, and had too great a recoil. The most common large long gun in service at the end of the eighteenth century, and only on ships-of-the-line, was the 36-pounder. The *Victory*, which had fought the Battle of Cape St Vincent (1797) with a lower-deck battery of 42-pounders, was armed at Trafalgar (1805) with 32s.

The 36-pounder was also the largest gun in common use aboard French ships-of-the-line. The US Navy, with only frigates, relied on the 24-pounder long gun and the 32-pounder carronade, although in the War of 1812 32-pounder long guns and 42-pounder carronades did see naval service.[18]

The table below compares US Navy cannon (the longest, or chase guns) and carronades:

	length ft-in	weight lbs	Powder charge lbs-oz	Bore diameter inches	Shot diameter inches
68-pdr carronade	5–2	4,032	6–0	8.05	8.000
42-pdr long gun	10–0	7,504	14–0	7.018	6.684
42-pdr carronade	4–3.5	2,492	4–8	6.85	6.684
32-pdr long gun	10–0	6,496	10–11	6.41	6.105
32-pdr carronade	4–0.5	1,918	4–0	6.25	6.105
24-pdr long gun	10–0	5,824	8–0	5.824	5.547
24-pdr carronade	3–7.5	1,456	3–0	5.67	5.547
18-pdr long gun	9–6	4,704	6–0	5.292	5.040
18-pdr carronade	3–3	1,008	2–0	5.14	5.040
12-pdr long gun	9–6	3,808	4–0	4.623	4.403
12-pdr carronade	2–2	654	1–8	4.50	4.403
9-pdr long gun	9–6	3,388	3–0	4.200	4.00
6-pdr long gun	9–0	2,688	2–0	3.668	3.498
4-pdr long gun	6–0	1,372	1–5	3.204	3.053
3-pdr long gun	4–6	812	1–0	2.913	1.775

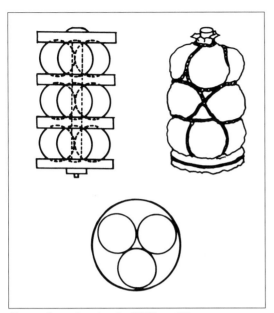

Grape shot, drawing by William Clipson.
(*Author's collection*)

Range of guns varied according to the powder charge and elevation. For example, in 1812 the shot for a long gun charged with powder one-third the weight of the ball and at an elevation of two degrees, reached 1,200 yards on the first graze. A charge of one-quarter and the same elevation propelled the shot to 1,000 yards for a first graze, although double shot with the same charge and elevation reached only 500 yards. At seven degrees elevation and a charge of one-quarter, a single shot reached 2,020 yards at first graze. The precise weight of powder charge was not fixed until the nineteenth century; often these were at the whim of the individual ship captain or even gunner.

Projectiles consisted of solid shot, explosive shell, and – for close-in action – canister and grape. All weighed approximately the same as a solid ball of the same size. Solid shot, commonly called 'shot,' was the projectile most often employed at sea during the period. It was designed not so much to damage a ship, which if taken was usually incorporated into the victor's navy, but to inflict personnel casualties. Solid shot could have a bowling-ball effect in the close confines of a ship, especially if it was being raked from bow or stern.

Shot produced the splintering of wood that was so lethal in the close confines of a ship. Reduced charges and lower velocity for the projectile maximized this splintering effect. In fact, 'man killing' rather than 'ship killing' won battles. Very few ships were actually sunk in battle.

Other projectiles included disabling shot, which was fired high to damage the sails and rigging of an opponent, and grape and canister shot for close actions. Grape consisted of smaller balls positioned around a stand and enclosed in canvas, wound with rope so that it rather resembled a cluster of grapes; the balls separated when fired. Grape was used at short range against personnel and small craft. Canister was scrap metal (langrage) and/or musket balls packed in tin canisters with sawdust. It was intended for use at the closest ranges against personnel. In close action, guns

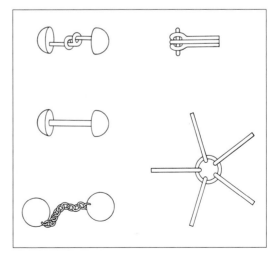

Disabling shot to be fired at masts and rigging, drawing by William Clipson. (*Author's collection*)

might be double- and even triple-shotted, but this meant a considerable loss in velocity for the projectiles.

At the end of the eighteenth century most guns were fired by means of a match to the touch hole, into which a tube filled with fine gunpowder had been inserted. In 1778 Royal Navy captain Sir Charles Douglas of HMS *Duke* paid to have guns aboard his ship fitted with musket locks. Among his other ordnance innovations was the use of powder-filled goose quill tubes to prime the guns; these were both cheaper and less dangerous than those of iron. He also installed flintlocks on his next ship, HMS *Formidable*. Flintlocks produced a faster and more reliable rate of fire and gave gun captains control over the timing of the fire, especially important at sea because the rolling of a ship affected gun elevation. The advantages were made clear to the rest of the fleet in the Royal Navy's victory in April 1782 at the Battle of the Saintes. Finally in 1790, when a new bronze model became available, the Royal Navy officially adopted the flintlock for its warships. Other navies followed suit and flintlocks were widely in use during the Napoléonic Wars, although at Trafalgar the French were still using the match. In 1818 Sir Charles's son Howard Douglas introduced an even more reliable double flintlock, later copied in other navies.[19]

Possibly the most important military innovation of the first half of the nineteenth century was the percussion cap, made possible by the discovery of fulminate of mercury in 1800. Seven years later a Scots Presbyterian minister, Alexander Forsyth (1769–1843), patented the use of mercuric fulminates as priming for firearms and so created the possibility of applying automation to the discharge of lethal projectiles. Before this, all guns – large and small – were fired by a priming charge of fine powder. Forsyth's fulminates did not need fire to set them off; they detonated when struck a sharp blow, and a gun fitted with a cap containing a small quantity of fulminate and placed over the fire hole, with a simple trigger-controlled hammer with which to strike it, could be fired and reloaded more rapidly than a flintlock and was reliable in all weather conditions. Efforts were made to apply this principle to cannon, and percussion firing devices were applied to ship batteries. In 1828 the *Vandalia* was the first US Navy warship to have its entire battery so equipped. The percussion cap replaced other ignition devices on small guns, and it brought near certainty of discharge and more precise timing of fire. Friction primers were also developed but rarely used at sea.[20]

NAVAL GUNNERY

Gun sights at sea were virtually unknown until the early nineteenth century. Guns were trained laterally by tackle and wooden handspikes and were elevated or depressed by a wooden wedge ('quoin') under the breech.

During battle all those aboard ship went to previously assigned stations or 'quarters.' Gun crews varied in size. For example, a 24-pounder in the US Navy was manned by between 9 and 14 men, depending on the weight of the gun and the size of the ship's company. Gun crews were nominally responsible for two guns: those in the respective positions on each side of the ship. But it was quite difficult to fight both sides of the ship at once because of the shortage of manpower; and, as battles progressed, men might become casualties or be required to man pumps, put out fires, or perform other duties. Usually ships fought only one side at a time. Well-trained Royal Navy crews could fire three rounds in five minutes, but that was the exception and could not be sustained for long. During the lengthy wars with France, British gun crews were, on a ship-by-ship basis, probably the best in the world. The fact that the British could reload and fire a gun at up to twice the speed of their French counterparts had much to do with the victory at Trafalgar in 1805.[21]

CREWS AND TRAINING

Warships were virtual floating cities. At the Battle of Trafalgar HMS *Victory* carried 821 officers and men. The large US Navy frigate *Constitution* carried a crew of 450–500.

Warships were complex, highly intricate organizations, and at sea long training and drill were essential to success in battle, let alone survival. Crews were trained by the officers, warrant officers and petty officers. Well-trained crews had a great advantage in battle, both in manoeuvring their vessels and in producing rapid and well-aimed fire against an opponent.[22]

A classic example of this is the case of the one-on-one frigate battle between HMS *Shannon* and USS *Chesapeake* on 1 June 1813, the bloodiest frigate action of the War of 1812. The battle also showed the disparity in rate and actual armament: the *Shannon*, rated at 38 guns, actually carried 52; while the *Chesapeake*, rated at 36, in fact carried 50 guns.

Captain James Lawrence of the *Chesapeake* foolishly decided to fight Captain Philip Broke's *Shannon*. Lawrence had been in command of the frigate less than two weeks, and his inexperienced crew was unused to its vessel; in contrast, Broke commanded the *Shannon* since 1806. His vessel was probably the most proficient gunnery platform in the entire Royal Navy. Broke had trained the crew in concentrated fire, whereby the deck was marked in degrees

and all guns were laid on the principle of converging lines. He had also spent his own money to equip his ship with the latest aiming devices and was a staunch advocate of realistic gunnery training reinforced by frequent drill. Broke was said to have directed his men during the action: 'Throw no shot away. Aim every one. Keep cool. Work steadily. Fire into her quarters. Don't try to dismast her. Kill the men, and the ship is yours.' This effectively summed up British gunnery practice of the period.[23]

Not surprisingly the artillery duel that ensued favoured the better trained side. Ultimately, the British lost 33 men killed in action and 43 wounded (including Broke), though many of these were lost while boarding. The Americans had 62 killed (including Lawrence) and 85 wounded. The *Chesapeake* was taken into the Royal Navy, where she served until 1815.[24]

TACTICS

Success in naval warfare depended on carrying out instructions quickly and accurately; rapid changes during a battle, upon which victory or defeat might hinge, could be carried out only by well-trained crews. Experience and effective training were thus immensely important. Before the French Revolution well-trained French crews could manage to steer six points off the wind when close hauled; British crews normally steered only seven points from the wind.[25]

French training fell off precipitously during the Wars of the French Revolution and Napoléon, and this was certainly a major factor in British success at sea. Royal Navy ships spent many months in blockade duties in all kinds of weather off the French-controlled European ports, and this denied the French crews sea experience in squadron manoeuvres.

At the beginning of a war, when a nation had to take its warships out of ordinary ('moth balls' is the term used today) and new ships had to be constructed, many seamen and officers were untrained. Admirals thus found it impossible to carry out complicated manoeuvres. It was only towards the end of a war when experience was high that this could be accomplished. An anonymous British admiral summed this up when he wrote of the Battle of the 'Glorious First of June' (1794) that it 'was the *first* general action fought in the course of the war, and led to many glorious results; had it been the last, not one of the French ships would have been allowed to return to port.'[26]

In part because of the lower level of experience aboard their warships in the Wars of the French Revolution and Napoléon, many French captains and admirals sought to preserve their own ships rather than try to destroy their opponent. They sought engagements that would allow them to preserve their options: to stand off at long range to lee (from the wind) and fire high in order to damage masts, spars, and rigging. In the opinion of British admiral Sir Philip Broke, this was more often due to accident than design:

> The effects of fire of the French ships of war upon our masts and rigging was partly owing to their acting upon the dismasting system and much also in latter times to bad gunnery – firing upon the line of metal (even when designing to hull a ship) and supposing it to be horizontal aim, and what was still worse, firing and loading in such a confused way when they began to feel alarmed that if the quoin [the wooden wedge used for elevation] jumped down the hatchway at the recoil of the gun it was often fired without one.[27]

British captains, on the other hand, usually sought the weather gage (position to windward of their opponent) to close to short ranges and so be able to fire into the hull of the opposing vessel and/or take her by boarding. Marines, who were aboard ships primarily to provide security, were of particular value in such circumstances. They used their small arms to shoot members of the opposing crew, especially their officers. Admiral Nelson met his death in this fashion. French ships often carried larger crews and even took infantry to sea in attempts to take opposing vessels by boarding. Such actions were often desperate, hand-to-hand affairs in which firearms were of less utility than swords, cutlasses and axes.

Although the sides of ships-of-the-line were heavily timbered, there were openings at the gunports. A well-placed shot, or concentration thereof, could create havoc inside, dismounting guns and causing horrible casualties among personnel. A chance shot could also damage the base of a mast. But aiming high was a valid tactic. A lucky shot there could bring down a mast, yards and sail, obscuring vision and disabling a vessel, enabling her to be raked and forced to surrender.

Individual ship actions were fought as circumstances dictated. With virtually all the heavy guns in broadside along the length of the two sides of the ship and effective ranges relatively short, most engagements took place at short distance, sometimes even gunport to gunport and with the ships lashed together. This was the case in one of history's best-known individual ship actions, the 23 September 1779 engagement between the American frigate *Bonhomme Richard* and the British ship *Serapis*.[28]

If possible a captain positioned his vessel so as to enable him to rake his opponent. This meant manoeuvring his own ship so

One of the bloodiest single-ship actions of the age of fighting sail. USS *Bonhomme Richard* vs HMS *Serapis* off Flamborough Head, England, 23 September 1779. Painting by William Elliott, RN, *c.* 1780, in US Naval Academy Museum. (*Naval Historical Foundation, NH 61851*)

that it was broadside to an opponent vessel's bow or stern to enable all of his port or starboard broadside guns to bear while the opposing vessel could respond with only a few bow or stern guns. The bow and stern of a ship were also much weaker than its sides, especially the stern, which had at least one row of windows. Raking also meant more opportunity to damage a vessel and inflict personnel casualties because the length of the target vessel was exposed. Raking was therefore the preferred way to engage another vessel.

Squadron and fleet tactics were notoriously difficult to execute properly, and admirals faced a considerable challenge in carrying out the highly standardized squadron tactics laid down in fighting instructions that had changed little over the centuries. Sailing vessels relied on the wind for their motive power. Even if the wind were blowing, and often it was not, at no time could the admiral make use of more than five-eighths of the sea because his vessels could not sail directly into the wind. Progress into the wind could be made only by tacking across from one side to the other, and never closer than six points of the compass (67.5 degrees).

In fleet engagements frigates scouted ahead to locate the enemy. A chief failing of admirals in this period was in not

A broadsides action off Trieste, 22 February 1812, between HMS *Victorious* and French 74 *Rivoli*. HM Brig *Weazel* in attendance to left. (*Royal Naval Museum, 1976/150*)

maintaining adequate reconnaissance to provide warning of the approach of an opposing fleet. This happened to Admiral Comte François-Joseph Paul de Grasse when he was surprised at Yorktown in 1781 by the arrival of a British fleet and was obliged to put to sea short-handed. Another French admiral, François Brueys d'Aiguilliers, also failed to use his frigates adequately before the 1798 Battle of the Nile and Nelson surprised him there.

Once enemy vessels were located, the frigates signalled with flags, often in relay over the horizon, as before the Battle of Trafalgar. When the two opposing fleets came within direct sight of each another, one was usually to windward and thus held what was termed the weather gage. This was a considerable advantage in that it allowed that side to choose whether, when, and how to attack. Because of this both sides usually tried to secure the windward, although the lee gage preserved the option of being able to escape if necessary. All this was complicated by the fact that wind and weather were subject to frequent, sometimes dramatic, change, and if the fleets were near land the admiral also had to take into consideration tides and currents. If the wind dropped altogether, as after the 5 September 1781, Battle of the Chesapeake, the two sides were left immobilized and unable to change position or close, let alone form in order of battle. If vessels on one side failed to maintain position, it could lead to defeat. Admiral Sir John Jervis, Earl of St Vincent, asserted, 'Two fleets of equal strength can never produce decisive events,

A ship being raked. Action off Trieste, 22 February 1812, between HMS *Victorious* and French 74 *Rivoli*. (*Royal Naval Museum, 1976/251*)

unless they are equally determined to fight it out or the Commander-in-Chief of one of them so bitches it as to misconduct his line.'[29]

French Admiral Charles-Henri Comte d'Estaing defeated Vice Admiral John Byron off Granada on 6 July 1779, largely because Byron's fleet had become dispersed during the night. Because of the need to maintain control, admirals generally avoided night actions. Nelson, however, risked this in the Battle of the Nile (Aboukir Bay), an engagement begun in the late afternoon that extended well into the night of 1 August 1798.

Fighting instructions specified linear tactics. These brought the greatest number of guns to bear and had the advantage of being pre-arranged and easy to enforce.

Battles were tightly choreographed according to near-rigid rules. Admiral Sir John Byng, loser of the 20 May 1756, Battle of Minorca, was court-martialled '*pour encourager les autres*,' or as Byng put it, 'They make a precedent of me such as admirals hereafter may feel the effects of.' The excuse for his conviction and execution was not that he had lost the battle; Byng was acquitted of disaffection and cowardice, but rather he was found guilty of 'neglect of duty in battle', i.e. violation of the fighting instructions.[30]

In a fleet action the two opposing fleets arrayed themselves similarly in three divisions: van, centre, and rear. Communication by signal flag, however, meant that captains along the line were unable to see a flag hoisted in the centre and so signalling was sequential rather than immediate. The larger the fleet, the more difficult it was to control and the longer it took to manoeuvre it into position. Tacking into the wind and wearing or gybing (changing course with the wind astern) were difficult manoeuvres and taxing for officers and crews. Each ship hoisted the flag shown by the ship ahead. Captains had to be able to hold their precise place in the battle line for their ship, on the course set by the admiral and at a set distance from the ship in front. Keeping exact station in the battle line was essential; in close order, collisions were a constant danger.

With each ship following the other and turning at the same place as its predecessor, it meant that the vans engaged before the centres, and the centres before the rears. This enabled a fleet downwind, if hard pressed, to break off the engagement. The result was a slow-to-develop battle with each ship following the one ahead of it in two long stately lines.

During the War of the American Revolution, except when led by Admiral Pierre André de Suffron, French fleets never attacked. Instead they relied on what had been their practice throughout the eighteenth century – when opposed by a fleet of comparable strength, they went on the defensive. Nonetheless, the French were able, until the very end of the war, to outpoint the British again and again.

Unlike the British, who had Home Popham's excellent new signalling system, the French slavishly followed the overly complicated method of tactics and signals developed by the Vicomte de Morogues in his, *Tatique Navale ou Traité des . . . volutions et des Signaux* (1763). As late as 1806 the French Navy rejected a numerical signalling system in favour of the complex scheme introduced by Captain du Pavillon in 1776. This continued in use until the end of the

Napoléonic Wars. The French Navy also rejected new tactics advocated by French naval theorists the Vicomte de Grenier, the Comte d'Amblimont, Ramatuelle, and Le Chevalier Delarouvraye.[31]

When one fleet attacked another already in line, the customary procedure was to make a slow and stately approach, maintaining alignment. This might mean an advance, even with a stiff breeze, of as little as four knots. Hours and even days might be spent getting into position, or trying to do so, as in the days of inconclusive manoeuvring following the 1781 Battle of the Chesapeake. This also meant that sometimes victors were incapable of pursuit, as after the 1782 Battle of the Saintes.

In 1697 Père Paul Hoste, a Jesuit who had been Vice Admiral Comte Anne-Hilarion de Tourville's chaplain, published *L'Art des armées navales*. The first great study of naval tactics under sail, it laid out three possibilities for fleet battles. The first of these was 'massing', in which the attacker concentrated the bulk of his ships against a segment of the enemy line. This was accomplished by reducing the interval between the ships in order to achieve a decisive mastery at one particular point in the line. The remainder of the ships either ahead or astern would be stretched thin in an effort to contain the remainder of the enemy line.

The second major tactic was 'doubling', whereby the attacker passed ships, moving in the same direction, on both sides of one end of an enemy line in order to take the enemy vessels under fire from both sides concurrently; this would force the enemy crews to work both the port and starboard batteries at once. De Tourville had doubled the Allied van in the 1690 Battle of Beachy Head. Doubling presumed a larger attacking force, however.

The third major tactic against an enemy fleet was 'breaking'. In this case the attacking fleet might be in line ahead formation, coming from the enemy rear. Sailing parallel, it would then break through the enemy line at some point, doubling the enemy line by passing back on its opposite side and forcing the enemy crews to fight both sides of their vessels simultaneously.[32]

As the opposing fleets closed, crews were called to battle stations and ordered to run out the guns. When the ships were in position, the two opposing fleets blasted away at each other until individual vessels sustained sufficient casualties or, less likely, were damaged, usually in their rigging, to the point that their captains surrendered or 'struck'. It was unusual for a vessel to be sunk by cannon fire. Wooden ships could absorb tremendous punishment from solid shot, as is shown in the case of the Royal Navy ship-of-the-line *Impregnable* (98 guns) at Algiers in August 1816. Hit by 233 large shot in her hull, she still sailed to Gibraltar for repair. On 30 March 1800, the British 80-gun *Foudroyant* fired 200 12-pounder, 100 18-pounder, 1,240 24-pounder, and 1,200 32-pounder shot – in all 2,740 shot – at close range at the 80-gun French warship *Guillaume Tell* before the latter struck; two other British ships, the 64-gun *Lion* and the 36-gun frigate *Penelope* were firing at the French ship at the same time. The *Guillaume Tell* not only survived but was later incorporated into the Royal Navy.[33]

Occasionally a ship caught fire and was lost from that or from an explosion of its magazine. On 22 September 1796, while completing repairs at Plymouth dockyard, the frigate *Amphion* suddenly blew up. She was scheduled to sail the next day and had many families on board. All but 12 of the 312 people on board her that day died, although her captain, Israel Pellew, survived when the explosion blew him out of a captain's cabin window at her stern!

Magazine explosions were rare but seamen feared them more than any other hazard.[34]

Captured ships were closely studied and had their lines copied off. They were then usually taken into the victor's navy. Early in the nineteenth century the Royal Navy forcibly incorporated a number of ships of other nations into its fleet, as after it attacked and seized the Danish fleet at Copenhagen in September 1807.

More often than not it seems, battle instructions produced indecisive results, such as in the 1781 Battle of the Chesapeake. In part because of a failure to coordinate signals, British Vice Admiral Samuel Graves and Rear Admiral Sir Samuel Hood were unable to bring all of their line to close with the French battle line; and the resulting engagement ended up little more than a stately promenade. Despite its inconclusive nature, the battle was decisive because it left the French in control of the Bay. Denied means of resupply or evacuation, Major General Charles Cornwallis was obliged to surrender his land force, a third of the British Army in North America.[35]

The revolutionary answer to line-to-line formations was 'breaking'. In the 1782 Battle of the Saintes, Admiral Sir George Rodney inadvertently struck a blow for innovation in naval tactics when he broke the French line of battle. This was not premeditated and was largely the result of circumstances: a shift in the wind caused the French ships to turn toward the British line to maintain steerage way, and inevitably gaps opened between them. Sir Charles Douglas, captain of Rodney's flagship, urged him to exploit the situation by breaking the French line. After hesitation, Rodney so ordered; five ships astern followed the flagship. In the confusion of the smoke of battle, the British penetrated the French line in three places. Although a melée did not result, this action allowed the British to capture five French ships. It was the Royal Navy's first tactical success in a stand-up fleet action since the Battle of Barfleur in 1692, and it had a profound influence, showing what might be accomplished with innovative tactics.[36]

This process was completed in the Royal Navy by new signals and fighting instructions, both thanks to Admiral Lord Richard Howe, who had charge of the North American Station during the War of the American Revolution. Howe issued the Navy's first *Signal Book for the Ships of War*, along with a separate set of instructions. By 1790 this evolved into a numerical system based on ten flags, numbered 0 to 9. As many as four could be displayed at one time, giving a possibility of 9,999 separate instructions, although in actual fact there were only a few hundred. Within a few years this system had been adopted, either *in toto* or with minor variations, by every British fleet commander.

Howe's new fighting instructions were also revolutionary because they included provision for breaking an enemy line. This was not new, of course, but in the old tactic the enemy line was pierced with each succeeding ship following its predecessor in line and moving through at the same point. Howe's innovation was to range his ships in line-ahead formation next to the enemy battle line and then have them all suddenly turn to pass under the stern of their counterpart vessels in the opposing battle line, coming about on the enemy's

previously unengaged side. In 1794 Howe, commanding the Channel Fleet, put his ideas into practice. In the Battle of the Glorious First of June, although only his flagship and six other ships managed to break the enemy line, the remainder pressed closely and the melée battle that ensued led to six French ships being captured and a seventh sunk. Nelson's later method was to break through at a single point or a few points. Most admirals, however, were either unsure of or reluctant to trust their subordinates and preferred to keep the close control of the line-ahead formation.[37]

Breaking an enemy line was possible in the Royal Navy thanks to the revolution in signals developed by Captain (later Rear Admiral Sir) Home Popham's new signalling system spelled out in *Telegraphic Signals or Marine Vocabulary* (1803). The Admiralty did not formally adopt this signals system, in more sophisticated form, until 1816, replacing that developed by Howe. It was, however, already in extensive use; and Nelson was able to exploit this preceding the Battle of Trafalgar, arranging his frigates so that they could relay information to him over the horizon. This allowed him to maintain a loose blockade in order to entice the French out, yet he was quickly informed when they did put to sea. This system also enabled him to control his ships perfectly in the resulting battle that established Britain as the dominant power at sea for the remainder of the nineteenth century.[38]

CHAPTER 2

THE WARS OF THE FRENCH REVOLUTION AND NAPOLÉON

BRITAIN VERSUS FRANCE AND NEARLY EVERYONE ELSE, 1793–1815

BALANCE OF FORCES

The great sea wars of the age of fighting sail were waged in the eighteenth and early nineteenth centuries between Britain and France. If there is truth to the statement that the British were sea creatures whereas the French were land animals, it was because of the accident of geography. With no domestic enemies save the Irish, Britain did not fear invasion as long as her navy remained strong. Even in the twentieth century the British regular army was small and fashioned for colonial requirements rather than the great wastages of continental war. With no need for a large army, Britain could concentrate her relatively limited resources on the navy. Save during the War of the American Revolution, which she fought alone, Britain resorted to subsidies to keep her continental allies in the wars against France on land.

Lacking natural frontiers in the north-east, France, however, was obliged to maintain a strong army, if only for defensive purposes. For this reason, and because during much of this period France was in fact waging war to push its frontier to the Rhine River in the north-east, its navy came in a poor second.

Also critical was the difference in the way in which resources were managed. Although France was by far the wealthiest state in Europe in 1789, its government was unable to utilize the national resources effectively because it was chronically poor – the result of an inefficient, corrupt and unfair system of taxation. Britain, with far less in the way of resources, was simply much better administered.

The War of the League of Augsburg (1688–97) was a turning point for France on the seas. In the 10 July 1690, Battle of Beachy Head, French Vice Admiral Count Anne-Hillarion de Tourville gained the greatest victory ever by a French fleet. With 75 ships he decisively defeated Admiral Arthur Herbert, Earl of Torrington's Anglo-Dutch fleet of 59 ships. The Allies lost 12 ships in the battle. Because the battle had occurred in the English Channel it had great strategic possibilities, but the French had not made any preparations for an invasion and could not exploit the victory.

During 29 May–3 June 1692, the situation was reversed. This time the French planned an invasion, but de Tourville was forced to put to sea despite unfavourable winds that prevented the Toulon fleet from making contact. A French fleet of 44 ships went up against an allied force of 63 English and 36 Dutch warships off Cape Barfleur. The French sank two ships without loss to themselves, but their battered fleet disintegrated in the allied pursuit, and fireships and boat parties destroyed 15 French ships that had taken refuge at Cherbourg and in the Bay of La Hogue. The Battle of Barfleur (also known as La Hogue) was arguably the most important of the war. In what was perhaps a crucial mistake in policy, France abandoned its effort to control the seas. Instead of pursuing a *guerre d'escadre* (squadron warfare, meaning fleet operations), France now adopted the policy of a *guerre de course.*

Following the Seven Years' War (1756–63) the French Navy did enjoy a brief renaissance. On the eve of the War of the American Revolution, France had 73 ships-of-the-line and 52 frigates. Together the French and Spanish had 90 ships-of-the-line, the British only 73. Taking advantage of her naval strength, in the War of the American Revolution France assisted the colonies in separating from Britain. France thus avenged the humiliation of the Seven Years' War but at prohibitive cost; and, much to the chagrin of France, after the war the former American colonies maintained and even increased their trade with Britain. Building and maintaining her revived fleet during the War of the American Revolution strained an already overburdened French treasury, and the resulting debt forced the crown to summon the Estates General, which led directly to the French Revolution.

In 1789, at the start of the French Revolution, France still had 63 ships-of -the-line and eight more under construction as well as 64 frigates. In 1791 the French had 70 ships-of-the-line and 65 frigates, while the British had 135 ships-of-the-line. For a variety of reasons, including the distraction of the Revolution, the loss of many capable Royalist captains, and the pre-eminent claims of the French Army, by 1793 the French Navy had only 53 ships-of-the-line.[1]

At the beginning of 1793, although many of the ships were in ordinary (mothballs) or undergoing repair, the Royal Navy had 279 rated ships manned by 88,500 men; in 1795, it had 326 and 100,000 respectively; and in 1796, 376 and 110,000. By 1803 the Royal Navy had increased in size to 770 ships (397 rated and 373 others). During this period the Royal Navy lost 73 rated ships and 153 others, and many were also broken up, so there was actually a greater gain in numbers of ships than is apparent above. One source estimates that as many as 1,250 ships and small craft entered the Royal Navy at this time.[2] The naval imbalance between Britain and France continued to grow under Napoléon Bonaparte, for in 1804 the French had only 60 ships-of-the-line and 32 frigates to contest 120 British ships-of-the-line.[3]

The inequity at sea between Britain and France was somewhat offset by the fact that some French ships were larger and hence carried more guns. British naval historian William James calculated the actual imbalance in total broadside weight of metal that could be thrown by individual guns at 88,957 lbs for the British and 73,957 lbs for the French.[4] But this does not address such matters as leadership and training.

During the Wars of the French Revolution and Napoléon, Britain's primary weapon against France and her allies was blockade. In more than two decades of war this effort provided the training for officers and seamen in all weathers so necessary for success in battle at sea. Certainly the blockade was costly and extraordinarily taxing on officers and men alike. Admiral Horatio Nelson went from June 1802 to July 1805 without leaving the *Victory* and Admiral Cuthbert Collingwood was once at sea for 22 months without dropping anchor; but such feats of endurance paid handsome dividends. Providing Royal Navy officers and seamen with invaluable experience, the blockade denied the same to the French.[5]

Superior training and leadership more than offset any inadequacies in British individual ship construction. Time and again the outcome of battles turned on better British seamanship. Equipped with Popham's new signals, aggressive British captains sought to close with and destroy an enemy vessel or fleet rather than be content with an exchange of long-range fire.

Although Britain and France were the chief sea powers at the end of the eighteenth century, many other states had sizable naval establishments. This table for 1790, published in 1810, is, however, only approximate and does not address the serviceability of vessels:[6]

Country	Ships-of-the-line	Frigates	Total vessels
Britain	195	210	661
France	81	69	291
Spain	72	41	222
Russia	67	36	803
Holland	44	43	187
Denmark	38	20	118
Turkey	30	59	180
Sweden	27	12	79
Venice	20	19	88
Portugal	10	14	53
Naples	10	10	32
Totals	594	515	2714

It is readily apparent from the above that although Britain eclipsed France in naval strength, if the latter could combine her navy with those of other powers she could threaten British mastery. British naval and political leaders were well aware of this fact, which helped dictate London's strategy at sea.

THE WARS OF THE FRENCH REVOLUTION AND NAPOLÉON

The Wars of the French Revolution and Napoléon began in the spring of 1792 when France declared war on Austria and Prussia. The war was prompted by the French desire for territorial expansion, chiefly a natural frontier to the northeast. French leaders also wanted to carry the Revolution to other countries of Europe so that it might be safe in France, and they sought to unite the French population behind the Revolution. The following February the conflict expanded to the seas when France declared war on Britain, the Netherlands, and Spain. This came from the French effort to annex the Low Countries and the January 1793 execution of King Louis XVI, an event that shocked King George III and caused London to expel the French ambassador.

In 1792 the French military was in wretched shape, a consequence of license and neglect during the early period of the Revolution. In this the Army fared somewhat better than the Navy, the ships of which were in poor repair. Also, dockyards were short of supplies, which worsened with the British blockade. The Navy also lost many capable former Royalist officers through emigration or purges, especially during the 1793–94 Reign of Terror. Among the victims was Admiral Henri d'Estaing. On being condemned he is said to have retorted, 'Send my head to the English; they will pay well for it.'[7]

French merchant captain replacements had no knowledge of handling men-of-war or of fleet tactics. Seamen were in short supply, and so only about half the French ships could be manned; and sharp divisions about the Revolution led to mutinies aboard some ships. Their lack of training resulted in poor performances, despite their ships often being in better condition from spending more time in port because of the British blockade. As French Admiral Louis Thomas Villaret-Joyeuse put it, 'Patriotism alone cannot handle a ship.'[8]

In the war against France the British concentrated their resources in the naval sphere. Not only was the Royal Navy much larger than that of France but its captains were highly motivated and capable. Although the Royal Navy was short of seamen, those that it had were well trained. This advantage increased as the wars continued, aided by the difficult task of carrying out the blockade in all types of conditions.

At varying times the British also had the support of Allied navies from Spain, Holland, Portugal and Naples. This was a mixed blessing. The largest of these was that of Spain, but it was in worse condition than the French Navy. The Spanish government put so little in the way of resources into its navy that when that country was added to the French imperial forces under Napoléon, there was no way it could recover on the seas. The Dutch Navy was small but competent, with excellent dockyards; this changed after 1795 when Holland was tied to France and suffered the rigours of the British blockade. Portugal played only a minor role at sea, contributing a squadron to the Royal Navy in the Mediterranean early-on. The Portuguese Navy played no significant role after the 1808 French occupation. The Neapolitan Navy was too small to have any major role, and at the turn of the century Naples was joined to France, although the British held Sicily.[9]

Historians distinguish no fewer than nine separate wars of the French Revolution and Napoléonic period: the War of the First Coalition (1792–97); the War of the Second Coalition (1799–1802); the War of the Third Coalition (1805); the War of the Fourth Coalition (1806–7); the War of the Fifth Coalition (1809); the Russian Campaign (1812); the German War of Liberation (1813); the Winter War (1813–14); and the Hundred Days (Waterloo) Campaign (1815). Britain and France remained at war on the seas throughout the period 1793–1814, save for a brief interlude during the Peace of Amiens (March 1802 to May 1803).

The British goals at sea were to destroy French and allied naval forces and merchant shipping, enforce a naval blockade of France and French-occupied territory, cooperate with Allied land forces by carrying out joint operations and amphibious raids, and secure trade and overseas possessions belonging to France and its allies. At the same time Britain sought to protect its own vital worldwide trading interests. The Royal Navy was remarkably successful in attaining most of these aims.

In 1793 the bulk of Britain's naval assets were in two forces: the Channel Fleet under Admiral Lord Richard Howe, perhaps England's most experienced sailor; and the Mediterranean Fleet, commanded by Vice Admiral Sir Samuel Hood, who had distinguished himself during the War of the American Revolution. French naval forces were also divided, between its Atlantic bases (notably Brest but also Lorient and Rochefort) and its principal Mediterranean base at Toulon.[10]

On the outbreak of war Hood established a loose blockade of Brest, utilizing frigates, and the first actions involved these ships. Frigate battles continued throughout the wars as each side sought to destroy the other's commerce.

In March 1793 experienced French Vice Admiral Morad de Galles put to sea from Brest with three ships-of-the-line, but his crews were poorly trained and refused to go aloft when the ships encountered a severe storm. De Galles recorded, 'Nothing can make them attend to their duties.'[11] For France it was a sign of things to come.

In August 1793 de Galles again put out, this time with 19 ships. Admiral Howe then had 17 ships. The two fleets came together off Groix, but the result was inconclusive manoeuvring. De Galles withdrew to Belle Isle in accordance with instructions to be available to escort a valuable West India convoy, and because his crews were so poorly trained and divided about the Revolution that he feared whole ship defections. Indeed mutinies occurred aboard some French ships in Quiberon Bay.

De Galles was soon in prison, his place as commander of the Atlantic fleet taken by Rear Admiral Louis Thomas Villaret-Joyeuse. The latter showed an ability to control his crews and, despite his noble birth, was not tainted politically. Nonetheless, the French ships remained in port.

British capture of Toulon (August 1793)

In the Mediterranean theatre Admiral Hood scored a notable success early on. Hood commanded 21 ships-of-the-line including two 100-rates, the *Victory* and *Britannia*. Opposing him at Toulon, French Rear Admiral the Comte de Trogoff had 58 warships, nearly half the French Navy. Seventeen of these were ships-of-the-line ready for sea, including the 120-gun *Commerce de Marseilles*, built the previous year. Trogoff had another four ships-of-the-line refitting and nine repairing.

In August 1793 Hood was able to take advantage of Royalist reaction in southern France against the radicalism of Paris. Only the month before, Toulon had overthrown

its Jacobin government and declared for the monarchy. When Paris dispatched troops, in desperation Toulon's counter-revolutionary leaders invited in Hood. Accompanied by a Spanish squadron of 17 ships-of-the-line under Admiral Juan de Langara, Hood arrived off Toulon. Many of the French crews were willing to fight, but a great many simply deserted to avoid being part of a civil war. On 27 August Hood's ships sailed into the port, and Spanish and other Allied troops went ashore. The British disarmed the French ships and put 5,000 captured French seamen on board four disarmed and unserviceable 74s to sail under passport to French Atlantic ports. On their arrival at Brest the men found themselves regarded as deserters for not having fought their ships.

In September French Republican forces invested the port from the land side. The Allied defenders consisted of Spaniards, Neapolitans, Sardinians, and French Royalists. Republican forces did little until December when a young artillery colonel, Napoléon Bonaparte, convinced his superiors of a plan to use land artillery to force the British from the port. He pointed out the obvious: securing the high ground surrounding the town and its anchorages would render the British position untenable. On 17 December, French reinforcements took the heights, and on the night of 18–19 December the British and Spanish forces sailed away, evacuating the Allied land force and some French Royalists.

Sir Sidney Smith, meanwhile, volunteered to burn the dockyard and those French ships that could not leave. This improvised effort was only partially successful. Although some smaller storehouses were fired, the large magazine escaped destruction. In all some 19 French ships (11 of them ships-of-the-line), including those building, were destroyed; the Spanish took off three small

Destruction of Toulon on the night of 18/19 December 1793. (*Musée de la Marine, PH 86433*)

French warships and the British secured 15, including three ships-of-the-line.

Few of the ships captured were of value. The *Commerce de Marseilles* immediately became the largest ship of the Royal Navy, although she was too weak structurally for fleet service and became first a storeship and then a prison hulk. The French recovered at least 16 warships largely intact, including 13 ships-of-the-line. Later these formed the nucleus of the fleet that carried Bonaparte's expedition to Egypt. This action at Toulon, in addition to marking the beginning of the meteoric rise of young Bonaparte, also marked the end of Spanish participation in the naval war on the British side.[12]

Following the fiasco at Toulon the French had only their Atlantic fleet and it was in appalling condition. Mutineers had taken over many ships and held them at Brest, abandoning the sea to the British. The

Committee of Public Safety in Paris sent two of its number, Jeanbon Saint-André and Pierre-Louis Prieur, to deal with the situation. They arrived at Brest in early October and, although Prieur soon departed, Saint-André remained to reorganize the 22 ships-of-the-line and other vessels.

Saint-André knew it was essential to get the fleet to sea as soon as possible. France was desperately short of food, and to meet this need the government assembled in the United States a flotilla of merchantmen to carry grain to France. Securing their safe arrival dominated all French naval operations.

Saint-André restored order in the fleet by a combination of punishment and inducement. Republicanizing the Navy and increasing its efficiency were much more daunting tasks than motivating armed forces on land, where dash and enthusiasm might make up for lack of training. Dissension among naval officers was rife, the consequence of the departure of many Royalists and an influx of merchant captains. Saint-André dismissed additional Royalist officers and advanced new men. He promoted a commoner, Thévenard, as vice admiral in command at Brest but, despite Jacobin outcries, he retained the former nobleman Villaret-Joyeuse in actual command at sea. Officers lost their special privileges and Saint-André held out the promise of advancement to admiral, to all, based solely on merit. A small army of schoolteachers came aboard the ships to educate the men and conduct propaganda. Saint-André also introduced a strict code of naval discipline. Brest itself was thoroughly purged and completely reorganized as an arsenal for war. Mass enthusiasm and hard work, coupled with dictatorial authority, worked wonders; within six weeks, Brest had reconditioned 12 ships-of-the-line, 3 frigates, and 12 corvettes.

Soon French ships were stealing out singly to raid British commerce. Six ships-of-the-line also ventured out under Rear Admiral Van Stabel, but Howe drove them back into port. Despite its brave front, the French Navy still suffered from serious problems, among them a lack of training, which manifested itself in frequent ship collisions.[13]

On most occasions British crews were able to outsail their adversaries, even in adverse conditions, and they were usually able to get off the first broadside. Indeed, British gun crews were the fastest in the world. This advantage was evident on 20 October 1793, when, in one of the first British victories of the war, Captain James Saumarez's Royal Navy frigate *Crescent* (36 guns) took Captain Francis A. Denian's French frigate *Réunion* (32 guns). Both vessels suffered damage aloft, but the French had 81 killed and wounded while the *Crescent* had only one man injured by the recoil of a gun.[14]

The Glorious First of June

In 1794 the Royal Navy scored a notable victory at sea. French authorities had managed to bring together more than a hundred merchant vessels in Chesapeake Bay and loaded them with foodstuffs purchased at great expense in the United States and the West Indies. To assure their safe arrival at Brest and perhaps the very survival of the French government, the Committee of Public Safety again dispatched Saint-André to Brest. On 25 December 1793, Van Stabel had sailed for the United States with four warships and was expected to return with the merchantmen toward the end of May. Meanwhile, British ships under Howe patrolled the Bay of Biscay and the coast to the north. The French fleet at Brest, although rebuilding over the past seven months, was not ready to contest the British, but it would now have to put to sea and break the blockade if the vital convoy were to reach France.

On 16 May the French fleet finally departed Brest: 22 ships-of-the-line, led by the 120-gun *Montagne*. Admiral Villaret-Joyeuse had command but Saint-André also went along. They hoped to link up with the grain convoy some 500 miles west of Brest, but Van Stabel had not received this information. Nonetheless the Committee in Paris had given explicit instructions that the fleet's sole task was to protect the convoy, and Villaret-Joyeuse was ordered to avoid all action unless the convoy were positively in danger. The fleet had to be preserved so that it could be ready for a planned invasion of England.

Saint-André cannot have been reassured by what he saw once the fleet was at sea. The French captains lacked experience in handling ships in formation and, in effect, trained as they sailed. Manoeuvres were indifferent, signalling was ineffective and frigate commanders often disobeyed instructions and chased after isolated merchantmen on their own. Being under

Battle of the Glorious First of June 1794. Engraving after painting by P.J. de Loutherbourg, published in London, 1832. (*Naval Historical Foundation, NHF NH 61764*)

sail also revealed deficiencies in hasty French ship construction.

On the morning of 28 May the French sighted Howe's fleet. Villaret-Joyeuse and Saint-André tried to obey instructions and withdraw, while Howe endeavoured to cut off the French fleet and force a battle. The British admiral succeeded only in cutting off the last ship in the French line, which fought well until its senior officers were dead. On 29 May the two fleets again came together, running parallel in the same direction. The resulting engagement was destructive but inconclusive; but the damaged British ships were able to continue in service, while some French vessels had to depart for immediate dockyard attention.

French losses were, however, made up by the arrival of four additional ships-of-the-line under Rear Admiral Neilly the next day.

Villaret-Joyeuse and Saint-André now tried to draw Howe away to the north-west in the hope that Van Stabel would then be able to pass to the south with the convoy unmolested. On the afternoon of 31 May both sides prepared for battle the next day. The resulting engagement, known to the British as the 'Glorious First of June', saw two evenly matched fleets in terms of numbers. The French had 26 ships-of-the-line and the British 25. French enthusiasm, however, encountered greater British experience and discipline.

Howe won a resounding victory by turning into the midst of the French line and piercing it in six separate places. In the resulting melée battle some French vessels were forced to fight both sides of their ships simultaneously, while other French ships had nothing at which to shoot. All fleet control was lost in the din and smoke of battle as the contest became one of individual ship engagements. Superior British leadership and gunnery carried the day, while on board many French ships enthusiasm gave way to panic. According to historian R.R. Palmer, only 11 of 26 captains performed credibly and these were chiefly those of the former French Royal Navy.

The French flagship *Montagne* was attacked by five and six British ships at a time, including Howe's flagship *Queen Charlotte*. Her 129 guns enabled her to survive, despite taking more than 318 casualties. The battle ended in the afternoon when Villaret-Joyeuse broke off contact to return to Brest. In all the British took six French ships. Another ship, the *Vengeur du Peuple,* sank as British ships approached her. The captured French vessels had all sustained extensive damage, and two were judged not worthy of repair.

Although the victory went to Howe, Villaret-Joyeuse achieved his goal of drawing the Royal Navy away from the convoy. The French Atlantic Fleet returned to Brest on 11 June, but there was no sign of the grain ships. The fleet then prepared to go out again, but Van Stabel was sighted the next day, and on the 13th the convoy of 116 merchant vessels arrived with 24 million pounds of flour. The French had been lucky. Howe's vessels suffered so much damage in the 1 June battle that he returned to Plymouth for repairs, but the remaining British squadron patrolling the coast was sufficient to deal with Van Stabel's warships. It was simply chance that the French convoy avoided detection.[15]

The war at sea was widespread in nature. This is shown in fighting in the East Indies and West Indies. British efforts in the East Indies were minor compared with elsewhere, but by the end of July 1796 Rear Admiral Peter Ranier's small squadron had captured the Dutch possessions of Ceylon and Malacca and secured control of the Asian trade.

Fighting began in the West Indies with the British recapture of the island of Tobago from the French in April 1793. The next spring London sent out Admiral Sir John Jervis and Lieutenant General Sir Charles Grey. They secured Martinique in March and St Lucia and Guadeloupe in April. Meanwhile, thanks to Howe's decision to keep the Channel Fleet at Spithead, a French squadron of two frigates and some transports escaped Brest. The French reinforcements, the preoccupation of Grey and Jervis with plunder, and the decimation of their garrisons by yellow fever, all led the British to evacuate Guadeloupe in December. Further reinforcements allowed the French to reconquer St Lucia and helped foment revolt on other British-held West Indian islands. Although the fighting in the West Indies seesawed back and forth, the British eventually secured the upper hand.

The wealth of the West Indies made it a favourite hunting ground for privateers of both sides, and in the process the British destroyed much of the French merchant marine. Both sides also employed frigates and sloops for commerce destruction. This war against the other side's merchant marine continued throughout the Wars of the French Revolution and Napoléon. Although the French seriously damaged the British maritime trade, the British won most of the single-ship contests.[16]

In 1794 the British took Corsica in a combined arms operation and managed to hold it until late 1796. The French conquest of the Netherlands also led London to send an expedition against the Dutch colony of the Cape of Good Hope, in order to protect communications around Africa with India and China. Vice Admiral Sir George Keith Elpinstone's squadron of five ships-of-the-line and two sloops carried troops commanded by Major General James Craig and arrived off the Cape in July. Following the Dutch governor's refusal to place the colony under British protection, the troops landed. Reinforcements helped force the colony's surrender in September.

In February 1796 a small Dutch squadron commanded by Rear Admiral Englebertus Lucas escaped the British blockade of the Texel. With 3 ships-of-the-line, 4 frigates, and a sloop, Lucas sailed to the Cape with the intention of retaking it. He arrived at Saldanha Bay in early August. Elphinstone had 8 ships-of-the-line, 2 frigates, and 4 sloops, and his ships-of-the-line were also much larger. Lucas surrendered without a shot being fired.[17]

In 1795 there were two minor actions in the Atlantic in conjunction with an ill-fated British amphibious operation in Quiberon Bay. The Royal Navy put ashore 17,000 men, mostly Royalist émigrés with some British troops, in an effort to spark an uprising in Brittany. Ultimately the French Army captured half the invaders, but, during 8–12 June, British Admiral William Cornwallis's 5 ships-of-the-line escaped Villaret-Joyeuse's 12 ships-of-the-line in the Bay of Biscay.

A week later the situation was reversed when the French ran into the larger British Channel Fleet, commanded by Admiral Lord Bridport while Howe was ashore. Bridport had 14 ships-of-the-line and some frigates and was providing cover for British troop transports carrying the French Royalist force to Quiberon. A small squadron under Commodore John Warren escorted the transports. Warren's daring prevented Villaret-Joyeuse from attacking the convoy and the French then came up against Bridport's ships. Villaret-Joyeuse, with only 9 ships-of-the-line, shifted his flag to a frigate

and the French tried to get away, but the next day, 23 June, there was an engagement near the Isle de Grois off the port of Lorient. The French ship-of-the-line *Alexander* was a slow sailer, which had led to her capture from the British the previous year, and Villaret-Joyeuse ordered his fleet to form on her, but only two of his captains obeyed. The three French ships were soon taken. Doubting his remaining ships would put up a fight, Villaret-Joyeuse ordered them into Lorient; later he succeeded in getting them back, three at a time, to Brest.[18]

In the Mediterranean, in 1795 Hood's successor Vice Admiral William Hotham twice duelled inconclusively with French Admiral Pierre Martin's refurbished Toulon fleet. In November, Admiral Sir John Jervis replaced the inept Hotham.

Naval operations in 1796 were inconclusive. The British blockades of Brest and Toulon were sufficiently porous that the French were able to get to sea. In September, Admiral Joseph de Richery's small squadron left Toulon for Newfoundland where Richery took a number of fishing vessels and merchantmen before returning safely to Toulon.

In December, France launched an effort to invade Ireland in support of Lord Edward Fitzgerald's United Irishmen. The plan was to transport a land force to Bantry Bay on the south-western Irish coast. The invaders were to march to Cork and destroy Royal Navy stores. Admiral Villaret-Joyeuse protested that the Brest dockyards were short of supplies and his men too poorly trained to undertake such an expedition. He was promptly replaced by Admiral de Galles. With Vice Admiral Sir John Colpoys not on station at Brest, de Galles sailed with 17 ships-of-the-line, 19 other warships, 7 transports, and a powder ship. They carried 13,000 troops commanded by General Lazare Hoche. One French ship, a 74, was lost when it ran aground. Storms scattered the poorly handled remainder, and not all of them reached Bantry Bay on 21 December, where in any case bad weather prevented a landing. The British took six of the French ships, five were lost to the weather, and the remainder returned to Brest.[19]

In the Mediterranean, meanwhile, British captain Horatio Nelson was destroying commerce along the Franco-Italian coast, seriously handicapping French land operations in Italy. In August, Spain joined France against Britain, and the British evacuated Corsica and Elba. In December Jervis collected the Mediterranean fleet at Gibraltar and transferred its activities to the Atlantic coasts of Spain and Portugal.

Battle of Cape St Vincent

On 14 February 1797, Spanish Admiral Don José de Córdoba and 27 ships-of-the-line sailed from Cartagena in the Mediterranean, past Gibraltar en route to Brest and a planned rendezvous with the French and Dutch fleets for an invasion of Britain. The aggressive Jervis, commanding the former Mediterranean fleet of 15 ships-of-the-line, had been sailing off Portugal to prevent just such a move, and, heading south, intercepted the Spanish off Cape St Vincent. Jervis formed his fleet from two columns into a single-line formation with his own ships between Córdoba's two divisions of 18 and 9 ships. With his men relatively untrained, Córdoba knew he could not unite the two divisions. He brought his own more westerly division onto a northerly heading with the intent of escaping astern of the British. Jervis responded by ordering his ships to tack in succession, reverse course, and engage the Spanish rear. In an hour of fighting only a small number of the ships were engaged, and it looked as if Córdoba might be able to bring most of his ships astern of the British line and escape.

Battle of Cape St Vincent, 14 February 1797. Engraving by J. Pass, published in England in 1797. (*Naval Historical Foundation, NH 61729*)

Jervis now made his famous signal Number 41, 'The ships to take suitable station for their mutual support and to engage the enemy as arriving up with them in succession.' This in effect abandoned the line-of-battle and freed each ship's captain to act on his own to form a new line-of-battle as quickly as possible. Nelson in the *Captain*, the third ship from the end of the British line, participating in his first fleet engagement, may or may not have seen the signal but had already acted in anticipation of it and turned the tide of the engagement. In defiance of the Fighting Instructions, he broke from the line and stood on the opposite tack into the path of the advancing Spanish line. Collingwood in the *Excellent*, the last ship in line, followed his friend's ship.

Almost at once the *Captain* fell in with the four-decker *Santísima Trinidad*, the largest warship in the world, with twice the firepower of Nelson's own vessel. Three other Spanish warships also joined in, including two 112-gun ships and an 80-gun ship. But Nelson's action forced the Spanish ships to alter course and this allowed the rest of Jervis's ships to close and join the fight. In the ensuing melée the British took

'Nelson's patent bridge for boarding first rates', Battle of Cape St Vincent, 14 February 1797. Nelson boarded and took from HMS *Captain* (74) the Spanish ships *San Nicolas* (84) and *San Josef* (112). (*Naval Historical Foundation, NH 61604*)

four Spanish ships, two of which fell to Nelson. The 84-gun *San Nicolas* and 112-gun *San Josef* had collided, and Nelson took them by boarding one from the other. This exploit, unique in the history of the Royal Navy, soon became known in the fleet as 'Nelson's patent bridge for boarding first rates'.

Although the Spanish escaped back to Cádiz the next day, the Battle of Cape St Vincent ended a possible invasion threat to Britain. It also showed the superiority of the melée battle over line-of-battle, at least for a more aggressive force with superior seamanship. Finally, it marked the rise of Horatio Nelson.[20]

During April to August 1797 serious and widespread mutinies broke out aboard Royal Navy ships in the Channel Fleet, at Spithead, the Nore, and other home ports. These protests were not against the war, and the mutineers said they would sail if the French appeared; rather the mutinies were a protest against appalling conditions aboard Royal Navy ships, although later mutinies were tinged with radicalism. From

Battle of Camperdown, 12 October 1797. (*Royal Naval Museum, 1976/207*)

1793 to 1797 the Royal Navy had increased in size from 45,000 seamen and marines to 120,000, and many rough and unruly people had been pressed into service in appalling circumstances. Low pay, ferocious discipline, impossible living conditions and inadequate food all led to the mutinies.

Ultimately more than 50,000 men in 113 ships refused orders in the largest naval insurrection in history. For a time the mutiny was so widespread that Admiral Adam Duncan had only his own flagship to maintain the blockade of the Texel. The mutinies were over by June, however; 36 ringleaders were hanged and others were flogged and imprisoned. The harshness of the punishments reflected Admiralty fears over disobedience among crews. In the long run, however, the mutinies did result in some improvements in conditions aboard ship.[21]

Battle of Camperdown

In the autumn of 1797 the Royal Navy clashed with the Dutch, who were then allied with France. Paris planned another invasion of Ireland from Brest, to be supported by the Dutch fleet from the Texel. Although the plan was shelved, on 11 October, Dutch Admiral Jan Willem de Winter with 15 ships-of-the-line and three frigates emerged in line from the Texel, probably in a gesture of defiance. Admiral Duncan, commanding the blockading squadron, had taken most of his ships to Yarmouth Roads to victual and refit.

Immediately on being informed of the Dutch foray, Duncan put to sea. With 16 ships-of-the-line he encountered the Dutch on 12 October off the town of Camperdown in the Netherlands. With the Dutch ships soon making for shoal water, Duncan knew that he had to attack quickly to get between them and the coast. After hoisting flags for 'General Chase', Duncan signalled 'Pass through the enemy's line and engage to leeward'. The British came up against the Dutch line in two loosely formed divisions, in effect breaking it into three groups. Each British ship steered for its opposite number so as not to impede the movement or fire of flanking ships. Although the two sides were evenly matched in terms of numbers of vessels, the Dutch ships were both smaller and weaker in gun size than their counterparts.

The Dutch fought bravely, but superior British gunnery and the mutual support tactics of the pell-mell carried the day. The British took seven Dutch ships-of-the-line (including the flagship), two 56s, and two frigates. The Dutch put up such resistance that the British ships suffered severe damage and many of the captured Dutch ships were unusable. In percentage of ships taken of total enemy force, the Battle of Camperdown was the most complete British victory of the French Revolutionary and Napoléonic Wars.[22]

Battle of the Nile

In May and June 1798 the Royal Navy returned to the Mediterranean when London dispatched a small fleet there under Rear Admiral Nelson to seek out a large French invasion force under General Bonaparte that had sailed east from Toulon. In pursuit, Nelson actually passed close by the French on the night of 15 June without realizing it. He guessed Bonaparte's objective as Alexandria, but when he arrived there and did not see the French he departed.

Finally on 1 August 1798, Nelson caught up with the French fleet at Aboukir Bay in Egypt. His ships came upon the French unprepared for battle. French commander Vice Admiral François Brueys, flying his flag in the 120-gun *Orient*, thought his position secure. His 13 ships-of-the-line were anchored in a line, protected by shoals, gunboats, and

shore batteries; but part of their crews were ashore. Nelson, who had written to his wife before the battle, 'Glory is my object, and that alone', ordered an immediate attack.[23]

Nelson had foreseen the situation and already explained to his captains what he expected; no new orders were needed and the attack occurred that same afternoon. The resulting Battle of Aboukir Bay, which the British remember as the Battle of the Nile, was a disaster for the French.

The French ships were anchored to allow them sufficient room to swing with the current. Noting that if there was room for a French ship to swing there was sufficient space for a British ship to manoeuvre, and guessing that the French ships were unprepared to fight on their port sides, Nelson sent his leading ships in from that direction. The risk to the British was revealed when the leading ship, the *Culloden* grounded, but three of Nelson's ships-of-the-line managed to get in between the French battle line and the shore, where they anchored. Brueys' ships could now be brought under attack from two sides. Such fighting was difficult in the best of circumstances, but it was made more so for the French because their ships were short-handed. The British doubled up on one French ship after another, systematically moving down the line.

The battle continued into the night. The *Orient*, which was being painted when the British arrived, caught fire. The flames finally reached the magazine, whereupon she went up in a great explosion that rocked the coast for miles. The flagship took down with her most of Bonaparte's treasury, some £600,000 in gold and diamonds alone. By dawn only two French ships-of-the-line remained; the rest had been burnt, sunk, or captured. One of those that did get away carried Admiral Pierre Charles Villeneuve, later Nelson's opponent at Trafalgar; the other took Admiral Dénis Decrès, subsequently Napoléon's minister of marine.

Battle of the Nile, 1 August 1798. (*Royal Naval Museum, 1976/218*)

Admiral Brueys was among those killed. More important from a strategic standpoint than the loss of the ships, Bonaparte's army was now cut off in Egypt. Bonaparte was in effect 'the prisoner of his conquest'.[24]

The British victory also led to the formation of a new coalition against France that added Russia, Austria, the Italian states, and Turkey. Subsequently the Royal Navy thwarted Bonaparte's land expedition into Syria. On 18 March 1799, Commodore Sidney Smith's squadron captured seven French ships bound from Alexandria and Damietta for Saint Jean d'Acre. These vessels, which mounted a total of 34 guns, were carrying the heavy guns, ammunition, and siege equipment for the French siege there. Largely as a result, in May, two months into the siege, Bonaparte gave up and returned to Egypt; British seapower had ended his dreams of Middle Eastern empire. In 1799 he abandoned his army in

Egypt, returning to France in a frigate in early October. The next month Bonaparte became First Consul in a *coup d'état*.[25]

In August the French attempted another invasion of Ireland. Ships transported 1,200 men to Killala Bay where they were disembarked on 22 August, but in early September British troops forced the French ashore to surrender. Then on 12 October Admiral Sir John Warren overtook and destroyed a French reinforcing squadron commanded by Admiral J. B. F. Bompard.

In September a revolt broke out on Malta against its French garrison, which Bonaparte had installed on his way to Egypt. Nelson sent ships and men to assist the rebels and the French were ultimately forced into Valetta and besieged. Starvation forced their surrender in September 1800.

While Bonaparte concentrated on the land war and made no major effort on the seas, the British expanded their naval control

Battle of Copenhagen, 2 April 1801. (*Royal Naval Museum, 1976/221*)

and tightened the blockade. The principal Royal Navy operation during 1800–01 was landing 18,000 British and Turkish troops at Aboukir Bay on 8 March 1801. They reconquered Egypt that summer, forcing Bonaparte's Army of Egypt to surrender.

In February 1801, after Bonaparte had forced Austria to sue for peace, Russia, Prussia, Denmark and Sweden joined in a League of Armed Neutrality to protect their shipping against Britain. The British saw this as a clear threat and decided on a show of force in the Baltic and if necessary a preemptive strike to break up the League.

Battle of Copenhagen

In March 1801 Admiral Sir Hyde Parker, with Nelson as his second-in-command, took 53 ships, 11 of them ships-of-the-line, into the Baltic. On 26 March the cautious and irresolute Parker gave Nelson command of 41 of his vessels, including 10 ships-of-the-line, and ordered him to approach

Copenhagen, bombard the Danish fleet, and perhaps land a regiment of troops. On 2 April Nelson ignored Parker's orders to disengage. Reportedly Nelson placed the telescope to his blind eye and remarked, 'I really do not see that signal.'

Despite some of his ships grounding, Nelson engaged Danish Commodore Johan Fischer's flotilla of ships, blockships at anchor and shore batteries. In a slogging three-hour gun fight, the Danes agreed to a truce after Nelson had taken 17 of their ships. Human casualties were heavy and approximately equal; of Nelson's battles only Trafalgar was fought at greater human cost. It was also Nelson's most difficult battle, the one in which he came closest to defeat. Negotiations then commenced and on 9 April, under threat of bombardment of Copenhagen, the Danes signed an armistice that in effect took them out of the League of Armed Neutrality.

The battle had been unnecessary. Nelson recognized from the start that Britain's chief enemy in the Baltic was Russia and that Denmark was only her unwilling ally. He had wanted to sail to Revel (Tallin) to engage the Russians, leaving only a squadron to keep the Danes in check. Had this plan been followed the British would have discovered that Tsar Paul had been assassinated on 24 March, and that his successor, Alexander I, had changed policies. Indeed, news of this, received at Copenhagen in the course of the armistice negotiations, enabled the Danes to conclude a satisfactory agreement.[26]

Peace (Truce) of Amiens

On 27 March 1802, after a decade of war, hostilities ended between France and Britain in the Peace of Amiens. But Napoléon used peace as he did war, to promote his own position, and on 16 May 1803, fighting resumed. Whether Napoléon was really serious about invading England is unclear, but he did collect an impressive array of small craft. He also concentrated on the north coast of France a sizable force of men in what he called the Army of England.

In early October 1804 Sidney Smith led a raid with fire and explosion ships against the mouth of the Rhine, destroying a number of vessels in the purported invasion fleet there. Elsewhere British naval units kept the French from concentrating their fleet for any cross-Channel attempt.

The Battle of Trafalgar

In 1805 Napoléon ordered another invasion effort based on a deception that he hoped would cause the British to leave the Channel unprotected. Admiral Villeneuve's fleet at Toulon and Spanish naval units under Admiral Federico Carlos de Gravina would sail to the West Indies. At the same time Admiral Honoré Ganteaume and his 21 ships were to break out from Brest and release Spanish ships at El Ferrol in north-west Spain. French hopes rested on the British following them west. The French fleets were to unite at Martinique under the command of Ganteaume, elude their pursuers, and make for the Channel. Napoléon, who understood simple arithmetic but not warfare at sea, assumed he would then have available 60–70 ships-of-the-line and at least a dozen frigates to provide the brief period of naval mastery in the Channel sufficient for a host of small vessels to ferry an invading army to England.

Nelson had been carrying out a loose blockade of Toulon in the hope of enticing his opponent out. On 30 March Villeneuve did indeed escape Toulon and sailed west into the Atlantic where he reached Cádiz and linked up with Admiral de Gravina. Their combined 20 ships-of-the-ine, 8 frigates, and some smaller vessels then sailed for the West Indies with Nelson's 10 ships in pursuit. Napoléon's orders were for Villeneuve to wait at Martinique no longer than 35 days. If Ganteaume was unable to break free of Brest, Villeneuve was to proceed to El Ferrol and then on to Brest to release Spanish and French ships for the invasion attempt.

After inconclusive manoeuvring, on 8 June Villeneuve panicked on the news that Nelson was in pursuit and left Martinique for Europe. Nelson followed and returned to Gibraltar on 20 July. Two days later Admiral Sir Robert Calder with 15 ships-of-the-line and two frigates clashed with Villeneuve's combined fleet off Cape Finisterre. The Spanish ships bore the brunt of the attack; the British dismasted two and took them as prizes, along with 1,200 seamen as prisoners. Poor visibility allowed the remainder of the combined fleet to escape, but five other Spanish vessels, including a frigate, were so badly damaged that they had to go into dry dock for repairs. Two British ships lost masts. Calder had won a nominal victory, but it was by no means decisive. London's negative reaction toward the engagement led Calder to demand a court of inquiry to clear his name, and he was subsequently acquitted and restored to command.[27]

Villeneuve, meanwhile, proceeded first to El Ferrol and on 13 August sailed south to Cádiz, where he was reinforced with additional Spanish ships. The British soon had the combined fleet under blockade. On learning the news, British Prime Minister William Pitt insisted that Nelson, then in England, take over command of British ships opposing the combined French-Spanish fleet from Calder.

Utilizing a line of frigates, Nelson rejected the previous more cautious close blockade in favour of a loose arrangement that kept his fleet out of sight of Cádiz. Frigates provided communication over the horizon to the main body of the fleet some 50 miles away. This had the possibility of enticing the French and Spanish out. It was a risky tactic because his enemies might get away, but Nelson preferred this to no action at all. He had, however, no way of getting the French and Spanish to oblige him. Napoléon arranged that. With little appreciation of the intricacies of sea warfare, in mid-September he ordered the combined fleet to the Mediterranean to support French operations in southern Italy: a recipe for disaster.

Villeneuve was aware that his ships were not ready. Many of the Spanish crews were untrained, a large number of his own men were sick, and dangers lay offshore. His Spanish colleagues also urged him not to sail on grounds of approaching bad weather. On the plus side the wind had backed to the south, which was to his advantage. Villeneuve was also aware that Nelson had recently detached some of his ships to escort a convoy through the Straits. Nelson had also committed the serious error of allowing Calder to sail home to his board of inquiry in a ship-of-the-line rather than a smaller vessel. Yet Villeneuve risked everything because he was stung by Napoléon's charges of cowardice and news from Madrid that he was about to be replaced as commander of the combined fleet.

On 19 October the French and Spanish ships began exiting Cádiz; in all 18 French and 15 Spanish ships-of-the-line straggled out over that day and the next. His lookout frigates soon informed Nelson off Cape Spartel that the French and Spanish ships had sailed. He explained his daring plan to his captains. Outnumbered by his opponents who also boasted the two largest ships, Nelson intended to split off the enemy centre and rear from its van by attacking in two or three columns so as to cut off some 20 or so ships in the van from the remainder. With the French and Spanish ships running before the wind, the others would find it difficult to tack back and rejoin the action. By the time they came up Nelson hoped to have the battle decided. This extraordinarily bold plan promised either great success or disaster.[28]

When Nelson approached the Franco-Spanish fleet Villeneuve realized the size of his opponent's force and ordered the combined fleet to turn back toward Cádiz, a decision that astonished his flag captain. The five-mile long irregular line of the Franco-Spanish fleet now became even more ragged as in places ships-of-the-line bunched up and even came abreast. Nelson's 27 ships in two divisions did not hesitate and sailed directly into the centre of the opposing line, cutting it in two.

In terms of numbers of guns, the British were inferior: 2,148 to 2,568. The combined fleet also had more men: some 30,000 as opposed to only slightly more than 17,000 for Nelson.[29] But the British ships were far in advance in terms of gunnery training and seamanship. As it turned out, these factors and superior leadership more than compensated for the deficiency in numbers.

Battle of Trafalgar, 21 October 1805. Engraving by J. Cousen after painting by Stanfield. (*Naval Historical Foundation, NH 61748*)

In the resulting five-hour battle of 21 October 1805, the British took 19 French and Spanish ships. Another, the *Achille*, blew up. No British ship was lost, but human casualties were heavy, among them the fleet's commander. Nelson's flag in the *Victory* had been easily visible to ships in the van of the combined fleet, and his ship became a principal target for French and Spanish gun crews and sharpshooters. Pacing the deck in full uniform, early in the battle Nelson fell mortally wounded from a musket ball fired by a sharpshooter in the *Redoubtable*. Carried below, he learned of the great victory before he died.

The British seamen did not have long to mourn their beloved leader or to savour their victory. A great storm came up and, despite valiant efforts, most of the prizes were lost in the fierce tempest that lashed victor and vanquished alike. Men who had just fought each other now struggled just as desperately to save one another and their ships. Only four of the prizes were saved, a cruel

disappointment to seamen who had hoped to profit from the hard-earned prize money.[30]

Of the original 19 prizes, excluding the four taken to Gibraltar, Collingwood ordered four scuttled, including the *Santísima Trinidad*; two others escaped to Cádiz. The remainder either sank in the storm or were dashed on the rocks with heavy losses to their crews. Although 13 ships of the combined fleet made it back to Cádiz, three of these soon broke up on the rocks. As a consequence of the Battle of Trafalgar, the Royal Navy had thus reduced the strength of its opponents by 23 capital ships.[31]

Napoléon, who had just won a great victory over the Austrian Army at Ulm, absurdly dismissed the Battle of Trafalgar in one sentence: 'some ships have been lost in a gale following an unwisely undertaken engagement'.[32] On 7 December the semi-official Parisian newspaper *Journal de Paris* did inform its readers that a great sea battle had indeed taken place, but it mistakenly gave the date as 19 October and reported

Victory under tow following Battle of Trafalgar, 21 October 1805. (*Royal Naval Museum, 1974/120*)

that the combined fleet had faced 33 British ships and had either sunk, wrecked on the rocks, or badly damaged 19 of them. It estimated British casualties in the battle at more than 10,000 men.[33]

In truth the Battle of Trafalgar shattered the French Navy for decades to come. As two French naval historians summed up, it put *finis* to the last warships of Louis XVI: 'poorly maintained, indifferently armed, and badly commanded, they had been lost in a battle without honour'.[34]

Trafalgar also marked the completion of the trend from the 'formalist' school of fleet tactics to the 'melée' school. Nelson's tactics, combined with Popham's signalling system, saw sailing ship warfare at its peak of perfection. Trafalgar was quite possibly the most important naval victory in British history and it raised Nelson to the status of the greatest of Britain's military heroes. It established Britain as mistress of the seas, which would not seriously be challenged until the end of the nineteenth century. More immediately, it confined Napoléon to the land. To get at the British thereafter, Napoléon resorted to a war

against their trade from the land side by denying British goods entry into all parts of Europe.

Meanwhile the war at sea continued. In a brief action on 4 November 1805, British captain Sir Richard Strachan with four ships-of-the-line and four frigates captured Rear Admiral Dumanoir's four ships-of-the-line that had survived the Battle of Trafalgar. Dumanoir had been about to escape when the two leading British frigates, in advance of the rest of the squadron, were able to reach his rearmost ship and bring it under fire, forcing Dumanoir to form a line-of-battle. Ignoring custom, the British frigates joined in, opposing ships-of-the-line.[35]

At the same time Britain strengthened the blockade and used her seapower to assist her allies fighting on land. In the Peace of Amiens, Capetown had been restored to the Dutch; in January 1806 Britain landed forces there and retook this important choke point from its Dutch and French defenders. Then in the 6 February Battle of Santo Domingo, Vice Admiral Sir John Duckworth with seven ships-of-the-line, two frigates, and two sloops defeated French Vice Admiral Leissègues' squadron that had broken out of Brest the previous December. It consisted of five ships-of-the-line (including the 130-gun *Impériel*), two frigates, and a corvette. Only the two frigates and corvette escaped. In March the British were also victorious over French naval units in the Indian Ocean. During 1806 and 1807 the British also conducted operations at Buenos Aires and Montevideo.[36]

In June and July 1806 the British mounted an amphibious attack on Calabria, Italy, putting ashore 5,000 troops to assist guerrillas fighting the French. Although the British troops defeated a French land force, they subsequently withdrew to Sicily. On 8 October 1806, Admiral Sidney Smith attacked the French Channel port of Boulogne with Congreve rockets.

The British were less successful against Turkey. In February 1807 London, fearful that Turkish naval resources would be added to those of France, ordered its commander in the Mediterranean, Admiral Collingwood, to have Admiral Duckworth capture the Turkish fleet, along with sufficient naval stores to maintain it. Duckworth's dilatory advance allowed the Turks time to mobilize and Sultan Selim III rejected his ultimatum. In short order the citizens of Constantinople collected 1,000 guns along the shore and opened fire on the British ships. Duckworth's vessels sustained considerable damage and he withdrew, his ships suffering further damage in repassing the Dardanelles. A Russian squadron under Vice Admiral Seniavin then joined him, but Duckworth rejected Seniavin's suggestion that they combine their fleets and return to Constantinople while a second Russian squadron blockaded Constantinople from the northern end of the Bosphorus. On 19 June 1807, the aggressive Seniavin virtually destroyed the Turkish fleet off Lemnos.[37]

That July, after Napoléon had defeated Prussia, France and Russia concluded a peace at Tilsit. Fearful that Denmark would add its fleet to that of France and Russia, London repeated its 1801 strategy by deciding to strike first. In great secrecy Admiral James Gambier sailed for Copenhagen in command of a powerful fleet of 29 ships-of-the-line and 53 frigates and smaller vessels. Lieutenant General Lord Cathcart commanded a land contingent of 29,000 men lifted in 380 transports. Arriving off Vinga, Gambier detached four of his capital ships, three frigates, and 10 brigs into the Great Belt to insure that no Danish reinforcements reached Copenhagen from the mainland, where most of their troops were located. On 3 August the main body anchored off Helsinger, where the transports joined them.

The Danish fleet then numbered 20 ships-of-the-line, 27 frigates, and 60 smaller vessels. Three additional ships-of-the-line were under construction and almost complete. The British had achieved such surprise, however, that none of the Danish ships were ready for combat.

When the Danes refused to negotiate, on 15 August Gambier moved the fleet off Skövshoved, four miles north of Copenhagen. The next day the British troops went ashore there and five miles to the north. Hostilities began on the 17th. Following an armistice during 28–30 August, the fighting resumed.

On 2 September the British fleet began a bombardment of Copenhagen. The British had learned from their experience against the Danes in 1801 and did not use ships-of-the-line in the bombardment. Instead they employed shore artillery and Congreve rockets fired from special ships. These rockets proved highly effective in circumstances where accuracy was not required, and parts of Copenhagen were soon in flames. On 6 September the Danes surrendered, agreeing to the British demand that they hand over their entire fleet as well as all cannon in the arsenal. Over the next six weeks the British removed the spoils of war and destroyed what they did not take, including the three ships-of-the-line and four other vessels on the stocks. Some other vessels were also burned and sunk. On 21 October the British sailed off with their prizes: 16 ships-of-the-line, 20 frigates, and 43 other vessels. The military booty the British carried off in the transports was estimated at 3 million thalers. Severe storms on the return trip to Britain resulted in the loss of 25 vessels and only four ships-of-the-line were eventually taken into the Royal Navy. In September the British had also taken the small Danish island of Heligoland, important in the economic warfare that now ensued.[38]

The Continental System

With neither the world's greatest sea power or the world's greatest land power able to get at the other, Napoléon resolved to change the situation. On 21 November 1806, following his defeat of Prussia, he inaugurated a plan to defeat Britain from the land by issuing a decree from Berlin that began the Continental System. This prohibited trade between the French Empire, including the German states, and Britain. In 1807 it was extended to Russia and the next year to Portugal and Spain. Napoléon's intention in the Continental System was to deny Britain trade and force her into ruinous inflation. He also hoped that being deprived of British manufactured goods would stimulate continental, especially French, industry.

London responded in January 1807 with Orders in Council that prohibited neutral ships from trading between French-controlled ports (i.e. the coasting trade) or those of her allies. Neutral ships bound for a French or French-held port first had to discharge their cargoes in Britain before obtaining an export license.

From Milan in November and December 1809 Napoléon authorized the seizure of ships that had called at British ports and the confiscation of cargoes not certified as originating outside of Britain or her colonies. London then warned that the Royal Navy would seize any ship that dared sail directly for a European port controlled by Napoléon. These policies directly affected the trade of all nations and were a chief cause of war with the United States in 1812.

The Continental System did not work and indeed was a major factor in Napoléon's defeat. It caused him to spread thin his limited resources and it angered the peoples of Europe, including the French middle class, who desired trade with Britain and British goods. Exports to Britain were also

vital to Russia. The British did everything they could to pry open the blockade, even on occasion, with Napoléon's blessing if goods were necessary for him, trading directly with France. To punish Russia for withdrawing from the Continental System, in 1812 Napoléon embarked on his most reckless enterprise, an invasion of that country.[39]

Surprisingly, the French somewhat rebuilt their naval strength after Trafalgar. In 1807 France was at its low point with only 35 ships-of-the-line; in 1810, it had 55; and in 1813, 71, with 42 building. And for the most part these were powerful vessels of 80 guns rating and three decks. But the British had during the same period increased their strength to an overwhelming 235 ships-of-the-line.[40]

Fighting overseas continued and on 30 June 1809, the British took Martinique and Santo Domingo when French admiral Villaret-Joyeuse surrendered the islands to a joint Hispano-British expedition. Spain controlled Martinique until 1814 and Santo Domingo until 1821.

In late July 1809 the British mounted a massive amphibious operation in Holland to divert Napoléon from land operations against Austria following his defeat in the 21–22 May Battle of Aspern. London pushed the plan despite the fact that all military advisors thought it was precarious. Even after news of Napoléon's crushing victory over the Austrians at Wagram on 5–6 July, the British government gave no thought to cancelling the operation.

Admiral Sir Richard Strachan commanded some 618 ships in the task force: 268 warships, including 37 ships-of-the-line, escorted 352 transports carrying some 44,000 officers and men, over 4,000 horses, and 206 pieces of artillery, all commanded by John Pitt, Earl of Chatham, elder brother of the late prime minister William Pitt. The British planned to attack up the West

Scheldt and take the key Belgian port of Antwerp.

The expedition was a dismal failure, repulsed without significant battle but by heavy casualties from disease in the Scheldt islands; it also suffered from an appalling lack of army-navy cooperation. As a diversion for Austria, it was too little too late, and the British withdrew by the end of the year. This operation, so costly in terms of men and money, did at least force the British to concentrate their efforts on land in the Iberian peninsula. Here the combination of the Royal Navy and British merchant shipping proved invaluable in supplying troops under Arthur Wellesley, the Duke of Wellington.[41]

In other operations during 1810–14 the British continued conquests in the West Indies, capturing Guadeloupe, which they held until 1816. Elsewhere, the British seized the islands of Mauritius and Réunion, two bases in the Indian Ocean that the French had used for commerce raiding.

In April 1814 Napoléon abdicated, succumbing to crushing Allied land superiority and an invasion of France. Save for the brief renewal of fighting during the Hundred Days in 1815, the Napoléonic Wars were over.

THE WAR OF 1812

Meanwhile, the British had to deal with another opponent, in the United States. The War of 1812 flowed directly from the Napoléonic Wars for, in their zeal to conquer Napoléon, the British pushed the Americans too far. One of the chief causes of the war was the British impressment of seamen. With conditions in the Royal Navy brutal and pay abysmal, many British seamen deserted when they had the opportunity, and a number of these found their way into American merchant ships and even aboard US warships. Royal Navy ships stopped US vessels to take back these deserters, but they also impressed many native-born Americans.

On 22 June 1807, the British ship *Leopard* stopped the US frigate *Chesapeake* that had just departed Norfolk, Virginia for the Mediterranean. When the American captain refused the British demand to examine her crew for deserters, the *Leopard* poured three broadsides into the unprepared American frigate, killing 17 men aboard her and rendering the *Chesapeake* helpless. The British then took off four men and sailed away. If President Thomas Jefferson had wanted war with Britain, he could have had it, and the war would have been more popular and successful than in 1812. But Jefferson favoured economic pressure on Britain and resisted the clamour for war.[42]

The other chief cause of the war was the British Orders in Council that allowed the seizure of any ship that dared sail directly for a European port controlled by Napoléon. By 1812 this had resulted in the capture of some 400 American vessels which played havoc with the American export trade. Other causes included the American desire to absorb Canada and the belief that the British were supporting Indians in the north-west.

Finally, US economic pressure began to tell and Foreign Secretary Lord Castlereagh announced suspension of the Orders in Council. However, two days later, without benefit of Atlantic cable, on 18 June 1812, the US Congress declared war.[43]

This war for 'Free Trade and Sailors' Rights' was fought mostly on land, beginning with a US invasion of Canada, which was turned back in 1812 by British regulars and their Indian allies. On the seas it was different. The US Navy was minuscule: no ships-of-the-line and only six frigates, three sloops-of-war, and seven smaller vessels, not counting 160 small gunboats. The money expended on this defensive programme under Jefferson and his successor James Madison would have been far better spent on ships-of-the-line and frigates; the gunboats also proved largely useless against the British in the war.[44] New American construction, only belatedly authorized by Congress, did not get to sea until after the end of the war. In 1812, however, the Royal Navy was so deeply involved in war with France that it could initially spare for North American operations only one ship-of-the-line, seven frigates, and a number of smaller vessels.

Pride of the US Navy were frigates *Constitution*, *United States*, and *President*. Rated at 44 guns, they were bigger than the contemporary frigates of other nations, threw a heavier broadside, and were heavily timbered and planked. With their great spread of sails, they could outrun ships-of-the-line. Their crews were volunteers, and the officers, trained and tested in the Quasi War against France

(1798–1800) and fighting in the Mediterranean against Tripoli, longed to avenge the *Chesapeake*. The British were overconfident, certain of besting vessels larger than their own. Hence the American victories in 1812 came as a great shock to the British. *Constitution* defeated the frigate *Guerriere* (19 August); *Constitution* also battered the frigate *Java* into a hulk (29 December); sloop-of-war *Wasp* defeated the *Frolic* (17 October); while *Hornet* sank the *Peacock*; the frigate *United States* also took the frigate *Macedonian* (25 October). Superior American gunnery and tactics were important factors in these battles. The military value of the early naval victories was slight, however; by 1813 the British had brought in naval reinforcements and imposed a highly effective blockade. The Royal Navy also gained a measure of revenge when, on 1 June 1813, HM frigate *Shannon* defeated the US frigate *Chesapeake* in the bloodiest frigate engagement of the war.[45]

USS *Constitution* vs HMS *Guerriere*, 19 August 1812. Painting by Thomas Birch in the US Naval Academy Museum. (*Naval Historical Foundation, NH 55424*)

USS *Chesapeake* vs HMS *Shannon*, 1813. Painting in the Collection of President Franklin D. Roosevelt. (*Naval Historical Foundation, NH 001995*)

Most of the American ships that put into harbour during the winter of 1812–13 never got out again. Thus the situation at sea for the United States in 1813–14 was much as it had been during the Revolutionary War but with no help from France, while the British were able to move troops by water from Halifax, Nova Scotia, at will.

During 1813 the Royal Navy was too busy with Europe to do more than hit-and-run raids on the Atlantic seaboard. In the winter of 1812–13 a naval construction race occurred on the Great Lakes. Finally on 10 September 1813, the showdown occurred in the Battle of Lake Erie. Captain Oliver H. Perry and his 10 warships (55 guns total) used long guns to stand off and batter Commodore Robert Barclay's six British vessels (65 guns total), armed mainly with short-range carronades. Light winds prevented the British from closing. Perry reported laconically, 'We have met the enemy and they are ours: Two Ships, two Brigs, one Schooner and one Sloop.'[46]

Land battles in 1813 were not decisive, but in 1814 the British went on the offensive. Thanks to the defeat of Napoléon that April, London could send out forces sufficient to carry the war into the United States and extend the naval blockade. The British planned a multi-pronged offensive: on the Niagara front, down Lake Champlain, and at New Orleans; while simultaneously raiding the Chesapeake Bay region.

On the Niagara front the Americans struck first, taking Fort Erie in early July, and later that month winning two land battles that forestalled a British offensive

Battle of Lake Erie, 10 September 1813, as drawn by Sam Maverick and engraved by P. Maverick. (*Naval Historical Foundation, NHF NH 2052*)

there. On the Lake Champlain front, a 10,000-man British expeditionary force moving south was blocked as a consequence of the 11 September naval Battle of Plattsburg, won by a US flotilla commanded by Captain Thomas Macdonough. The British land force then withdrew to Canada.

In June 1814 British admiral Sir Alexander Cochrane sailed into the Chesapeake with a substantial contingent of troops. He instructed his commander to ravage those points ashore that were assailable. This led to the British assault on Washington, DC (24 August) and the burning of its public buildings in retaliation for the American destruction of York (now called Toronto) and Newark in Canada. The British then proceeded to Baltimore, where they were rebuffed at Fort McHenry, after which they withdrew to Jamaica to refit and be reinforced to 7,500 men. A powerful British squadron accompanied these troops on their attack on New Orleans, where the land force was defeated on 8 January 1815. This battle actually occurred after peace had been signed at Ghent on 24 December 1814.[47]

Despite the inconclusive and somewhat frustrating nature of the War of 1812, in 1815 the Royal Navy could look back with great pride on over two decades of accomplish-ment. William James gives naval losses by country for the period 1793–1815 as follows:

	Captured	Destroyed
Britain		
Line-of-battle	5	–
Frigates	16	–
France		
Line-of-battle	59	20
Frigates	125	29
Netherlands		
Line-of-battle	11	11
Frigates	13	2
Spain		
Line-of-battle	20	3
Frigates	17	5
Denmark		
Line-of-battle	18	–
Frigates	9	–
Russia		
Line-of-battle	1	–
Turkey		
Line-of-battle	–	1
Frigates	1	4
United States		
Frigates	3	–

In sum, the Royal Navy had lost 5 line-of-battle ships and 16 frigates, while her enemies had lost 92 line-of-battle ships and 172 frigates.[48] During 1793–1815, in combat alone, the Royal Navy lost 166 warships of all types. In turn it had captured or destroyed 1,201 enemy warships of all types, as follows:[49]

France	712
Netherlands	172
Spain	196
Denmark	85
Russia	4
Turkey	15
United States	17

It was one of the most remarkable combat records in history.

Naval warfare was also occurring in other parts of the world, notably in Latin America as new states there struggled to establish independence from Spain and Portugal. The most dramatic episode in this was probably Lord Thomas Cochrane's masterful leader-ship of the Chilean Navy, beginning in 1818. Cochrane was vital in securing Chilean independence from Spain.[50] For the most part, however, these Latin American conflicts involved only small numbers of ships. The last large naval contest of the age of fighting sail occurred in the 1820s, in the unlikely venue of Greece.

THE GREEK WAR FOR INDEPENDENCE

In the early nineteenth century the Balkans entered into a period of turmoil and war. The decline of the Ottoman Empire and a rise in nationalism led the Ottoman subject peoples to seek their freedom. Austria and Russia fanned the flames in order to expand their own influence in the region. Russia had long sought direct access to the Mediterranean and control of the Bosphorus and Dardanelles. Britain and France were alarmed by Russian and Austrian designs on the Ottoman Empire and wanted to maintain a balance of power there, but the Greek cause attracted such enthusiastic support in Europe that both Western powers aligned themselves with Russia against Turkey.

The war began with a Greek uprising in the Morea (Peloponnese) and massacre of the Turkish garrison at Tripolitsa in October 1821. The Turks responded with their traditional savage reprisals, and all Greece was soon aflame. In January 1822 the Greeks proclaimed their independence and in April a Turkish squadron under Kara Ali took the island of Chios (Scio). The Turks massacred or enslaved its inhabitants. This event provided considerable grist for the Greek propaganda mill, including a famous painting by French artist Eugène Delacroix. On 18–19 June in the naval Battle of Chios, Greek sailor-patriot Constantine Kanaris sailed two fire ships into the Turkish squadron and blew up its flagship with all on board.

In 1823 after an unsuccessful land siege of Missolonghi, the Turks withdrew. Instead of pressing their advantage, the Greeks quarrelled among themselves. In February 1825, following a deal struck with Sultan Mahmud II, the Egyptian ruler Mehemet Ali intervened with both a sizable fleet and expeditionary force. The Egyptians landed 5,000 troops in the Morea and quickly overran the peninsula at the same time that a Turkish army invaded the north and again laid siege to Missolonghi, this time with success. The Turks then took Athens in June, and soon controlled all continental Greece.

In these circumstances and under pressure from pro-Hellenic public opinion, in July 1827 the governments of Britain, France, and Russia demanded that the Egyptians withdraw from Greece and that the Turks agree to an armistice. Both Egypt and Turkey refused and, on 8 September, a large Egyptian squadron landed reinforcements at Navarino, where the Turks also had a squadron. The three allied governments then dispatched naval units to Greece, and these rendezvoused in Greek waters at Zante.

Battle of Navarino Bay (20 October 1827)

The Allies moved their fleet to Navarino Bay, where they arrived on 14 October. British vice admiral Sir Edward Codrington had his flag aboard the *Asia* (84 guns). He also had two 74-gun ships-of-the-line, four

frigates, and four brigs. French admiral Henry Gauthier de Rigny had four 74-gun ships-of-the-line, a frigate, and two schooners. Admiral Count Heidin's Russian squadron consisted of four 74-gun ships-of-the-line and four frigates. The Allies thus had in all 11 ships-of-the-line and 15 other vessels. Codrington, the senior officer present who also happened to have the most ships, took command. In Navarino harbour the Egyptians and Turks had 65 or 66 warships: three Turkish ships-of-the-line (two of 84 guns each and one of 76); four Egyptian frigates of 64 guns each; 15 Turkish frigates of 48 guns each; 18 Turkish and 8 Egyptian corvettes of 14–18 guns each; four Turkish and eight Egyptian brigs of 19 guns each; and five to six Egyptian fire-

Battle of Navarino Bay, 1827. (*Royal Naval Museum, 1984/449*)

brigs. There were also transports and smaller craft.

On 25 September Codrington and de Rigny met with Turkish commander Ibrahim Pasha to discuss a mediation arrangement already accepted by the Greeks. London had instructed Codrington to avoid battle if possible, and Ibrahim Pasha agreed to an armistice while awaiting instructions from the Sultan. At this time the Greek squadron under British admiral Lord Cochrane, commander of the Greek Navy, arrived at nearby Patmos. The Turko-Egyptian fleet tried to leave Navarino harbour for Patmos, but Codrington's force turned them back. The situation was complicated by reports of Turkish troops in the Navarino area committing atrocities against civilians.

About noon on 20 October, after consultation with the other Allied comm-anders, Codrington sailed the joint force in two lines into Navarino Bay. The British and French formed one line, the Russians the other. The Turks demanded that Codrington withdraw, but the British admiral replied that he was there to give orders, not receive them, and that if any shots were fired at the Allied ships he would destroy the Turko-Egyptian fleet.

The Turkish-Egyptian vessels lay at anchor in a long horseshoe-shaped form-ation with the flanks protected by shore batteries. The Allied ships dropped anchor in the midst of this formation. Codrington

dispatched the frigate *Dartmouth* (32 guns) to a Turkish ship which was in position to command the entrance of the bay, with an order that she move. The captain of the *Dartmouth* sent a dispatch boat to the Turkish vessel, which opened musket fire on it, killing an officer and several seamen. Firing then immediately became general as vessels on each side opened fire on the other and the shore batteries fired on the Allied ships.

The resulting engagement was more a slaughter than a battle; it was essentially a series of individual gun duels by floating batteries at close range, without overall plan. Three-quarters of the vessels in the Turko-Egyptian fleet were either destroyed by Allied fire or set alight by their own crews to prevent capture. Only one, the *Sultane*, surrendered. After four hours Allied personnel losses were 177 killed and 469 wounded; the Allies estimated Turkish and Egyptian killed and wounded in excess of 4,000. Recalled to Britain, Codrington was acquitted on a charge of disobeying orders.

The Battle of Navarino Bay removed any impediment to the Russian Black Sea Fleet, and in April 1828 Russia declared war on Turkey. That August, Egypt withdrew from hostilities, virtually ending the war; in the Treaty of London, May 1832, Greece secured her independence. The Battle of Navarino Bay, which had made this possible, is noteworthy as the last major engagement by ships-of-the-line in the age of fighting sail.[51]

CHAPTER 3

THE REVOLUTION IN SHIPS, ARMAMENT AND PROPULSION, 1815–65

Following the defeat of France in the Wars of the French Revolution and Napoléon, Britain cut back on its navy. Its battlefleet of some 200 ships was reduced by half with emphasis placed on repair and reconstruction rather than building new ships. In these circumstances Sir Robert Seppings, surveyor of the Navy from 1813 to 1832, carried out a revolution in ship construction. Thanks to Seppings, Britain took the lead in structural design.

Seppings' system of diagonal framing substituted a stronger triangulated plan for the old rectangular one. He also increased the use of knee pieces and employed iron straps. In exterior design Seppings developed stronger round bows and circular sterns, important given the new Nelsonian tactic of breaking an enemy line that exposed these relatively weak parts of a ship to fire more so than had the old line-of-battle tactic. Seppings' reforms produced ships that were a quarter larger and far stronger than their predecessors. The changes made possible construction of the 90-gun two-deck steam battleships of the 1850s.[1]

Following the Napoléonic Wars the Royal Navy built no more 74-gun third rates, formerly the mainstay of the battlefleet. The smallest ships-of-the-line were now 80- and 84-gun second rates. In response to new American and French designs, in the late 1820s the Navy Board ordered the building or reconstruction of ten 120-gun first rates to mount a heavier uniform battery. Despite receiving a wider beam, these 'Caledonia'-class ships were incapable of carrying a battery of 32-pounders.

Rodney

This led to the building of the *Rodney*, the first of three such second rates and the culmination of Seppings' work. The first British 90-gun two-decker, she was laid down in 1827 but was years on the stocks and not completed until 1833. At 2,598 tons builder's measurement, the *Rodney* was shorter than the 'Caledonia'-class 120-gun three-deckers, 206 versus 252 feet. She had almost the same beam, 54.5 versus 57 feet; but she lacked the extra deck. The *Rodney* was the first British ship-of-the-line able to carry a battery of 32-pounders. Rated at 92 guns, she in fact carried 10 × 8-inchers and 82 × 32-pounders. In 1860 she was converted into a screw battleship.[2]

THE STEAM SHIP

Even as it was reaching the peak of its development, the dominance of the wooden sailing ship was coming to an end. The introduction of steam engines revolutionized not only the construction of ships but the entire practice of naval warfare. Steam engines freed warships from the whims of the wind and allowed a captain to take his vessel where he pleased.

Although primitive steam engines were known to the ancients, the modern steam engine evolved from the late seventeenth century to the second half of the eighteenth, when it was largely perfected in 1764 by James Watt, an instrument maker at the University of Glasgow. Watt patented his steam engine in 1769.

Watt's steam engine was soon applied to maritime uses. This trend was apparent well before the Wars of the French Revolution and Napoléon. In 1783 the Marquis de Jouffroy constructed a practical small stern-wheel steamship, the *Pyroscaphe* that plied the Sâone near Lyons. In 1787 American John Fitch tested his own steamboat on the Delaware River; and in 1788 wealthy Scottish banker Patrick Miller and engineer William Symington constructed Britain's first steamboat, the *Charlotte Dundas*, and tested her on the Firth of Forth. Other steam-powered vessels followed. In 1807 American inventor Robert Fulton built the *Clermont*. The first commercially successful steamboat, it carried passengers on the Hudson River between New York and Albany at a speed of five knots. Europe's first merchant steamboat was Thomas Bell's twin-paddle, 30-ton *Comet* of 1812. Powered by a 3 hp engine, she steamed at 6–7 knots on the Clyde between Glasgow and Greenock.[3]

The first serious attempt at a steam-powered warship came in the 1790s in Britain, when the Earl of Stanhope proposed a vessel powered by feathering paddles (not paddle-wheels) or, as he called them, 'duck feet'. Although the Admiralty encouraged Stanhope in his endeavour, his ship, the *Kent*, was built at his own expense. Constructed on the Thames in 1793, she had a flat bottom and straight, flared sides. Her paddles feathered on the return stroke, but her engine proved a failure.[4]

The British were slow to embrace a change that would render obsolete the world's largest navy. As the Lords of the Admiralty put it in 1828, 'Their Lordships find it their bounden duty to discourage to the best of their ability the employment of steam vessels, as they consider the introduction of steam is calculated to strike a fatal blow at the naval supremacy of the empire.'[5] Resistance to change prevailed in all navies. US Secretary of the Navy James K. Paulding (1838–41) said that he would 'never consent to let our old ships perish, and transform our navy into a fleet of sea monsters'.[6]

Demologos

Despite such attitudes, change went forward. Robert Fulton had already experimented with steamboats, submarines and mines when, in 1813 during the war between the United States and Britain, he submitted plans for a steam warship. Secretary of the Navy William Jones and some influential captains supported him, and Congress authorized such a vessel in March 1814 with Fulton to oversee her construction. Named the *Demologos* ('Voice of the People'), she was launched that October and commissioned in June 1815. After the inventor's death in February 1815, she was renamed the *Fulton*.

Although not completed in time to take an active part in the War of 1812, the *Fulton* was the first steam frigate in any navy. Hardly a frigate in the sense of the sailing ship of that name, she was intended as a

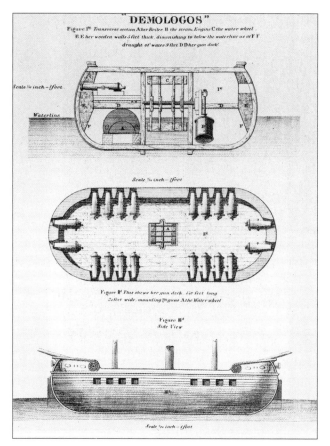

Demologus (*Fulton* I), US Navy steam battery. Rough plan from Charles B. Stuart, *Naval & Mail Steamers of the US.* (*Naval Historical Foundation, NH 74702*)

adding masts and sails. This necessitated building up her sides to protect the men working the sails, and the extra weight detracted from her sailing qualities.

With the war over, the *Fulton* became a receiving ship at the Brooklyn Navy Yard. She served in that capacity until 1829, when she succumbed to the accidental explosion of her magazine, which killed 24 people outright and wounded another 19.[7]

It was not until 1837 that another steam warship, the *Fulton II*, was launched. A 700-ton side-wheeler, 180 feet in length, with a beam of 35 feet, she was powered by two engines totalling 625 hp. She could make 12 knots under steam but carried only nine guns: 8 × long 42-pounders and one long 24-pounder. Commanded by Captain Matthew Perry, she was primarily an experimental vessel.[8]

All early steam vessels were hybrids and employed sail rigs as well as steam power, a practice that continued late into the century. During the American Civil War, for example, the Confederate commerce raider *Alabama* used her sails the vast majority of the time and steam only for close-in manoeuvring. All but a half-dozen of the *Alabama*'s 66 prizes were taken under sail alone.[9]

As development of steam warships lagged in the United States, experimentation went forward in Europe. The British Post Office ordered two mail packets, the *Lightning* and *Meteor*. Built under Admiralty supervision, they entered service on the Irish Sea in 1821. After she carried King George IV across the Irish Sea that August *Lighting* was renamed *Royal Sovereign George IV*, later shortened to *Sovereign*.

In 1821 the Admiralty ordered its first steamship, as a tender and tug for towing warships. Designed by Oliver Lang, the master shipwright at Woolwich Dockyard, the 115 × 21-foot paddle-wheel steamer (known as a 'paddler') *Comet* was launched in May 1822. Two slightly larger steamers followed: the *Lightning* (1823) and *Meteor* (1824). Such

harbour defence vessel for New York City. Fulton conceived her as a floating battery utilizing steam power to move about. This ship-rigged catamaran was 156 × 56 feet with a depth of 20 feet, and displaced 2,475 tons. With her paddle-wheel well protected between twin hulls, her 120 hp engine propelled her at 5.5 knots, greater than the 4–5 knots Fulton had promised. Armed with 30× 32-pounder guns, the *Fulton* had 58-inch wooden bulwarks and was considered shot proof. Fulton conceived of her as being propelled by steam alone, but Captain David Porter, who took command of the vessel when she was being built, insisted on

Karteria, Greek Navy steam warship. Model belonging to Greek Navy. (*Naval Historical Foundation, NH 85312-KN*)

ships usually carried a light armament, and these were rated at three guns.[10]

In fairness to their critics, early steam vessels had serious shortcomings. They were subject to boiler explosions, their engines frequently broke down, they were slow, and their high rate of fuel consumption reduced cruising range, (for example, the early Royal Navy steamer *Rhadamanthus* required 188 tons of coal to steam only 10 days[11]). Side-wheels were also an inefficient means of propulsion, and their drag inhibited the ship's speed when under sail. Paddle-wheels were also large and vulnerable to enemy fire, and they took up much room on the side of the vessel. This prevented standard broadside batteries, forcing the re-location of the guns on the upper deck. Accommodating the engines, boilers, fuel and boiler water also meant reductions in other areas, including the numbers of crewmen and thus the numbers of men available to work guns. As a consequence, most early side-wheelers carried a few powerful

guns on pivot mounts at bow and stern that were capable of much longer-range fire than the old broadside battery guns.

The first steam paddle warships were those for African service. The Royal Navy built the *Congo* in 1816 to explore the river of the same name. She mounted a single 12-pounder. Probably never used under steam, the *Congo*'s engine was removed that same year. In 1818 the French built the *African* and *Voyager* for service on the Senegal River. Then in 1821 Lord Cochrane ordered the 20-gun *Rising Star* (10 guns per broadside), for Chile in its war of independence, but she did not reach there until the war was over.

Karteria

The first purpose-built war steamer actually known to have participated in high-intensity combat was the British-built *Karteria* (Perseverance) of the Greek Navy, which underwent trials in May 1826 and took part in the Greek War of Independence against

Turkey. Inferior to the *Rising Star* in almost every respect, this 400-ton side-wheeler was armed with 4 × 68-pounder guns. She owed her existence to former Royal Navy officer and philhellene Frank A. Hastings. He persuaded the Greeks to order two, later three, steam warships. Hastings served as the *Karteria*'s commander from September 1826 until he was mortally wounded in combat in May 1828. He claimed that in 1827 she had taken or destroyed 24 Turkish vessels, conducted shore bombardments, and acted as a transport. Hastings used her paddle-wheels to turn her at rest, probably with one disconnected, then fired each gun in turn. Although the performance of the *Karteria* against Turkish forces afloat and ashore was probably exaggerated and she achieved little under her subsequent captains, she nonetheless demonstrated the great potential of steam propulsion in warships. The *Karteria* suffered an untimely end, being blown up in 1831 during the Greek Civil War.[12]

Another effective propaganda instrument for sea power was the Dutch *Curaçao*. Built at Dover in 1826, she was the first steam warship to cross the Atlantic. Other early war steamers included the East India Company packet *Diana*, which transported troops and launched rockets in the First Burma War (1824). The first US Navy steamer was the 200-ton *Sea Gull*, the former New York ferryboat *Enterprise*; she took part in anti-piracy operations in the Caribbean. These warships had come into service on the initiative of individual commanders, in these cases Captain Frederick Marryat and Commodore David Porter.[13]

EARLY ROYAL NAVY PADDLE-WHEEL WARSHIPS

In December 1827 the Lord High Admiral the Duke of Clarence decided to include steamers on the Navy list under commissioned officers. The *Dee*, ordered a month before he took office, entered Royal Navy service in 1832. At 700 tons and 167 × 30.5 feet, she was twice the size of the previous steamers. Sometimes known as the first practical steam warship, the *Dee* mounted 2 × 32-pounders.[14]

The *Dee* and another steamer, the 813-ton *Rhadamanthus*, proved their worth in 1832 during Royal Navy operations blockading the Netherlands coast, in support of French land operations to expel Dutch troops from Belgium. The next year the *Rhadamanthus* was the first British steamer, warship or commercial vessel, to cross the Atlantic, although steam was used only intermittently. She remained in service as a transport until 1864. Four other steamers were built during 1833–34; by 1837 nearly 30 had been built expressly for the Navy, with others purchased for minor duties.[15]

Gorgon

Before 1840 most early naval steamers were used for towing purposes or as dispatch boats. The paddle-wheel frigate *Gorgon* was a considerable improvement. Entering service in 1837, she was 1,111 tons, 178 × 37.5 feet, and mounted 2 × 10-inch guns and 4 × 32-pounders. She could make up to 10 knots under steam. A successful sea-boat, the *Gorgon* took part in the 1840 Syrian campaign, including the bombardment of Acre, and won praise for her service there. Reportedly one of her shells touched off the Egyptian magazine and decided the battle early.

The *Gorgon* was followed in 1839 by the paddle-wheel frigate *Cyclops*. Closely modelled after the *Gorgon*, she displaced 1,195 tons, was 190 × 37.5 feet, and mounted 2 × 98-pounders and 4 × 68-pounders. The Royal Navy built 18 *Gorgon* and 6 *Cyclops* derivatives through 1846. Additional steamships also entered service, the largest of which was the frigate *Terrible* of 1845. At 3,189 tons she was 226 × 42.5 feet and mounted 8 × 68-pounders, 8 × 56-pounders, and 3 × 12-pounders. The *Terrible* served with distinction in the Crimean War.

Terrible, Royal Navy paddle frigate. (*Royal Naval Museum, 1985/32 (457)*)

Attack on Turkish ships at Sidon, Lebanon, led by Commodore Sir Charles Napier, 27 September 1840, from left, HMS *Gorgon* (flag), HMS *Thunderer*, Turkish corvette, Austrian frigate *Guerriera*, HMS *Wasp*, HMS *Stromboli*. English engraving. (*Naval Historical Foundation, NH 61742*)

The Royal Navy's last paddle steamer was launched in 1852.[16]

FRENCH PADDLE-WHEELER STEAM WARSHIPS

France was the only other nation to make a serious commitment to steam in this period. As noted, the first French naval steamers were for African service. France launched its first effective steam warship, the aviso (dispatch boat) *Sphinx*, at Brest in 1829. A paddle steamer, she was 151 feet 6 inches × 26 feet 4 inches and had a displacement of 777 tons. The *Sphinx*'s 160 hp engine propelled her at 7 knots. She also had a sail rig. Her steam engine came from England; not until 1848 did France produce its own steam engines. The *Sphinx* was one of two steamers to take part in operations against Algiers in 1830.[17]

Over the next ten years France built 23 small, 910-ton, 166-foot 'Sphinx'-class aviso dispatch boats. In the 1840s France also built a few larger paddle-wheel frigates to match the British 'Gorgon'-class. France actually built more paddle warships than Britain, although they tended to be smaller.[18]

US NAVY PADDLE STEAMERS

US Navy steamer construction languished. Although another steam battery, the *Fulton II* was built in 1837, it was not until the early 1840s, in part the result of rising tensions with Britain, that US steamer construction dramatically increased. Congress authorized a home squadron of two steam warships and these, the *Missouri* and *Mississippi*, marked the real beginning of the US steam navy. Launched in 1841 these powerful steamers were 3,200 tons displacement, 229 × 40 feet, and 11 knots. They carried 2 × 10-inch pivot guns and 8 × 8-inch guns in broadsides. The *Missouri* was destroyed by fire at Gibraltar on 15 August 1843, but the *Mississippi* had a

distinguished career. Commodore Matthew Calbraith Perry's flagship during the Mexican War and in the opening of Japan in 1853, she was lost during the Civil War on 24 April 1863, while trying to pass the guns of Port Hudson.

By the early 1850s the United States had a significant steam fleet. The Navy ordered three other successful side-wheel frigates: the *Saranac* and *Susquehanna*, commissioned in 1850; and the *Powhatan*, commissioned in 1852. There were also three side-wheel sloops. Paddle steamers saw extensive use during the Civil War, especially in riverine warfare as gunboats, rams, transports and supply vessels.[19]

Paddle fighting ships had only a brief period of service and none fought in major battles. With the advent of the screw steamer they were thought obsolescent, despite the fact that the later types carried a heavy armament and had about the same capabilities as screw vessels. The chief role of the paddlers was to prove the value of steam warships.

OTHER NAVIES

Russia, the third largest naval power, did little to develop a steam navy. The Russian Navy acquired its first steamer, the *Skorij*, in 1817, but as late as the start of the Crimean War in 1854 Russia had fewer than 30 steam warships, most of these quite small. A number were built abroad and most had foreign-built engines. Grand Duke Constantine's efforts to update the navy beginning in 1850 were incomplete when war came. Of smaller powers, Denmark, Sweden, the Netherlands, Naples, Sardinia and Spain all acquired steam warships. Ironically, the first all-steam fleet was the British Imperial Indian Navy.[20]

SCREW-PROPELLER

The change from paddle-wheel to screw propulsion was essential for steam-powered warships. Although there were a number of

Mississippi, US Navy side-wheel frigate. Engraving from Charles B. Stuart, *Naval & Mail Steamers of the US.* (*Naval Historical Foundation, NH 60656*)

Powhatan, US Navy side-wheel frigate. Photograph taken after the Civil War. (*Naval Historical Foundation, NH 48103*)

earlier experiments, in 1836 Francis Petit Smith and John Ericsson, working independently, took out patents for screw propellers. Smith's design was helical in shape and placed between the sternpost and the rudder. He secured commercial backers and in 1838 fitted a propeller to a ship of his design, the *Archimedes*. A 237-ton vessel, she was 125 feet × 22 feet 6 inches. After successful river trials, in 1839 the *Archimedes* became the first seagoing screw-propeller vessel. In a series of cross-channel races beginning in 1840 she proved a match for the Dover paddle-wheel packets. Smith's propeller was also fitted on I. K. Brunel's Atlantic liner, the *Great Britain* (1843), the first large commercial ship of iron construction. Her employment of the screw-propeller did much to advance its popularity.[21]

Princeton

Meanwhile Ericsson was testing his propeller. His first design consisted of a pair of contra-rotating drums aft of the rudder. It was fitted on the 40-foot launch *Francis B. Ogdon*, which in April 1837 towed a barge of senior Admiralty officials down the Thames at a steady 10-knot clip. The officials were unmoved, but several American observers, including US Navy captain Robert Stockton, were much impressed.

Ericsson's first design was too complex and affected steering. He improved it by removing one of the drums and mounting the propeller before the rudder. Meanwhile, Stockton ordered an iron ship, the *Robert F. Stockton*, launched at Liverpool in July 1838. She underwent trials that September with Ericsson's propeller, her engine acting directly on the propeller without gearing. In a public trial in January 1839 she towed four coal barges lashed alongside at 5.5 knots. In April 1839 the *Robert F. Stockton* crossed the Atlantic under sail alone; in 1840 she was sold to the Delaware and Raritan Canal Company, where she remained in service for many years. Stockton was also instrumental in getting Ericsson to bring his inventive genius to the United States.[22]

One problem with the screw-propeller was technical. The single expansion engine, in use until the 1860s, only worked at about 20 psi. This slow-running engine was better suited to running the paddle-wheel; to run the propeller with sufficient speed it required considerable gearing.

The United States Congress made funds available for a prototype vessel to combine the innovations of a new heavy armament and screw-propeller. This was the 672-ton steam sloop *Princeton*, launched in 1843. Stockton oversaw her construction and designed her sail rig and hull. Ericsson designed the engine and six-blade screw-propeller. The *Princeton* was the first screw-propeller warship in any navy, the first warship with machinery entirely below the waterline, and the first to burn anthracite coal and use fan blowers for her furnace fires.[23]

In 1843 the Royal Navy ordered its first screw-propelled vessel, the *Rattler*. Of 888 tons, she was 176.5 × 32.5 feet. The screw-propelled sloop mounted one 68-pounder bow gun and 4 × 32-pounders, and she could steam at 8–9 knots.[24]

Doubts over which was the superior form of propulsion – the screw or the paddle-wheel – were resolved by tests in 1845. In a series of races the screw-sloop *Rattler* proved faster than her rival, the paddle-sloop *Alecto*. Proponents of the paddle-wheel claimed it had superior towing capabilities; this too was disproved in a tug-of-war between the two ships on 30 April 1845, which the *Rattler* won.[25]

STEAM BLOCKSHIPS

By mid-nineteenth century the screw-propeller and improved engines led to wooden steam-powered battleships. At first steam engines and the propeller were simply added to wooden sailing warships already in commission, transforming them into hybrids capable of being driven by both wind and steam. In the Royal Navy the first ships so converted, beginning in 1845, were some old 74-gun ships-of-the-line and 44-gun frigates. These were transformed into harbour defence vessels, known as blockships. The plan was to give them minimum screw steam propulsion to enable them to manoeuvre from place to place in all types of weather. They had full, although reduced, sail rigs.

The world's first steam battleship was the *Ajax*, completed in September 1846. The *Blenheim* was close behind and actually was the first such ship to go to sea. These conversions were quite successful and the ships gave effective service in the Crimean War.[26]

FRENCH NAVY

The French Navy underwent a renaissance beginning in the 1840s. This halted with the 1848 Revolution, but resumed and reached culmination under Emperor Napoleon III after 1851. The French first tried to build a wooden steam battlefleet to match that of Britain, with the result that a brief naval building contest occurred between the two countries in the early 1850s. Despite the expenditure of some 3 billion francs on its navy between 1851 and 1869, much of this by imperial decree, and efforts to learn as much as they could in Britain, the French were never able to compete effectively with the British experience in iron shipbuilding or with their superior wealth and resources.[27]

Napoléon

The *Valmy*, a 120-gun ship-of-the-line launched at Brest in 1847 was the last sailing three-decker of the French Navy. Although she had been ordered as early as May 1847, in 1848 the French started work on the two-decker, 90-gun, screw-driven *Napoléon*, the first purpose-built steam battleship. A two-stacker designed by

Napoléon, French Navy steam battleship. (*Musée de la Marine, PH 33982*)

St George, Royal Navy converted screw battleship. (*Royal Naval Museum, 1985/32 (443?)*)

Agamemnon, Royal Navy screw battleship. (*Royal Naval Museum, 1963/74*)

Euryalus, Royal Navy screw frigate. (*Royal Naval Museum, 1985/32 (347)*)

Phoebe, Royal Navy screw frigate. (*Royal Naval Museum*)

Stanislas Dupuy de Lôme of just over 5,000 tons displacement and 234 feet × 55 feet 1.5 inches, she was launched in 1850 and completed in 1852. With her propeller she could make 13.5 knots; in fact, de Lôme designed her primarily as a steamer with sail as auxiliary power only. Intended to secure France's Mediterranean communications between Toulon and Algiers, the *Napoléon* had no rivals when launched.[28]

Agamemnon

In 1847 the Royal Navy had ordered its first screw battleship, the 80-gun *Audacious*, but she was never started. In October 1848 the Navy decided to convert a ship already building, the *Sans Pareil*. She was not very successful. The British answer to the *Napoléon*, however, was the Isaac Watt-designed second rate, 91-gun, screw-propeller, *Agamemnon*, ordered in July 1849 and completed in 1852. At 5,080 tons, she was 230 feet × 55 feet 4 inches and mounted 36 × 8-inch and 54 × 32-pounder guns. Like the *Napoléon*, she was a successful design and played a leading role in the Crimean War; later she laid the first, although unsuccessful, Atlantic cable. The *Agamemnon* was the prototype for the majority of Royal Navy purpose-built wooden steam battleships to follow.[29]

Britain and France had the only steam battlefleets of the period. During 1850–60 France built 10 new hybrid ships-of-the-line and completed 28 conversions, while Britain completed 18 new ships, 41 conversions, and 9 blockships. Ultimately more than 100 two- and three-deck hybrid wooden battleships were either built or converted to steam power before that type of ship disappeared. The last British wooden steam battleship was the first rate three-decker *Howe*, completed in 1860. She measured 260 × 60 feet, displaced 7,000 tons, mounted 121 heavy guns, and was capable of more than 12 knots.[30]

Both France and Britain built smaller screw ships. In 1842 the French ordered an experimental frigate, the *Pomone* of 2,010 tons, to be completed with a screw propeller; Ericsson furnished the plans for her machinery. Several other small screw ships were also begun, and in 1845 the French ordered their first large screw-propeller frigate, the *Isly*, for purposes of comparison with paddle steamers.[31]

The Royal Navy responded in 1846 with its own screw-propeller frigate, the *Amphion*, converted from a 36-gun all-sail frigate laid down in 1830. By 1858 Britain had a total of 421 paddle and screw warships of all types, France perhaps 219. In wooden steam battleships, while Britain had 69 and France had 38, the rest of the world together had only 17: Russia nine, Turkey three, Sweden two; and Austria, Denmark, and Italy one apiece.[32]

US NAVY SCREW STEAMERS

Although the US Navy had only 19 steamers in 1860, most of these were new. They included six first-class screw frigates authorized in 1854. The first five were the John Lenthall-designed 'Merrimack'-class: the *Merrimack, Roanoke, Colorado, Minnesota,* and *Wabash*. Each displaced some 4,650 tons. The *Merrimack* was the smallest, at 256 feet 10.5 feet × 50 feet 2 inches; the *Minnesota* the longest, at 264 feet 8.5 inches. They were all excellent sailers, their steam power being auxiliary only. Many considered them the most powerful frigates in the world, and they generated more public interest than any other US ships since the frigates authorized in 1794.[33]

Instead of the usual 32-pounder armament the frigates carried a battery of 8- and 9-inch shell guns, the latter new guns designed by John Dahlgren. This was an innovation, as in both Britain and France shell guns were merely auxiliaries in batteries composed largely of 32-pounders. The 'Merrimack'-class frigates each mounted 40 guns: the main deck had 24 × 9-inch shell guns; the spar deck, 14 × 8-inch shell guns in broadsides and 2 × 10-inch

Merrimack, US Navy first-class screw frigate. Engraving by L.H. Bradford after drawing by G.B. Pook. (*Naval Historical Foundation, NH 46248*)

guns, one each fore and aft. Although somewhat slower than the Royal Navy 'Euryalus' and 'Shannon' classes, the 'Merrimacks' had the decided advantage in weight of battery. The two British screw frigate classes had a throw weight of 1,066 and 1,167 lbs respectively, while the 'Merrimacks' had 1,424 lbs.

Also authorized in 1854 was the *Niagara*, designed by George Seers. At 5,540 tons and 345 feet overall, and classed as a frigate, she was actually a large sloop-of-war. For most of her career she mounted 12 × 11-inch Dahlgren shell guns on pivots on her upper deck, with a maximum broadside of seven guns.[34]

Of more use during the US Civil War were 12 large sloops-of-war authorized by Congress in 1857 and 1858. These entered service beginning in 1859. They included the five 'Hartford'-class: the *Hartford, Brooklyn, Richmond, Lancaster* and *Pensacola*. They were sister ships in classification only – all differed sharply in dimensions and armament. They ranged from 225 feet to 235 feet in length, from 42 feet to 46 feet in breadth, and from 2,688 to 3,290 tons in weight. The *Hartford* was the most famous of these ships and the one with the longest service life. At 2,550 tons, she was 225 × 44 feet and her initial armament was 16 × 9-inch guns.[35]

With her funnel lowered, only her greater length betrayed the fact that the screw steamer was not a traditional sailing warship. Unlike the paddlers, which carried a reduced armament of a few heavier guns on the upper deck and relied on long-range fire, screw steamers could, and did, have the traditional broadsides armament; but most retained the paddler arrangement of a few heavy guns on the upper deck.

Steam warships conclusively demonstrated their great utility in the wars of mid-century: the US-Mexico War, and the Crimean War. In 1856, summing up the lessons of the Crimean War, French Minister of Marine Vice Admiral Baron

Hartford, US Navy screw sloop. Photographed during the Civil War. Note sails and laundry drying. (*Naval Historical Foundation, NH 90535*)

François Hamelin, who had commanded the French fleet in the Black Sea in 1854, said: 'Any ship that is not provided with a steam engine cannot be considered a warship.'[36]

IRONCLADS

While steam power was being applied to warships, experiments were going forward with iron-hulled vessels. The boom in railroad construction in Britain reduced the price of iron and sharply increased the number of men skilled in its manufacture. Iron ships first appeared in civilian use. Iron canal boats were in use at the end of the eighteenth century and in 1819 an iron passenger barge, the *Vulcan*, began service on the Forth and Clyde Canal. The first ocean-going iron ship was the *Aaron Mercy*. In June 1822 she steamed from the Thames across the Channel to France, then up the Seine to Paris. She made regular runs on the Seine between Le Havre and Paris, remaining in some type of service until 1855. In 1838 the British transatlantic liner *Great Britain* proved the durability of iron construction. The next step was to apply this to warships.[37]

The British firm of Laird had already built several iron ships for the East India Company. In 1839 Laird launched the first iron warship, but that company's 28th iron steamship. The *Nemesis* was built for the Bengal Marine, the naval arm of the East India Company. An iron paddler, 184 × 29 feet, that initially mounted 2 × 32-pounders and 4 × 6-pounders, she later received an additional 6-pounder and a rocket launcher. Her successful employment in the First China War (1841–43), especially on the Canton River and in the bombardment of Whampoa, was widely publicized and was said to be a deciding factor in the Royal Navy's decision to order iron frigates for its own use.

Early in 1840 the Royal Navy ordered three iron shallow-draught (4- to 6-feet draught) ships from Laird's for duty on the River Niger in Africa. These two-masted topsail schooners, the *Wilberforce*, *Albert*, and *Soudan*, were commissioned in October. The first two mounted 3 × 12-pounders and 4 × 1-pounders. The third, a smaller vessel, mounted a single 12-pounder howitzer. None of the ships was long in service; the *Soudan* was wrecked in 1844 and the others were sold during 1844–45.

The Admiralty also ordered an iron ship, the *Mohawk*, for the North American Great Lakes. Built by the firm of Fairbairn, she was shipped overseas in sections and assembled at Kingston, Ontario. The *Mohawk* mounted one small gun and was in service until 1852.[38]

Stevens Battery

In the United States, Robert L. Stevens of Hoboken, New Jersey, came up with the idea of attaching iron plates to a vessel to protect it from enemy fire. Stevens and his brother experimented with laminated iron plate 4.5 inches thick and discovered that it could, at 30 yards, withstand shot from a 64-pounder gun.

In April 1842 Congress made the world's first appropriation for a seagoing ironclad vessel when it authorized a contract with Stevens for a revolutionary war steamer that preceded the French *Gloire* by fifteen years. Stevens wanted his steamer to be shot- and shell-proof, faster than any other ship afloat, and capable of firing shot and elongated shell that would explode after penetration. But the Stevens Battery, as the project came to be called, was never completed. John Ericsson arrived in the United States with a heavy wrought-iron 12-inch gun, and its projectiles could smash through 4.5 inches of wrought iron. This forced the Stevens brothers to increase the thickness of their armour to 6.75 inches. The ship had to be enlarged to take the extra weight, one reason why it was never finished; ultimately more than $700,000 was expended on the project. During the Civil War there was talk of finishing it, but the cost was estimated at $812,000, and in the 1870s the Stevens Battery was sold for scrap.[39]

The first iron-hulled warship actually built in the United States was the side-wheeler first-class steamer *Michigan*. Ordered in 1842, she was launched in 1844. Parts of the ship were built in Pittsburgh and assembled at Erie. When commissioned, she was armed with 2 × 8-inch and 4 × 32-pounder guns. This was found a violation of the Rush-Bagot

Michigan, US Navy first-class side-wheeler steamer. Painting by Charles Patterson in Dossin Marine Museum, Belle Isle, Michigan. (*Naval Historical Foundation, NH 46269-KN*)

Agreement providing for disarmament on the Great Lakes, and in 1825 her armament was reduced to only one gun, an 8-incher. The *Michigan* remained in service until 1923. Interest in ironclads in the United States then languished, not to revive again until the start of the Civil War in 1861.[40]

The world's first significant iron warship was the steam frigate *Guadeloupe*, which Laird built in Britain for Mexico in 1842 and which Dupuy de Lôme considered to be the strongest ship built at that time. At 788 tons, she was 175 × 30 feet, developed 180 hp, and was armed with 2 × 68-pounder pivot guns. Two years later the Royal Navy added six iron steamers of 334–378 tons and five steam frigates of 1,391–1,953 tons. The *Guadeloupe* and another Laird-built steamer, the *Montezuma* of 203 × 24 feet, 1,164 tons, and 280 hp, proved their worth in fighting against Texas. Under fire almost daily over a period of four to five weeks the *Guadeloupe* was repeatedly hulled, but the shot passed through cleanly with few dangerous splinters and the holes were easily patched. Royal Navy officers who served on the two ships thought them excellent fighting vessels.

Iron was brittle, however, and experiments revealed that it tended to fracture under the impact of shot, whereas wood merely

Guadeloupe, Mexican Navy iron steam frigate. Colour lithograph by G. Hawkins after Horner. (*Anne S.K. Brown Military Collection, Brown University Library*)

absorbed it. This, and the loss of the iron-hulled troop ship *Birkenhead* on 26 February 1852, with the death of 455 people, resulted in a temporary move away from iron hulls.

The Crimean War changed this thinking. On 30 November 1853, at Sinope, a Russian squadron destroyed a Turkish fleet at anchor. The Russians fired both shot and shell, but shell did the most damage, tearing large irregular holes when it exploded in the wooden sides of the Turkish vessels. While the effects of shell at Sinope were exaggerated – the Turks were simply overwhelmed in every category – the battle renewed interest in iron as armour for wooden vessels. Emperor Napoléon III proposed a system of iron protection, and British Chief Naval Engineer Thomas Lloyd demonstrated that four inches of iron could protect against powerful shot.[41]

France was first to develop floating batteries armoured with sheets of forged iron. Initiated by Napoleon III following the Battle of Sinope, the first ironclad vessels were literally 'ironclad' in that iron armour was applied as plates over the wooden sides. The emperor, who was knowledgeable about artillery, wanted ten such vessels for the 1855 Crimean campaign; but with French yards able to build only five, he asked Britain to construct a like number. These virtually rectangular vessels were 170 × 42.5 feet and drew about 8.7 feet of water. They were 1,600 tons displacement and were protected by 4-inch iron plate backed by 17 inches of wood. Each mounted 16 × 50-pounder guns and 2 × 12-pounders, was powered by a 225-hp engine, and could make 4 knots. Not seagoing vessels, they were designed solely to batter Russian land fortifications.[42]

On 17 October 1855, three of these *batteries flottantes cuirassées* (armoured floating batteries), the *Dévastation*, *Lave*, and *Tonnante*, took part in an attack on Russia's Kinburn forts in an estuary at the mouth of

Dévastation, French Navy armoured floating battery. (*Musée de la Marine, PH 37215*)

Gloire, French Navy screw frigate. Lithograph by and after Le Breton. (*Anne S.K. Brown Military Collection, Brown University Library*)

the Dnieper and Bug rivers. The Russian fortifications, three of which were of stone and two of sand, housed 81 guns and mortars. From a range of between 900 and 1,200 yards, in an engagement lasting from 9:30 in the morning until noon, the French vessels fired 3,177 shot and shell and reduced the Russian forts to rubble. Although they were repeatedly hulled the vessels themselves were largely impervious to the Russian fire. The *Dévastation* suffered 67 hits and the *Tonnante* 66. Two men were killed and 24 wounded, but the casualties resulted from two hot shots entering gunports and another passing through an imperfect main hatch. The vessels' armour was only dented. At noon an Allied fleet of ships-of-the-line shelled what was left of the forts from 1,600 yards range and in less than 90 minutes the Russians surrendered. Undoubtedly the success of the floating batteries was magnified because they were the emperor's special project, but many

observers concluded that the Kinburn battle proved the effectiveness of wrought-iron and marked the end of the old ships-of-the-line.[43]

Five British floating batteries were ordered in October 1854, but they were delayed by the First Sea Lord Sir James Graham and not completed until 1856. One was destroyed by fire before launching. These self-propelled 1,954-ton vessels were each armed with 14 × 68-pounders. The *Erebus*, *Glatton* and *Aetna* were from 172 feet to 186 feet in length and from 44 feet to 48.5 feet in beam. Their sides were to have four inches of iron protection, but a good bit of this was rolled as much as half an inch under the desired thickness. The armour extended from the gunwale to a point two feet below the waterline and was supported by six inches of oak. The upper deck was of nine-inch wood.[44]

Gloire

French leaders most fully understood the implications of the ironclad, and again they sought to challenge Britain by new designs. France halted construction of wooden ships-of-the-line (their last was laid down in 1855) and began converting their first-line fleet into fast, single gundeck ironclads. They also carried out a series of armour experiments. The French were spurred to action by the realization that wooden ships-of-the-line were obsolete, and they saw a chance to outflank their rival, Britain.

In January 1857 Dupuy de Lôme, a staunch advocate of iron ships and armour plate, as well as one of the most brilliant naval designers of the period, became chief naval constructor. The steam screw frigate *Gloire*, which he designed, began the revolution. Laid down at Toulon in May 1858, she was launched in November 1859 and fitted out in August 1860. Described both as an 'armoured frigate' and a 'cut-down two-deck ship-of-the-line', she was in fact altogether a new class of ship. The *Gloire* was a three-masted ship of nearly 5,618 tons, 254 feet 5 inches × 55 feet 6 inches. Slightly longer than the wooden steam battleship *Napoléon*, she had finer lines that enabled her French-built 900-hp engine to drive her at a high, 13.5-knot, speed. Dupuy de Lôme sharply reduced her sail area; sails were to help her movement under certain conditions but were designed for only a secondary role.

Because the French lacked the British iron shipbuilding experience and resources, the *Gloire* was built of wood; indeed she was constructed basically along the same lines as her wooden predecessors; the difference was that she was protected by a 4.5-inch belt of iron that ran her entire length and extended from six feet below the waterline to the upper deck. This iron belt was supported by 17 inches of wood. The *Gloire* mounted 14 × 22 cm (8.8 inch) and 16 cm (6.4 inch) rifled, breech-loading guns. She was, however, not a good seaboat; rolling badly, she was an ineffective gun platform. Dupuy

de Lôme had not designed her for high-seas operation, admitting that she was 'not destined to act far from European waters'.[45]

Magenta and *Solferino*

Even before the *Gloire* had entered service the French government decided in March 1858 to order a total of six ironclads. The *Gloire*'s sister ships, *Normandie* and *Invincible*, were launched in March 1860 and April 1861. They were followed by the *Magenta* and her sister ship *Solferino*, launched in June 1861.

These two ironclads, named for two hard-won French victories in a recent war with Austria, were the only two-decker broadsides ironclads ever built. They were also the first with a ram bow. Displacing 6,715 tons, they were 282 feet × 56.5 feet. They were easily identified by their pronounced ram bow and tumble-home to the hull. They mounted 2 × 22 cm (8.8 inch), 34 × 16 cm (6.4 inch), and 16 × 55 pounder guns. Their 4.7-inch armour belts were narrower than the *Gloire*'s and were concentrated amidships protecting the two decks of guns, which were also protected by transverse bulkheads. The two-tier placement of the guns gave those on the top deck increased elevation and range. *Magenta* blew up on 31 October 1875, as a result of a fire. *Solferino* was broken up in 1884.[46]

Couronne

In September 1858 the French Navy approved plans for an iron-hulled capital ship, but she was not begun until February 1859 and not launched until March 1861, four months after the British ironclad *Warrior*. The new ship, the *Couronne*, was a strong, seaworthy vessel of 6,076 tons and 261 feet 4 inches × 54 feet 6 inches. Her 900-hp engine enabled her to make 13 knots in her trials. She mounted 40 guns in broadsides. In addition to a side belt of 3.2- to 4-inch armour she had an armoured deck of sheet iron, which did not, however, extend over the engines and boilers, where there were large openings to admit air and light. *Couronne* had a long service life – she was hulked only in 1910 – and demonstrated conclusively the advantages of the iron-hulled ship.[47]

Warrior

The British were slower to act. Although well aware of the new developments from their own experiments with new ordnance and armour plate aboard the ordnance ship *Excellent* and elsewhere, the Royal Navy continued to build wooden ships-of-the-line until the so-called naval scare of 1858, when the French decision to build six seagoing ironclads spurred them into action. The French did not gain long-term advantage. Britain led the world in metallurgical techniques and her armour plate was superior to that of France; Britain also led her rival in the development of rifled ordnance.[48]

The British did not have all that much confidence in ironclad vessels. Surveyor of the Navy Admiral Sir Baldwin Walker dominated British naval construction in this period and deserves principal credit for the creation of the Royal Navy steam battlefleet and specifically the *Warrior*. Walker did not see the ironclad vessel as

the inevitable future of the warship, and he waited on developments while trying to keep ahead in technology. Indeed, in 1856 the British responded to the US Navy's new large 'Merrimack'-class of steam frigates with the *Mersey* and *Orlando*, the largest and most powerful single-deck wooden warships ever built. Completed in 1858, they were approximately 3,740 tons (builder's measurement) and 300 × 52 feet. They were powerfully armed with 28 × 10-inch shell guns and 12 × 68-pounders. Despite the best construction methods, the two vessels were strained by their engines and demonstrated the limits of wooden construction. News of the construction of the *Gloire*, which reached Britain in May 1858, however, created something akin to panic and goaded the British into action.[49]

The *Warrior* was very much a counter to the *Gloire*, and her construction demonstrated British determination to retain the lead in technology at sea. All major warships of the era had been built at the Royal Dockyards, which lacked the experience and facilities to build large iron ships. In an unprecedented step the government called on eight ship builders to submit designs. Ultimately these were rejected and Chief

Warrior, Royal Navy armoured ship. (*Royal Naval Museum, 1987/403 (20)*)

Irresistible, Royal Navy screw second rate. (*Royal Naval Museum*)

Orlando, Royal Navy steam frigate. (*Royal Naval Museum, 5868*)

Constructor of the Navy Isaac Watts came up with his own plan, assisted by Chief Engineer Thomas Lloyd, to Walker's very specific requirements. In May 1859 the order for her construction went to the Thames Ironworks Company of Blackwall, London. The novelty of her construction and modifications to the original design led to delays in building the new ship; the *Warrior* was not launched until December 1860; she went into service in June 1862. At 9,210 tons, she was larger than the *Gloire* and longer than any wooden warship: 380 × 58.5 feet. In all respects the *Warrior* was more advanced. Whereas the *Gloire* was merely a wooden ship protected by iron plate, the *Warrior* was virtually an iron vessel. She was in fact a great advance in ship design and immediately made every other warship in the world obsolete.

The first large seagoing, iron-hulled warship, the *Warrior* was protected by 4.5-inch band of iron bolted to 0.625-inch plating and 18 inches of teak running from six feet below to six feet above the waterline. Walker feared that pushing the armour belt to the ship's extremities would cause plunging in a heavy sea, so the ends of her hull were divided into watertight compartments, a major innovation made possible by her iron construction. The heart of the design was the 'citadel', a 210-foot long 'armoured box' that protected her guns and machinery. Powered by a 1,250-hp engine (10 boilers and 40 furnaces), the *Warrior* retained a full sail rig.

The *Warrior* had just one gundeck, but she carried a powerful battery of 10 × 110-pounder and 4 × 70-pounder Armstrong breech-loading rifled guns and 26 × 68-pounder muzzle-loading smoothbores. This was more than ships-of-the-line, the guns of which could not penetrate her armour.

With her long, sleek lines the *Warrior* was the prototype of the new warship. Much faster than conventional ships-of-the-line, she could escape what she could not destroy. *Warrior*

could make up to 13.75 knots under sail, 14.33 under steam, and 17.5 knots combined. Properly handled, with her superior speed, armour and long-range guns, she could have destroyed any other ship in the world.[50]

The French may have begun the new period, but as one historian has noted:

Despite the exaggerated hopes of the French and the absurd fears of the British, *Warrior* was a far better ship. *Gloire* was constructed in an attempt to overturn British naval mastery of the sea, *Warrior* demonstrated that the hope was unreal. By taking naval architecture into the industrial age the French played into the hands of Britain, already the leading industrial nation.[51]

Sister ship to the *Warrior*, the *Black Prince* was launched in February 1861 and commissioned in June 1862. The Admiralty also let contracts for smaller ironclads, the *Defence* and *Resistance*, also designed by Watts. Both were launched in April 1861 and commissioned that December. At 3,668 tons, they were designed to be 'suitable for Channel and Home Service'. They were 280 × 54 feet and had the first conspicuous ram. Their initial armament consisted of 16 × 68-pounders on the main deck and 2 × 68-pounder pivot guns and 4 × 40-pounder Armstrongs on the upper deck. As with the *Warrior* and the *Black Prince*, the new ships had 4.5-inch iron plate backed by 18 inches of teak for more than half their length, from the upper deck to five feet below the waterline. Armoured transverse bulkheads were located at the extremities of the side armour belt. Unlike the *Gloire* and *Couronne*, which were armoured for their entire length, both ends of the first four British ironclad frigates were unprotected, being only divided into watertight compartments. Their 600-hp engines gave them a speed of nearly 12 knots in their trials.

Watts next produced the *Achilles*, a perfected *Warrior* and one of the finest

Black Prince, Royal Navy armoured frigate. (*Royal Naval Museum*)

Minotaur, Royal Navy iron screw ship. (*Royal Naval Museum, 1985/32*)

ironclads ever built. Of 9,820 tons, she was 380 × 58 feet with a 1,250-hp engine and speed in excess of 14 knots. Launched in December 1863, she was completed in November 1864. Her initial armament consisted of 20 × 100-pounder guns.[52]

Britain's largest ironclads were the three five-masted 'Minotaur'-class ships. *Minotaur*, *Agincourt* and *Northumberland* were completed for sea in 1867 and 1868. They were 6,621 tons, 400 × 59.5 feet, and were powered by 1,350-hp engines. Originally designed for 40 heavy Armstrong guns, they carried 24 × 7-inch guns and 8 × 24-pounders. In order to allow the chase guns to be worked from behind belted armour, they had a transverse armour bulkhead some 25 feet aft of the bow. The Admiralty also reduced the wood backing of the side armour from 18 inches in the *Warrior*, while increasing the iron plate from 4.5 to 5.5 inches, although this tapered down to 4.5 inches at bow and stern.

By early 1861 the Admiralty programme had reached a total of 16 ironclads. The Admiralty had not concluded that wooden ships were totally obsolete for every purpose, especially for service on distant station, but it nonetheless recognized that the French had revolutionized naval architecture.[53]

Virginia (ex-*Merrimack*)

The first clash between ironclad ships came in the United States during the American Civil War (1861–65). It was only natural that the Confederacy, which lacked both a navy and the potential to keep up with the North in building warships, and which needed to break the Union blockade, would turn to ironclad ships. Unfortunately for the South it had neither the financial resources nor manufacturing facilities to match the North in this regard. The Confederates did, however, raise the US Navy steam frigate *Merrimack*, scuttled in the Union abandonment of the Norfolk Navy Yard, and rebuilt her into an ironclad.

The *Merrimack*'s hull had largely escaped damage and her engines and boilers could also be used. Renamed the *Virginia*, she was armoured with 4-inch-thick iron plate. When completed, she mounted ten guns: 6 × 9-inch Dahlgrens and 2 × 6.4-inch Brooke rifles in broadsides, and 2 × Brooke 7-inch rifles in pivot at bow and stern. These were protected by a slanted casemate, which became the style for most Confederate ironclads. The *Virginia* also had a 1,500-lb iron ram.[54]

Both sides in the Civil War began construction of ironclads for coastal and riverine operations. In the west where the Union and Confederacy contested control of the Mississippi and other great rivers, the US Army contracted for conversion of three Mississippi steamers. Their decks were reinforced to enable them to carry heavy guns, and 5-inch thick oak was installed as protection against rifle fire; as a result they became known as 'timberclads'. But little could be done to protect their vulnerable machinery. On commissioning, the *Conestoga* mounted 4 × 32-pounder smoothbores; the *Lexington* had 2 × 32-pounders and 4 × 64-pounders (8-inch shell guns); and the *Tyler* had one 32-pounder in the stern and 6 × 64-pounder (8-inch shell) guns in broadside.[55]

The US Army also beat the US Navy to ironclad construction, hastily contracting for seven ironclads to serve on the Mississippi and other western rivers. These 'City'-class ships, all named for western river ports, entered service in January 1862. They were also known as 'Pook Turtles' for the Samuel M. Pook-designed rectangular casemates that covered the entire ship with sloped, armoured sides. The seven were the *Cairo*, *Carondelet*, *Cincinnati*, *Louisville*, *Mound City*, *Pittsburg*, and *St Louis* (renamed the *Baron de Kalb* when she was transferred to the Navy, as there was already a *St Louis* in naval service). These 512-ton vessels were 175 feet × 51 feet 2 inches and drew only six feet of water.

Virginia, Confederate Navy ironclad under conversion from the hulk of the US Navy steam frigate *Merrimack* in drydock, Norfolk Navy Yard. (*Naval Historical Foundation, NH 58712*)

Designed for 10 knots, they were powered by two engines and propelled by a single stern paddle-wheel. They often had trouble when steaming against the current.

The gunboats were heavily armed, although with fewer than the 20 guns each, as originally planned, probably as a consequence of the weight of their iron armour plating. In January 1862 each mounted 13 guns: 3 × 8-inch smoothbores, 4 × 42-pounder Army coast defence rifled guns (7-inch bore), and 6 × 32-pounder rifled guns. Three of these guns fired forward. Each gunboat was protected with 2.5 inches of armour on the casemate and 1.25 inches on the conical pilot-house forward. Although underpowered and vulnerable to plunging fire, they gave excellent service in support of army operations ashore.[56]

Galena

In response to reports of Confederate ironclad construction, in August 1861 Congress appropriated $1.5 million for ironclad construction and authorized a special board of naval officers to examine proposals and make recommendations on those to be built. In September the board recommended construction of three experimental ironclads. The first of these, designed by S. H. Pook, was the *Galena*, 210 feet × 16 feet 11 inches, and 950 tons. Commissioned in April 1862, she was armed with 4 × 9-inch Dahlgren smoothbores and 2 × 100-pounder rifles. Equipped with a two-mast schooner rig to supplement her single-screw propeller, the *Galena* had 3.25-inch side armour of interlocking iron bars. Disappointing as a ship type, she was severely damaged at Drewry's Bluff on the James River, Virginia, on 15 May 1862, when her armour proved susceptible to plunging fire striking at almost straight angles against her tumble-home sides. The next year the armour was removed and the *Galena* was converted into an unarmoured screw sloop with three-mast sail rig.[57]

Monitor

The second of the experimental ironclads was John Ericsson's revolutionary *Monitor*. Ericsson had offered his services to the Federal government. In one of the most unusual government contracts in history and because his warship was so revolutionary, Ericsson agreed that he was not to be paid until the *Monitor* had proven successful. The board accepted the revolutionary design because of the threat posed by the *Virginia* and because Ericsson promised quick delivery.

Laid down in October 1861 and commissioned on 25 February 1862, the *Monitor* revolutionized naval warfare. Entirely of iron, she incorporated 47 patentable inventions. The *Monitor* was the first ironclad warship built without rigging or sails and she incorporated a turret. She was just 987 tons displacement and 179 feet × 41.5 feet × 10.5 feet. Her two engines delivered 320 hp to her one screw, enabling a speed of 9 knots. She was crewed by only 49 officers and men. Armed with 2 × 11-inch smoothbore Dahlgren guns, she had 8 inches of armour on the turret, 4.5 inches on the sides, 2 inches on the deck, and 9 inches on the pilot-house.

The *Monitor* had only slight freeboard, and her turret was the principal visible part. This led to her being called 'a hat on the water' or 'cheesebox on a raft'. Most of her machinery was below the waterline with only the turret and the small pilot-house forward as targets. Her revolving spindle-type turret, the first such use of a turret in warfare, enabled her gun ports to be moved away from enemy fire while her guns were being reloaded.[58]

The heavy weight of early turrets precluded their use high in the ship, and for that reason Ericsson designed the *Monitor*, and other 'monitors' to follow, with very low freeboard. The other difficulty with the turreted warship was that the inefficiency of early steam propulsion meant that sails were still required. With sail rigs impractical on a turreted monitor, the early monitors were coastal vessels rather than seagoing ships.

New Ironsides

The third of the experimental Union ironclads, the *New Ironsides*, while not as experimental as the *Monitor*, was actually a more successful ship type. The *New Ironsides* was launched in May 1862 and commissioned in August. Designed by Barnabas Bartol for Merrick & Sons of Philadelphia, she was much more conventional in appearance. An armoured, broadside vessel, she was closely patterned after the French

USS *Monitor* vs CSS *Virginia*. The first duel between ironclads in history. (*Naval Historical Foundation, NH 51793*)

New Ironsides, US Navy ironclad. (*Naval Historical Foundation, NH 66759*)

Gloire. With a beam of 56 feet, the *New Ironsides* was 230 feet between perpendiculars, of which 170 feet was armoured in a 4.5 feet iron belt. She also boasted an iron ram. She had a draft of 15 feet 8 inches and displaced 3,500 tons.

The *New Ironsides* had a formidable battery of 14 × 11-inch Dahlgren smoothbores and 2 × 150-pounder Parrott rifles. Capable of ten times the fire of the single-turreted monitors, she was, in fact, the most powerful warship of the US Navy in the Civil War. The *New Ironsides* was slow – only seven knots instead of the design-specified 10 knots – but this was a consequence of her bulky hull, necessary to insure shallow draught, a prerequisite for coastal operations. The *New Ironsides* was far superior to the *Monitor* and her successors in seaworthiness, armament and even armour. The *Monitor* had laminated armour, which Ericsson chose because of the need for speedy construction, while the *New Ironsides* utilized superior solid plate.[59]

In 16 months of service with the South Atlantic Blockade Squadron off Charleston, South Carolina, the 'guardian of the blockade', as the *New Ironsides* came to be known, proved an effective deterrent to Confederate ironclad attacks against the wooden Union blockading fleet. Her service there was unmatched by any other Union warship. Always the primary target for return fire during Union bombardments of Confederate shore positions, the *New Ironsides* came off with only minor damage while the monitors often suffered severely and even fatally.

Other Union monitors

Following the battle between the *Monitor* and the *Virginia*, the North succumbed to 'monitor fever'. Of 84 ironclads laid down in the North during the war, 64 were of the turreted monitor type. Both the 'Passaic' and 'Canonicus' classes were essentially modified monitors. The ten-ship 'Passaic'-class monitors displaced 2,335 tons each and were 200 feet between perpendiculars and 46 feet in beam. They drew only 11.5 feet. Most were armed with one 15-inch and one 11-inch Dahlgren smoothbore. The nine-ship 'Canonicus'-class monitors, only seven of which were commissioned, were 2,100-ton ships. Most were 235 × 43 feet 8 inches and mounted 2 × 15-inch Dahlgren smoothbores.

Ericsson also designed the large single-turreted monitors *Dictator* and *Puritan*. Commissioned in November 1864 the *Dictator* displaced 4,438 tons, was 312 × 50 feet, and was armed with 2 × 15-inch Dahlgren smoothbores. She had 15 inches of armour on her turret, 12 inches on the pilot-house, 6 inches on the sides, and 1.5 inches on her deck. The *Puritan* was the largest of the Ericsson monitors; she displaced 4,912 tons, was 340 × 40 feet, and was designed to carry two 20-inch smoothbore Dahlgren guns. Launched in July 1864, she was never commissioned and was rebuilt as a new ship in 1874.[60]

Not all Union monitors were successful. The 20 'Casco'-class ironclads with a turtleback deck, designed by Stimers, were 1,175 tons and 225 feet × 45 feet 9 inches. They floated with only three inches of freeboard before being fitted for their turrets, and therefore had to have their decks sharply raised. Most were delivered after the war's end. Some later served without turrets and were armed with spar torpedoes; all were scrapped within a decade.[61]

Among later Union ironclads were the *Keokuk* and *Dunderberg*. The *Keokuk* proved so hopelessly vulnerable to hostile fire that she sank after her first day in battle. The ram *Dunderberg*, a 7,060-ton warship, was a brigantine-rigged casemate ironclad designed for broadside fire. She had a double bottom, a collision bulkhead, and a massive solid-oak ram. Although laid down late in 1862, she was so delayed in construction that the Navy rejected her in 1865. Her builder then sold her to France, where she was renamed *Rochambeau* and took part in the naval blockade of Prussia in 1870.[62]

During the Civil War, the monitor craze inhibited construction of seagoing ironclads and, after the war, low budgets until the 1880s prevented it. As noted, broadside ironclads were the exception; the US Navy had only the *New Ironsides* during the Civil War, despite the fact that this type had a considerable tactical advantage in offensive firepower over the monitors, and this fire could be concentrated.

While the 15-inch guns of the 'Passaic'-class monitors were more powerful individually than the 11-inchers on the *New Ironsides*, the monitors were at a severe disadvantage in fighting at sea. The earliest types had only 1–2 feet of freeboard, and even the 'sea-going' monitors had only 2 feet 7 inches. The *New Ironsides* had 13 feet of freeboard, putting the bores of her guns 9 or 10 feet above water, where there was no fear of interference by the sea. Her higher freeboard also enabled the *New Ironsides* to keep speed at sea. And, despite her unarmoured ends, she was the equal of any monitor defensively. Her solid-plate armour was superior to the much thicker laminated armour on the monitors, the turrets of which were vulnerable to jamming. The only advantages of the monitors was their shallow draft and small target area.

The advantages of the *New Ironsides* would have been critical had the Confederacy been able to acquire the 'Laird rams' being built in Britain. Although smaller than the *Gloire* or *Warrior*, the *New Ironsides* was their equal in armour protection and superior to them in armament. Her European counterparts had the advantage only in speed.[63]

Colbert

In 1875 France launched her last wooden-hulled battleships, the *Colbert* and her sister ship *Trident*. The *Colbert* was fully rigged to save coal, but she had an armour belt that varied in depth between 7 and 8.7 feet, located above and below the waterline. The *Colbert* displaced 8,750 tons, was 317 feet 7 inches × 57 feet 3 inches, and was armed with 8 × 10.8-inch (270 mm), 2 × 9.4-inch (238 mm), and 8 × 5.5-inch (140 mm) guns. Russia, Austria-Hungary, and Italy also built ironclads. The new era was fully established.[64]

Chapter 4

Dramatic Changes in Naval Ordnance

In the half century following the Wars of the French Revolution and Napoléon the evolution in ship design was closely tied to changes in naval ordnance. These included uniform batteries of the same calibre guns, the shift from solid shot to shell, extensive tests of guns and armour, and improved training resulting from the establishment of gunnery schools.

Fewer but Heavier Guns

At the end of the Napoléonic Wars virtually all naval ordnance was still muzzle-loading and smoothbore. Batteries were mixed, with a variety of calibres and mix of long guns and carronades. The many lighter guns mounted in broadsides now gave way to fewer and heavier guns of new types.

In the Royal and US navies this meant a change to all 32-pounder armament, and in the French Navy to 36-pounders. This was prompted in part by the US Navy practice during the War of 1812 of utilizing the largest and most powerful batteries possible. Large guns mounted in pivot bow and stern could fire over a wide arc and project heavier shot and shell before a broadsides-armed vessel could close and engage with its more numerous but smaller guns. The introduction of steam warships, the side-wheels of which precluded extensive broadside batteries, accelerated this trend. New types of guns also appeared.

Explosive Shell

The great naval ordnance innovation of the period, beginning in the 1820s, was the use of explosive shell in place of solid shot. This helped bring about the change from wooden ships to ironclads. In the late eighteenth century one of the promoters of the carronade, General Robert Melville, had suggested that it fire shells and hollow (cored) shot as well as solid shot; but this proposal remained an exception. The idea of firing shells was not new; they had long been an ordnance staple, principally on land. In the mid-eighteenth century King Frederick II of Prussia had popularized the howitzer, which was designed principally to fire shell in a trajectory between that of cannon and mortars. Explosive shells were

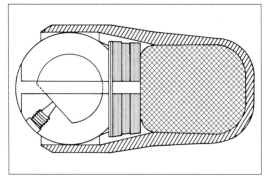

Shell with sabot and powder. Drawing by William Clipson. (*Author's collection*)

not commonly used at sea, however, except in heavy mortars aboard specially designed ketches known as 'bombs' for shore bombardment. Many naval officers rejected their use as barbarous and cowardly.

Still, the idea of projecting shell in a flat trajectory persisted. As early as 1756 the British conducted a trial at Gibraltar and the great French artillerist Gribeauval suggested it in a memoir on coastal defence. In 1795 at Toulon the French conducted trials with shell, and two years later carried out an experiment by firing 24- and 36-pounder shells against target ships at Cherbourg. Napoléon was sufficiently impressed to order shells cast for all 36-pounder coast defence guns and to have some 48-pounder guns cast specifically for firing shell.

Meanwhile Sir Samuel Bentham conclusively demonstrated the effects of shell. While a lieutenant colonel in Russian service Bentham fitted out a flotilla of small galleys armed with 32- and 48-pounder cannon and 8- and 13-inch howitzers mounted on a non-recoil principle to fire explosive and incendiary shell either at point-blank or with very little elevation. In the 17 and 27 June 1788, naval battles of the Liman (lagoons near the mouth of the Dnieper River), Rear Admiral John Paul Jones, commanding the Russian Black Sea Fleet, employed a few larger ships and a number of Bentham's galleys firing shell against Hasan el Ghasi's Turkish flotilla. The first battle was inconclusive, but, in the second, the Turks lost 15 ships and had 3,000 men killed and more than 1,600 taken prisoner. The Russians lost only one frigate, 28 men killed, and 67 wounded. The battle virtually finished off Turkey as a naval power.[1]

Henri Paixhans

French colonel Henri Joseph Paixhans is generally credited with developing the shell gun. Rather than invent anything new,

Paixhans brought scattered technological elements together in a new system. He advanced his theories in two books: *Nouvelle force maritime et artillerie* (1822) and *Expériences faites sur une arme nouvelle* (1825). Paixhans' idea was to do away with solid shot altogether in favour of exploding shell fired in a flat trajectory from a few large-calibre guns. He also argued for uniformity in the calibre of guns, replacing the mixed armament then in place with 36-pounders of different weights for the various decks. The lighter 36-pounders could be reamed-up 24-pounders. All would fire charged shell.[2]

Solid shot had been the mainstay at sea for centuries. Shot was used to hole a vessel, wound and destroy spars and masts, and kill enemy crews. But wooden warships with their thick oak sides could absorb a tremendous number of hits. Even if it penetrated, shot tended to leave a regular rounded hole easily plugged by a ship's carpenter, especially as the wooden fibres tended to close after the shot had passed through. In any case it took many such holes

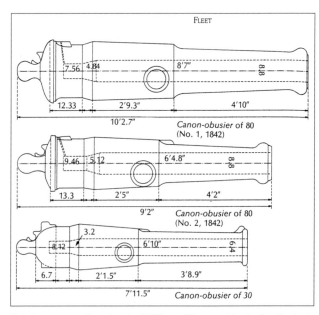

Paixhans guns. Drawing by William Clipson. (*Author's collection*)

to sink a wooden warship. Occasionally ships were lost by a magazine explosion, but most captured vessels were first disabled through damage to masts, spars and rigging or from heavy personnel casualties that enabled them to be taken by boarding.[3]

The anti-personnel effects of shot occurred when it exited the wood and produced showers of splinters. The effects of this were greatest when the force of the shot was only slightly more than that required to pass through the wood. But far too often shot failed to penetrate the wooden side of a ship at all.

Shell, however, was designed not to penetrate. It moved at a slow velocity in order to lodge and explode *in* the side of a ship, causing an irregular hole that was difficult to patch and large enough that it might even sink the vessel. Shot had greater accuracy and range, but shell was much more destructive. Shell guns also had the advantage of being lighter than shot guns, as shell was fired with smaller charges. This meant that the weight of metal that a warship fired in broadside might actually be increased at the same time the weight of its ordnance was reduced. Shot guns were heavier in order to take large powder charges and project shot at a high velocity and longer range.[4]

That the French took the lead in developing a new system should not be surprising. They had less to lose than the British in an entirely new naval ordnance system. Inferiority in overall number of ships might be offset by superior ordnance, which Lieutenant John Dahlgren, the principal US Navy advocate of switching entirely to shell guns, pointed out. The British position was summed up by Thomas Simmons in 1837:

So long as the maritime powers with which we were at war did not innovate by improving their guns, by extending the invention of carronades, or above all, by projecting shells horizontally from shipping, so long was it in the interest of Great Britain not to set the example of any improvement in naval ordnance, since such improvements be adopted by other nations, and not only would the value of our immense materiel be depreciated if not forced out of use, but a probability might arise that these innovations might tend to render less decisive our great advantages in nautical skill and experience.[5]

In 1821 the French government approved production of two 22-cm, 80-pounder bomb cannon (86.5-pounder English) according to Paixhans' designs. These guns underwent trials at Brest in 1823 and 1824. In the first trial a powder charge of nearly 20 lbs threw shot a distance of 4,100 yards. The second trial saw shell fired at ranges of up to 1,280 yards. The exploding shell tore irregular holes several feet in diameter in the target, quite sufficient to sink an ordinary wooden ship. These tests were conclusive. Not only was shell found to have adequate range, it had proven quite accurate. Although the tests had been conducted under optimum conditions, the implication was obvious: armed with a few heavy Paixhans guns, a frigate could sink a ship-of-the-line.

In 1824 France introduced the Paixhans gun into its navy as a part of the regular armament. An 1837 regulation established the 22-cm (80-pounder) shell gun as a part of every ship battery and six were aboard every ship-of-the-line. The French Navy Paixhans gun, officially the '*canon-obusier* of 80, No. 1, 1841', was easily distinguished from every gun of the time by its peculiar form and straight muzzle. The gun was of medium length, 9 feet 4 inches in length (about 12 calibres) and large bore of 8.95 inches. It weighed about 8,300 lbs or approximately that of a much smaller bore 36-pounder truck gun. Ratio of gun weight to that of shell was quite high, 137 to 1.

The Paixhans gun continued the trend toward greater simplicity in ordnance design. The outside diameter sharply increased just forward of the trunnions to a point back about two thirds the distance to the base ring where the gun shrank to a diameter narrower than normal because the chambering at the end of the bore held what was, for its size, a small charge of powder. Improved models in 1842 and 1848 had larger powder chambers and the guns were slightly shorter. In addition to the *canon-obusier* of 80, the French also introduced a smaller one for solid or cored shot.[6]

French success with the shell gun goaded the British into action. The British had employed shell in the past and used them extensively in firing at Napoléon's troops besieging Acre in 1799. In 1824, the year the French Navy adopted the Paixhans gun, the British tried out a 10-inch gun of 9 feet 4 inches, weighing 86 cwt (about 9,600 lbs). Found too heavy for all but the largest ships, this gun led to experimentation with an 8-inch shell gun of 5 feet 8.5 inches, weighing 5,600 lbs. But this was found too light and short for the larger ships. Finally in 1838 the British adopted the 8-inch shell gun, 9 feet in length and weighing 65 cwt (some 7,300 lbs).

GUNNERY SCHOOLS

In 1817 Sir Howard Douglas published his *Treatise on Naval Gunnery*. It soon became *the* naval gunnery manual and went through many editions into at least the 1850s. Then in 1830 the Royal Navy commissioned HMS *Excellent* both as the first naval gunnery school and as a centre for ordnance experiments.[7]

The validation of this scientific and practical training came in the effective bombardment of Acre, on 3 November 1840. Historian Andrew Lambert claims it was 'the high point of combat efficiency with wooden

sailing warships armed with muzzle-loading smooth bore artillery'.[8] Other powers, including the United States, followed suit with their own gunnery schools.

In 1835 the Royal Navy carried out a series of gunnery experiments against the old three-decker *Royal George* of 1772, noting the effects of solid shot, hollow shot, and shell. These confirmed Paixhans' trials of 16 years before. The British then experimented with a shot gun developed by Monk, manufactured on the principle that the weight of the gun ought to be about 1.75 cwt per pound of shot. This led to a 56-pounder of 11 feet, weighing 98 cwt. Monk reduced the thickness of metal in the chase of the gun and increased it around the breech, the point of greatest strain. Nonetheless the gun was quite light in relation to its shot. Monk also reduced the windage (the difference between the diameter of the projectile and that of the bore) from 0.235 inch to 0.175 inch. Monk had intended the gun for coast defence purposes, and its weight was reduced to 87 cwt for naval service.

At this time the 42-pounder had been discarded and the heaviest shot gun in the Royal Navy was the 32-pounder, 9.5 feet long and weighing 56 cwt. It is not clear whether Monk intended his 56-pounder as a rival to the 8-inch shell gun, but his gun and a 68-pounder of 95 cwt designed by Colonel Dundas joined the fleet in the 1840s and early 1850s. The 56-pounder Monk gun compared quite favourably with the larger shell guns and was more effective in long-range firing, and was therefore preferable as the bow guns of steamers. The range of its shot, 5,720 yards, exceeded that of the old 32-pounder by 860 yards. By 1851 the 56-pounder Monk had become the favourite gun in the Royal Navy and was part of the broadside battery of all rates and classes of ships and as a pivot gun aboard steamers.[9]

The US Navy also experimented with new ordnance. The first US Navy Paixhans guns

HMS *Excellent*. (*Royal Naval Museum 1984/640*)

HMS *Excellent*, gunnery training school.

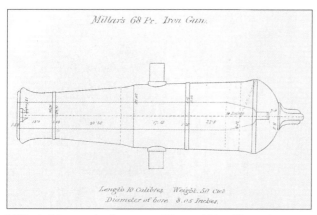

Millar's 68-pounder iron gun, 50 cwt, 120 calibres, bore 8.05 inches. Sketch from a gunnery manual on HMS *Excellent*, 1839. (*Royal Naval Museum*)

were 64-pounders of 60 cwt with an 8-inch bore and 32-pounder powder chamber. The Navy first ordered these in 1841. At the same time a number of old 42-pounders were bored up to an 8-inch diameter, while retaining a 32-pounder chamber; but, as with bored-up guns in British service, these were found too weak

and were condemned in 1847. Other guns were also reamed up. Some 24-pounders were bored up to 32-pounders to fire hollow shot and shell. By the early 1850s US Navy warships were armed with a few 8-inch (or 64-pounder shot guns) or 10-inch shell guns.[10]

John Dahlgren

John Dahlgren was the most influential figure in the development of nineteenth-century US Navy ordnance. His work marked the beginning of scientific techniques in its design and employment. Dahlgren's ordnance work began when, as a lieutenant in 1847, he was assigned to conduct ranging experiments at the Washington Navy Yard.

While best known for the heavy guns that bore his name, Dahlgren also developed a new lock, primer and sights graduated in yards. He also designed a highly effective bronze boat howitzer, his first major ordnance triumph. It appeared as 12- and 24-pounder smoothbores and a 4-inch (20-pounder) rifle

Two US Navy 32-pounders of 33 cwt, cast in 1846, now at the Washington Navy Yard. (*Photograph by Malcolm Muir, Jr*)

and was for a generation one of the finest of its type in the world. The howitzer could be rapidly fired and easily changed from boat carriage to field carriage and back again. Its effectiveness was proven in assaults on the Barrier forts near Canton, China, in November 1856, and it was widely used during the Civil War in Union operations along the Western rivers. It was also copied by other navies, including the Japanese.[11]

But Dahlgren is chiefly remembered for the system of heavy smooth-bore, muzzle-loading ordnance that bears his name. Even as his boat howitzers underwent trial, Dahlgren was designing a new heavy shell gun. This was prompted by the explosion in November 1849 of a 32-pounder being tested for accuracy, which blew up and killed the gunner. Dahlgren then obtained permission to design a new gun to incorporate both greater power and safety.

In January 1850 Dahlgren submitted a draft for a 9-inch gun. The first prototype was cast at Fort Pitt Foundry and delivered to the Washington Navy Yard in May 1850. The original 9-inch Dahlgren had a more angular form and only one vent. Later the design was modified in favour of a curved shape and double vent. In 1856 the side vents were restored. The second vent was to extend the life of the gun. When repeated firings had enlarged the vent opening beyond a desirable point, the second vent, which had been filled with zinc, was opened and the original vent was sealed with zinc. Dahlgren guns, with their smooth exterior, curved lines and weight of metal at the breech, resembled soda water bottles, and were sometimes so called. Dahlgren designed them so as to place the greatest weight of metal at the point of greatest strain, the breech.

The 9-inch remained the most common broadside, carriage-mounted gun in the US Navy until well after the Civil War; the 11-inch, the prototype of which was cast in 1851,

was the most widely used pivot-mounted gun of the war. Its shell could pierce 4.5 inches of plate iron backed by 20 inches of solid oak.

Dahlgren guns appeared in a variety of sizes: 32-pounder (3,300 and 4,500 lbs), 8-inch (6,500 lbs), 9-inch (12,280 lbs), 10-inch (12,500 lbs for shell and 16,500 lbs for shot), 11-inch (16,000 lbs), 13-inch (34,000 lbs), and 15-inch (42,000 lbs). There was even a gun of 20-inch bore (97,300 lbs), designed for the monitor *Puritan*. The first of these, named 'Beelzebub', was cast in May 1864. The 20-inch gun did not, however, see service aboard ship during the war.

The 15-inch Dahlgren was mounted in both the 'Passaic' and 'Roanoke' classes of Union monitors. It was a formidable weapon, especially against Confederate ironclads, as

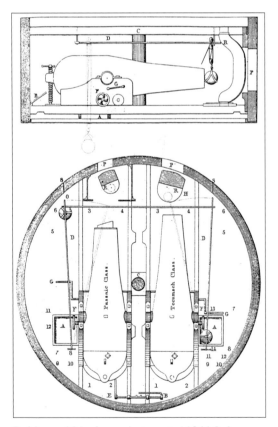

Dahlgren 16-inch gun in turret. (*1866 Ordnance Instructions*)

View on gundeck of US Navy screw sloop *Hartford*, 1864, showing Dahlgren 9-inch shell guns in broadsides. (*Naval Historical Foundation, NH 53678*)

11-inch Dahlgren aft pivot gun aboard USS *Kearsarge*. (*Naval Historical Foundation, NH 52025*)

was proven when its shot smashed through the four inches of armour plate and compelled the surrender of the *Atlanta* in June 1863 and of the *Tennessee* in August 1864. Its projectiles consisted of a 440-lb solid shot fired with a 60-lb powder charge, a 400-lb cored shot for use against masonry fired with a 50-lb charge, and a 330-lb shell fired with a 35-lb charge.[12]

Dahlgren summed up the difference between Paixhans' system and his own when he wrote, 'Paixhans' guns were simply shell-guns, and were not designed for shot, nor for great penetration or accuracy at long ranges. They were, therefore, auxiliary to, or associates of, the shot-guns. This made a mixed armament, was objectionable as such and was never adopted to any extent in France.' The same was true in Great Britain and the United States. His system, on the other hand, was 'to have a gun that should generally throw shells far and accurately, with the capacity to fire solid shot when needed. Also to compose the whole battery entirely of such guns. The omission of shot is thus accounted for. The proclivity to fire

them was such, and the avoidance of shell practice so great, that I asked that no shot should be kept on board, and then the practice with shells would be compulsory'.[13]

Dahlgren smoothbores were extra-ordinarily reliable. One captain said that the 9-inchers were 'the best . . . ever made', and he noted that their crews handled them 'with as much confidence as they drink their grog'.[14]

INTRODUCTION OF SHELL

The first real test of the new shell guns came in the Crimean War. As noted earlier, in the November 1853 Battle of Sinope the Russians had destroyed a Turkish squadron. The Russians had used both shot and shell, but shell did the most damage, tearing large irregular holes in the wooden sides of the Turkish vessels and setting many of them on fire. Sinope both provided ample proof of the effectiveness of shell and spurred the development of the ironclad.

Battle of Sinope, 30 November 1853, *see also* page 101–2. Wood engraving, *Illustrated London News*, 7 January 1854. (*Anne S.K. Brown Military Collection, Brown University Library*)

Despite this demonstrated success, for a variety of reasons shell guns formed only a part of the armament of the world's navies. For example, the largest French warship, the *Bretagne* (completed in 1856) had only 36 × 22 cm shell guns out of her total of 130 guns; and the Royal Navy *Victoria* (completed in 1861) had 62 × 8-inch shell guns out of her total armament of 121 guns. The standard shot guns remained the 36-pounder in the French Navy and the 32-pounder in the Royal Navy. The use of shell guns was restricted because of simple resistance to change, the unfortunate legacy of switching to an all-carronade armament, because shell was largely untried, the failure to seat cartridges properly in the chambers led to misfires, and because crews were apprehensive of shells and fearful of accidents.[15]

An example of the danger of shells to one's own vessel occurred on 14 May 1799, when the Royal Navy was helping to defend Acre against French attacks. The 74-gun ship-of-the-line *Theseus* was firing unexploded French shells in its own guns when some 70 of them suddenly blew up, killing 26 men, including her captain, and causing considerable damage to the ship.[16]

By the 1850s there were two basic kinds of guns aboard warships: those to fire solid shot and those for the projection of shell. In both the Royal and US navies, shot guns were designated by weight of their shot; shell guns were designated in the Royal Navy by the diameter of their shot and in the US Navy by the diameter of their bore. Thus a gun of the same calibre might be a 64-pounder if it were a shot gun or an 8-inch if it were a shell gun. But an 8-inch gun in the Royal Navy had a bore of 8.05 inches and fired an 8-inch projectile; its US Navy counterpart had a bore of 8 inches and fired a projectile with a maximum diameter of 7.82 inches.[17]

Shot guns were much heavier. An 8-inch 63 cwt shell gun of 1856 weighed 7,056 lbs; its counterpart 64-pounder shot gun weighed 105 cwt or 11,760 lbs. Shell guns were not only lighter but many had chambered bores for the smaller powder charges. While designed to fire shell, they were also fully capable of firing shot. By the time of the Civil War the US Navy had adopted the shell gun exclusively. It is thus ironic that in naval engagements of the war the most effective means of dealing with an ironclad vessel was a shell gun firing solid shot with a much heavier charge than originally thought possible.

RIFLED GUNS

The major naval powers also experimented with rifled guns aboard ship. Rifling had found an enthusiastic advocate in Englishman Benjamin Robins, who may be said to have begun the scientific study of ordnance. Robins also invented the ballistic pendulum, a device to measure the velocity of projectiles. In 1742 he published his important book, *New Principles of Gunnery*. His theories of atmospheric resistance to the flight of a projectile led him to favour rifled, elongated projectiles and larger-calibre guns at the expense of range.[18]

In 1745 Robins conducted experiments with rifled field pieces. He predicted that:

> whatever state shall thoroughly comprehend the nature and advantages of rifled barrel pieces, and, having facilitated and completed their construction, shall introduce into their armies their general use, with a dexterity in the management of them; they will by this means produce a superiority which will almost equal anything that has been done at any time by the particular excellence of any one kind of arms.[19]

By the 1850s there was renewed interest in rifling for large guns at sea. The rifle offered the advantages of longer range, greater projectile penetration, and more accurate fire. There were, however, difficulties in developing larger rifled guns. For one thing they had to be quite strong to sustain the higher pressures created by the smaller windage.

A gun blowing up could be disastrous, particularly in the close confines of a ship. An example of this was the bursting of an old Army 42-pounder converted to a rifle on board the *St Louis* during the 1862 Union siege of Island No. 10. It killed or wounded 15 officers and men. Rifled guns were also hard to aim accurately on the heaving deck of a vessel underway, and they could not fire in ricochet. The latter was important at sea because gunners were routinely instructed to fire low for fear that shot would go high and miss the target vessel entirely. Ricochet fire also greatly increased the range of shot; on hitting the water, the round ball from a smoothbore gun would continue on line, whereas a rifle projectile might take off at any angle. Early rifle projectiles also tended to tumble in flight. Finally, rifled guns were quite expensive.

It was not until the 1820s that serious efforts were made to apply rifling to cannon. The pioneers in this were Baron Wahrendorff in Sweden and Major Cavalli of the Sardinian Artillery. Both introduced breech-loading rifled guns in the 1840s. The Cavalli shell had raised projections on opposite sides of the length of the cylindrical projectile. These ran in two grooves cut spirally into the bore that made a half turn over its length. In both guns the breech was secured after loading by means of a rectangular metal wedge working in a mortise slot in an extension of the gun beyond the breech. In the Cavalli, the chamber was sealed by means of a 'culotte,' an iron cup placed at the mouth of the chamber after the shell and cartridge had been loaded. Both guns also had unusual carriages. The Cavalli was secured in a non-recoil mount, while the Wahrendorff recoiled up an inclined plane, with gravity returning it to battery. In 1852 the English conducted tests with both guns. The Wahrendorff performed well, but the Cavalli became unserviceable after only four rounds.[20]

The Lancaster breech-loading gun, developed in Britain in 1850, also offered promise. It weighed 95 cwt (16,640 lbs) and had an elliptical eight-inch bore with a spiralled rifling of one-quarter rotation. Elongated rifle projectiles were heavier than round shot of comparable diameter and, since they were in greater contact with the barrel and fit it more tightly, developed more friction. Rifled gun barrels were therefore under more strain than the smoothbore barrels firing round shot with a heavier charge. To be safe, spherical projectiles could be fired only with small powder charges.

The first trial of the Lancaster gun took place in August 1851. The strain of the firing broke six out of seven shells, even with small charges. Better results were obtained a year later when seven shells were fired with 10 and 12 lbs of powder for a range of 5,600 yards at 17 degrees elevation. On the eighth fire, however, the shell stuck in the gun.

After these trials the Lancaster gun was shelved until the Crimean War, when it was seen as a weapon capable of striking Russian defences at distances beyond the range of Russian shore batteries. Some Lancasters installed in land batteries took part in the shelling of Sevastopol beginning on 17 October 1854. One of them, firing at the Russian ship-of-the-line *Dvenadtzat Apostolov*, failed to register a hit. Two burst in the attack on the Kinburn forts and another in England.

The French conducted experiments with a 22 cm gun bored for a 30 lb shell. Rifled with two spiral grooves, it fired a cylindro-conical projectile weighing 54.5 lbs. The latter had two nipples that fit into grooves in the bore. Forty of these guns were ordered from the

Ruellese foundry, and by 1856 30 had been cast. They achieved ranges of 5,400 yards and that same year were used on gunboats in Baltic operations against Russia. The French also employed rifled pieces on land in their 1859 war with Austria.[21]

Daniel Treadwell

In the 1840s Harvard University Professor Daniel Treadwell introduced a new gun design. It took advantage of the fact that wrought iron had about twice the tenacity of cast iron. The Treadwell was a built-up gun in which the body was of cast iron, the thickness of which was only about half the diameter of the bore. On top of this were placed successive rings or hollow cylinders of wrought iron welded together. Each ring was made up of bars wound spirally and then welded and shaped in dies. A hydrostatic press forced the rings together. The rings, made slightly smaller than the final fit, were then heated so that the expanded iron could be put on the gun before cooling and contracting. The gun was light for its calibre, with a ratio of shot to gun metal about the same as for a carronade.

Subsequently the softness of wrought iron induced Treadwell to change the process, beginning with a steel band about a third the thickness of the whole. Wrought-iron bars were then wound around it. The object in this was to arrange the metal fibre in a direction opposite to that of tangential rupture – in other words, to produce a gun of equal strength in all directions.

Between 1841 and 1845 upwards of 20 Treadwell-designed guns were manufactured. Both the US Army and Navy tested them and found them satisfactory, although the gun was never adopted. Factors in its rejection were its high cost and doubts about reliability. While wrought iron guns had great tensile strength, they also tended to be weak. As Chief of the Bureau of Naval Ordnance, Captain Henry A. Wise noted in 1864, 'You may make one gun that will stand ten thousand rounds, and the next gun may not stand ten rounds. You cannot get the uniformity desirable.'[22]

'Peacemaker'

This seemed borne out in the infamous 'Peacemaker' explosion. In 1841 Swedish engineer John Ericsson arrived in the United States. A 12-inch wrought-iron gun named the 'Orator' that he had designed, and had manufactured at the Mersey Iron Works near Liverpool, was placed aboard the steam sloop *Princeton*. The gun had been strengthened in the United States by the addition of 3.5-inch wrought-iron bands shrunk on the breech. The gun's shot could penetrate 4.5 inches of wrought iron.

Captain Robert Stockton, who had command of the *Princeton*, now ordered a second gun built in the United States. Forged by Ward and Co. of New York, it was bored and finished at the Phoenix Foundry under Ericsson's direction. The second gun, named the 'Peacemaker', had the same bore and chamber as the first but was greater in diameter to compensate for the bands on the first gun. In January 1844 it and the first gun, renamed the 'Oregon', were mounted on the *Princeton*.

There was much interest in these powerful new guns and the sloop made several trial runs to demonstrate them. On 28 February 1844, 400 people, including President John Tyler, his department heads and their families, were taken on board the sloop for a trip from Washington to Alexandria, Virginia. Stockton fired the gun successfully several times and, on the return trip upriver, agreed to fire it again. This time it burst. The explosion killed eight people, including Secretary of State Abel Upshur and Secretary of the Navy Thomas Gilmer. Stockton and a number of others

Explosion of the 'Peacemaker' on board the US steam frigate *Princeton*, 28 February 1844. (*Naval Historical Foundation, NH 58906 KN*)

were injured. President Tyler, below deck, escaped harm.

A subsequent scientific inquiry into the explosion urged that attempts to use large wrought-iron guns be abandoned. It found fault with the welds and held that the iron had been weakened by long exposure to intense heat in the manufacturing process. The 'Oregon' was then removed from the *Princeton*.

Although the explosion may have led Congress to hold up funds for naval ordnance and ship development, it also led to new casting techniques and quality control. Another effect was a reduction in powder charges for guns aboard ship. By the time of the Civil War, the maximum powder charge was 15 lbs, and this was for the 11-inch Dahlgren. This had its effect in the 1863 Civil War battle between the *Monitor* and the *Virginia*.[23]

Armstrong, Whitworth and Blakely

Probably the most successful rifled cannon of this era was the breech-loading gun developed by Englishman William G. Armstrong, an engineer known for hydraulic machinery. Armstrong made use of the Treadwell principle. In both Treadwell and Armstrong guns, the requisite strength was obtained by coiling wrought iron and welding this in place. Designed in 1854 in response to ordnance shortcomings in the Crimean War, the first Armstrong gun appeared in July 1855. The prototype 3-pounder had a two-inch bore in a steel tube with several spiral grooves of rifling. This was then covered by ribbons of wrought iron wound on spirally and welded together. The breech unscrewed for loading. The projectile had a soft coating of lead to enable it to engage the grooves of rifling.

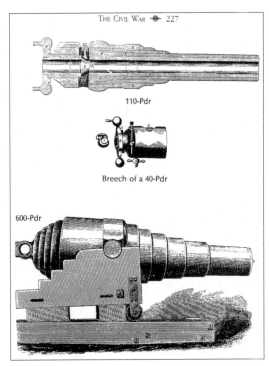

THE CIVIL WAR ◆ 227

110-Pdr

Breech of a 40-Pdr

600-Pdr

Armstrong guns. (*Alexander Holley*, A Treatise on Ordnance and Armor, *1865*)

Following the prototype's success, a larger gun, all of wrought iron, was manufactured.

In 1858 the British Army accepted an 18-pounder Armstrong field gun. At 1,000-yards range its projectile regularly hit the target, while the conventional muzzle-loading smoothbore did so only once every 57 shots. Although Armstrong was later knighted and made superintendent of the naval gun factory, the naval version of his gun was not as successful. Armstrong conducted tests with a 6-inch version weighing 65 cwt, firing projectiles weighing between 80 and 100 lbs. Its velocity was less than a conventional 32-pounder gun, and the projectiles could not penetrate 4-inch wrought iron, even from 50 yards. Nonetheless, the Ordnance Com-mittee placed orders for 7-inch Armstrong guns to fire 110-lb shells. These guns were ready by the time the *Warrior* was launched and the Admiralty placed ten of

them aboard the new ship, along with 4 × 70-pounder Armstrongs and 26 × 68-pounder conventional guns. A 9-inch, 12-ton Armstrong rifle was tested in 1864 and its shells penetrated 5.5-inch armour. This gun was first mounted in the *Prince Albert* and *Bellerophon* in 1866.[24]

The Armstrong gun's relative lack of velocity because of the small charge, meant that its shells could not penetrate substantial armour. There were also problems in breech jamming during the August 1863 Royal Navy bombardment of Kagoshima, Japan. Another disadvantage was the gun's vulnerability to enemy fire; even a small shot could put it out of action. In 1864 US cannon founder Charles Knap described the Armstrong as 'a very good gun, but excessively expensive, and not very durable'.[25]

Another Englishman, Sir Joseph Whitworth, designed breech-loaders as well as muzzle-loading guns. The Whitworth gun's bore was a hexagonal spiral. The gun was made of cast iron bored from the solid but also from steel, with wrought-iron rings shrunk on. By 1862 Whitworth guns were of 3-, 12-, and 80-pounder sizes and ranged in weight from 208 lbs to four tons. The 3-pounder could, with an 8 oz charge of powder, throw a projectile 9,688 yards.

A third British rifled gun was the Blakely, designed by Royal Artillery captain Theophilus Alexander Blakely. It used the same principle as the Armstrong and Whitworth, with wrought-iron rings shrunk around a cast-iron core. The Blakely differed from the other two only in appearing as a muzzle-loader. Probably the most famous Blakely was the 7-inch (150-pounder), one of two pivot guns aboard the CSS *Alabama*. During the American Civil War the Confederacy purchased all three of these rifled gun types as well as the inferior Clay breech-loader.

John Dahlgren also designed rifled guns, somewhat similar in shape to the

Rear Admiral John Dahlgren standing next to one of his 4.4- or 5.1-inch rifled guns aboard the *Pawnee*, Charleston Harbor, 21 April 1865. (*Library of Congress, B8171-3417*)

smoothbores although some had separate bronze trunnion and breech straps. Dahlgren rifles appeared in these sizes: 4.4-inch/30-pounder (3,200 lbs), 5.1-inch/50-pounder (5,100 lbs), 6-inch/80-pounder (8,000 lbs), 7.5-inch/150-pounder (16,700 lbs), and 12-inch (45,520 lbs, only three of which were cast). Dahlgren's rifled guns were not successful, and in February 1862 during the Civil War most were withdrawn from service.[26]

Rifled guns for sea service were for a long time a work in progress. During the American Civil War the favourite Union rifled gun was the Parrott, designed by Robert P. Parrott, a former US Army ordnance officer who operated the West Point Foundry. The Parrott was essentially a muzzle-loading, cast-iron rifle with a wrought-iron band shrunk over the breech. The band had a thickness of one half the

6.4-inch (100-pounder) Parrott rifled gun aboard USS *Teaser* during Civil War. Note compressor gear and shell in foreground. (*National Archives, 90-CR1-482*)

bore diameter. The 3.67-inch and 4.2-inch guns were rifled with five grooves; the 2.9- and 3-inch had 3, the 6.4-inch 9, the 8-inch 11 and the 10-inch, 15 grooves. Parrott guns were used at sea in a variety of sizes, and by 1864 Parrott was the only founder producing rifled guns for the US Navy. The Navy then had about 650 of them in service, about a fifth of its ordnance inventory. The 8-inch Parrott, which weighed 16,300 lbs, fired projectiles of between 132 and 175 lbs and was used in the turrets of some monitors alongside the Dahlgren smoothbores.[27]

John M. Brooke

During the Civil War Confederate Navy lieutenant John Mercer Brooke, who surprisingly had little ordnance experience, designed a variety of guns. These included 8- and 9-inch smoothbores, 10- and 11-inch double-banded smoothbores, and an 11-inch triple-banded smoothbore. Brooke is best known, however, for his double- and triple-banded rifled guns, produced in 6.4-inch, 7-inch, and 8-inch bore sizes. They were probably the finest rifled naval guns on either side in the Civil War. As with Dahlgren, Brooke understood that a hemisphere offered the strongest cap for a cylindrical pressure vessel. He also understood, as did Parrott, the gain in strength from a wrought-iron band shrunk around the breech of a cast-iron gun. Brooke-designed guns are identified, with

Confederate 10-inch Brooke double-banded smoothbore gun, reportedly cast for the ironclad *Columbia*. In the background is the Ericsson 12-inch wrought-iron smoothbore navy gun, made at the Mersey Iron Works in 1845 as the replacement for the 'Peacemaker'; it apparently never saw service. (*Washington Navy Yard, photograph by Malcolm Muir, Jr*)

few exceptions, by a fully hemispheric breech contour; layers of welded-on reinforcing bands; a plain tapered chase extending from the reinforcing bands to the muzzle; the Confederate practice of not turning and merely leaving the exterior of the guns rough; and, save in the smoothbores, seven-groove rifling of right-hand twist.[28]

The Confederates particularly favoured rifled guns. They converted a number of smoothbores to rifles and purchased rifled guns in Europe. Captured Union guns and their own limited ordnance production were sufficient to meet the Confederacy's more modest requirements, although the lack of manufacturing facilities and skilled labour led to difficulties in mounting guns, and in shortages of shells and wrought-iron bolt projectiles.

TRIAL ADOPTION OF BREECH-LOADING GUNS

Breech-loading guns had been around since the first use of cannon but the problem had always been in sealing the breech against the escape of gases. Modern metallurgical and machining techniques helped to surmount this. Even so, the heavy breech block had to be unscrewed and then screwed back on after each shot, a process that became progressively more difficult with powder fouling. Also, the problem in preventing the escape of gases at the breech was not completely solved until the invention of the interrupted screw breech block. This allowed the block to be inserted, then screwed and locked into place. This invention is usually credited to American Ben Chambers, who patented a slotted screw in 1849.

Over the next years there were many experiments and modifications in breech block design. French ordnance designer Treuille de Beaulieu built on Chambers' work and helped secure the French Navy's adoption of breech-loaders in 1858. Three years later the French introduced some breech-loading guns aboard the *Gloire*. The Royal Navy countered by introducing breech-loading Armstrong guns as the heaviest ordnance aboard the *Warrior*, as well as on other ships. But problems with the Armstrong gun, already referred to, and accidents, owing to the fact that it was possible to fire it without the breech-block being completely screwed down, led in 1864 to breech-loaders being withdrawn from service, replaced by muzzle-loaders. The Royal Navy did not change back to breech-loaders until 1881.[29]

In the American Civil War the breech-loading Armstrongs, Whitworths and Blakelys did not prove successful. As late as 1861 one ordnance expert concluded, 'Breech-loading cannon to command the settled confidence of military men . . . never will be made at least in considerable numbers for general service . . . Popular favour now sustains the Armstrong breech-loading cannon. In time it will sink to a level corresponding with its true merit.'[30]

A year later another writer concluded similarly that 'the endeavor to produce breech-loading cannon is an effort to obtain uncalled for and superfluous facility in gunnery'.[31] Dahlgren himself wrote in 1865, 'The plan of loading at the breech is

exploded and dismissed.'[32] Effective breech-loading heavy ordnance had to await advances in technology and manufacturing.

By the 1850s some were also having second thoughts about the shell gun. Many agreed with Sir Howard Douglas' conclusion: 'distant firing with powerful solid shot guns will be the most effectual means of avoiding or counteracting the destructive effects which hollow shot and shells would unavoidably produce if the ship which uses them were by any chance to gain the requisite proximity'.[33] Despite controversy over the relative merits of shot and shell guns, by the 1850s shell had earned permanent place at sea. Prior to the Civil War, US Navy regulations called for captains to practice firing loaded shells 'in preference to shot'.[34]

GUN CARRIAGES

As the debate between type of gun went forward, gun carriages were changing. The old truck carriage had lasted for so long because it had proved so durable, but the new, larger guns subjected it to strains it could not take. One innovation was the American Marsilly carriage, which increased friction on the deck by substituting wooden skids for the rear trucks. But the new mounts evolved from those built for the carronades.

These had introduced a screw for elevation in place of the wooden wedge or quoin, and the mount itself recoiled in a slide anchored to the side of the ship by means of a pin. The slide also had small trucks set at right angles to it that allowed easier lateral training. This system was now applied to long guns even of the largest size, with their recoil arrested by means of a compressor, possibly invented by Royal Navy admiral Sir Thomas Hardy, that increased

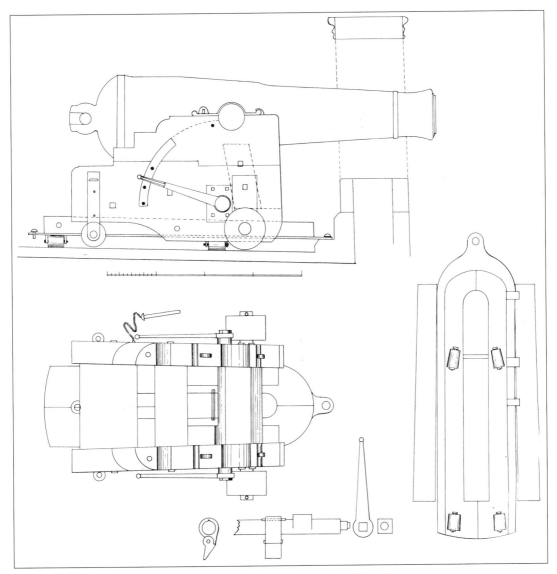

Friction carriage, designed by Van Brunt for the US Navy in the 1850s. Note compressor.

friction and reduced the recoil. The idea was not to reduce it altogether, as muzzle-loading guns needed to be brought back a sufficient distance after firing in order to reload them.

The next step was to replace the wooden carriages and slides with those of iron. Following trials with both wooden and iron carriages, in September 1865 the Royal Navy adopted iron carriages for all guns weighing more than five tons. Also, with new breech-loading guns it was no longer necessary to have the gun recoil a considerable distance for reloading purposes.[35]

Armoured turret

The logical next step following the development of large-bore pivot-mounted

Even during the Civil War old guns and truck carriages were widely used, as may be seen in this photograph of US Navy steam tug *Thomas Freeborn* of the Potomac Flotilla in May 1861, shortly after the start of the war. (*Naval Historical Foundation, NH 60990*)

Erzherzog Ferdinand Maximilian, Austrian armoured frigate with ram, drawing depicting her at the 1866 Battle of Lissa, *see also* pages 131–2. (*The International Research Organization, Karl Goff Collection, Naval Historical Foundation, NH 86032*)

Hotspur, Royal Navy armoured ram. (*Royal Naval Museum, 5019*)

guns was an armoured turret to protect the guns and their crews, especially during the lengthy reloading process. This invention is variously credited to Captain Cowper Coles in Britain, Dupuy de Lôme in France, and John Ericsson in the United States. The first actual employment in battle of a revolving turret occurred during the American Civil War in the 9 March 1862, engagement between the USS *Monitor* and the CSS *Virginia.*

THE RAM

The ram bow also made a comeback. A weapon utilized in the ancient and early modern periods for sinking an opposing warship, it was fitted at the bow either above

or below the waterline. Its utility seemed proven during the American Civil War when on 8 March 1862, the CSS *Virginia* used her underwater ram to sink the USS *Cumberland.* Unfortunately for the Confederates, the ram broke off in the *Cumberland* and so was not available for her important duel with the Union *Monitor* the next day. During the war both sides built ram warships.

The Austrians also used the ram in the 20 July 1866, Battle of Lissa during the Austro-Prussian War, when the *Erzherzog Ferdinand Maximilian* sank the Italian ship *Re d'Italia.* Despite these few successes and the fact that rams continued to be utilized aboard warships during the remainder of the century, they could not take the place of the gun at sea.

CHAPTER 5

THE TECHNOLOGICAL REVOLUTION IN PRACTICE

NAVAL WARFARE AT MID-CENTURY

A series of wars at mid-century demonstrated the new naval technologies of steam power, ironclad ships, and heavier ordnance. The wars also gave rise to new weapons systems, such as the submarine and mine, that would later appear in more advanced forms.

MEXICAN WAR (1846–8)

On 11 May 1846, the United States Congress declared war on Mexico. President James K. Polk sought the Mexican province of California; and, after the Mexican government rebuffed his efforts to purchase it, Polk engineered the war to gain California by force. Fighting took place principally on three fronts: California, northern Mexico and central Mexico. Unlike the Army, the Navy was ready for the war.

In June in California, US citizens there proclaimed a republic. The arrival of the US Pacific Squadron at Monterey and a cavalry regiment overland insured that California would stay in American hands. The campaign in northern Mexico was more complicated. Major General Zachary Taylor's inability to bring the war to a successful conclusion there led Polk to agree to Major General Winfield

Scott's plan to move against the capital of Mexico City from the port of Vera Cruz. As Taylor's forces were drawn off for Scott's expedition, President/General Santa Anna attempted to destroy a weakened Taylor, but in the Battle of Buena Vista (22–3 February 1847) Taylor was victorious.

Commodore David Conner's Home Squadron, meanwhile, secured control of the Gulf of Mexico. The Mexican Navy was negligible and posed no threat; it had only two warships of consequence, the steamers *Guadaloupe* and *Montezuma*, and Great Britain repossessed both at the start of the war.[1]

Conner's orders were to blockade the principal Mexican ports, protect US commerce from privateers, and assist army operations. The Navy was successful in all three, but its most important contribution and its principal task in the war was the blockade of the Mexican coasts, chiefly in the Gulf of Mexico.

The blockade applied political and economic pressure on the Mexican government, but it also protected US commerce against privateers, which Mexico tried to commission in Cuba. Only one privateer with a Mexican commission is known to have seized a

US vessel during the war, and the Spanish government subsequently returned her.

The blockade was a considerable achievement given the distances involved, for the nearest US Navy base was Pensacola, Florida, 900 miles from Vera Cruz. Conditions were daunting: tropical diseases (especially yellow fever), the lack of accurate coastal charts, and extremes of weather from summer heat to sudden and violent winter storms.

There were few harbours on the Mexican Gulf coast and those that did exist had shallow bars passable only in calm conditions. This necessitated operations in shoal waters too shallow even for the smallest sloops. Indeed, one goal of US Navy coastal operations was to capture Mexican vessels suited to coastal conditions.

Initially Conner had available the powerful steamers *Mississippi* and *Princeton*, two heavy frigates, three sloops, five brigs, and a schooner. Soon the Navy purchased five small fast-sailing schooners, equipping each with a single heavy gun and additional armament. Other warships were added later.

Conner soon established a floating advance base near Vera Cruz; for a blockade to be legal at this time, the blockaders had to be actually stationed at the ports to be blockaded. In conformity with the traditional US position toward neutral rights, the Navy confiscated only those ships actually flying the Mexican flag; foreign flag vessels were allowed to pass freely. In spite of difficulties, the blockade was effective. Certainly some Mexican ships got through, but no large quantities of war matériel reached Mexico during the war.

Control of the seas was also vital to the US war effort in another way. Supply by sea was much easier than by land, and the Navy

Mississippi, US Navy side-wheel frigate. Wash drawing by Clary Ray showing the ship during the Civil War. (*Naval Historical Foundation, NH 60655*)

Naval bombardment of Vera Cruz, March 1847. Lithograph by N. Currier. (*Naval Historical Foundation, NH 001306*)

made possible the Army landing at Vera Cruz. On 9 March 1847, using 65 'surf boats' shipped in the holds of transports, the Navy put ashore Scott's entire army of 12,000 men with artillery, horses, vehicles and supplies near Vera Cruz. Siege guns manned by sailors were sited to bombard the city, which surrendered on 27 March. Scott then marched inland 260 miles to Mexico City in a brilliant six-months' campaign that forced the Mexican government to conclude peace in February 1848.

The war proved the effectiveness of steamers in fast resupply, in blockade, and in shelling coastal targets where tide and wind proved difficult for sailing craft. The light-draught steamers *Scorpion*, *Scourge*, *Spitfire*, and *Vixen*, all purchased at New York and converted into warships, were especially effective in river operations, including two forays up the Tabasco River and the Army landing at Vera Cruz. Steamers frequently towed sailing ships into position, as during the Tabasco River expeditions.

The Mexican War therefore provided a powerful boost for expanding the numbers of steamers in the world's navies. The *Mississippi* and *Princeton*, the largest steamers in the US Navy, were particularly useful in the Home Squadron during the war. Although too deep in draught to participate in river expeditions where there was usually a bar, they provided fast and reliable service regardless of wind conditions. Proof of this came in November 1846 when the *Mississippi* steamed from Tampico to Matamoros and then on to New Orleans to obtain troops and supplies, returning to its starting point in only 13 days, a record for that time.

Taking note of the success of steamers during the war, in March 1847 the US Congress authorized construction of four steamers. These were the *Susquehanna*, *Powhatan*, *Saranac*, and *San Jacinto*. The US Navy's experience in the war, especially in blockade, undoubtedly assisted it during the Civil War 15 years later. But the Mexican War also hastened the coming of that great sectional conflict, for as a consequence of victory, the United States secured not only the Rio Grande boundary for Texas but California and New Mexico (which yielded the future states of New Mexico, Arizona, Colorado, Utah and Nevada). The paramount issue now became whether the new states would be slave or free.

CRIMEAN WAR (1854–6)

While sectional pressures were building within the United States a major war erupted on the periphery of Europe. Fighting began from a quarrel over control of the Christian holy sites in Turkish-ruled Jerusalem. This pitted France, representing Roman Catholics, against Russia, supporting Orthodox Christians. But the real cause of the war was the continuing decline of Turkey and Russia's efforts to divide up the European possessions of what was now referred to as the 'Sick Man of Europe'. Russia had long sought a warm water outlet to the Mediterranean. This could be accomplished either by securing de facto control of the eastern Balkans or outright control of the Turkish-held Bosphorus, Sea of Marmara and the Dardanelles in order to access the Mediterranean from the Black Sea.

In July 1853 Tsar Nicholas I ordered Russian troops to begin occupation of Turkey's Romanian principalities. In October Turkey declared war on Russia and crossed the Danube, defeating the Russians in the 4 November Battle of Oltenitza. That same month France, followed by Britain, dispatched fleets to Constantinople to encourage Turkey. Neither power wanted to see Russia gain access to the eastern Mediterranean.

Battle of Sinope (30 November 1853)

Russian warships based at Sevastopol had been active in the Black Sea since the beginning of the war with Turkey, but there had been little naval action, apart from the

Russian capture of an Egyptian frigate. That changed in November. Late that month Turkish vice admiral Osman Pasha was en route to Serbia with a force of seven sailing frigates, two corvettes, and several transports to relieve Turkish forces short of provisions, when he was caught in a storm in the Black Sea and took refuge in the port of Sinope (Sinop). Osman flew his flag in the 60-gun *Avni Illah*. The largest Turkish guns were 24-pounders, but the anchorage was protected by 84 guns, some of them possibly landed from the ships.

A Russian force under Admiral Paul S. Nakhimov now arrived at Sinope. Nakhimov had three ships-of-the-line and several smaller craft, but he secured from Sevastopol four 120-gun three-deckers: the *Grossfurst Constantin*, *Tri Sviatitla*, *Paris* and *Zvolf Apostel*. Their main armament was in new 68-pounder shell guns.

A thick mist on the morning of 30 November masked the approach of the Russian vessels into the harbour. The Turks barely had time to clear for action before battle was joined at 10:00 a.m. Within half an hour the *Grossfurst Constantin* had sunk a Turkish frigate and silenced the Turkish shore batteries. The battle (*see also* page 85) raged until 4:00 p.m. Only one Turkish vessel – the paddle steamer *Taif* – managed to escape; the remainder were sunk. The Russians admitted to 37 dead; the Turks lost upwards of 3,000.

Although the Turks had been badly outgunned at Sinope, the inequity of the losses conclusively demonstrated the superiority of shell over shot against wooden vessels. The Russian ship *Imperitritza Marie* had been struck by 84 cannon balls without major damage, but the Turkish fleet had been destroyed. As noted in Chapter 4, the battle led to heightened world interest in the construction of ironclad warships for protection against shell.[2]

British and French ships in the Baltic, Crimean War. (*Royal Naval Museum, 1976/253*)

Sinope also produced a wellspring of support for Turkey in Britain and France. The British Press labelled this legitimate act of war 'a foul outrage' and a 'massacre'.[3] In early January, French and British warships entered the Black Sea, and in March both nations agreed to protect Turkey's coasts and shipping against Russian attack. That same month a strong Russian land force invaded the Turkish territory of Bulgaria.

On 28 March 1854, both France and Britain declared war on Russia, and early the next month they concluded a formal alliance. The Western Allies then sent an expeditionary force to assist in repelling the Russian invasion force besieging Silistra. At this point virtually the entire French Navy and much of the Royal Navy was in the Black Sea. Overall the Allies enjoyed an advantage of more than three to one over the Russian Navy in terms both of line-of-battle ships and frigates.[4]

On 16 April Russian shore batteries at Odessa opened fire on the British frigate *Furious* as it tried to enter the port under a flag of truce. In retaliation, on 22 April the Allies bombarded Odessa and inflicted serious damage. In June two British steam gunboats raided a Bessarabian village at the mouth of the Danube and destroyed Russian fortifications. But there was little for Allied ships to do, apart from blockade and patrol activities, until the time came to escort the Allied troop and supply ships across the Black Sea to the Crimea.

Meanwhile Austrian threats to enter the war caused Russia to abandon its siege of Silistra and withdraw troops from the area. The object of the Allied expedition seemed to have been accomplished, but Russia rejected demands that it renounce claims against the Ottoman Empire, and the war continued.

Although the Allies had achieved their principal objectives of getting Russia to evacuate her land conquests and uphold the territorial integrity of Turkey, British and French goals shifted to include destruction of Russian naval power in the Black Sea. To accomplish this the Allies had to take the great Russian naval base of Sevastopol, although they entered into this without any real thought of what it might entail.

In early September a great convoy of some 150 Allied ships departed Varna in present-day Bulgaria for the Crimean Peninsula, and finally landed about 30 miles north of Sevastopol. Russian commander Prince Alexander Sergeievich Menshikov made no effort to oppose the landing.

The advance toward Sevastopol was badly handled, and it was not until early October that the Allies began siege operations. Allied control of the sea should have greatly aided their Crimean operations; while the Russians had a land route open, their logistics system was primitive and they had problems supplying the beleaguered fortress.

The Allies were confident, therefore, that they would soon take Sevastopol and end the war. Reports from Russian deserters of low morale among the defenders gave hope. The Allied commanders planned a concerted land and naval bombardment to begin on the morning of 17 October. Inasmuch as the Allied forces ashore were entirely dependent on the fleet for resupply and, in a worst case scenario, evacuation, British naval commander Admiral Sir James W. Dundas was opposed to risking his ships against the Russian shore batteries. French naval commander Admiral Hamelin then threatened to act alone and Dundas gave way. The French were first into the action, their sailing ships brought into position by steamers lashed to their sides. Although there was a terrific cannonade the Allies inflicted little damage on the Russian stone forts. So as not to risk the vessels unduly, they were kept at the extreme limit of their range and, after the first few shots, the targets were

Bombardment of Odessa, April 1854, Crimean War. (*Royal Naval Museum, 1977/381*)

Sevastopol from the sea, from deck of HMS *Sidon*. (*Royal Naval Museum, 1977/380*)

obscured in thick smoke. Fortunately for the ships, the Russian gunners also had trouble locating their targets.

When the engagement ended, however, the ships had suffered more than the forts. They had fired 700 tons of shot from 500 guns, but the forts were still in action; the few Russian guns dismounted were replaced or back in action by the morning of the 18th. Ships-of-the-line *Albion* and *Arethusa* were badly damaged; the *Retribution* had lost her mainmast, the *Firebrand* had also been much cut up, and the *Rodney* was nearly lost when she ran aground. Forty-two British and 32 French sailors were killed and 266 British and 180 French wounded. The operation had been a failure, but the admirals had learned their lesson and made no further attempts to bombard Sevastopol's harbour fortifications.[5]

The Allied commanders now settled in for a long siege. They had made no provision for a winter campaign in Russia, and normal difficulties were abetted by a severe storm on 14 November that wrecked some 30 transports at Balaklava and destroyed stores of rations, forage, and clothing. To add to the misery and suffering on the peninsula, cholera broke out. It was not until early 1855 that the Allied supply situation improved.

Finally, on 8 September 1855, the Allies breached the Russian defences. That night Russian commander Prince Mikhayl Gorchakov, who had replaced Menshikov in early February, evacuated Sevastopol and blew up what remained of the fortress.

On 17 October the French employed the steam ironclad batteries *Dévastation*, *Lave* and *Tonnante* to bombard and demolish the heavy sand and masonry Kinburn Forts at the mouth of the Dnieper and Bug rivers. The first use of ironclad vessels in warfare, it made a considerable impression in naval circles.

Allied operations in the Baltic

There was also fighting in the Caucasus region and in the Baltic. With most of their naval strength deployed in the Black Sea, London and Paris were worried about the threat posed by 27 Russian ships-of-the-line in the Baltic. To prevent the Russian ships from leaving the Baltic, London assembled a scratch fleet of 25 ships under Vice Admiral Sir Charles Napier and dispatched it from Portsmouth on 10 March 1854, even before war was declared. The squadron's composition reflects the transformation then in progress from sail to steam. Napier flew his flag in the ship-of-the-line *Duke of Wellington* (131 guns); the other vessels ranged from first rates all the way down to a warship of just six guns. All of the bigger ships, save two, had previously been fitted for screw-propellers, but at the same time they retained their full sail rigs. The nine smaller ships were all paddle-wheel (paddler) steamers. Although, reportedly, Napier had told Queen Victoria that he would take Kronstadt, he knew that the powerful Russian base was well defended and that it would be too difficult for his force to accomplish. His orders merely called on him to seal the Baltic and destroy such Russian ships as possible.

Napier split his ships into three squadrons and positioned them so as to watch the Gulf of Danzig, the Gulf of Riga and the mouth of the Gulf of Finland. His ships carried out a series of small raids, destroying several Russian dockyards and forts.[6]

The Russians used mines in an effort to the protect their forts. On 9 July 1855, some 2.5 miles off Kronstadt, the paddle packet/survey vessel *Merlin* was the first ship to be mined in naval warfare. Although the *Merlin* struck two Russian mines she was little damaged.[7] Later Napier's fleet destroyed a small Russian dockyard at Brahestad, along with a number of gunboats on the stocks.

In June, Paris sent its own fleet into the Baltic under Vice Admiral Parseval Deschenes. This, and some additions to his own force, led Napier to review the idea of a strike against Kronstadt, but the only action there was a brief appearance by the Allied force on 29 June.

The French agreed to send out 11,000 troops for raiding operations if the British would provide the transports. On 11 July a French division under General Achille Baraguay d'Hilliers sailed for the Baltic. Earlier, on 21, 26, and 27 June, the Allies had shelled Bombarsund, one of the fortified towns in the Aland Islands guarding the Gulf of Finland, but without success. On 10 August Napier returned and put some 6,000 French troops ashore in two locations. They worked their way overland and bombarded the town from the land side while British ships also shelled the Russian lines. After four days the Russians surrendered and were taken off as prisoners-of-war. The Allied troops destroyed the fortifications, but with the approach of winter the fleets sailed for home.

In June 1855 the Allies were surveying approaches to Kronstadt when they discovered a large Russian minefield. In probably the first mine-sweeping operation in history, the Allies recovered several Russian mines. In the process HMS *Firefly* hit a mine, but because the powder charge was small, she suffered little damage.

In 1855 the British had a proper force for the Baltic. Admiral Dundas, former British commander in the Black Sea, replaced Napier; French Rear Admiral Penaud replaced Deschenes. With little naval activity in the Black Sea, Dundas was able to draw off some of the better ships there. Although the Allies paid lip service to an attempt against Kronstadt, Dundas was determined not to squander men or ships there. He was well aware of the limited effect of ship bombardment against the masonry and stone forts of Sevastopol, while his own ships were being battered by return fire.

Although Dundas rejected an Admiralty plan for an attack on Kronstadt he did agree to a joint attack against the five-island complex known as Sveaborg Fortress several miles from Helsinki, which was defended by more than 800 guns and 12,000 men. Beginning on 9 August the Allied fleet shelled the Sveaborg complex for three days and two nights, lobbing thousands of shot, shell and rockets, the French alone firing more than 4,000 projectiles. Two gunboats mounting Lancaster 68-pounder rifled guns opened up on the ship-of-the-line *Russia* and claimed several hits. Heavy explosions ashore indicated several Russian magazines blown up. The Allies claimed to have killed 2,000 Russians, but the actual tally was probably 55 killed and 199 wounded. This ended naval operations in the Baltic. The British also kept a squadron in the White Sea to blockade Archangel, and in the Pacific an Anglo-French squadron also saw some action.[8]

By 1856 both the Allies and the Russians were exhausted; each side had lost close to a quarter-million dead, many from disease. In February 1856 Russia agreed to a preliminary peace settlement, the final terms of which were worked out at the Congress of Paris (28 February–30 March).

In the peace settlement Russia gave up her aspirations regarding Turkey. She lost control of the mouth of the Danube, had to cede the southern part of Bessarabia to Turkey, and was forced to demilitarize the Black Sea. Another consequence of the war was the Declaration of Paris that outlawed paper blockades and privateering and placed restrictions on commerce raiding in general.[9] Of the world's major naval powers, only the United States and Spain refused to sign the treaty.

In the naval sphere the Crimean War provided final proof of the effectiveness and reliability of the steamship in war; but it also showed the importance of iron armour. The threat posed by mines was less clear.

AMERICAN CIVIL WAR (1861–5)

In the United States, the great Civil War began in April 1861. Usually identified as the first modern, industrial war, it had many causes, including differing economic development and outlook. A sense of nationalism developed among whites in the South, but the issue of slavery forced the war. Most Northerners wanted to restrict slavery to the areas where it then existed and not allow it in the new territories to the west. A vocal minority of Northerners favoured outright abolition.

Immigrants to the United States could not compete with free slave labour in the South and most settled in the North. By the time of the Civil War the North had 22 million people, the South but 9 million and over a third of these were slaves. Manufacturing was even more imbalanced. In 1861 the North had some 85 per cent of total US manufacturing. The South, for example, had only one facility, the Tredegar Iron Works in Richmond, Virginia, capable of producing the heaviest guns and armour plate. Given the difference in manufacturing capacity it is hardly surprising that the war turned out as it did.

In November 1860 Republican Party candidate Abraham Lincoln was elected president, and at the end of the next month South Carolina seceded from the Union. Alabama, Georgia, Florida, Mississippi, Louisiana and Texas all followed. On 8 February 1861, delegates from these states met at Montgomery, Alabama, and formed the Confederate States of America.

President Lincoln decided to resupply two isolated US garrisons at Fort Sumter, South Carolina, and Fort Pickens, Florida. This difficult decision precipitated the war. To forestall the resupply of Sumter in Charleston harbour, on 12 April 1861, Southerners opened fire on it. The war was on.

At the outset, both sides were militarily weak. The Union did have a clear advantage at sea, although its widely scattered force of 80 warships was totally inadequate for what lay ahead. But by 1865 the US Navy would include some 700 vessels of all types and be second in the world in number of warships only to Great Britain.

The Union Blockade

When the war began Southern leaders adopted a defensive strategy; they hoped to tire the North, causing it to let the South go. The Northern war aim was to end Southern secession. The South had a much smaller population and a vast territory to defend, including some 3,500 miles of coastline; but a lot would depend on where and how the North attacked.

On 17 April the president of the Confederacy Jefferson Davis issued a proclamation inviting applications for letters of marque and reprisal, an action subsequently confirmed by the Confederate Congress. Davis believed he was legally free to do this because the United States had not ratified the 1856 Treaty of Paris. In retaliation, on 19 April Lincoln proclaimed a blockade of the Confederate coasts and warned that anyone attacking a US vessel would be treated as a pirate. This threat did not deter applications for letters of marque, although few of these vessels ever took to the seas.

The Confederates missed an opportunity at the beginning of the conflict. Although it was never officially announced as government policy, Davis supported withholding the cotton crop from Europe. The assumption was that this would force Britain to send warships to assist in breaking the Union blockade. This did not occur, and

the British government even issued a proclamation calling on its citizens not to break a legally constituted blockade. The catch-phrase of the Declaration of Paris was that, 'Blockades, to be binding must be effective, that is to say, maintained by a force sufficient really to prevent access to the coast of the enemy.'[10]

As it worked out precious time and a great deal of money was lost as much of the cotton crop deteriorated on Southern wharves. The South lost money to buy arms and supplies abroad.

Meanwhile Union Secretary of the Navy Gideon Welles was busy converting a small, mostly obsolete, collection of ships into an effective force. He also launched a large naval construction programme, which included ironclads; but for immediate use, Washington purchased ships of all types, many of them steamers, and assigned them to the blockade.[11]

The power of the blockade was derived from steam engines. Steamers were faster than sailing vessels and could eventually overtake them. Although Welles's new converted steamers were weak as fighting vessels, they were sufficient to deal with Confederate sail-driven blockade runners. By mid-summer the Union blockade of the South was well underway.

Davis's mistaken belief in the power of cotton had caused the South to go slow with its own construction of ships to run the blockade. The potential of this was demonstrated in September 1861, however, when a privately-owned British vessel, the iron-hulled screw steamer *Bermuda*, arrived from England with 81 rifled field pieces, four heavy smoothbore guns, 6,500 Enfield rifles, and 20,000 cartridges for the Confederate government.[12]

Unfortunately for the Confederacy the government in Richmond left most of this effort in the private sector and much of the trade was in consumer goods rather than military supplies. Because a fortune could be made on one successful voyage, too often patriotism took second place to profit. Even the British got involved, organizing private firms for blockade running operations. Speedy, low silhouette, grey-painted ships were built specifically to run the blockade. With their powerful engines burning the best coal to give off little smoke, many easily eluded Union blockaders. One such ship, lost after eight trips, nonetheless returned a profit of 700 per cent.[13]

As the Union blockade strengthened, the South was forced into reliance on small, fast, shallow-draught vessels. Union warships seized ships of any nation, even on the high seas, that could be proved as bound for Southern ports. As a result, large ships carried cargoes to Nassau, Bermuda, Havana or Halifax. Here their cargoes were transferred to smaller steamers for the run to the South.

Union sailors found blockade duty difficult, frustrating and hazardous, as they were forced to contend with the blockade runners in coastal shoal waters. Gradually, the Union pressure tightened, aided by joint naval and military expeditions. By January 1865 the Union Navy had 471 ships with 2,245 guns in blockade service, and in the course of the war these took as many as 1,500 blockade runners.[14]

Fall of Port Royal (7 November 1861)

Apart from Charleston, Port Royal, South Carolina, was the Confederacy's best natural harbour along the Atlantic coast. On 7 November 1861, US Navy flag officer Samuel Du Pont arrived off Port Royal from Hampton Roads with about 75 ships, most of which were supply vessels and transports lifting 12,000 Union soldiers under Brigadier General Thomas W. Sherman. Port Royal was well protected by two Confederate earthworks, Forts Beauregard and Walker, on

either side of the harbour entrance. But these had only 41 guns between them, and Du Pont steamed his warships in a great oval to attack both simultaneously. Superior firepower gave the Union the victory. The seizure of Port Royal was an important step in the blockade because it provided a perfect base for the South Atlantic Blockading Squadron; great stretches of Southern coastline were now within easy reach of Union gunboats.

Although penetrating the Union blockade became increasingly difficult, blockade runners continued to supply the South until the end of the war. The diminished quantity of military goods they brought was nonetheless sufficient to keep the Southern military effort going. One scholar concludes that home production never reached 50 per cent of military needs and that without the supplies brought by the blockade runners the South could not have survived as long as it did. Blockade runners also brought clothing, chemicals and medicines. Defeat did not come from lack of materials; the Confederacy simply ran out of manpower.[15]

At the onset of the war the Confederacy secured one major naval asset. In April 1861, on the secession of Virginia, the South gained control of the largest pre-war US Navy yard at Gosport (Norfolk). Withdrawing Union troops made only a half-hearted attempt to destroy both the facility and its stores, and the South secured at Gosport some 1,200 heavy guns, including 52 9-inch Dahlgrens, valuable naval stores, and some vessels. Among the latter was the powerful modern steam frigate *Merrimack*. Set on fire by retreating Union forces, she burned only to the waterline before sinking. The Confederates then raised and rebuilt her as an ironclad.

Confederate commerce raiding

Confederate Secretary of the Navy Stephen Mallory sought to offset the Northern naval advantage by constructing ironclads to break the blockade; he also advocated commerce raiding. He recalled the great success of the Americans in sending large numbers of privately owned warships to sea against the British in the War of the American Revolution and War of 1812. The US Navy had devoted itself largely to a *guerre de course* in both conflicts. For the Confederacy the situation was analogous to these earlier American wars: a nation weak on the seas faced a powerful foe with a formidable fleet but with an extensive and vulnerable merchant marine.

Mallory reasoned that a strong blow against Union merchant shipping would wound the North financially and weaken its resolve. Even modest successes would force up insurance rates and minimize profits, and a few raiders might force the US Navy to shift warships from blockade duties. The first Confederate privateers initially found easy hunting, but most were gone within a year. The Union

blockade made it difficult for them to bring their prizes into Southern ports, and many were simply converted into blockade runners.

To continue the war against Union commerce the Confederacy turned to commerce raiders. The first of these, the *Sumter*, commanded by former US Navy lieutenant Raphael Semmes, evaded the Union squadron at New Orleans and got to sea at the end of June 1861. She took 18 prizes before she was forced to put in at Gibraltar in January 1862 and was there abandoned. During the war no fewer than a dozen such ships attacked Union merchantmen. The *Alabama* was by far the most successful. Built in Great Britain on secret Confederate order, she was commissioned in August 1862. Commanded by Semmes, the *Alabama* took 66 Union merchantmen and sank the US Navy steamer *Hatteras*. Ultimately her toll of

Confederate States raider *Sumter* running past US Navy screw sloop *Brooklyn* at the mouth of the Mississippi and escaping into the Gulf of Mexico. (*Naval Historical Foundation, NH 51797*)

Alabama, Confederate Navy commerce raider. (*Naval Historical Foundation, NH 57259*)

prizes nearly equalled the combined total of the two next most successful raiders: the *Shenandoah*, with 38, most after the end of hostilities; and the *Florida*, with 33.[16]

During the Civil War the *Alabama* and other Confederate commerce raiders destroyed some 257 Union merchant ships, or about 5 per cent of the total. They drove up insurance rates substantially and destroyed much of the US whaling fleet, but they hardly disrupted US trade and they did not disturb the Union blockade, which became steadily more effective. Their main effect was to force a substantial number of vessels into permanent foreign registry. During the four years of war more than 700 US ships transferred to British registry alone.[17]

Historian George Dalzell stated that the *Alabama* and her sisters inflicted 'irreparable injury' on the US merchant marine, with more than half of the total US merchant fleet permanently lost to the flag during the Civil War. The cruisers burned or sank 110,000 tons of Union shipping, but

another 800,000 tons was sold to foreign owners, and these were the best ships.[18]

Early fighting

The first fighting on land occurred in the East. Hopes in the North of a quick war, culminating in a Union victory, were dashed in the First Battle of Manassas (Bull Run) in July 1861, when the Confederates sent attacking Union troops streaming back to Washington. Both sides now settled in for a long war.

Each side built ironclads. The first were actually warships built by the Union in the West to aid in securing control of America's great interior rivers, especially the Mississippi. Thanks to its superior manufacturing resources, the Union got its river fleet built first. The first vessels were converted river steamers, known as 'timberclads', but in August 1861 the Army ordered seven ironclad gunboats. The ships, built by James B. Eads, were actually the first vessels in the Western Hemisphere built specifically as ironclads. All were completed that autumn.

Commodore Andrew H. Foote's US Navy ironclad gunboats shown attacking Fort Henry, 6 February 1862. (*Naval Historical Foundation, NH 60823*)

Bombardment of Island No. 10 by Commodore Andrew H. Foote's US Navy squadron, 7 April 1862. Shows the ironclad gunboats, mortar boats along the shore, and one 'timberclad' gunboat. Lithograph by Currier & Ives. (*Naval Historical Foundation, KN-969*)

Detail of mortar boats during bombardment of Island No. 10 by Commodore Andrew H. Foote's US Navy squadron during night attack of 18 March 1862. Note position of the crew during firing. (*Naval Historical Foundation, NH 59021*)

Tennessee, with its important natural resources, food and men, was vital to both sides. At the beginning of February 1862 a joint Army-Navy operation combining troops under Brigadier General Ulysses S. Grant with a gunboat flotilla under Commodore A.H. Foote, took the offensive against Confederate positions on the Tennessee and Cumberland rivers.

Utilizing the timberclads and new ironclads, Foote took Fort Henry on the Tennessee (6 February), although most of its garrison escaped to nearby Fort Donelson on the Cumberland. The Union success at Henry was something of a fluke; the Confederates had been outgunned and their principal battery had been badly sited too close to the water.[19]

Although Confederate theatre commander General Albert S. Johnston believed that forts could not stand up to the ironclads, he regarded Fort Donelson as the major defence

of Nashville and foolishly reinforced it to buy time for his flanking garrisons to withdraw. A week later Foote's gunboats were rebuffed at Donelson and a number were damaged. This time the Confederate guns were well sited on high ground and their projectiles struck the sloping armour of the ironclads at right angles.[20]

Despite this failure Grant had Donelson cut off on the land side and was reinforcing. On 16 February Donelson fell along with 14,000 Confederates. This opened the way for Union forces to take Nashville, the first Confederate state capital in Union hands. The Union now had access to middle Tennessee and some of the richest territory of the Confederacy.[21]

When the Confederates withdrew from Columbus, Kentucky, this cleared the way for Union forces to move down the Mississippi. In March a Union army under General John Pope forced the Confederates to evacuate positions at New Madrid and a water-land siege of nearby Island No. 10 in the river began. By now 13-inch mortars mounted on specially designed mortar boats had joined the Union fleet. The mortar weighed 17,250 lbs and rested in a 4,500-lb bed. With a 20-lb charge of powder and at elevation of 41 degrees, it could hurl a 204-lb shell with a bursting charge of 7 lbs of powder three miles. At this range, the shell took 30 seconds in flight. The mortars were also used in the reduction of Fort Pulaski, Georgia.[22]

Battle of Plum Point Bend (10 May 1862)

After taking Island No. 10, Foote's squadron, mortar boats in tow, pressed down the Mississippi and laid siege to Fort Pillow. On 10 May eight Confederate gunboats staged a surprise attack on the Union squadron. Confederate commander Captain James Montgomery hoped to cut out or destroy one or more of the Union mortar boats and her covering ironclad. The arrival of more powerful warships in the Union squadron,

THE TECHNOLOGICAL REVOLUTION IN PRACTICE

now under the command of Commodore Charles Davis, caused the Confederates to retire, but not before they had rammed two Union ironclads, the *Cincinnati* and the *Mound City*. Both went down in shallow water and were easily refloated and soon repaired. As the Confederate warships fled downriver Union shells smashed into the boilers of three and disabled them.

During the hour-long battle the Union suffered only four wounded, one fatally; the Confederates probably had over 100 dead. Apart from its heavy losses in personnel, the South had achieved a tactical victory. Its flotilla had temporarily disabled two of the much more powerful Union gunboats. This Battle of Plum Point Bend was the war's first real engagement between naval squadrons.[23]

For three weeks the Union mortar boats and ironclads continued a slow bombardment of the Confederate positions. In mid-May the

seven steamers of Colonel Charles Ellet's Union Army Mississippi Ram Fleet arrived. Known as 'Ellet's Rams' these converted Ohio River steamers, conceived solely as rams with no ordnance, were the Union answer to the Confederate river rams.

Ellet was keen for an immediate strike against Fort Pillow, which Davis resisted, but the Confederates took the decision out of Union hands. On 29–30 May Confederate troops abandoned Corinth, Mississippi. This left Fort Pillow untenable, and on 4 June the Confederate defenders abandoned it.[24]

Battle of Memphis (6 June 1862)

On 5 June Davis' flotilla, reinforced by Ellet's rams, moved south to attack the Confederates at Memphis, arriving just above the city that evening. On the morning of 6 June, as thousands of Memphis citizens lined the shores to watch, a running battle occurred in

Battle of Memphis, 6 June 1862, from *The Illustrated London News*. (*Naval Historical Foundation, NH 89626*)

US Navy ships running past forts St Philip and Jackson on their way to New Orleans, 24 April 1862. Lithograph by Currier & Ives, 1862. (*Naval Historical Foundation, NH 76369-KN*)

which the Union gunboats and rams destroyed all but one of the eight Confederate vessels, which escaped to Vicksburg.

The naval Battle of Memphis was perhaps the most lopsided Union victory of the war. At a cost of only four casualties and one badly damaged ram, the Union had ended Confederate naval power on the Mississippi River and added additional vessels to its flotilla. The mighty river was now open to Vicksburg, and the Union had control of the fifth largest city in the Confederacy along with control of four key rail lines and important manufacturing resources, including a former Confederate naval yard, which soon became a principal Union base. The Confederates had been forced to destroy their one ironclad, the *Tennessee*, building there, although they were able to

remove downriver a second uncompleted ironclad, the *Arkansas*.[25]

Capture of New Orleans (April 1862)

While the northern Mississippi was being secured, Union forces were moving against New Orleans, the Confederacy's most important seaport. On 16 April Commodore David G. Farragut, flying his flag in the screw sloop *Hartford*, moved his fleet from the Gulf into the Mississippi River estuary. He had 17 ships, 8 steam sloops and corvettes and 9 gunboats, mounting a total of 115 guns. He also had 20 mortar schooners under Commander David D. Porter. Some 10,000 Union troops under Major General Benjamin F. Butler accompanied the expedition.

Guarding the southern Mississippi and barring the way to New Orleans were two

A 13-inch mortar aboard a US Navy mortar schooner. (*Library of Congress, B8184-10067*)

Confederate forts, St Philip and Jackson, mounting in all 115 heavy guns. A potentially powerful Confederate ironclad, the *Louisiana*, her engine not yet complete, was moored as a floating battery above St Philip. Confederate naval commander Commodore John K. Mitchell also had a number of small, makeshift gunboats and fire rafts ready to set loose against the Union fleet. The Confederates completed their defence by spreading a great chain, supported by hulks, across the river. High water in the river had flooded both forts, but Confederate engineers worked around the clock to control the water and strengthen the forts against the expected Union attack.

On 18 April Porter's mortar boats began a bombardment from a point some 3,000 yards from Fort Jackson, protected by a bend of the river and woods. For six days and nights they fired at the fort without much effect, while Confederate gunners heroically kept to their positions. The Confederates managed to sink one of the mortar schooners in counter-battery fire.

On the night of the 20th crews on two Union vessels, under heavy but inaccurate Confederate fire, managed to cut the chain and breach the Confederate obstructions below the forts. This action cleared the way for Farragut's fleet to pass. The Confederate land commander subsequently complained that Mitchell had not sent any fire rafts down to light the river at night and that he had not stationed any vessel below the forts to warn of the Union approach. The lack of cooperation between Confederate land and naval commanders proved costly.

On 24 April Farragut ran his squadron past the forts. Heavy land fire was answered by broadsides from the flotilla. Meanwhile, a dozen Confederate warships sortied out to engage the Union ships. The *Hartford* grounded in the swift current near Fort St Philip and a Confederate fire ship soon set her alight, but Farragut's leadership and the discipline of the crew saved the flagship. The *Varna* was not so lucky; rammed by two Confederate warships, she soon sank. In turn, Union warships sank nine Confederate vessels including the ram *Manassas*; two Confederate ships surrendered, and their crews destroyed two others to prevent capture.

With the Union fleet past the forts and the Confederate gunboats destroyed there was no barrier between the squadron and New Orleans. The next day Union ships steamed to the city. With the river up, Union guns could easily bear on New Orleans from over the levee top. Faced with the inevitable, the city fathers surrendered New Orleans the same day, and Butler's troops occupied the city.

The loss of its largest and most important seaport was a heavy blow to the Confederacy. Following the subsequent surrenders of Forts St Philip and Jackson the Mississippi was free for Union shipping to New Orleans. Vicksburg and Port Hudson were the only remaining Confederate river strongholds.[26]

Monitor versus *Virginia* (9 March 1862)

In the East the Union objective was to secure the Confederate capital of Richmond. President Lincoln preferred a push directly south to Richmond, but Union general-in-chief Major General George McClellan thought he had a better plan. Utilizing Union naval assets, he planned to enter Chesapeake Bay to land a large force on the peninsula between the James and York Rivers and advance on Richmond from that direction. As he closed on the Confederate capital from the east Major General Irvin McDowell's corps that had been guarding Washington would push south to help take Richmond and so end the war.

The so-called Peninsula Campaign set up history's first battle between ironclads. Union transports gathered at Hampton Roads were now threatened with destruction by the Confederate ironclad *Virginia* (10 guns), commanded by Commodore Franklin Buchanan. On 8 March she sallied forth and off Hampton Roads sank the Federal sloop *Cumberland* with her ram, which however broke off in the Union ship. The *Virginia* then attacked and burned the frigate *Congress*. In the haste to escape, other Union vessels, including the flagship *Minnesota*, ran aground. As night fell and with her pilots uncertain of the shoal water, the *Virginia* retired, her crewmen confident they would complete the destruction of the Union vessels the following day.

As the Confederates departed they saw by the light of the burning *Congress* a strange craft put into the Roads. It was the Union ironclad *Monitor*, one of the experimental ironclads ordered in response to Confederate ironclad construction. The *Monitor*, commanded by Lieutenant John Worden, was far more manoeuvrable than her Confederate opponent, but she was only a fraction of the *Virginia*'s size and mounted only two guns. Not quite finished and with workmen still aboard, she had nearly sunk the day before while being towed south. There were serious doubts on the Union side that she would prove a worthy opponent for the *Virginia*.

The next morning, 9 March, the *Virginia*, now commanded by Lieutenant Catesby ap Roger Jones, steamed out to engage the *Minnesota*. The *Monitor* sortied and placed herself in front of the grounded Union flagship. The two ironclads then joined battle, which lasted from about 8:00 a.m until noon. The battle was fought at very close range, from a few yards to about 200; both warships were constantly in motion. The *Virginia* rammed the *Monitor* but, because of the loss of her ram, did little damage. The *Monitor* sought to cripple her antagonist's vulnerable propeller and rudder.

The *Monitor* was able to fire her guns only about every seven or eight minutes, but her rotating turret meant that they were a target only when they were about to fire. Almost all of the shots from the *Monitor* registered and the *Virginia* sustained damage. Although the more numerous Confederate guns fired more shots, most went high and did little damage. Worden was temporarily blinded by the direct hit of a shell that struck the pilot house, however. In the resultant confusion the *Monitor* drifted away from the battle, and when her new commander, Lieutenant Samuel Greene, brought her back into position he saw the *Virginia* in retreat. Jones had interpreted the *Monitor*'s actions as meaning that the Confederates had won, and he returned to Norfolk for repairs.

Tactically the inconclusive battle was a draw. It might have ended quite differently had the *Virginia*'s fire been concentrated on the *Monitor*'s pilot house or if she had fired solid shot instead of shell, the type of projectile best suited against the wooden warships at Hampton Roads that she had expected to engage. On the other hand, the *Monitor*'s fire should have been directed at her opponent's waterline where the *Virginia*'s armour was weakest; and her 11-inch guns could have used 30-lb powder charges instead of the 15 lbs decreed as a consequence of the 'Peacemaker' explosion. But the *Virginia* had been hit 50 times and was leaking. The *Monitor* had sustained only 21 hits and was virtually undamaged.[27]

The battle between the two vessels was not renewed, but by surviving the *Monitor* had assured the safety of the Union transports and supply ships and hence McClellan's operation. The battle signalled a new era in naval warfare. The first time that ironclad vessels had fought, it also demonstrated the demise of the wooden vessel.

Only a small percentage of Civil War warships were ironclads, however. In December 1864 the Union fleet numbered 671 vessels. Of these just 71 were ironclad steamers. There were also 113 screw steamers and 52 paddle-wheel steamers, all expressly constructed for naval purposes; 323 steamers, purchased or captured and fitted out for naval use; and 112 sailing vessels. Of the 671 vessels, 559 were powered by steam.[28]

The Confederates countered with casemated vessels along the lines of the *Virginia*. The best known of these were the *Arkansas*, *Manassas*, *Atlanta*, *Nashville* and *Tennessee*. The Confederacy secretly contracted in Britain for two powerful seagoing ironclad ships. Built under the guise of construction for the Egyptian Navy, these so-called Laird Rams were turreted vessels superior to any Union Navy warship. When the war shifted decisively in favour of the Union the British government took them over. Intended to be the *Mississippi* and *North Carolina*, the two were completed as the HMS *Warren* and *Scorpion*.[29]

The engagement between the *Monitor* and the *Virginia* also led to a frantic effort to manufacture larger calibre guns capable of penetrating the new iron armour. As for the two ships themselves, the *Virginia* was scuttled on 11 May 1862, when the Confederates were forced to abandon Norfolk and were unable to move her up the shallow water of the James River. The *Monitor* sank in a gale while under tow off Cape Hatteras, North Carolina, on 31 December 1862.

General McClellan, meanwhile, failed to press his numerical advantage. Dubbed the 'Virginia Creeper', he was halted by the

CSS ram *Arkansas* running through US Navy squadron above Vicksburg, 15 July 1862. (*Naval Historical Foundation, NH 73378*)

Army of Northern Virginia under its new commander General Robert E. Lee. Lincoln then ordered McClellan to bring his army back north in favour of a direct push south from Washington toward Richmond. Before the North could concentrate its forces, however, the Confederates inflicted another defeat in the Second Battle of Manassas (Bull Run) at the end of August. Lee then invaded the North but Union forces halted him and the Army of Northern Virginia at Sharpsburg (Antietam) on 17 September.

The Union now took the offensive again but was rebuffed at Fredericksburg in December, Lee's most lopsided victory of the war. Lee won a brilliant victory against heavy odds at Chancellorsville on 2–4 May, and then invaded the North for a second time in a spoiling attack, only to be stopped

by Major General George Meade's Army of the Potomac at Gettysburg during 2–4 July.

In the West, Union forces were attempting to take the Confederate fortress of Vicksburg and free the remainder of the Mississippi. Farragut ran his fleet north past Vicksburg on 28 June 1862, but in the process he suffered casualties and considerable damage to his ships, with scant return. Vicksburg, located high on bluffs along the east bank at a bend of the mighty river, seemed impervious to naval assault.

On 1 July Farragut linked up with Davis's squadron off the mouth of the Yazoo River. Two weeks later, on 15 July, the powerful Confederate ram *Arkansas* of 10 guns sallied from the Yazoo and battered her way south through the entire Union fleet to Vicksburg. On 21–22 July Farragut again ran south past the gauntlet at Vicksburg in an effort to destroy the *Arkansas*. She took considerable damage in an exchange of fire with the *Essex* on 22 July and on being rammed twice by the *Queen of the West*. Both Union ships, however, were also damaged in the exchange, especially by fire from shore batteries.

With the failure to destroy the *Arkansas*, Farragut gave up. Two days after the abortive attack on the Confederate ironclad he embarked Union troops on transports, and the entire fleet headed downriver. Farragut returned to New Orleans but left two gunboats, along with the *Essex* and the *Sumter*, at Baton Rouge in case the *Arkansas* ventured south.

Although damage from the 22 July attack was still being repaired and her engines were in terrible shape, on 3 August the *Arkansas* got under way for Baton Rouge with executive officer Lieutenant Henry K. Stevens in command. The ironclad had been ordered to support an attack at Baton Rouge by 3,000 Confederate troops under Major General John C. Breckinridge. About the same number of Union troops held the city, while four Union vessels including the *Essex* protected it from the river side.

A day after the *Arkansas* got under way, her engines broke down. As the ironclad anchored for repairs Breckinridge's troops were breaching the Union lines and driving the Federal troops back against the river. The *Arkansas*, which finally got under way again, suffered another engine breakdown within sight of Baton Rouge. As her crew desperately tried to effect repairs, the Union gunboats kept up a steady fire against the advancing Confederate troops and forced them back.

During the night of 5 August Captain William Porter of the *Essex* learned of the presence of the *Arkansas*, and at 8:00 a.m. he led the small Union squadron upriver against her. Her crew completed repairs to the *Arkansas* just as the *Essex* was getting up

steam. But as the *Arkansas* moved to attack the Union warship her engines again broke down, and she drifted back to the shore. Stevens then ordered his vessel fired and his men to abandon ship. The *Arkansas* drifted back into the river and downstream for more than an hour before she blew up. On learning of her destruction Breckinridge decided not to renew the land attack and withdrew his men.[30]

In November and December 1862 General Grant made several attempts with his Army of the Tennessee to take Vicksburg by amphibious operation. He sent General William T. Sherman and 40,000 men south, supported by Rear Admiral David D. Porter's gunboats. But Grant's attempt was stymied because of Vicksburg's defences. The heavily fortified city was protected by the nature of the terrain to the north and west. Confederate raids on Union supply bases also had an effect. The year ended with the Confederates still in control of a stretch of the river from Vicksburg south to Port Hudson. That all changed in 1863.

Grant now took personal command. Union probing attacks in January 1863 against Vicksburg's increasingly formidable defences produced little. In February, Porter ran two warships, the ram *Queen of the West* and ironclad gunboat *Indianola*, past the fortress to attack Confederate shipping between Vicksburg and Port Hudson. Although they succeeded in disrupting the shipping, the *Queen of the West* was eventually captured and the *Indianola* destroyed.

As Grant built up his strength, in mid-March Farragut set out upriver from New Orleans for an operation planned in cooperation with Major General Nathaniel Banks. Only Farragut's flagship *Hartford* and one other vessel were able to fight their way past Port Hudson's strong defences. Although the inept Banks failed to cooperate, Farragut's two ships soon swept

Confederate shipping from the central Mississippi.

Vicksburg was most vulnerable from the south and east, and Grant now decided on a bold step. In late March Union ships carried his troops south from his base at Memphis. The troops disembarked above Vicksburg and marched by land along the west bank to a point south of the Confederate stronghold. At night Porter ran his gunboats and the transports south past Vicksburg's batteries to Grant's new base at Hard Times. On 30 April Porter's gunboats and transports ferried Grant's troops across the Mississippi.

Grant, now deep in enemy territory, adopted the indirect approach. In defiance of instructions he marched inland with 20,000 men, living off the land as much as possible. He first moved against Vicksburg's link to the east, the key railhead of Jackson. He took that city, held by 6,000 Confederates, and destroyed it as a communications centre, then turned west toward Vicksburg. In a hard-fought battle at Champion's Hill (16 May), Grant and 32,000 men defeated Lieutenant General John C. Pemberton's 25,000 men. Pemberton then retired into the Vicksburg perimeter.

After two futile assaults against the fortress Grant settled down to a siege. Following a six-week bombardment, on 4 July Pemberton surrendered the city and 30,000 troops. With Vicksburg lost and his own remaining Mississippi stronghold surrounded by 14,000 Union troops, the commander of Port Hudson surrendered on 9 July. The entire Mississippi was under Union control and the Confederacy split. A joyful Lincoln could write, 'The father of waters again goes unvexed to the sea.'[31]

Control of the Mississippi greatly benefited the Union. Supplies from the Trans-Mississippi West were not a major factor for the Confederacy but Midwestern farmers could use the river for their goods and were now solidly behind the Union war effort. With his north–south axis secure, Grant was now free to split the Confederacy from west to east.

In the meantime, another major ironclad battle had occurred, in Wassaw Sound, Georgia. On 17 June 1863, CSS *Atlanta* (commanded by Commander William A. Webb), accompanied by the wooden steamers *Isondiga* and *Resolute*, sought to engage two US Navy 'Passaic'-class monitors, the USS *Weehawken* (commanded by Captain John Rodgers) and the USS *Nahant* (commanded by Commander John Downes). The *Atlanta* mounted two 6.4-inch and two 7-inch rifled guns. The former were in broadsides, while the latter were on pivot mounts able to fire to either side. The *Atlanta* also had a percussion spar torpedo fitted to her bow, which Webb hoped to explode against the *Weehawken*. But the *Atlanta* grounded in coming out, and although her crew got her free she failed to obey her helm. *Weehawken* and *Nahant* worked in close to her, Rodgers waiting until the *Weehawken* was only about 300 yards away to open fire. The Union monitor, armed with one 11-inch and one 15-inch Dahlgren smoothbore, fired five shots in 15 minutes at relatively close range. Four of these struck, smashing through the *Atlanta*'s armoured casemate. They disabled her guns, caused casualties, and forced her surrender. The next year the *Atlanta* was incorporated into the US Navy.[32]

Charleston

At the same time Union naval commanders worked to tighten the blockade. Charleston, South Carolina, and Wilmington, North Carolina, were the principal points of entry for blockade runners, and Union strategists believed they could be closed only by occupation.

The great Southern port of Charleston, fount of the Rebellion, was a symbol for both sides. The Union siege there ended up as the

US Navy bombardment of Fort Sumter, 7 April 1863. (*Naval Historical Foundation, NH 59274*)

longest campaign of the war. Commander of the South Atlantic Blockading Squadron Rear Admiral Samuel Du Pont showed a marked reluctance to attack either Charleston or Fort Sumter, but under repeated prodding from Secretary Welles agreed to try. On 7 April 1863, Du Pont sent nine of his ironclad monitors against Fort Sumter. The Richmond *Whig*, editorialized, 'At last the hour of trial has come for Charleston.'[33]

Battle was joined at noon. The Union monitors soon came under heavy fire from guns at Sumter and Fort Moultrie, and a number of the Union warships sustained heavy damage. The ironclad *Keokuk* was hit 90 times, many of the shots piercing her at or below the waterline. Her crew was able to keep her afloat that day only because the water was calm. (Anchored overnight outside the range of Confederate guns, she sank the next day when a wind came up.)

Du Pont broke off the action at dusk. He reported to Welles that he had intended to resume the battle the next day but was persuaded not to do so on receiving damage reports from the monitor captains. The Confederates had beaten back a major Union effort and gained a stunning victory.

Du Pont now declared that Charleston could not be taken by naval attack alone. This became widely known and led to calls for his removal. Welles replaced Du Pont at Charleston on 10 July with Rear Admiral John Dahlgren. The US Navy's chief ordnance expert, Dahlgren had long sought a command afloat and had used his influence with Lincoln to become the new commander of the South Atlantic Blockading Squadron.[34]

From July to September Dahlgren kept up a naval bombardment of the Charleston defences, this time in cooperation with land attacks by troops under Major General

Quincy A. Gillmore. Fort Wagner, the principal Union target, repulsed several attacks with heavy Union losses. Finally, on 6 September, the Confederates abandoned Wagner. Its loss greatly diminished Charleston as a haven for blockade runners.

Mines and submarines

In the fighting for Charleston the Confederates used mines and a submarine to attack the Union fleet. On 5 October 1863, they sent out into the harbour a small, 50-foot long vessel, the *David*. Designed to operate low in the water, she resembled a submarine but was in fact strictly a surface vessel. Propelled by a steam engine and manned by a crew of four, the *David* mounted a spar torpedo – a mine at the end of a long pole – that contained 60 lbs of powder inside a copper casing.

Commanded by Lieutenant W. T. Glassell, the *David* approached the Union ironclad *New*

Ironsides, the most powerful warship in the US Navy. The *David* got to within 50 yards of her target before she was discovered. Hailed from the Union ship, she responded with a shot gun blast and then placed her mine.

Although the explosion damaged the *New Ironsides*, she did not sink. The same blast sent up a great wave of water that washed into the *David* and put out the fire in her steam engine. Believing she was sinking, Glassell and two other members of her crew abandoned ship; one subsequently returned to the *David*, where the engineer succeeded in restarting her furnace fire. Glassell and another man were captured. The *David* and others like her made other attempts against Union ships at Charleston, but without success.[35]

On 17 February 1864, the submersible CSS *H.L. Hunley* sank the 1,934-ton screw sloop *Housatonic*. When she went down off Charleston from the explosion of the *H.L. Hunley*'s 130-lb spar torpedo, the *Housatonic*

David torpedo boat, Confederate Navy, photographed at Charleston, South Carolina in 1865. (*Naval Historical Foundation, NH 165-C-750*)

CSS *Alabama* vs USS *Kearsarge*, 19 June 1864, off Cherbourg, France. Painting by Xanthus Smith, 1922. (*Naval Historical Foundation, K-29827*)

became the first ship sunk by a submarine in the history of warfare. The unstable *H.L. Hunley* went down shortly thereafter (for more on mines and submarines of the Civil War see Chapter 7).

Alabama versus *Kearsarge* (19 June 1864)

On 19 June 1864, one of the most famous of nineteenth-century naval battles occurred, but on the other side of the Atlantic. In nearly two years since her commissioning, the Confederate cruiser *Alabama* had travelled an incredible 75,000 miles. Her widely reported exploits were a considerable boost to Confederate morale, and Secretary Welles was determined that she be hunted down and destroyed. At one point or another 25 Union warships were searching for her.

The prey was, however, worn out. In March 1864 Semmes took her north from Cape Town to find a European dry dock to

effect repairs. On 11 June the *Alabama* arrived at Cherbourg, France. Both Paris and London were well aware of the changing fortunes of the war, and French officials refused Semmes' request, pointing out that the dockyard was for French government ships only. Semmes believed that Emperor Napoleon III, who had sent a considerable military force to Mexico and thus had great interest in a Confederate victory, would ultimately grant approval.

While Semmes waited, news of the *Alabama*'s arrival reached the Dutch port of Flushing, where the third-rate screw steam sloop *Kearsarge* (commanded by Captain John A. Winslow) was monitoring Confederate raiders *Georgia* and *Rappahannock* at Calais. Winslow and his well-trained crew had spent a year searching for the *Alabama*. The *Kearsarge*, two months out of a Dutch dockyard and in excellent condition, was soon underway for Cherbourg, arriving there on the 14th.

Despite the fact that his ship was in poor condition Semmes did not hesitate to do battle. It was partly a matter of pride; the war was about over and there had been little glory in sinking merchantmen, but in fact he had little choice. Delay would only bring more Union warships. On 19 June the French ironclad *Couronne* accompanied the *Alabama* as she left Cherbourg harbour about 9:30 a.m.

Despite Semmes' later claims that the *Kearsarge* had the advantage, the two ships were closely matched. The *Kearsarge*'s 11 knots maximum speed made her slightly faster than her opponent. She had 4 × 32-pounder (42 cwt) guns, a 30-pounder rifled gun, and a 12-pounder boat howitzer. Her strength, however, was in 2 × 11-inch pivot-mounted smoothbore Dahlgrens that threw 135-lb shell. While the *Kearsarge* mounted seven guns, she could fight only five on one side. Her broadside weight of metal was about a quarter greater than that of her opponent (364 lb to 274 lb). The *Alabama* also fought five guns on a side. Her armament consisted of eight guns: 6 × 32-pounders in broadside, and two pivot-guns amidships: a 100-pounder rifled Blakeley and an 8-inch smoothbore.

As the *Alabama* came out Winslow had the *Kearsarge* steam off to the north-east to insure that the battle would occur outside French territorial waters and to enable the Union warship to prevent the *Alabama* from running back to the French shore. Semmes and the *Alabama* followed. The *Couronne* took up position to mark the three-mile French territorial limit.

Semmes expected to use his starboard guns in broadside and shifted one 32-pounder from the port side to strengthen that battery. The added weight, however, caused the *Alabama* to list about two feet to starboard. This was, however, thought to be an advantage, as it exposed less of that side

to enemy fire. When the two ships were about a mile and a quarter apart Winslow reversed course and headed for the *Alabama*. He too planned to use his starboard battery, so the two ships met proceeding in opposite directions.

The entire action lasted a little over an hour. Just before 11:00 a.m. Semmes opened with a broadside at somewhat less than a mile. Several minutes later, at about a half mile, the *Kearsarge* replied. Winslow ordered a port turn to try to place his own ship in position to rake his opponent. Semmes veered to port to avoid this but the manoeuvre allowed Winslow to close the range. As the *Alabama* turned back to starboard the *Kearsarge* mirrored her movement. The *Kearsarge* was faster and, as Winslow narrowed the range, the circles grew progressively smaller, down to a quarter of a mile, with each ship firing her starboard batteries only.

The *Alabama* had the early advantage as her large Blakeley rifle had greater range than any of the *Kearsarge*'s guns. One Blakeley shell lodged in the *Kearsarge*'s wooden sternpost but failed to explode. Had it done so, it would have destroyed her steering.[36]

The *Kearsarge* enjoyed an advantage in having cable chain strung over her vital midships area to protect engines, boilers and magazines. This technique had been proven in fighting on the Mississippi River and the chain had been in place on the *Kearsarge* for some time. In effect, the *Kearsarge* was a partial ironclad. An outward sheathing of one-inch wood painted the same colour as the rest of the hull concealed this from Confederate observation. The *Alabama* had chain in her lockers that could have been used for the same purpose. Later Semmes claimed he had been unaware of the *Kearsarge*'s chain mail, which he said was an unfair advantage. This is not true, as French officials had told him about it. But Semmes seems to have convinced himself that this was the only reason he lost the battle.[37]

With the *Alabama*'s shot having no effect on the chain-protected side of the *Kearsarge*, Semmes ordered the gun crews to fire higher. One shell then tore through the Union ship's smokestack; another sheared off the top of her engine-room hatch, but only one shot caused personnel casualties aboard : a Blakeley shell that exploded on the quarterdeck and wounded three men at the after pivot gun, one mortally.

As the range narrowed, both sides substituted shell. Semmes hoped to close on his opponent sufficiently to take the *Kearsarge* by boarding, but Winslow kept to a range that allowed his own guns to be most effective. Because his own vessel was both faster and more manoeuvrable, he was able to dictate the range. Meanwhile shell from the 11-inch Dahlgren guns tore large holes in the *Alabama*'s hull and had a terrible effect on her crew.[38]

At the beginning of the eighth circle, when the two ships were about 400 yards apart, Semmes saw that his ship was sinking and turned out of the circle in hope of making the French shore. He also opened fire with his port battery, but the *Alabama* was taking on too much water and Semmes was able to bring only two of her port guns to bear. The *Alabama* was now completely at the mercy of the *Kearsarge*.

With his vessel going down fast, Semmes ordered all hands to abandon ship. Since most of the *Alabama*'s boats were destroyed or damaged in the battle, most men simply leaped in the sea. The *Alabama* sank at 12:24 p.m.[39]

Broadside fire from each ship had little effect on the outcome. Perhaps surprisingly the *Alabama* got off many more shots, 370, but less than 10 per cent of them struck their opponent (13 in and about the hull and 16 in the masts and rigging). These did

little damage and only three men were wounded, one fatally, aboard the *Kearsarge*. The Union warship was perfectly ready to fight again. Winslow reported that during the battle his ship had fired 173 shots, and that a high percentage of these struck. One shot alone killed or wounded 18 men at the *Alabama*'s after pivot gun.[40]

Shell fire from the heavy 11-inch pivot guns of the Union vessel had decided the engagement, especially a fortunate shot that damaged the *Alabama*'s steering. The Confederates did have the disadvantage of weakened cannon powder from long months at sea. In all there were 41 casualties aboard the Confederate vessel: 9 dead, 20 wounded, and 12 drowned.[41]

An English yacht that had been about a mile away during the battle rescued 42 Confederates, including Semmes, and took them to Southampton, where they were released. Semmes later returned to the Confederacy, where he commanded the James River Squadron of three ironclad rams and seven wooden steamers for three months, until early April 1865 when Confederate forces abandoned Richmond and he had to destroy his ships.

The defeat of the *Alabama* signalled the beginning of the end for Confederate commerce raiders. In October the *Florida* was taken. Commissioned at the same time as the *Alabama*, she had ravaged the Atlantic coast for some time. One of her prizes, converted to a warship, sailed into Portland, Maine, and blew up a Federal revenue cutter before being captured. Federal warships finally cornered the *Florida* in Bahia Harbour, Brazil, and, on 7 October 1863, boarded and captured her in defiance of Brazilian neutrality.

Battle of Mobile Bay (5 August 1864)

The Union Navy, in the meantime, was taking the remaining Confederate seaboard ports. Early on the morning of 5 August

1864, Rear Admiral Farragut led 18 ships, including four ironclad monitors, against heavy Confederate defences guarding Mobile Bay, Alabama. Shortly after 6:00 a.m. the Union ships crossed the bar and moved into the bay. Monitors *Tecumseh*, *Manhattan*, *Winnebago* and *Chickasaw* formed a column to the right of another of wooden ships in order to mask them from the heavy guns of Fort Morgan. Farragut also employed the tactic used against Port Hudson; he ordered the seven smallest wooden ships lashed to the port side of the larger wooden screw steamers to provide additional protection.

Shortly before 7:00 a.m. the lead Union ironclad, the *Tecumseh*, opened fire at Fort Morgan, and the engagement became general. Confederate admiral Franklin Buchanan now ordered his squadron to attack the advancing Union ships. His most powerful vessel by far was the ironclad ram *Tennessee*. Supporting her were the *Gaines*, *Selma* and *Morgan*. The captain of the *Tecumseh* headed his warship right for the *Tennessee* in order to engage her at once.

Suddenly there was a great explosion as the *Tecumseh* struck a mine and blew up. She sank within half a minute, stopping the Union fleet in front of the guns of Confederate Fort Morgan. Ninety-three officers and men died aboard the Union ironclad; only 21 escaped. Both sides were so stunned by the explosion that the fire slackened for a few moments before it was resumed.

Lashed in the rigging of the *Hartford*, Farragut saw the sloop *Brooklyn* in front of him slow to a crawl and then reverse engines. The *Brooklyn* now blocked the channel, and behind the *Hartford* Farragut could see the Union ships begin to bunch up as Confederate gunners at Fort Morgan continued their fire. Had it not been for Farragut's orders that the Union fleet run close to the fort and keep up a steady fire of grape and shrapnel against it, the ships would have been hard hit.

This was the decisive point in the battle, and Farragut knew it. He also knew that if he could get a sufficient number of his ships into the bay, he could close it to blockade runners forever. Farragut chose to take the risk of additional mines with his own ship, calling out, 'I shall lead.' The *Hartford* got up speed and, as she passed on the port side of the *Brooklyn*, Farragut shouted, 'What's the trouble?' 'Torpedoes', was the reply. 'Damn the torpedoes', Farragut yelled out. He then ordered his ship to get up speed, and finally, he called to the captain of the gunboat lashed to the side of the *Hartford*, 'Go ahead, Jouett, full speed!' Farragut's words have passed into history in shortened version as, 'Damn the torpedoes; full speed ahead.'

Although men below decks on the *Hartford* that day could hear primers going off beneath them, none of the remaining Confederate mines exploded. Some of the Union warships were damaged by Confederate shore fire, but all passed safely through into the bay and beyond the range of Fort Morgan's guns.

Buchanan saw Farragut's pennant flying from the *Hartford* and ordered the ironclad ram *Tennessee* toward her. The Confederate gunboats also joined in. The *Tennessee* did not have sufficient speed up, however, and passed by the Union flagship with both vessels firing at each other. As the *Tennessee* swept on, firing at the remaining pairs of Union ships and inflicting some damage and casualties, Farragut ordered the *Metacomet* and smaller vessels cut free to attack the Confederate gunboats, which now hauled off and steamed up the bay.

The three remaining Union monitors, which had been covering the passage of the wooden Union ships into the bay, now joined the fray. Buchanan, seeing his own warship surrounded, withdrew the *Tennessee* as the smaller Union vessels concentrated on the Confederate gunboats. After a hard fight the *Selma* surrendered to the *Metacomet*; the *Gaines* was hit several times below the waterline; her captain tried unsuccessfully to make Fort Morgan, but the *Gaines* went down about 400 yards from the fort. The *Morgan* managed to reach the fort and took refuge there under its guns. That night she escaped to Mobile.

The *Tennessee* also gained the protection of Fort Morgan, where Buchanan considered his next move. He correctly assumed that Farragut would block his escape over the bar and attempt a night attack. Rather than wait to be attacked, at 9:00 a.m. Buchanan brought the *Tennessee* back against the entire Union fleet in what was virtually a suicide mission. The Confederate admiral hoped to catch the Union ships off guard, inflict what damage he could, then ground the *Tennessee* as a stationary battery under Fort Morgan.

As the *Tennessee* came out Farragut ordered the monitors and larger vessels to attack. Both the *Monongahela* and *Lackawanna* rammed the *Tennessee* but received more damage than they inflicted. The *Hartford*, with Farragut again in the rigging, also crashed into the *Tennessee*. While circling for another try, she was by mistake rammed by the *Lackawanna*.

The Union monitors now arrived, and a shot from the *Manhattan*'s 15-inch Dahlgren gun ripped through the *Tennessee*'s side, tearing away over two feet of solid wood backing five inches of iron. It was the only Union shot during the battle to penetrate the *Tennessee*. The monitor *Chickasaw* also took up position astern and her twin 11-inch Dahlgrens began to pound the Confederate ironclad. Their shot jammed her port shutters and cut the exposed wheel chains. Several of her crewmen were killed, and

Surrender of the CSS *Tennessee*, Battle of Mobile Bay, 5 August 1864. (*Naval Historical Foundation, NH 1276*)

Buchanan and others were wounded. The ram's smokestack was shot away, her steering was gone, and she was dead in the water. Her ammunition was also nearly depleted. Given these conditions, Buchanan surrendered.

Farragut's capture of Mobile Bay cost the Union side 145 killed and 170 wounded. Many of his wooden ships were heavily damaged, but the only one lost was a supply vessel hit by fire from Fort Morgan as she attempted to follow the fleet into the bay. The Confederates lost 12 killed, 20 wounded, and the crews of the *Tennessee* and *Selma* captured. For all practical purposes the battle ended blockade running in the Gulf.[42]

CSS *Albermarle*

Along the South Atlantic coast the powerful Confederate ironclad ram *Albermarle*, constructed at Edward's Ferry on the Roanoke River, had for months dominated the North Carolina sounds. She was finished in time to participate in a Confederate Army assault led by General Robert F. Hoke on the Union blockading base at Plymouth, North Carolina. On 19 April 1864, the *Albermarle* sank one Union gunboat and drove off another, and on 5 May she dispersed a squadron of seven Union gunboats. The ram was a considerable threat to Union coastal operations because her shallow draft enabled her to escape the larger Union ocean-going ships and she easily outgunned smaller Union coastal craft.[43]

On 27 October 1864, 21-year-old Lieutenant William B. Cushing led a boat expedition against the *Albermarle* in the Roanoke River at Plymouth. With the approval of Secretary Welles, at New York Cushing purchased two 30-foot steam

Attack by US Navy *Steam Picket Boat No. 1* against CSS ironclad ram *Albermarle*, 27 October 1864. (*Naval Historical Foundation, NH 57267*)

launches and fitted each with a 12-pounder Dahlgren howitzer and a 14-foot spar and torpedo. As the two launches proceeded south by the inland water route, one of them, *Steam Picket Boat No. 2*, developed mechanical problems and was forced to put ashore in Wicomico Bay, Virginia, where the Confederates captured it.

Steam Picket Boat No. 1, commanded by Cushing himself, arrived safely in the North Carolina Sounds on 24 October. Cushing then revealed his plan to the crew and asked for volunteers; all seven men joined him.

Cushing set out on the night of 26 October, but the launch grounded at the mouth of the Roanoke River. The crew finally freed her, but the mishap forced Cushing to postpone the attack until the next night.

The night of the 27th was dark and foul. Cushing was accompanied by fourteen men; the additional crewmen were volunteers from the blockading squadron. *Steam Picket Boat No. 1* towed a cutter to be used to take the picket vessel *Smithfield* in order to prevent Confederates aboard her from giving the alarm by signal rocket. A former Union vessel taken in an earlier action with the *Albermarle*, the *Smithfield* had been positioned as a hulk in the river about a mile from the *Albermarle*'s berth.

A heavy tarpaulin helped to muffle the noise of the launch's steam engine during her approach, and Cushing was able to get in close to the wharf before the alarm was raised. He ordered the cutter to cast off and take the *Smithfield*. At the same time he ordered his own launch to get up steam and make for the *Albermarle*.

The Confederates had now opened fire from both the ram and the shore. A large illuminating fire blazed up on the shore but this enabled Cushing to see a protective boom of logs floating in the water around the ram. Coolly ordering his launch about, Cushing

then ran it full speed at the obstruction, while firing canister from his boat howitzer against the Confederates ashore.

At high speed the launch rode over the log barrier and was quickly next to the *Albermarle*. Its torpedo boom with the charge at the end was lowered under the Confederate ram. Almost simultaneously a shot from the *Albermarle* crashed into the launch and the mine exploded, the resulting wash of water swamping the Union launch.

The explosion of the torpedo tore a gaping hole in the *Albermarle*, which now began to sink rapidly. She settled quickly, so that soon only her superstructure and smokestack were visible. Cushing ordered his own men to swim to safety. In the morning Cushing managed to secure a skiff, which he then rowed eight miles to Albermarle Sound, where he was picked up by a Union ship. Only one other man aboard the launch escaped death or capture.

Destruction of the *Albermarle* enabled Union forces to capture Plymouth and gain control of the entire Roanoke River area. It also released Union ships stationed there for other blockade duties. Congress subsequently commended Cushing and promoted him to lieutenant commander.[44]

Union capture of Fort Fisher (13–15 January 1865)

Wilmington, North Carolina, was now the last remaining principal Confederate port for blockade runners and a main overseas supply link for General Lee's Army of Northern Virginia. With the *Albermarle* disposed of, aggressive Vice Admiral David D. Porter, who now commanded the largest number of ships in US Navy history to this point, wanted to move against Wilmington. It took some time for Grant to release the troops, two Union army divisions commanded by incompetent Major General Benjamin Butler.

The Union commanders first attempted to destroy the principal Confederate defensive works of Fort Fisher by blowing up a ship filled with powder under its walls on 23 December, but this failed. Porter's squadron also began a bombardment to cover a landing over the next several days by 6,500 of Butler's men. But after a brief demonstration Butler re-embarked the men and sailed back to Fort Monroe. A furious Porter demanded that Butler be removed from command, and General Grant agreed, replacing him with able Major General Alfred H. Terry.

On 13 January 1865, Terry landed 8,000 men in three divisions north of Fort Fisher and prepared to attack it in conjunction with an intense naval bombardment from Porter's ships. While the Confederate defenders succeeded in repulsing a Navy-Marine landing against the fort's sea face, Terry's troops, covered by naval gunfire, took the outer works. On 15 January, after some of the most bitter fighting of the entire war, Colonel William Lamb and 2,000 Confederates surrendered. This last great maritime effort of the war closed the remaining sea gate of the Confederacy.

End of the war

On land Union general-in-chief Grant accompanied the Army of the Potomac as it drove south toward Richmond. Lee parried Grant's blows and inflicted casualties equivalent to the size of his own force, but his own Army of Northern Virginia never recovered from the relentless attacks. Grant sought to get in behind Lee at Petersburg, south of Richmond, but Lee was too quick for him, and the two sides settled down to a long siege, a harbinger of First World War trench warfare.

As Grant attempted to take Richmond and destroy Lee, Major General William T. Sherman took Atlanta and then drove east to the sea, cutting a swath of destruction through Georgia to Savannah. He then turned north through the Carolinas to join Grant. Lee broke out of Petersburg and attempted to escape west. Cornered at Appomattox Court House, he surrendered on 9 April 1865. The Civil War was over.

Some Confederate ground units held out for weeks, and the Confederate raider *Shenandoah* (commanded by Lieutenant Commander James Waddell) continued her depredations against the Union whaling fleet. Waddell's last eight captures came at the end of June, some two months after Lee's surrender at Appomattox. Finally convinced in early August by the captain of a British ship that the war had indeed ended, Waddell dismounted the *Shenandoah*'s ordnance and sailed her to England. Evading Union warships, he arrived at Liverpool on 6 November, fully six months after the end of the war, and turned his ship over to British authorities.

After the war the issue of the British government having allowed the fitting out of Confederate cruisers became a major stumbling block in Anglo-American relations. Washington believed that London's proclamation of neutrality and then persistent disregard of it in the early period of the war had heartened the South and prolonged the conflict. There were those in the US government who proposed taking British Western Hemisphere possessions, including Canada, as compensation.

In January 1871, when the European balance of power decisively changed with Prussia's defeat of France, British statesmen concluded that it might be wise to reach an accommodation with the United States. An international tribunal met in Geneva beginning in December 1871 over what became known as the '*Alabama* claims'. In September 1872 it awarded the US government $15.5 million in damages. This settlement came to be regarded as an important step in the peaceful settlement of international disputes and a victory for the world rule of law.[45]

The Civil War marked a turning point in military history. Although most European observers did not recognize it at the time, in many ways it was the first modern, total war, with military strength counting less than industrial output.

Apparently Americans had had enough of war. The US Army went from 1,000,000 men under arms at Appomattox to only 25,000 by the end of 1866. In January 1865 the blockading squadrons had 471 ships mounting 2,455 guns; in December 1865 they numbered only 29 ships carrying 210 guns.[46]

AUSTRO-PRUSSIAN WAR (1866)

A year after the end of the American Civil War, Austria and Prussia went to war. Prussian Minister-President Otto von Bismarck engineered the conflict. At the suggestion of French ruler Napoleon III he secured an alliance with Italy, which hoped to wrest Venetia from Austria. The war began on 20 June 1866, with Austria and virtually all the smaller German states pitted against Prussia and Italy.

The naval part of the war took place in the Adriatic Sea, between Italy and Austria. Italy had built up her navy before the war, adding ironclads acquired from Britain and the United States. Unfortunately for Italy, at the insistence of King Victor-Emmanuel, the incompetent Admiral Count Carlo Pellion di Persano commanded the Italian fleet, based at Taranto. On 25 June Persano moved the fleet to Anconas, only 90 miles across the Adriatic from the Austrian base of Pola (Pula).

Energetic 38-year-old Rear Admiral Wilhelm von Tegetthoff commanded the Austrian Fleet. He believed strongly in the ram and preferred it to naval gunfire, especially as his ships did not possess any of the new shell guns. As in the time of the Greek trireme, the ship itself would be the chief weapon. Yet not one of Tegetthoff's warships had a true ram bow. Instead they had hastily fitted joined-armour bow plates.

Thanks largely to Tegetthoff's leadership the Austrian Navy was operational first. His orders were to cover the flank of Austrian land forces by defending the coast against Italian attack. On 27 June Tegetthoff took six ironclads and seven large wooden ships to Ancona, where the Italian fleet was assembling. The Italians were unready, and Persano refused to take his ships to sea. Tegetthoff then removed his squadron to Fasana, near Pola. This sortie raised Austrian morale, while depressing that of the Italians.

Italian Minister of Marine Agostino Depretis then ordered Persano to join battle or be replaced. As a consequence, on 15 July Persano took 29 of his ships to sea, but not to Pola. Instead he sought an easy victory, making south-east for Lissa, an Austrian-held Adriatic island defended by 88 guns.

Italy's newest warship, the British-built *Affondatore* ('sender-to-the-bottom') with a 30-foot-long pronounced bow ram, had left Naples escorting 10,000 troops. This iron-hulled, schooner-rigged vessel had two Cowper Coles-designed turrets. The *Affondatore* was to rendezvous with the remainder of the fleet at sea. For two days the Italian fleet bombarded Lissa with little effect; the Austrian batteries returned fire and badly damaged the *Formidabile*, which also suffered 60 casualties.

Naval Battle of Lissa (20 July 1866)

News of the Italian attack soon reached Pola. When Tegetthoff learned that virtually the entire Italian Navy was at Lissa he set out on 19 July for the island, his flag in the ironclad *Erzherzog Ferdinand Maximilian* (for illustration, *see* page 96). His ships were in three wedge-shaped divisions: the flagship and six other ironclad frigates led; they were followed by seven large wooden ships headed by the screw ship-of-the-line *Kaiser*; seven wooden gunboats made up the third division. Small dispatch boats to relay messages were posted in the intervals. Tegetthoff had 27 vessels, seven of them ironclads. They displaced 57,300 tons, mounted 532 guns, and carried 7,870 men. Persano had 31 ships: 12 ironclads and 11 large and 8 small unarmoured ships. They displaced 86,000 tons, mounted 645 guns, and carried 10,900 men. The Italians had the advantage in everything save leadership and discipline.

At dawn on 20 July, in a rough sea with mist, lookouts aboard the Italian scout boat *Esploratore* spotted the approaching Austrian fleet. She immediately made for the Italian fleet to warn Persano, who had no contingency plans and was, moreover, involved in landing troops on Lissa. The alarm was quickly sounded, however; by 10:00 a.m. the Italian ships, although somewhat scattered, were underway toward the approaching Austrians. Eleven of the Italian ironclads began to form up in column. The wooden ships held back and did not participate in the action. The misnamed ironclad *Formidabile*, damaged during an exchange of shells with the Austrian shore batteries, also did not participate. Persano, however, unexpectedly transferred his flag to the *Affondatore* without informing his ship captains. The result was a high degree of confusion on the Italian side during the resulting battle.

At 10:30 Tegetthoff signalled for his armoured ships to charge the enemy ships and attempt to sink them. Considerable smoke from the gunfire led to much confusion on both sides. As a result, Tegetthoff's ironclad rams missed their targets. Their return charge damaged four of the Italian ships, however.

Austrian cannon fire also damaged the *Re d'Italia*'s exposed steering apparatus, and a shell hitting the stern of the *Palestro* set her on fire and caused her to leave the line. Tegetthoff then spied the *Re d'Italia* to port and ordered his *Erzherzog Ferdinand Maximilian* to ram her. The Austrian ship struck the Italian vessel at a speed of about 11.5 knots and tore a gaping hole in her side, causing the *Re d'Italia* to sink in only five minutes. Aboard the *Affondatore*, Persano signalled to inquire after the *Re d'Italia*. The reply from another Italian ship was, ironically, 'affondato' (sunk). The sinking of the *Re d'Italia*, which had a pronounced influence on naval architecture for decades to come, was actually a fluke; she had been virtually dead in the water and hence vulnerable to the ram.

Persano also ordered the *Affondatore* to ram, but these efforts were largely ineffectual. The wooden *Kaiser* rammed the *Re di Portogallo*, sister ship of the *Re d'Italia*. This actually did more damage to the Austrian vessel, wrecking a funnel, starting a fire, and forcing the *Kaiser* to retire. At about 2:30 p.m. the blazing *Palestro* suddenly blew up with the loss of 204 officers and men. Persano then broke off the action. The Italians had lost two ships and four others were badly damaged. They had also suffered a total of 619 dead and 39 wounded. Later the *Affondatore* foundered in a squall off Ancona, largely as a result of damages sustained in the battle. Austrian losses were slight: several ships damaged but only 38 men killed and 138 wounded.

Tegetthoff had not only saved Lissa, thus denying Italy a bargaining chip at the peace conference, but he had defeated a superior naval force. Vienna promoted him to vice admiral immediately after the battle and later decreed that the Austrian Navy would always have a ship named Tegetthoff.

Lissa was the first battle in history between oceangoing ironclad fleets at sea. It was also the only major fleet encounter of ironclads in which the principal tactic was ramming. Even though only one ship had been sunk by this method during the battle, for the next three decades the world's navies made the ram standard equipment in battleship construction.[47]

Unfortunately for the Austrians their victory in the Battle of Lissa went for nought. The war was decided to the north, in fighting on land between Austria and Prussia.[48] Here the Prussians had the clear edge, particularly with their new breech-loading rifle. The Seven Weeks' War turned out to be a nineteenth-century version of the Blitzkrieg. Despite Austrian victories on both the land and sea against Italy, one big Prussian triumph on land, Königgrätz (Sadowa) in Bohemia on 3 July 1866, decided the war.

FRANCO-PRUSSIAN WAR (1870–1)

The Austro-Prussian War ended 120 years of rivalry between Austria and Prussia and set up Bismarck's next great challenge, the defeat of France in order to bring about the unification of all German states under Prussia. He accomplished this in the Franco-German War of 1870–1. Fighting was almost exclusively on land, as the French Navy had a crushing superiority over the Prussian Navy, which stayed in port. Two French squadrons of 13 armoured frigates of the *Gloire* type, built over the previous decade, quickly imposed a total naval blockade of the North Sea and Baltic. Although shots were fired in other instances, the only real ship engagement of the war occurred between the French aviso (dispatch vessel) *Bouvet* and the Prussian gunboat *Meteor* off the coast of Cuba.

Bouvet versus *Meteor* (9 November 1870)

The *Bouvet* was already at Havana when the *Meteor* arrived there on 7 November. The next evening French captain Franquet and his Prussian counterpart, von Knorr, arranged a ship duel, and Franquet took his vessel to sea to await his opponent. The two vessels were about the same strength; each mounted one 16 cm rifled gun, although the *Bouvet* also had four 12 cm guns while the *Meteor* had only two. The French vessel was faster but the German ship had a stouter hull.

The battle began in international waters off Havana in poor visibility and at a range of some 800 yards. The two ships circled and gradually closed the range. At about 300 yards, the *Bouvet* rammed. The *Meteor*'s captain managed to position his ship so as to avoid the main force of the blow, which fell at about a 45-degree angle; but the *Meteor* still got the worst of it, losing her main mast, the shrouds of which fouled her propeller. Both ships were now very close and the two crews opened up with small arms. The *Bouvet* then took a shot from the *Meteor*'s stern gun, which disabled her boiler and caused her to retire to Havana. The *Meteor* was not able to pursue the *Bouvet* before she regained Spanish waters because of the fouling of her propeller.[49]

France's control of the sea did enable it to maintain lines of communication with Algeria and with neutral states, and to obtain equipment and supplies from abroad. If the war had been protracted, this naval mastery might have been critical, but it went badly on land for France almost from the beginning. This also precluded the possibility of mounting amphibious operations along the Baltic coast. Prussia's crushing victory over France in 1871 decisively altered the European balance of power.[50]

CHAPTER 6

THE PERIOD OF EXPERIMENTATION, 1865–90

The two decades following the American Civil War saw great experimentation in ships and ordnance. The world's navies produced a succession of new designs, usually of a single ship or several ships, which did not end until 1890 with the standardization of the pre-dreadnought era. Because of the great expense involved, only Britain, and to a lesser extent France and Russia, built many capital ships in this era. Most other naval powers built only a few, and some, including the United States, built none at all. Part of this was cost; armoured ships were much more expensive. Also, frequent changes in design led to rapid obsolescence.

BROADSIDE VERSUS TURRET

One aspect of this was the placement of guns aboard ship. The ironclad era opened with a return to broadsides armament, but monitors had appeared in the American Civil War. Their much heavier guns meant larger projectiles, and this necessitated greater thicknesses of armour; but it was not feasible to place heavy armour over the entire ship. One of the chief advantages of the monitor was that the turret could be heavily armoured.

Sharp division between those who favoured the revolving turret and supporters of broadside armament continued. Renewed interest in the ram as a consequence of the Battle of Lissa, and bigger, more powerful guns helped decide the matter in favour of the turret. The ram meant that ships had to fire ahead as they prepared to attack an opposing vessel; heavier guns meant that ships needed fewer of them and that these should have the widest arc of fire possible. Although the growing range of naval gunfire and the torpedo increased fighting ranges and dramatically reduced the possibility of ramming an enemy vessel, for many years ramming and 'bow's on' fighting, in which ramming was to be an important part, heavily influenced naval design.

Cowper Coles

The two chief proponents of the turret were John Ericsson in the United States and Royal Navy captain Cowper Coles in Britain. Ericsson had sent plans for a turreted ship to Napoleon III in 1854; certainly he had the first shipboard armoured turret actually used in battle, in the March 1862 clash between the USS *Monitor* and CSS *Virginia*. Ericsson's turret was all above the upper deck, on which it rested. Before the turret could be turned it had to be lifted by rack and pinion from contact with the deck. A steam engine operating through gearing turned the turret around a central spindle. Ericsson's design was for a raft-like vessel, while Coles favoured a conventional ship.

The Coles turret was the more successful of the two. Easier to operate, it was also less susceptible to damage. It turned on a circumferential roller path set in the lower deck. Its upper 4.5 feet of armour came up through the main or upper deck and formed an armoured glacis to protect the lower part. The crew and ammunition entered the turret from below, through a hollow central cylinder.[1]

Coles had become interested in axial fire during the Crimean War. While in command of the paddle steamer *Stromboli* he had been faced with the problem of close-range, shallow-water operations against Russian shore batteries and hit on the idea of designing a floating battery. This was basically a raft made of casks, partially planked over, to carry a single gun. Built in one night, the *Lady Nancy* was 45 × 15 feet and, despite carrying a long 32-pounder gun weighing 42 cwt, 100 rounds of ammunition, and 18 men, she floated in only 20 inches of water.

Coles successfully employed the *Lady Nancy* in operations against Taganrog in the Sea of Azov. Encouraged by this, he made another raft, again supported by empty casks, to carry a 68-pounder 95 cwt gun protected by a hemispheric iron shield. During action it was partially submerged by filling some of the casks with water, and the large number of casks employed made it largely impervious to hostile fire.[2]

In March 1859 Coles patented the idea of turrets aboard ship. His idea of centreline mounted guns that would have wide arcs of fire on both broadsides, hence halving the number of guns, made eminent sense; but Coles did not understand problems inherent in marrying his armament ideas to a ship that had to incorporate sails as well as

steam. He certainly had no sense of ship design: his proposal for a warship carrying 20 heavy guns in 10 armoured cupolas had only token masts, no rigging, and only one small funnel.

Coles nonetheless continued to bombard the Admiralty with plans. His persistence, coupled with the powerful support of Prince Albert, finally led the Admiralty in March 1861 to install an experimental armoured turret on the floating battery *Trusty*. This test was a success, as 33 hits from 68-pounder and 100-pounder guns failed to disable it.[3] In an a series of letters to the Admiralty Coles proposed building a ship not more than 320 × 48 feet, and 23 feet in draught, of 5,600 tons displacement. It would carry a broadside of at least 16 × 100-pounders under cupolas and be equal to the *Warrior* in speed and fighting powers.[4]

In April 1862 Coles threw down a public challenge in a letter to *The Times* that in essence repeated his earlier challenge to the Admiralty. It stated in part:

I will undertake to prove that on my principle, a vessel shall be built nearly 100 feet shorter than the *Warrior*, and in all respects equal to her, with one exception, that I will undertake to disable and capture her within an hour. She shall draw four feet less water, require only half the crew and cost the country for building at least £100,000 less.[5]

Prince Albert

The Prince Consort also supported Coles' proposal, and in February 1862 the Admiralty ordered construction of the ship to be named the *Prince Albert*. Designed by Chief Constructor Isaac Watts, she was the first British sea-going iron turreted ship. Launched in 1864, she was in fact very much a precursor of things to come. She displaced 3,687 tons and was 240 × 48 feet.

She mounted 4 × 9-inch muzzle-loading rifles, one each in four centre-line circular turrets, which were turned by hand; 18 men could complete a revolution in one minute. She also had a raised superstructure forward of the funnel and full armour protection. Her two masts and simple gaff sails allowed her guns a wide arc of fire. Far more effective as a seagoing vessel than the US Navy *Miantonomoh*, the *Prince Albert* did not have a square rig and was really a coastal defence vessel.[6]

Miantonomoh

While the *Prince Albert* was under construction, in 1862 the United States laid down the US *Miantonomoh*, billed as a seagoing monitor. Designed by Lenthall, she was launched in August 1863 and commissioned in September 1865. This twin-turreted vessel displaced 3,401 tons and was 250 × 50 feet. Powered by two screws, the *Miantonomoh* was armed with 4 × 15-inch Dahlgren smoothbores. After service with the North Atlantic Squadron the *Miantonomoh* cruised to European waters during 1866–67 to prove her seagoing capabilities. This was hardly a success, as she was towed for much of the voyage. During 1865–66 another twin-turreted monitor, the *Monadnock* (commissioned in October 1864), did travel from the east coast to the west coast of the United States, steaming around Cape Horn. But despite efforts to prove their seaworthiness, the monitors remained basically coast defence vessels.[7]

Similar vessels appeared in other navies, including the Danish coast defence ship *Rolf Krake*, with four 8-inch, 68-pounder guns in two turrets. Designed by Coles, she was built in Britain. A similar ship, the *Huascar*, built for Peru, fought British armoured cruisers in 1877 and surrendered to two Reed-designed Chilean box-battery battleships in 1879. The *Huascar* still survives in Chile.

CENTRAL BATTERY AND CASEMATE SHIPS

Two alternatives to the turret were the central casemate (sometimes called 'box') design and the casemate. In both vessels the battery was reduced so that the armour in effect protected a short rectangular box in the centre of the ship. Early central battery ships mounted their guns in broadside, while the casemated warships had angled corner ports to allow greater arcs of fire.[8]

The central battery may have originated with the *Minotaur* of 1863 with its transverse armour bulkhead that allowed the chase guns to be fought behind armor protection. France took this a step further. Both the *Magenta* and *Solferino* incorporated armour protection for the entire central battery.

The battleship *Bellerophon*, completed in 1865, was the first major warship constructed on the central battery principle. Edward J. Reed's first design as chief constructor, she displaced 7,551 tons and was 300 × 56 feet. Her box casemate had 6-inch side armour and 5-inch bulkheads. Her principal armament consisted of 10 × 9-inch and 5 × 7-inch Armstrong muzzle-loading rifles. The *Bellerophon* was built on a new 'bracket-frame' system designed to give greater strength for small expenditure in weight. Reed saved additional weight by using mainly steel in her construction. She also had an extensive system of watertight compartments as a defence against the ram and a double hull (the first) to protect against the new automotive torpedo. Quite manoeuvrable, she incorporated the newly introduced balanced rudder and had a ram, although it was of U- rather than V-form in order to give buoyancy and minimize the tendency toward plunging in V-bow ships.[9]

The French battleship *Océan* of 1868 mounted its main armament of 4 × 10.5-inch guns in a central armoured redoubt. The

Bellerophon, Royal Navy battleship. (*Royal Naval Museum*)

Sultan, Royal Navy battleship. (*Royal Naval Museum, 1984/154 (9)*)

Audacious, Royal Navy battleship. (*Royal Naval Museum*)

guns themselves were in open armoured barbettes, large protective structures that looked like a turret. This meant that the heavy armour could be concentrated to protect the ship's vitals: the biggest guns, the engines, magazines and shellrooms.[10]

In Britain the *Bellerophon* was followed by ten more casemated ships. The *Sultan*, launched in 1870, was one of the most powerful central battery ships built. Displacing 9,540 tons, she was 324 feet 10 inches × 59 feet and had an armour belt that varied from 6 to 12 inches, backed by 10–12 inches of wood. Her armament consisted of 8 × 10-inch and 4 × 9-inch guns.[11]

Four smaller' Audacious'-class battleships, built in response to a growing number of French armoured cruisers, were also casemated battleships. The *Audacious* was commissioned in 1869. Of 6,010 tons, these were 280 × 54 feet vessels that carried 10 × 9-inch and 4 × 64-pounder muzzle-loading rifles. The *Alexandra* of 1875 was the last Royal Navy casemated battleship. Her design provided for as complete all-round fire as was possible in a central-battery ship. At 9,490 tons and 325 × 64 feet, she was armed with 2 × 11-inch and 10 × 10-inch muzzle-loading rifles and 6 × 64-pounders, the latter in broadsides on the main deck. The bulk of her armament was located so as to fire for end-on battle. Other countries also experimented with this type of warship.

SEAGOING TURRETED SHIPS

After the successful demonstration of Coles' turret and with Denmark and the Latin American states ordering turreted ships from British builders, the Admiralty took a wooden first rate 121-gun ship-of-the-line, the *Royal Sovereign* of 1857, and during 1862–4 converted her into an armoured turret ship of 5,080 tons mounting 5 × 9-inch guns.

Again under challenge from Coles, supported by Prince Albert and much of the British Press, the Admiralty agreed to build a seagoing iron turret ship from scratch, the *Monarch* of 1868. Displacing 8,320 tons and 330 × 57.5 feet, she was the first British ship to be armed with 12-inch guns, which now became standard for British battleships. These 25-ton guns were mounted two each in two centreline turrets at either end of a central armoured box. She also carried 3 × 7-inch guns, two fore and one aft. The *Monarch*'s retention of a sail rig, however, inhibited her arcs of fire.[12]

Coles criticized the design of the *Monarch* for her high poop and forecastle that prevented axial fire. He also attacked her overly high freeboard. The *Monarch*'s guns were mounted 3 feet above upper deck level and 17 feet above the waterline. High freeboard added to the roll of the ship and made it a less satisfactory gun platform; a lower freeboard also saved weight that could be diverted into heavier armour over the decks to protect the ship from plunging shot. Coles erred, however, when he asserted that, 'A good sea boat does not altogether depend on height out of water.' In fact, carrying the guns high was necessary in a ship under full sail; it increased the range of stability, that is the angle to which a ship could heel before it began to right itself.[13]

In 1863 Reed had become chief constructor, at only thirty-three. During his entire career he designed 95 warships, 25 of them ironclads.[14] Reed understood the need for the high freeboard, and he disagreed sharply with Coles over this and the latter's suggestions for another turreted ironclad. Reed regarded the low freeboard on the new design as potentially hazardous, given the fact that the Admiralty insisted that the ship retain a full sail rig. Even with little or no sail set, she was likely to roll heavily. Reed believed that heavy weather would likely carry away her funnel casings and open her large engine and boiler hatches to the sea.[15]

Captain

Each man had his supporters, but Coles had the backing of the First Lord of the Admiralty, the Duke of Somerset, and many in Parliament. Finally the Navy agreed to a second seagoing turreted ship to be built to Coles' specifications. He was allowed to select the shipbuilder from a shortlist selected by the Admiralty and chose Lairds, which submitted proposals in July 1866. Reed protested the designed freeboard of only 8 feet; he also held that the estimate of her weight was too low and that her centre of gravity was likely to be higher than estimated by Lairds. Controller Spencer Robinson also strongly objected to the ship's low freeboard, but Somerset approved the design, probably so that Coles could no longer complain in public about the Admiralty.

It was clear when the new ship was floated out of the drydock in March 1869, however, that she was well overweight. Completed in 1869 as the *Captain*, she underwent sea trials in 1870. Her design was modified to add to the height of the bow area in order to give her the necessary seagoing qualities, but this meant the sacrifice of ahead fire.

At 6,950 tons and 320 × 53 feet the *Captain* was smaller than the *Monarch*; she was also less beamy. She had two turrets mounting 4 × 12-inch muzzle-loaders, and she also carried 2 × 7-inch muzzle-loaders. Although similar in design to the *Monarch*, the *Captain* differed in the important respect that her actual freeboard was only 6 feet 7 inches instead of the 14 feet on the *Monarch*. The *Captain*'s trials were satisfactory and she proved stable at sea; but, designed as a full-rigged ship, she was overmasted and top heavy.

Captain, Royal Navy battleship. Contemporary artist's impression, showing her under the sail she was carrying the night she foundered. (*Royal Naval Museum, 1869*)

On 6 September 1870, only four months after commissioning, the *Captain* was cruising off Cape Finisterre when a storm came up. About midnight, with the sea lashing over her deck edge, the *Captain* capsized. She went down with 473 people, including Coles, out of 490 on board. The death toll was greater than that sustained by the Royal Navy in the Battle of Trafalgar.[16]

BREASTWORK MONITORS, 1870–80

Cerberus

Another type of battleship was the breastwork monitor, in which there was a centrally built superstructure or 'breastwork' amidships, on which turrets were mounted, one at each end. This arrangement provided a clear field of fire over the bow for the forward turret and over the stern for the after turret; between them, the two turrets could fire in either direction. Breastwork monitors had a low freeboard main deck but a higher armoured deck containing the turrets in the middle of the ship, that afforded protection for the funnel, turret bases, and airshafts; it also kept these and the hatchways clear of the sea.

Typical of breastwork monitors was the *Cerberus*, the first low freeboard battleship after the *Captain*. Reed, who designed her, was not worried about the low freeboard because she was mastless and a coastal defence monitor intended to defend Melbourne harbour. The *Cerberus* displaced 3,344 tons, was 225 × 45 feet, and mounted 4 × 10-inch muzzle-loading guns. Laid down in September 1867, nine months after the *Captain* had been begun, the *Cerberus* was completed in September 1870, the same month the *Captain* was lost. The genesis of all battleship design in the period to 1905, the *Cerberus* excited little interest in Britain because she was a special-purpose ship intended for distant service.[17]

Devastation

The last British battleship with a full sail rig, the *Shannon*, was completed in September 1877, but modern battleship design advanced significantly with Reed's 9,387-ton *Devastation*. A somewhat larger *Cerberus*, she

was begun in November 1869 and completed in 1873, incorporating design changes by Nathaniel Barnaby, Reed's successor.

The *Devastation* incorporated a good balance of speed, protection, and armament. Reed's instructions called for a smaller ocean going turret ship with sailing rig; but, given the weight of the armour required and the fact that rigging would hinder the turreted guns from being able to fire in a wide arc, the *Devastation* was built to be powered by steam alone. As Reed wrote in 1869, 'My clear and strong conviction at the moment . . . is that no satisfactorily designed turret ship with rigging has yet been built, or even laid down.'[18]

The *Devastation* was, in fact, the first oceangoing mastless man-of-war and thus the forerunner of all twentieth-century battleships. Powered by twin screw trunk engines, the iron-hulled and armoured *Devastation* was 285 × 62 feet. Her twin

Hercules, Royal Navy battleship. (*Royal Naval Museum*)

Devastation, Royal Navy battleship. (*Royal Naval Museum, 1981/136*)

propellers allowed a speed of 12.5 knots. With a midships superstructure, she mounted her principal armament of 4 × 12-inch muzzle-loading guns in two centre-line turrets fore and aft. She also was heavily armoured: her side armour belt alone was 12 inches tapering to 8 inches, all supported by 18 inches of teak and two layers of 0.75-inch iron plates. The total weight of armour in the ship came to 2,540 tons, or 27 per cent of total displacement! Before the *Devastation*, the standard was about 15 per cent.

Another feature was a great increase in bunkering space; the *Devastation* could carry up to 1,800 tons of coal. Since she was powered by steam alone the *Devastation* needed the extra coal capacity. With her large superstructure, she appeared to be top heavy. When she was commissioned at Portsmouth, someone placed a note on her gangway that read, 'Letters for the *Captain* may be posted aboard.' In fact, she performed well at sea in her trials and had little roll, even in a gale with 20–26-foot waves.[19]

ADVANCES IN PROPULSION

As ship design changed, so too did their engines. Down to 1870 most of the world's merchant fleets were sailing ships, and as late as 1880 there was as much tonnage driven by wind as by steam. But more powerful marine engines made the use of screw propellers truly practical. At the same time engines became smaller, yielding more space for ordnance and other requirements. Improved metallurgical techniques led to a series of innovations after 1870, including the compound engine, which greatly improved on the simple single expansion engine. An improved condenser also appeared.

These inventions reduced the consumption of coal and the cost of operating steamships. Equally important, by reducing the space required to carry coal and water, increased space became available for cargo, crews, and ordnance. All this had a considerable impact on naval construction.

Triple-expansion engine

The *Devastation* benefited from these changes. During 1891–2 she received triple expansion engines and cylindrical boilers. The triple expansion engine, first utilized in the *Aberdeen* in 1881, developed steam in three stages and improved engine economy. Instead of a normal pressure of 25–30 psi, it could produce steam at 60 psi; this meant that vessels so equipped could go much greater distances without recoaling. This was the last step before the introduction of the steam turbine.

During her 1879 refit the *Devastation* also received torpedoes, searchlights, and machine guns. This was typical of the period to the end of the century; capital ships all had mixed armaments to enable them to fight at short, intermediate, and long ranges. Naval theorists held that battles would occur at relatively short ranges, well within that of secondary armaments, which could be used to smother an opponent with rapid fire. This conclusion seemed borne out in the sea fights at the end of the century. In the Battles of Manila and Santiago during the Spanish American War, US warships closed to within 2,000 yards of the Spanish vessels in ideal, calm conditions yet scored only 3 per cent hits.[20]

The *Thunderer*, which followed the *Devastation* and was quite similar to her, was even more successful. A stable gun platform, she had faster engines and larger guns. She also incorporated a new loading system for her two forward 12.5-inch muzzle-loading guns. The guns were loaded externally, with steam power rotating the turret until it was in the correct location over the loading tube. The guns were then depressed hydraulically, and their 700-lb projectiles were rammed into the muzzles by a telescopic hydraulic rammer. Another innovation was the ability to fire her guns electrically from the bridge. The *Devastation* and *Thunderer* never did see battle and were broken up in 1908 and 1909.[21]

Dreadnought

The *Dreadnought* was directly descended from the *Devastation* and *Thunderer*. Originally designed by Reed and started in 1870, work on her was halted in 1871

Dreadnought, Royal Navy battleship. (*Royal Naval Museum, 1876*)

pending the outcome of the investigation into the *Captain* disaster. Although the basic design was kept, following Reed's retirement W.H. White made modifications.

The *Dreadnought* was one of the last true British ironclads. Of 10,820 tons, she was 320 × 64 feet with a main armament of 4 × 12.5-inch guns. She also shows how much progress was being made. The guns of the *Devastation* were loaded and worked by hand, and the forward turret of the *Thunderer* employed the hydraulics for its forward guns only; but both of the *Dreadnought*'s turrets employed the hydraulic system. The *Devastation* also had non-compound, trunk-type engines working with a maximum steam pressure of 30 lbs psi. The *Dreadnought* had compound three-cylinder vertical engines, working with 60

lbs psi, with the two engine rooms divided by a watertight bulkhead. She had an overall flat deck with two turrets, one each fore and aft of the central superstructure. Commissioned in 1879, she was in service for 25 years and became one of the best loved ships of the Royal Navy.[22]

CENTRAL CITADEL SHIPS

Duilio and *Enrico Dandolo*

The period saw something of a naval building contest as each new capital ship incorporated improvements in design, engines, armour, and heavier ordnance. Italy, as an emerging naval power, produced some magnificent ships in both the late nineteenth and twentieth centuries. In 1872 Italy laid down two vessels that advanced battleship design,

Duilio, Italian Navy battleship, photographed at La Spezia Naval Yard at the time of completion. Note depressed angle of her main guns in turrets *en echelon* amidships. (*Naval Historical Foundation, NH 88710*)

Inflexible, Royal Navy battleship. (*Royal Naval Museum, 1984/640*)

the *Duilio* and *Enrico Dandolo*. Designed by Benedetto Brin, these ships maintained the central citadel, but their armoured turrets diagonally placed amidships were separated by only a single-pole mast.

Brin saw them as heavily armed, well-protected, fast capital ships. On their completion they were the most powerful warships in the world. They also mounted the largest guns: 4 × 100-ton, 450 mm (17.7-inch) guns designed by Armstrong, two in each turret.

The major innovation in them was their two twin-mount midships turrets protected by 17-inch armour, which made up some 25 per cent of the ship's total weight. Brin relied on watertight bulkheads to protect the rest of the ship. The *Duilio* and *Enrico Dandolo* were in fact the first modern battleships built on the 'all or nothing' principle of protection.

Powered by twin-screw, vertical compound engines, the 358 feet 2 inch × 64 feet 8 inch, 12,071-ton *Duilio* could make 15 knots. Laid

down in 1873, she was not completed until 1880. She underwent several upgrades but was stripped of her armament to become a floating oil tank in 1909. The *Enrico Dandolo* was slightly heavier at 12,265 tons, but her twin-screw triple expansion engines could drive her at 15.6 knots. She also had a long service life; she was a floating battery during the First World War and was not broken up until 1920. A prolific designer, Brin also came up with ships exported to Argentina, Spain, and Japan.[23]

Inflexible

Before the *Duilio* was even commissioned the British responded with the *Inflexible*. Laid down in 1874 and designed by Barnaby in direct response to the *Duilio* and French moves to build new heavy ships, the 11,880-ton *Inflexible* was 320 × 75 feet. Completed in 1881, she mounted 4 × 16-inch, 81-ton muzzle-loading Armstrong guns. These were set two each in two 750-ton turrets, off the centre line so as to allow ahead fire. But the possibility of blast damage limited this to 30 degrees off axis. The turrets were at opposite corners of the citadel, which had a single breastwork of armour completely surrounding the turrets and superstructure. The guns were too long to be reloaded in the turrets, so this was accomplished by depressing them into an armoured glacis on the main deck, with hydraulic reloading. In optimum conditions they could fire a 1,700-lb shell every 2.5 minutes.

The *Inflexible* had the distinction of carrying the thickest armour of any battleship ever built. Her citadel had two thicknesses of 12-inch iron plate, backed by 36 inches of teak, which altogether weighed 1,100 lbs per square foot! The citadel contained the machinery, turrets, and magazine, and it was long enough to remain afloat and upright if the ends of the ship were flooded. The *Inflexible* also had a 3-inch armoured deck, and she carried two 60-foot torpedo boats and was fitted with the first underwater torpedo tubes.

The *Inflexible* was also the first battleship fitted with electric lights. Powered by twin-screw, compound engines, she made 14.75 knots in her trials, but she carried auxiliary sails. Despite her armour, in 1882 the *Inflexible* sustained damage during the shelling of Alexandria, Egypt. She was scrapped in 1903.[24]

For a time emphasis was placed on ships of smaller displacements and less armour. The *Inflexible* was followed by derivative ships *Agamemnon* (1879) of 8,510 tons and *Ajax* (1880) of 8,660 tons; each was some 3,000 tons lighter than the *Inflexible*. The two mounted 4 × 12.5-inch, 38-ton guns and had 18-inch armour. The *Colossus* and *Edinburgh* were significantly improved ships. They had largely steel hulls and introduced large breech-loading guns. They also carried a substantial secondary armament, the first for a modern British capital ship.[25]

BARBETTE

A third major means of carrying ordnance was the barbette, introduced by the French. They initially disregarded the new Italian designs and continued with construction of oceangoing ships of the casemate design. The lead battleship in their 1872 programme, the *Redoubtable* (launched in 1876), was followed by two more ships of the same type: the *Dévastation* and *Courbet*. Their answer to Brin's innovations came in 1877 with a new design that was a mix of previous practice and new technology. From 1877 to 1879 France laid down seven barbette ships, a new fleet that caused alarm in Britain in the 1880s as its scope became known.[26]

The barbette was simply an armoured shield behind which the gun crews served the guns, which were left exposed and mounted on a turntable. The chief advantages of this mount were its light weight, meaning that heavy guns could be mounted other than on the lower levels and centre of the ship, and the ease of working the gun for the crew. The disadvantage of the barbette was that it was an open mount, which meant that gun crews and the guns themselves were vulnerable to enemy fire.

Dupuy de Lôme had come up with the new barbette arrangement at the end of 1862 for coast defence vessels and rams. The French first introduced the barbette in their ocean going ships in the *Alma* of 1867. The English also experimented with a barbette arrangement on the *Téméraire* in 1876, but the first true barbette ship was the French battleship *Amiral Duperré*, laid down in 1877 and completed in 1883.

Amiral Duperré

The *Amiral Duperré* was the French response to the *Duilio*. Initially she had a sail rig, but this was removed before she was completed. The French insisted on a true seagoing ship that

Redoubtable, French Navy battleship. (*Naval Historical Foundation, NH 66089*)

carried her guns high above the waterline. Displacing 11,800 tons, the *Amiral Duperré* was 320 feet long. In order to render invulnerable such armour as was retained aboard their ships, the Italians and English removed it from part of the waterline. The French continued to favour a complete waterline belt and took their savings in weight in armour from the sides of the ship above the waterline. Although the *Amiral Duperré* retained a complete belt 22 inches thick, it was only 8 feet high; as with the *Duilio*, the sides of the ship above the belt were unarmoured. The *Amiral Duperré* had an armoured deck and her main battery consisted of 4 × 13.4-inch guns, each in a heavily armoured barbette; two of these were located abreast forward and two were on the centreline aft. Unlike most other

contemporary designs the French battleship also carried a significant number of 5.5-inch guns entirely unprotected in broadside mounts.

A key factor in this design was the French determination to retain the ability to ram. Brin wanted to keep his ship afloat and its guns firing; the French wanted to retain mobility in hope of ramming the enemy. A complete waterline belt was thought to improve chances of protecting the ship's mobility, whereas in the Italian citadel system a single shot from even a light gun to the ship's bow might inhibit its ability to manoeuvre. Also, ramming a citadel ship at bow or stern could produce serious, possibly fatal, damage; but the ramming ship would herself be in jeopardy without the additional structural support of

Amiral Duperré, French Navy battleship. (*Naval Historical Foundation, NH 66056*)

the armoured belt. These conclusions seemed borne out by experience. The British battleship *Victoria* lost its ability to manoeuvre and ultimately sank after being rammed accidently in her unprotected bow by the *Camperdown* off Tripoli on 22 June 1893. And on 17 September 1894, two Chinese battleships were so badly damaged in the Battle of the Yalu that they could manage only 4 knots and might easily have been finished off by ram or torpedo.[27]

In 1876, with the race for the heaviest guns aboard ship well underway, the minister of marine informed the French Chamber that 100-ton guns were imminent and that the two new battleships would be built to carry them. They were the last French barbette-design battleships.

Amiral Baudin and *Formidable*

The *Amiral Baudin* and *Formidable* followed the *Amiral Duperré* and were France's final answer to Brin's *Duilio* and *Italia*. Laid down in 1879, these 11,720-ton French ships were 323 feet 10 inches × 70 feet in size and had no sails. Their steel armoured belts varied from 14 to 22 inches, but only 12 inches of this was above the waterline. They also had a protective deck. Their 3 × 371 mm (14.6-inch) main guns were mounted in single barbettes on the centre line and protected by 16-inch armour. One mount was forward, one was between the two masts and aft of the stack, and the third was aft of the second mast. During 1896–97 the ships were reconstructed and the centre barbette was replaced by a casemate.[28]

The Italians also experimented with the barbette. In 1876 Brin began construction of two large, fast battleships, the *Italia* and *Lepanto*. When the *Italia* entered service in 1880 she was among the fastest vessels afloat. These two warships displaced 15,654 tons each and were 409 feet × 73 feet 10 inches in size; they could steam at up to 17.8 knots. They mounted 4 × 430 mm (17-inch), 102-ton guns, placed two each on turntables on a large oval-shaped armoured barbette amidships. The guns were protected by compound (steel-faced iron) 482-mm (19-inch) armour.

The high speed of the two ships resulted in large part from Brin's decision to do away entirely with side armour. Among the first battleships of steel construction, the *Italia* and *Lepanto* had no armoured belt; instead a 102-mm (4-inch) thick armoured deck curved down to the waterline. Indeed, a protective deck found increasing favour among naval architects. Brin's design also incorporated a large number of watertight compartments and cork-filled cells backed by coal to assist with ship survivability should the armour be breached. The ships also had an elaborate pump system to remove water in case of a hit below the waterline. Shells for the guns had to be trundled up from below deck, and it took five minutes between firings.

The ships were easily identified by their six funnels, three forward and three aft. By the time the two ships had entered service the quick-firing gun and new high explosive shell had rendered them obsolete. Large, fast, lightly armoured yet heavily gunned, these two ships were forerunners of the later battle cruisers.[29]

Formidable, French Navy battleship. (*Musée de la Marine, PH 32924*)

Collingwood, Royal Navy battleship. (*Royal Naval Museum*)

Trafalgar, Royal Navy battleship. (*Royal Naval Museum, 5078*)

In 1887 the French laid down the *Caiman*, 278 feet long with a speed of 14.5 knots. She carried two guns in barbettes, one 42-cm (16.5-inch) breech-loader each at bow and stern. She also carried 4 × 10 cm guns in broadsides. The *Caiman* had the traditional French heavy armour belt at the waterline with a maximum thickness of 19.5 inches, tapering toward bow and stern. The middle of the ship was also protected by a 2.8-inch steel deck.

The Royal Navy *Collingwood*, laid down in 1880 and completed in 1887, 9,500 tons and 324 feet 10 inches × 68 feet, was in part a response to the *Caiman*. Also employing barbette mounts for her main armament, she was the first of the so-called 'Admiral' class. The *Collingwood* set the overall design of British battleships until the *Dreadnought* in 1906. She was protected by an 18-inch armoured waterline belt and armed with 4 × 12-inch guns, which became the British battleship standard for the next 25 years. These were set in pairs in barbettes on turntables fore and aft on the centreline. She also carried a secondary armament of 6 × 6-inch guns, three per side on the upper deck amidships. Because of the introduction of new hydraulic machinery to work the guns, crew size was reduced. The powerful secondary battery in large part resulted from the threat posed by French torpedo craft. Powered by her twin screws and inverted compound engines, the *Collingwood* could make 17 knots.[30]

The Reed era of ship construction in Britain ended with the *Trafalgar*, also with barbette mounts. Laid down in 1886, she entered service in 1890. This 345' × 73 feet battleship was the last British single citadel turret ship built. At 12,500 tons she was also the largest British battleship thus far. Her main armament consisted of 4 × 13.5-inch, two per turret. She was the first British battleship to mount a secondary armament

of quick-firing 6-inch guns, of which she had six. She also had 8 × 6-pounders, 9 × 3-pounders, and 5 torpedo tubes.[31]

Other nations also experimented with different mounts. Germany came up with the 'reduit', an armoured deckhouse. Usually oval in shape, it had tracks that allowed the guns to be moved to different ports. The gun mount was not solved until the 1890s, when the barbette principle was retained but with an armoured hood over it. Among the more boldly experimental but curious vessels of this period were the two Russian *Popoffka*; circular, 120-foot diameter, coastal defence vessels constructed in the 1870s for use on the Black Sea. They had 11- to 18-inch armour.[32]

Most naval theorists in the 1870s still favoured the ram and broadside fire, while passing an enemy vessel, although opinion was slowly changing to the need for bow fire. The firing of heavy guns forward as the ship moved to ram an opposing vessel was held undesirable, however, because the smoke would obscure vision. Watertight subdivisions and manoeuvrability were considered the best defence against the ram and the torpedo.[33]

The French *Jeune École*

During this period arguments were advanced both for a few large capital ships and for more numerous smaller vessels. In 1869 French Captain Baron Louis-Antoine-Richild Grivel wrote *De la guerre maritime avant et depuis les nouvelles inventions* ('Naval war before and after the new inventions'). His discussion of changes in naval technology, mixed with his own personal experiences and work by his father, led to the set of ideas known as the *Jeune École* ('Young School').

Grivel said naval war was of three categories: on the high seas (what Mahan called 'command of the sea'), on the coasts, and the *guerre de course*. The first was to enable a navy 'to acquire an influence and supremacy on the great roads of the sea, which will open the way for coastal and commercial warfare'.[34]

Grivel posited that in the case of war between France and Prussia it would be possible for France to secure command of the sea and carry out operations against the Prussian coasts. But in the event of war with Britain, France could not gain command of the sea, thanks to superior British numbers of warships and level of training. The futility of competing with Britain had been shown in the huge sums expended in the failed naval building contest of the 1850s and 1860s.

Grivel believed, therefore, that in the event of war with Britain the solution was to attack it economically: 'Commercial warfare, the most economical form of war for the poorer fleet, is at the same time the one best suited to restore peace promptly, in that it strikes directly . . . at the very sources of the prosperity of the enemy.'[35] Grivel advocated both coastal attacks and a war against commerce. He did not see how this ran contrary to his own statement regarding command of the sea.

Neither Grivel nor his successors in the *Jeune École* saw this fundamental problem. Dupuy de Lôme had failed to show that technological change could bring France control of the high seas, and the *Jeune École* had failed to show how attacks against the British coasts could succeed without first securing control of the English Channel, but at least the torpedo made the argument seem more plausible.[36]

In 1886 Admiral Théophile Aube became minister of marine. Aube and the *Jeune École* held that the torpedo had ended the dominance of the big gun at sea; fast torpedo boats could attack and destroy the slow-moving battleships. The *Jeune École*, with its emphasis on a *guerre de course* aimed against British trade, stressed construction of cruisers, torpedo boats, and submarines. It dominated French naval thinking in the 1880s.[37]

CRUISERS

Cruisers underwent considerable change in this period – the term 'cruiser' was not really established until the 1880s. Cruisers replaced the old steam-and-sail screw frigates of the 1860s and 1870s. They retained much the same roles of scouting and independent action, such as attacking enemy commerce. Cruisers were differentiated from battleships by their smaller size, higher speed, and moderate armament. Because of their greater speed they received only such armour as was deemed sufficient to resist shells thrown by their own class of vessel.

During this period, reflecting their myriad roles, different cruiser classes proliferated: armoured, semi-armoured, belted, protected (first and second class), light, and scout cruisers. Armoured cruisers, those deemed capable of standing in the main battle line, were the largest; they had vertical side armour and sometimes armour on their superstructure. The smallest cruisers, scout or unarmoured, relied on speed for their protection. Protected cruisers were a compromise, without armour plate on their sides but with an armoured arched deck to cover the ship's vital machinery and magazines, and armour on the gun positions.

The US Navy screw cruiser *Wampanoag*, begun in 1863 during the Civil War but not completed until 1867, is sometimes considered the first cruiser type. Developed to deal with Confederate commerce raiders, she displaced 4,215 tons and was 335 feet × 45 feet 2 inches. She mounted 3 × 60-pounder rifled guns and 10 × 9-inch smoothbores. The *Wampanoag* averaged 16.75 knots in her trials, making her the fastest ship in the world. The Royal Navy responded with the 5,880-ton Inconstant-class frigates, beginning in 1868; 337 × 50 feet, they had 6 × 7-inch muzzle-loading rifles and 10 × 9-inch guns.[38]

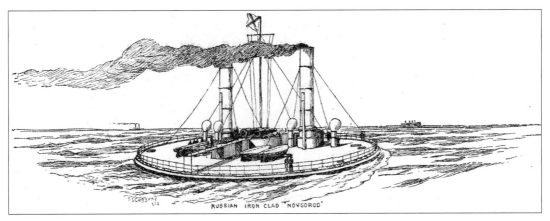

Novgorod, Russian coastal defence ship. Sketch by Fred S. Cozzens, 1894. (*Naval Historical Foundation, NH 74565*)

French protected cruiser *Sfax* (laid down in 1882), starboard view, 1898. (*Imperial War Museum, Q22305*)

The first 'armoured cruiser', in the sense that she carried a side armour belt, was the 5,030-ton *General Admiral*, a Russian ship with 8-inch guns. Laid down in 1870, she was completed in 1878 and was not removed from the Soviet Navy list until 1938. The British steam frigate *Shannon* entered service in 1875. At 5,390 tons and 260 × 54 feet, she carried 2 × 10-inch, 7 × 9-inch, and 6 × 20-pounder guns. She was the first 'protected

153

New York, US Navy armoured/first-class cruiser (CA-2), *see also* page 204. (*Naval Historical Foundation,*

cruiser', with an armoured deck to protect her vital machinery and magazines.[39]

One of the first modern cruisers was the *Esmeralda*, built in England for Chile in 1883. At 2,950 tons she was 270 × 45 feet and mounted 2 × 10-inch guns fore and aft in barbettes and 16 × 6-inch guns in broadsides. That same year the United States laid down three protected cruisers, the *Atlanta*, *Boston*, and *Chicago*, or the 'ABCs', as these first vessels of the new US Navy were called. *Atlanta* and *Boston* were only 3,190 tons and mounted 2 × 8-inch guns. The *Chicago* was almost 5,000 tons with 4 × 8-inch guns. The ABCs carried no armour but had a steel deck up to three inches thick to give the interior of the ship some protection. The ships were constructed of steel and could be propelled either by their compound steam engines or by sails.

In 1883 Britain launched two cruiser classes, the first of which was the four-ship 'Leander' class. These 4,300-ton ships were 300 × 46 feet and mounted 10 × 6-inch guns. Originally known as dispatch vessels, they were later classified as second-class cruisers. The larger 'Imperieuse'-class armoured cruisers were 8,400 tons, 315 × 62 feet, and mounted 4 × 9.2-inch, 10 × 6-inch, and 8 × 6-pounders.[40]

France built many cruisers, a consequence of *Jeune École* emphasis on cruiser warfare against commerce. Italy also built them. The *Piemonte*, an Italian cruiser built in Britain in 1887, was the first fitted with quick-firing guns. She carried 6 × 6-inchers and a like number of 4-inchers. In 1888 the Russians completed the armoured cruiser *Admiral Nakhimov*, the first cruiser to carry her main battery in turrets. That same year the United States authorized its first armoured cruiser, the *New York*, and the protected cruiser *Olympia*. In 1885 the British began building seven 'Orlando'-class armoured cruisers. Completed three years later, these were designed for world-wide cruising to protect trade and were the largest cruisers of the period. At 5,600 tons, they were 300 × 56 feet and mounted 2 × 9-inch, 10 × 6-inch, and 10 × 3-pounder guns.[41]

STEEL HULLS AND OTHER INNOVATIONS

Dividing a ship's hull into watertight compartments separated by bulkheads was an innovation of this period, but even more important was the introduction of steel in the construction of warships. Steel, both stronger and lighter than iron, had been known for some time, but was too expensive. New steel-making processes developed by Siemens, Martin (1865), and Thomas and Gilchrist (1878), dramatically lowered its cost. Because the displacement of steel ships was less in proportion to their carrying capacity than that of those of either iron or wood, steel-hulled vessels could carry more cargo or ordnance than the latter before their load lines were reached. Ships of steel were safer than those of wood and cheaper than those made of iron. Watertight doors were now possible. Equally important was the use of steel in boiler construction.

Steel also helped partially counteract the effects of the torpedo at sea. When a warship was at anchor, a steel net apron could be boomed out around the ship to

Olympia, US Navy cruiser (C-6), *see also* page 204. Photographed after 1901. (*Naval Historical*

Iris, Royal Navy dispatch boat (later second-class cruiser). (*Royal Naval Museum, 5332*)

protect against torpedoes. When not in use the net was hoisted aboard and tied to a shelf constructed on the ship's side. Such torpedo nets were employed into the Second World War.

Once again the French were in the forefront. In 1873 they laid down the steel-hulled *Redoubtable*. Completed in 1878, she was a 9,200-ton central battery ship. The *Redoubtable* was 315 × 64.5 feet and had a main battery of 8 × 10-inch guns.

The first British steel ships were the much smaller *Iris* and *Mercury*, of 3,730 tons. Completed in 1877 and 1878 respectively, they were 300 × 46 feet. Unarmoured, they carried 10 × 64-pounder guns. Capable of 17 knots and first known as dispatch boats, later they were called second-class cruisers. They are often identified as prototypes of

the modern cruiser. Italy also used steel for its new large 'Italia'-class battleships. By 1880 most of the world's navies had switched to all-steel hulls.[42]

Water-tube boiler

As the ships themselves changed, marine engineers were extending the limits of the steam engine. The water-tube boiler was another major advance. In an ordinary cylindrical boiler the water was heated by copper tubing carrying hot air. The water-tube boiler in effect reversed this process. In it the water was carried in tubing that passed through the furnace. Steam pressure was thus inside instead of outside the tube, and this minimized the danger of boiler explosions. It also saved considerable weight as the amount of

Mercury, Royal Navy dispatch boat (later second-class cruiser). (*Royal Naval Museum*)

metal necessary to resist bursting was relatively light. And it meant that, because the volume of water involved was much less, steam pressure could be increased more rapidly. This was important in warships that often had to get underway quickly or increase their speed.[43]

To facilitate marine transportation, fuelling stations, where steamships could replenish their supplies, were established along the world's principal shipping routes, and mechanical appliances for rapidly loading and unloading were installed in the important harbours. Two great obstacles to ocean transportation were also removed. The Isthmus of Suez was pierced in November 1869 with the opening of the Suez Canal. This 100-mile long canal connected the Mediterranean with the Red Sea and shortened by thousands of miles the sea voyage from the North Atlantic and the Mediterranean to the East. In the summer of 1914 the route to the Pacific was similarly shortened when the Panama Canal was opened across the Isthmus of Panama in Central America.

New weapons appeared, such as the automotive type torpedo, high-speed torpedo boats, and 'torpedo-boat destroyers' (see Chapter 7). The threat of underwater attack during fog or at night led to increased compartmentalization of ships' hulls for greater security. Searchlights appeared as detection equipment.

Armour

Armour for ships also underwent rapid change, growing in thickness from 4.5 to

24 inches. The race between ordnance and armour dominated this period. Originally the armour consisted of wrought-iron plates bolted against the wood. About 1865 rolled-iron armour on double layers of wood, all stiffened with iron girders, came into use. In 1870 sandwich armour appeared; it consisted of several layers of rolled-iron armour alternating with wood, all backed by an inner skin of sheet iron. It was followed in 1877 by compound armour that consisted of steel-clad wrought-iron plates.[44]

ORDNANCE DEVELOPMENTS

Major developments were registered in naval ordnance that helped re-establish the dominance of the battleship at sea. From 1860 to 1885 there was a tremendous change in the big guns carried aboard ship, from one firing an 8-inch, 68-lb shot in 1860, to a gun that fired a 16.25-inch shell weighing 1,800 lbs in 1884. The latter could penetrate 34 inches of wrought iron at 1,000 yards. But problems with the larger guns, including the short lives of their barrels, led most navies to drop back to a smaller size: for example 12-inch guns in the Royal Navy.

Ordnance experiments around 1870 involving testing pressures in gun bores had shown that performance could be greatly enhanced by the adoption of slower burning gunpowder and a longer barrel. Slow-burning large-grain powder, known as prismatic powder, prolonged the length of time that the charge acted on the projectile and hence increased both muzzle velocity and range. If the gun were to be chambered, that is making the powder chamber larger than the charge, a greater amount of the slow-burning powder could be utilized without increasing the pressure on the gun tube while at the same time increasing the pressure on the projectile as it moved down the barrel.

The problem with this was that the projectile left the barrel before all the powder was consumed. This could, of course, be solved by longer barrels, but that would make muzzle-loading next to impossible. The slower burning powders also required a powder chamber of diameter larger than that of the bore. These factors and the need to protect gun crews involved in the loading process led to a renewed search for an effective breech-loading gun.

Breech-loading guns

Although breech-loaders had been tried at sea in the modern era, beginning in 1858 on the *Gloire* and later on the *Warrior*, problems had led to them being discarded. In 1864 the Royal Navy reverted definitely to muzzle-loading ordnance, but other nations, especially the French, moved ahead with breech-loaders.

The old problem of ineffective sealing at the breech was only slowly overcome. Krupp breech-loading field guns as late as the Franco-Prussian War of 1870–71 emitted smoke and flame from the breech when they were fired. Finally in 1872 Captain de Bange of the French Army came up with a 'plastic gas check' that helped prevent escape of gases at the breech. Tests were successful, and in 1875 France adopted the breech-loader. At the same time brass cartridge cases, already used for smallarms, came into use for the smaller breech-loading guns.[45]

An accident aboard HMS *Thunderer* in the Sea of Marmora in January 1879 helped hasten the Royal Navy's decision to return to breech-loading guns. Simultaneous firing was underway, with the main guns fired in salvo; during this, one of the battleship's 12-inch muzzle-loading guns misfired. This was not detected from the force of the discharge of the one gun, and both guns were run back in hydraulically to be reloaded. They were then fired again,

French 27cm breech-loading gun on casemate mounting. Painting by G. Bourgain. (*Musée de la Marine*)

whereupon the double-charged gun blew up, killing 11 men and injuring 35 others. This could not have happened with a breech-loading gun, and in May the Admiralty set up a committee to investigate the merits of breech-loading versus muzzle-loading guns.[46]

In the summer of 1879 the British public also took notice of several gunboats built by Armstrong for the Chinese government. Each carried two 12-ton breech-loading guns that were as effective as any muzzle-loading guns in the Royal Navy. In August a committee of naval officers travelled to Germany to witness and report on trials of new Krupp breech-loaders. These and the realization of the need for a longer barrelled gun led the Royal Navy to decide in August 1879 to readopt the breech-loader for the three already-begun battleships *Colossus*, *Edinburgh*, and *Conqueror*, which entered service in 1881–82.

Two breech-closing systems were available: the Krupp wedge and the 'interrupted screw' originated by American inventor Ben Chambers, who patented a slotted screw in 1849. French General Treuille de Beaulieu modified the Chambers' system and played a key role in the French Navy adoption of the breech-loader in 1858. A steel tube with polygroove rifling formed the body of the gun; hoops of iron or steel shrunk on strengthened it at the breech.[47]

Steel guns

Another change in this period was to guns of steel, which accompanied the enormous increases in gun size. Krupp in Germany began producing cast steel rifled guns in 1860. Britain and Italy built their first large guns of iron and began to change to steel only after the guns reached 100 tons. In

France the Navy first turned to steel and then worked toward larger sizes, although France lagged behind her rivals in that regard. The change to steel guns was made possible both by the production of higher quality steel and new slower burning cannon powder. At the same time the Royal Navy went to the breech-loader it adopted the all-steel gun, in which a steel jacket was shrunk over a steel tube and layers of steel hoops were then shrunk over this. The system of jackets and hoops over an inner steel tube was followed by one in which steel wire was spun on under tension varying with the distance from the bore. This helped eliminate 'barrel droop'. 'Wire guns' continued in British service until the 1930s.[48]

Bore lengths of the guns increased from 35 to 45 calibres and even to 40 to 45 calibres. This change increased difficulty of production, although longer and more reliable steel forgings were now possible. Following the demonstrated success of the new Krupp steel guns during the Franco-Prussian War the French ordered production of 20 experimental steel guns. Although these proved successful the French Navy continued to use iron guns from the Navy's Ruelle foundry, largely for reasons of economy. Pressure from French steel manufacturers, however, caused the minister of marine to decide in favour of steel guns. The first great French Navy steel gun was the 48-ton, 13.4-inch Model 1875. It was installed on all French ships designed for the 38-ton, 12.6-inch iron gun. The next step up for France came with 371-mm (14.6-inch) guns for the *Amiral Baudin* and *Formidable*.[49]

The larger guns of the period required mechanized ammunition hoists and complex breech-loading gear. Their metal carriages recoiled on inclined metal slides that pivoted under the gun port. The slides could be trained laterally by means of transverse truck wheels moving on 'racers', – iron paths set into the ship's deck.

Cannon powder

Prior to the mid-nineteenth century most cannon powder was in grains of 0.09 to 0.12 inch. In the United States, Lieutenant (later Brigadier General) Thomas J. Rodman of the Army Ordnance Corps began experiments to determine the best type of powder for the large guns he had designed. He learned that the larger the gun, the larger the powder grain had to be. This led to 'mammoth powder', pressed powder grains of between 0.6 and 0.9 of an inch in size. When ignited this tended to burn more slowly at first, building up to a higher pressure. This reduced the strain on both the gun and the shell. Britain followed this with 'cocoa powder', in which the charcoal was only partially charred, thus producing a brown rather than black colour for the cannon powder. It, too, burned more slowly.[50]

In the 1880s smokeless powder came into use. Guncotton (nitrocellulose) had first been produced in 1845. Made of the action of nitric acid on cotton, it had four times the explosive power of gunpowder and was virtually smokeless. It had two chief drawbacks: it burned too quickly, and thus was not an effective propellent; and it was unstable, and thus a threat to friend and foe alike.

Then Swedish chemist and inventor Alfred Nobel discovered that a combination of nitroglycerine and an absorbent inert substance such as *kieselguhr* produced a safer explosive that was easier to manipulate. In 1866 he patented this as dynamite. Nobel then combined nitroglycerine with guncotton, producing a jelly-like substance even more powerful than dynamite. In 1876 he patented this as blasting gelatin. It combined the explosive power of nitroglycerine with the comparative handling safety of dynamite. In the late 1880s Nobel produced ballistite, one of the earliest nitroglycerine smokeless powders. The British developed cordite, which was 58 per cent nitroglycerine, 37 per cent nitrocellulose, and 5 per cent vaseline. The latter enabled the cordite to be produced in semi-gelatinous cords or threads.

Cordite, which came into widespread use in the 1890s, removed one of the obstacles to accurate long-range gunfire at sea – the massive clouds of smoke that accompanied firing. This was particularly important to accurate fire by the new quick-firing guns against fast-moving torpedo boats. The new powders also had a considerable advantage in weight: a 12-inch gun required only 88.5 lbs of cordite to produce the same muzzle velocity as 295 lbs of prism brown powder.[51]

Projectiles

Projectiles were also improved. In Britain Captain William Palliser, who had already suggested the conversion of old iron smoothbore guns into rifles by inserting a liner, now came up with a stronger shell. He suggested casting iron shell not in a sand mould but in a chilled steel mould. This had the effect of cooling the iron much faster, producing a harder projectile. A trial in August 1864 was successful, and within a year Palliser was a major; ultimately he was Sir William Palliser. In 1867 Palliser shot was issued to the Navy; it continued in use until the early years of the twentieth century.[52]

Quick-firing guns

Of great importance to warships of the period was the development of small calibre, 4- to 6-inch, quick-firing guns. Smaller rapid-fire guns had been an integral part of ship armament for some time. All navies utilized machine guns; the Royal Navy had its 0.45 Gardner gun, fired by a hand crank, in both two- and five-barrelled models. It also utilized the 1-inch Nordenfelt, which had two to four barrels fixed horizontally. With a lever operated breech mechanism the four-barrelled model

could fire 216×7.25 oz solid steel shot a minute, 40 in aimed fire.[53]

The quick-firing guns operated on the principle of 'fixed ammunition': the cartridge cases utilized in small-arms that contained both propellent and round. Fixed ammunition had a number of advantages: ease and rapidity of loading, keeping the powder charge well protected, reducing erosion on the chamber of the gun, and sealing the breech. The quick-firers had sliding breech blocks and a recoil mechanism that returned the gun rapidly back into firing position with a minimum of jar. Beside their rapid fire, such guns required smaller crews, only three men each for the smaller calibres.

Developed to deal with the threat of torpedo boat attack and to riddle the unprotected portions of ships, the quick-firing gun resulted from an 1881 Admiralty advertisement for a gun to fire 12 aimed shots a minute. The 47 mm revolving Hotchkiss gun, which fired a 2.37-lb high-explosive shell out to 4,000 yards range, was adopted by several major navies. The 53 mm Hotchkiss fired a 3.5-lb shell out to 5,500 yards but failed to achieve the popularity of the smaller models.

In 1886, 57 mm (2.24-inch) 6-pounder single-barrel guns by Hotchkiss and Nordenfelt were introduced in Britain. Later the quick-firing gun was made larger to deal with armoured vessels. A 4.7-inch quick-firing gun was tested and proven successful on the cruiser *Piemonte*, built in Britain for Italy in 1887. By the end of the decade Hotchkiss had built a 33-pounder and had a design for a 55-pounder; Armstrong had 4.72-inch, 5.5-inch, and even 6-inch rapid-fire guns. The larger quick-firing guns soon became standard secondary armament on British battleships.[54]

Because of the short battle ranges that prevailed in pre-range-finder days, the quick-firing 6-inch gun could easily riddle the unarmoured sections of the old battleships. Henceforth to use wood as material for a ship's superstructure was to invite disaster, as the Chinese learned in their war with Japan in 1894.

Communications

Changes in communications had a great effect on naval warfare, both in the ability of battle fleets to respond rapidly to international events and in the control of individual vessels during a battle. The telegraph had proved its importance on land in the American Civil War and in the Austro-Italian-Prussian War of 1866. The trans-Atlantic cable of 1866 was soon followed by a network of underwater cables connecting the world's major ports. No longer did it take weeks or months for communications to reach distant stations; instructions could be almost instantaneously sent to the nearest cable station.

An even greater revolution came with the wireless or radio, invented by the Italian engineer Guglielmo Marconi around 1895. In 1899 the Royal Navy used radio between ships and shore during fleet manoeuvres. Despite its limited initial range, nearly every one of the world's navies adopted the radio for communication. In 1901 Marconi even managed to get a message across the Atlantic. For the first time in naval history, communications could be effected between vessels over the horizon from one another. The first use of the radio in war came during the 1904–05 Russo-Japanese conflict.

CHAPTER 7

MINES, TORPEDOES, TORPEDO BOATS AND SUBMARINES

The nineteenth century saw development of the mine and torpedo. Both of these new weapons came to have a profound impact on war at sea.

MINES

'Torpedo' was the early term for a mine; it comes from the electric ray fish that shocks its prey.[1] Such a device was not new in history. Modern underwater mine warfare may be said to have originated with Yale University student David Bushnell during the War of the American Revolution; Bushnell had a workshop near Saybrook, Connecticut. On 5 January 1778, he released floating mines of his own invention in the Delaware River with the hope that they would drift downstream and destroy ships of the British fleet at anchor. These 'contact' mines were kegs of powder triggered by a flintlock arrangement inside the keg. The hammer was released by the shock of the mine striking an object, which set off the mine.

The mines took more than a week to reach the British anchorage; by that time many of the British ships had moved. During the attempt some boys spotted one of the kegs in the river. In the effort to retrieve it, it blew up and killed them. Thus warned, the British then fired at anything floating in the water. The Patriot press derisively referred to this as the 'Battle of the Kegs'.[2]

Following the Revolutionary War investigation into the use of mines went forward in both Europe and in the United States. Beginning in 1801 during the Napoléonic Wars, American Robert Fulton tried to interest Napoléon Bonaparte in employing submarine-laid mines of his invention against the British. Fulton told him that the only sure means of defeating Britain was to interrupt all commerce on the Thames. He believed France should deploy torpedoes off the principal British ports. These would be of two kinds: those detonated by means of a timer set for as little as four minutes to a maximum of four hours; and spar torpedoes released by a submarine underneath British vessels to explode on contact. Fulton concluded, 'There is not a pilot in the navy who could avoid these unseen blows, which can then close the enemy's ports, and at very little expense.'[3]

Bonaparte rejected Fulton's ideas, and in April 1804 the undaunted American travelled to London in an effort to sell his scheme to the British. Prime Minister William Pitt agreed to meet with him and the British government ultimately extended a contract to Fulton to attack the French fleet with 'submarine bombs'. London was particularly concerned over the concentration of military assets across the Channel for an invasion of Britain, and this seemed one means of dealing with the threat.

During 2–3 October 1804, Fulton carried out an attempt against French ships at Boulogne, using mines set to explode on 10-minute fuzes. Deployed from cutters, the mines were secured together in pairs by means of a long line. Fulton hoped the line would catch on the cable of an enemy vessel and the current would then cause the two mines to drift along and rest against the ship's sides. Although many of the mines exploded, they went off without apparent effect. Fulton mounted another attack off Boulogne shortly after midnight on 1 October 1805. This second attack was also largely unsuccessful, although four French sailors were killed when one of the mines they were towing to the beach exploded.

On 15 October 1805, Fulton attempted to demonstrate his mines by blowing up the 200-ton captured Danish brig *Dorothea*. There were many doubters among Royal Navy officers, one of whom even offered to remain aboard the brig during the test. Fulton used two mines, again secured to one another and set to explode after 18 minutes. They were dropped from a cutter, and this time they were kept buoyant by cork-filled boxes. Their line was grappled to the brig's cable, and the mines duly exploded against her hull. The blast lifted the brig out of the water and broke her completely in two, the first time in history that such a large vessel had been destroyed by a mine.

The Admiralty was sufficiently impressed by this demonstration to advance Fulton

additional funding. But Pitt, broken by the Austro-Russian defeat in the December 1805 Battle of Austerlitz, died the next year and Fulton lost his chief patron. Admiral the Earl St Vincent dismissed him. St Vincent noted, 'Pitt was the greatest fool that ever existed, to encourage a mode of war which they who commanded the seas did not want, and which, if successful, would deprive them of it.'[4]

In 1807 Fulton returned to the United States and presented plans to the American government for a moored mine. The Navy provided funds, and during a test in July 1807 Fulton blew up a 200-ton brig in New York harbour. This required several attempts before it was successful, however, leading to a loss of faith in his plans. In 1810 Fulton carried out another experiment against a sloop, but this was unsuccessful because the defenders were permitted to deploy a net. While admitting failure, Fulton pointed out the immobility such defensive schemes would impose on an enemy. He also believed that moored mines could close American ports to an attacking force.[5]

During the War of 1812, in July 1813, Sailing Master Elijah Mix used Fulton's mines in six attempts to attack the HMS *Plantagenet* (74 guns), moored in Lynnhaven Roads near Norfolk. On the seventh attempt, the mines went off prematurely in the water. A similar attempt was made against the British on Long Island Sound. During the war Fulton himself made numerous proposals to the US government to plant moored sea mines in US harbours, and for a harpoon system with mines for offensive purposes.[6]

Because mines are principally defensive weapons, nations under attack made most use of them. During the Crimean War of 1854–56 the Russians used mines to try to prevent Allied access to their coastal forts.

Fulton's method of destroying a ship riding at anchor with two floating mines connected by a line.

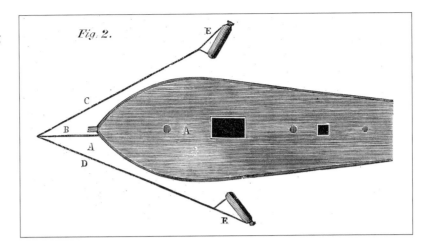

Fig. 2.

Fulton's destruction of the brig *Dorothea* by a mine of his invention, 15 October 1805.

PLATE 1.

In 1839 Tsar Nicholas I had appointed Prussian emigré Moritz-Hermann Jacobi as head of a scientific committee to conduct experiments in the development of a galvanic (electric) mine. As early as 1782 Tiberius Cavallo had demonstrated that gunpowder could be detonated by means of an electric current. Cavallo summed up his work in *Treatise on Magnetism in Theory and Practice* (1787). Building on the work of Cavallo, Americans Fulton and Samuel Colt, and the Russian Baron Pavel L'vovich Schilling von Cannstadt, Jacobi developed working mines by the time of the Crimean War. The Russians subsequently deployed these mines to help protect access to St Petersburg. Jacobi's mines were zinc canisters filled with gunpowder and set off by a detonator, a glass tube filled with acid, which when broken ignited the main charge of gunpowder. During the war the Russians used chemical, contact, and electrical command-detonated mines in both the Baltic and Black Seas. Crimean War mines were, however, too small to inflict much damage.[7]

The Confederacy made extensive use of mines during the American Civil War. The South employed land mines in the 1862 Peninsula Campaign. At the time such activity was considered quite controversial and outside the bounds of civilized warfare, but as the war increased in destructiveness, such prohibitions were ignored. During the war many Southern strategists saw sea mines as a means to reduce the Union naval advantage; influential Confederate Navy officer and scientist Matthew Fontaine Maury was an early proponent of mines and conducted experiments with them.

Civil War naval mines/torpedoes were of a variety of types. Either scratch-built or constructed from barrels as casings, they were essentially stationary weapons, a sort of buoy held in place at an appropriate distance from the surface by a cable anchored to the sea bottom by a weight. The Confederates positioned them in rivers or harbours to explode against the hulls of Union warships. There were two basic types of detonation: contact and electric. The first type were detonated when 'horns' surrounding the charge were broken; this set off a chemical reaction that ignited the charge. The second were fired by means of electrical connections from batteries on shore. The first type were more certain to explode but were unable to distinguish their victim and hence were also dangerous to friendly vessels. The second type could only be used close to shore.

More often than not such early mines failed to explode as a result of faulty detonating equipment or by becoming waterlogged, or they were swept away by the current. Even so they had a profound psychological effect on sailors aboard ship, producing 'torpedo fever' among Union crews.

One of the first uses of mines during the Civil War came during the February 1862 Union assault on Fort Henry on the Tennessee River. The wife of a Confederate officer inadvertently revealed their presence in a conversation with some Union scouts, and Union sailors swept for them. They discovered a number of mines several miles downriver from Fort Henry and used cutters to bring eight of them to the surface. Sheet-iron cylinders some 5.5-feet long and pointed at the ends, each containing about 75 lbs of gunpowder, the mines were fired by contact-type detonators. All of those recovered were waterlogged and harmless.

On 12 December 1862, the 512-ton Union ironclad *Cairo* succumbed to a mine while in the Yazoo River.[8] The first loss in an actual battle was the 2,100-ton *Tecumseh*, which went down on 5 August 1864, during the Battle of Mobile Bay. On 15 January

Depiction of the explosion of a Confederate electrically fired mine close to the USS *Commodore Barney* on the James River, 5 August 1863. Engraving from *The Soldier in Our Civil War*. (*Naval Historical Foundation, NH 51932*)

1865, despite precautionary sweeps by boats with drags, the 1,335-ton Union monitor *Patapsco* succumbed to a large mine or mines in the channel off Fort Sumter.[9]

Powder charges in Civil War mines ranged from approximately 50 lbs to large mines with up to a ton. One of the latter type, detonated electrically sank the 542-ton Union gunboat *Commodore Jones* in the James River on 6 May 1864. Her captain said the mine exploded directly under the converted ferryboat, 'absolutely blowing the ship to smithers'. The explosion claimed some 40 lives. A landing party captured two of the Confederate torpedomen and the galvanic batteries that had detonated the mine. One of the captives refused to divulge the location of other torpedoes until he was placed in the bow of the forward Union ship as a personal minesweeper.[10]

Mines were also used offensively as spar torpedoes at the end of a spar or pole. The Confederates built a number of craft designed to operate very low in the water and carry a spar torpedo in their bows to attack Union warships. On the night of 5 October 1863, one such craft, the *David*, damaged the Union ironclad *New Ironsides*.

The *Davids* were not submarines; they merely took in water as ballast to run awash on the surface.

The Union also employed spar torpedoes, and on 18 October 1864, Union *Steam Picket Boat No. 1* sank the Confederate ironclad ram *Albermarle*. This mine was affixed to the end of a 14-foot spar lowered by a windless. Once it was in position under the target's hull, a tug on a line released the mine, which floated up under the bottom of the ship. A second line activated the firing mechanism. Both sides during the war used similar spar torpedoes and equipped small boats as well as ironclad rams with them.

The largest ship sunk by a mine during the war was the 1,934-ton Union steam sloop *Housatonic*. On 17 February 1864, she sank off Charleston, the victim of a 130-lb spar torpedo on the partially submerged Confederate submarine *H.L. Hunley*, which sank shortly after her victim. Although only five Union sailors were lost, the *Housatonic* was the first ship sunk by a submarine in the history of warfare. In all, fifty ships were sunk or damaged by mines during the war. Four-fifths of these were Union vessels; only one Confederate ship, the *Albermarle*, was lost to a Union mine; most of the Confederate vessels lost were victims of their own mines.[11]

The Royal Navy in 1870 brought into service a towed mine known as the Harvey torpedo after its inventors, Captain John Harvey and Commander Frederick Harvey, both of the Royal Navy. They merely updated the Fulton concept. The advantage of the Harvey torpedo was that the control vessel could deliver it from a range of 150 yards. The Harvey torpedo made use of the principle that an object towed from the bows of a ship usually diverges from the vessel's course at a 45-degree angle. The towing vessel approached the target vessel at a maximum speed of 10 knots and then veered off to the side while the torpedo swung in a wider arc, struck the target ship, and exploded against it. Various chemical fuzes were used to ignite the 33 lbs of gunpowder in the torpedo explosive charge; later this was increased to 66 lbs of wet guncotton. Another version was fired by electricity. But there were many problems with the Harvey torpedo, including the low approach speed by its delivering vessel and difficulties with the torpedo parting its tow and exploding prematurely.[12]

All powers developed small, fast boats to deliver such devices. One Russian torpedo boat of 1878 was 75-feet long and 10 feet in beam. Powered by steam and capable of some 20 knots, it was also compartmentalized to lessen the chance of it sinking if damaged by enemy fire. It had three torpedo spars of hollow steel; at the tip of each was a mine encased in copper or steel loaded with between 40 and 50 lbs of dynamite. The spar was lowered underneath the target vessel and its mine exploded by means of electricity.[13]

Mines were used extensively during the 1904–05 Russo-Japanese War. The Russians employed them to defend the approaches to their Pacific ports and laid the first mines of the war; but the Japanese also had modern mines, laying them in groups and attempting to lure Russian ships over them. During the war the Russians lost one battleship, one cruiser, two destroyers, a torpedo boat, and a gunboat to mines. On 8 March 1904, the Russian battleship *Petropavlovsk* hit two mines and sank when she crossed over a Japanese minefield. She went down with Vice Admiral S. Ossipovitch Makarov and 635 officers and men. Because they were conducting offensive operations at sea the Japanese fared the worst, losing more ships to mines than to naval gunfire. In all, the Japanese lost two battleships, four cruisers, two destroyers, one torpedo boat, and a minelayer. The minelayer, the

Yenisei, sank when she blundered into her own minefield and was blown up.[14]

During this period electrically detonated mines became more common and new contact mines were also deployed. During the First World War both sides used mines extensively. The British developed the first magnetic influence mine, activated by the magnetic 'fingerprint' generated by steel ships during construction. But these mines were little used during the war.[15]

Mines played a key role in the war and may have altered the course of history. In early 1915 the Allies assembled a formidable task force to push through the Dardanelles and steam to Constantinople in order to force Turkey from the war and open up a southern supply route to Russia. On 18 March a small undetected Turkish minefield claimed several Allied battleships, and this caused Admiral John de Robeck to break off his effort to force the Dardanelles by naval power alone. Ultimately this decision had tragic consequences for Russia in the war.[16]

Both sides deployed mines extensively as offensive weapons. The Germans used both submarines and surface vessels to lay mines off British ports, but the Allies sowed great belts (barrages) of mines to inhibit German access to the North Sea. Mines claimed 30 per cent of all German submarine losses in the war.[17]

Sweeping techniques were developed to deal with the mines. In 1910 French admiral Ronarc'h invented a method that employed a single vessel, usually a converted trawler, to cut the main mooring wires by means of shears at suitable distances along the sweep. Mines floating to the surface were exploded by rifle or shell fire.[18]

MODERN TORPEDO

The success of stationary mines led to efforts to develop a propelled mine. The first modern automotive mine or torpedo

was developed by Captain Luppis of the Austro-Hungarian Navy in 1865 and perfected two years later by Scottish engineer Robert Whitehead, who managed an engine works in Fiume. The Luppis-Whitehead torpedo was a long cylinder, streamlined for movement through the water, with an 18-lb dynamite warhead and powered by an engine that ran on compressed air. The torpedo moved just below the surface at a speed of 6–8 knots and had an effective range of only several hundred yards. Its secret was a 'balance chamber' that enabled the torpedo to keep a constant depth beneath the surface.[19]

Whitehead travelled to Britain to demonstrate the new weapon. In September–October 1870 trials, the Admiralty was sufficiently impressed with some 1,000 test firings that it purchased rights to his invention for £15,000. In 1872 Whitehead opened a torpedo factory in England.[20] The British concentrated on a 16-inch, 1,000-yard-range version driven by contra-rotating screws at a speed of 7 knots, or 300 yards at 12 knots.[21]

Naval strategists believed that the torpedo was ideally suited for use by small, fast vessels, and all naval powers built large numbers of them. The British first used the new torpedo in combat in 1877 when the frigate *Shah* attacked the Peruvian monitor *Huascar*. The *Shah* launched its torpedo within 600 yards, but the *Huascar* easily changed direction and escaped.

Whitehead made other improvements in his torpedo, further streamlining it and fitting it with fins to stabilize its movement toward the target. He also increased the explosive charge three-fold by replacing gunpowder with guncotton. A three-cylinder, gas-powered Brotherhood engine improved torpedo speed to 18 knots, making it more difficult for a targeted vessel to escape.[22] The addition of a gyroscope, adapted for torpedo use by the Austrian Ludwig Obry, made the torpedo more accurate. Range also increased, so that by 1877 torpedoes could reach 800 yards.

Disappointment over torpedo performance in the Russo-Japanese War led to a new propellant to replace compressed air. In 1904-05 both the Whitehead factory at Fiume and the Armstrong Whitworth at Elswick in Britain came up with heaters to produce hot gas to drive the torpedoes. This had a dramatic effect on both speed and range. A typical 18-inch torpedo driven by compressed air could range out about 800 yards at a speed of 30 knots. The new hot gas torpedoes of the same size could travel over 2,000 yards at 34 knots, or 4,400 yards at 28 knots. By 1909 the British Mk VII '18-inch' (actually 17.7-inch) torpedo could range out to 3,500 yards at 45 knots, or 5,000 yards at 35 knots. Torpedoes also grew in size. The German 500-mm (19.7-inch) Type G of 1906 could reach 6,000 yards at 36 knots and its charge of 440 lbs was double that of an 18-inch weapon. The British Mk II 21-inch torpedo of 1910 could carry a 400-lb charge some 5,000 yards at 35 knots.[23]

The first successful torpedo attack occurred during the Russo-Turkish War of 1877–78. On 26 January 1878, off Batum on the Black Sea the Russian torpedo boat *Constantine* fired two torpedoes at a range of some 80 yards to sink a Turkish patrol boat.[24]

Torpedoes had a more spectacular result in 1884, during the Indo-China Black Flag/Tonkin Wars (1882–85), when France conducted naval operations against China. Paris ordered Admiral Amédée Anatole Courbet to threaten the Chinese naval base at Fuzhou (Foo Chow) on the Min River. Passage to the base was protected by two strongly fortified narrows and Courbet was unable to use his two armoured cruisers because of their draught. Courbet had five unarmoured cruisers, three gunboats, and two small torpedo craft at his disposal. In addition to shore batteries the Chinese had 11 ships (including two cruisers), junks and fireships, but their warships were sharply inferior to those of the French. On 23 August 1884, Courbet initiated battle by using motor boats Nos *45* and *46* to torpedo and sink the Chinese flagship and damage a second vessel; the flagship went down in about a minute. The engagement then became general and, within an hour, all Chinese ships were either sunk or on fire and drifting. Courbet put Chinese casualties at 2,000–3,000 men and his own at 10 dead and 48 wounded.[25]

TORPEDO BOATS

The torpedo meant that, for the first time in naval history, small vessels could threaten large ships. Successes with torpedoes led to the development of new vessels to deliver them. This was very much the age of the torpedo boat and there was even talk in the 1880s that the battleship was obsolete. Such vessels had to be fast and nimble, for they launched their weapons well within range of the opposing ship's guns.

Lightning

In 1874 the Royal Navy employed the torpedo on the *Vesuvius*, 244 tons and 90 × 22 feet, but capable of only 9.7 knots. The first purpose-built vessel to carry the torpedo was the *Lightning* of 1877. Displacing 27 tons, she was 84.5 × 11 feet. Powered by a 478-hp engine, she could make 19 knots and was fitted with a bow-launching tube for a single 14-inch torpedo. This meant that at launch the torpedo boat would be bow-on to her target and present the smallest silhouette to enemy fire. The *Lightning* served until 1910; impressed by her early performance, in 1878 the

Destruction of two Chinese cruisers by torpedo motor boats at Fuzhou (Foo Chow), 23 August 1884.
(*Musée de la Marine, PH 54139*)

Admiralty ordered 11 similar boats from the same builder, John I. Thornycroft, and eight others from seven different firms.[26]

The French were almost first with a torpedo boat. *Torpilleur No. 1* was actually ordered in 1875 but was not completed until 1878. Six additional torpedo boats followed, but the French were impressed with the British boats and ordered three, two from Thornycroft. By 1880 the French Navy had 30 torpedo boats built and another 30 under construction. Heavily influenced by the *Jeune École* that placed emphasis on smaller ships, France built the largest number of torpedo boats. By 1890 it had 220, Britain 186, Russia 152, Germany 143, and Italy 129. But torpedoes became standard armament on all classes of warships. All Royal Navy ships launched after 1872 carried them, and in 1876 the Royal Navy established the Torpedo School HMS *Vernon* at Portsmouth.[27]

The French *Jeune École* particularly embraced the torpedo, and ultimately France built more than 350 torpedo boats in only 25 years. Although all major naval powers built such vessels, they never reached their potential. An essentially offensive weapon was being carried by small coastal defensive craft. Early torpedo boats were sharply limited, and their failure as scouting vessels and poor performance during manoeuvres led to the construction of larger vessels of that type. Torpedo boats were made about 50 per cent longer, while at the same time preserving their slim, narrow lines. These lengthened craft were technically capable of ocean work, although their crews often did not think so. All navies built such vessels, which came to be

Hotspur, Royal Navy armoured ram, with deployed torpedo nets. (*Imperial War Museum, Q21360*)

regarded as a serious threat to blockading ships.

The initial French torpedo boats were 114.9 feet long and weighed 58 tons; but the failure of such boats led the Navy to decide not to build any of less than 80 tons, even for coastal defence. In 1889 France also decided to build larger boats of about 125 tons each to accompany a squadron at sea. All boats built after 1890 fell in those two categories. In 1892–93 the French successfully tried out *No. 147*, an 80-ton boat that made 24 knots. In 1893 the *Chevalier* achieved 27.5 knots, and two years later the 136-ton 144.4-foot *Forban* reached 31 knots, a world record.[28]

The threat posed by torpedo boats was partially countered by deploying torpedo nets and the development of quick-firing Nordenfelt and Gatling machine guns. At night they were used in conjunction with the newly developed searchlight. In a close action with other ships quick-firing guns might be used to fire at the gunports of an opposing vessel and to repel boarders.

Precursors of the torpedo boat destroyer

Finally a new type of warship appeared to defend against the torpedo boat; known first as the 'torpedo boat destroyer', later it was called simply a 'destroyer'. The precursor to this new class of ships may well have been the Royal Navy *Polyphemus* of 1881, although she was designed primarily for torpedo attacks. Known as a torpedo ram, she was 2,640 tons and 240 × 40 feet, and was capable of 18 knots. She carried a 2-pounder gun as well as 18 torpedoes for the five torpedo tubes in her largely submerged hull. She also had 3-inch armour.

In 1885 the Royal Navy purchased the *Swift* from a private builder. Although classed as a torpedo boat and equipped with three torpedo tubes, at 125 tons and 153 × 17.5 feet she was larger than existing torpedo boats. She also carried six quick-firing 3-pounder

guns to deal with them. In 1887 the *Rattlesnake* appeared. Classified as a torpedo gunboat, she was considerably larger than even the *Swift*. At 550 tons and 200 × 23 feet, she was armed with 1 × 4-inch and 3 × 12-pounder guns, in addition to four torpedo tubes. Seventeen of this class were built, but at 19 knots they were too slow to catch the torpedo boats.[29]

THE SUBMARINE

Although naval thinkers were slow to embrace the concept, the ideal would be to combine the new automotive torpedo with a submersible delivery system. The concept was not new. In the 1620s Charles von Drebbel, a Dutch physician living in London, built a combination wood and greased leather craft that could submerge and that was propelled by oars fitted in watertight sleeves.[30]

The first real submarine was invented by American David Bushnell during the War of the American Revolution. He had already developed an underwater mine; after the war began in 1775 Bushnell came up with the means to deliver it, building at Saybrook on the Connecticut River what he called a 'sub-marine'.

Because of its appearance, this 7.5 × 6 foot craft was known as the *Turtle*. Hand-powered by a crew of one, it was to fasten a mine containing 150 lbs of gunpowder to the hull of an enemy vessel. On 7 September 1776, an attack by the *Turtle* against Admiral Lord Richard Howe's flagship, the *Eagle*, at New York went awry. Several other attempts were made to sink British ships in the Hudson without success. The Turtle was later destroyed, probably to prevent her from falling into British hands.[31]

Nautilus

The next attempt to employ a submarine came in December 1797 during the Wars of the French Revolution and Napoléon, when

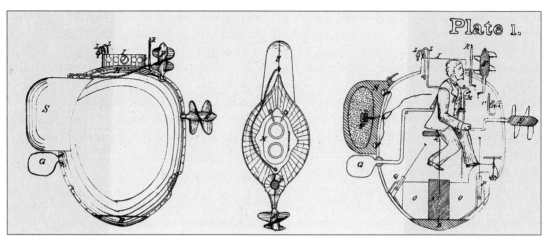

Turtle, David Bushnell's submarine, 1776. Drawing made by F.M. Barber in 1885 from description left by Bushnell. (*Naval Historical Foundation, NRL (O) 3294*)

Robert Fulton submitted plans to the French Directory for a 'plunging boat'. Fulton's motivation was in part monetary; he insisted on payment of 500,000 francs for the destruction of the first British ship and set payments thereafter. Fulton reasoned that the British would consider such a craft to be outside the accepted practices of war and would treat its crew as pirates if caught.

In November 1799 the French government changed again, and Napoléon Bonaparte came to power. When Fulton supporter P.A.L. Forfait became minister of marine, Fulton began constructing his submarine, which he called the *Nautilus*. Built by the Perrier workshop near the Seine, it was finally completed in June 1800. The *Nautilus* was a quantum advance over the *Turtle*, although the goal was the same: transporting a mine to be released against an enemy vessel. Some 21-feet long and cigar shaped, the *Nautilus* had a double hull of copper over an iron frame. Fitted with a sail, she had a collapsible mast. Fulton added a deck 20 × 6 feet to be used by the three-man crew when the submarine was on the surface. The *Nautilus* was powered by hand cranks that drove a propeller; she also had a system to control ballast.

Successfully tested on the surface and underwater on the River Seine at Paris on 13 June, with Forfait in attendance, the *Nautilus* remained submerged for some 45 minutes. Forfait was enthusiastic in his report to Bonaparte. Because the Seine was too shallow, in July Fulton had the submarine transported to Rouen and then to Le Havre, where that August he submerged to a depth of 15 feet and remained underwater for an hour. Fulton also successfully tested a contact mine against a barrel target.

Fulton was now ready to try the *Nautilus* against the Royal Navy. During 12–15 September the submarine was at sea. On two separate occasions Fulton tried to approach English brigs near the Marcou Islands, but each time they got underway before he could close the range. The *Nautilus* performed well during her sea cruise, although at one point rough water forced her to remain submerged for six hours, the crew receiving oxygen through a metal tube. Bad weather and approaching winter forced Fulton to end his tests and return to Paris. He communicated the test results to French mathematicians Gaspard

Monge and Pierre Simon de Laplace, who recommended Fulton to the First Consul. The three men then met with Bonaparte; both Monge and Laplace supported additional governemtn funding.

Fulton conducted further tests on the *Nautilus* at Brest in late July 1801, and at one point he took the submarine down to a depth of 25 feet. He also added a window topside at the bow. In addition to work on the submarine Fulton developed copper 'submarine bombs' containing 10 to 200 lbs of gunpowder each. Fulton spent much of the summer at Brest, cruising off the port and looking for English warships. Apparently warned, the British posted extra lookouts and used ships' boats to circle the warships as additional precautions.[32] Although Monge and Laplace wanted him to bring the submarine to Paris for a demonstration before Bonaparte, Fulton stunned them by writing on 20 September 20 that the *Nautilus* no longer existed:

When I finished my experiments, She leaked very much and being but an imperfect engine, I did not think her further useful. – hence I took Her to pieces. Sold Her Iron work lead and cylinders and was necessitated to break the greater part of her movements in taking them to pieces. So that nothing now remains which can give an Idea of her combination . . .[33]

At least in part because Fulton's submarine no longer existed Bonaparte removed his support. Fulton then went to Britain to sell his services there, but his work for the British government was in mines rather than submarines.[34]

Other submarines followed. During the War of 1812 a submarine built by a resident of Norwich, Connecticut, was taken to New London, where it made several attempts to

attach a mine to the hull of the 74-gun HMS *Ramillies*.[35] In 1850 during fighting between the German states and Denmark, Bavarian artilleryman and inventor Wilhelm Bauer came up with a 26.5-foot long submarine, *Le Plongeur Marin*. Powered by an internal handwheel that turned a screw propeller, the submarine submerged by letting water into a double bottom; to rise, the water was expelled by means of a pump. Weights moved forward and aft were used to adjust trim. Bauer and his crew nearly died in February 1851 when the weights shifted and the submarine temporarily stuck in the mud of Kiel Harbour in 50 feet of water. Bauer courageously let in additional water until the pressure built up and blew the hatches, expelling the crew to the surface like corks from a champagne bottle.

In 1856 Bauer constructed a much larger, 56-foot submarine in Russia. The *Diable-Marin* was powered by a treadmill and was capable of transporting a 500-lb mine. We know little else about Bauer's invention, but during coronation ceremonies for Tsar Alexander II (1855–81) Bauer transported underwater a small orchestra that played the Russian national anthem. The reaction of the musicians to the experience is unknown.[36]

The side in war without a major surface fleet is invariably the one most interested in new technology to offset the advantage held by their opponent. It was no surprise, therefore, that during the American Civil War the Confederacy developed primitive submarines.

As early as March 1862 Robert R. Barrow, James R. McClintock, and Baxter Watson applied for a letter of marque for a submarine craft named the *Pioneer*. Only about 20 feet long and intended for a crew of two, she was propelled by means of a crank shaft turned by her crew. The *Pioneer* was sunk to avoid capture when Union

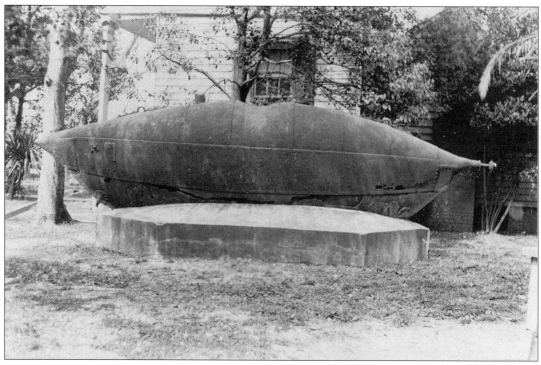

Pioneer, Confederate Navy submarine. The propeller vanes are broken off and the hatch or conning tower is missing. (*Louisiana State Museum, New Orleans. Naval Historical Foundation, NH 42854*)

forces took New Orleans. Horace L. Hunley, one of the sureties on the *Pioneer*, McClintock and Watson went to Mobile, Alabama, to continue experiments. In mid-February 1863 they tested another submarine along the same lines as the first, this one designed for five men and to deliver a spar torpedo. She went down in rough water off Fort Morgan but no lives were lost.

Undaunted, Hunley and his friends built a third submarine. In early August 1863, with Charleston under heavy Union attack, Confederate General P.G.T. Beauregard requested that she be sent there, large rewards having been offered for the destruction of Union ships. On 15 August the submarine arrived at Charleston on two covered railroad flat cars.

The *H.L. Hunley* was built from an iron steam boiler with tapered bow and stern sections added. Some 40 feet in length, 3.5 feet in breadth at her widest point, and 4 feet in depth, she resembled a long thin cigar. She was designed for a crew of nine: one man to steer and eight positioned along the length of the centre section to power the submarine. This was done by hand turning a crankshaft that moved the propeller, pushing the craft forward at about 4 knots. The *H.L. Hunley* was to run awash until close to her target, when she would submerge with the aid of rudders. The submarine was difficult to control, and the men needed fresh air, a supply of which was available only when she was awash.

On 29 August, after several practice dives in Charleston Harbor, the submarine sank at the dock. Her commander, Lieutenant John J. Payne, had ordered her to get underway when he was climbing into the forward hatchway. Apparently he became fouled in a hawser and then got his foot on the lever that controlled the fins. She moved from the dock and dived; as her hatches were open, she rapidly filled with water. Five men drowned, but three others, including Payne, escaped. The *H.L. Hunley* was raised and refitted. Another crew volunteered, this time with Hunley in charge; but on 15 October the submarine sank again in Charleston Harbour. Again she was apparently a victim of human error; Hunley had evidently left the valve to the front ballast tank open. This time Hunley and seven others perished. The submarine was again recovered, and a third crew, commanded by Infantry Lieutenant G.F. Dixon, volunteered.

The *H.L. Hunley*'s destructive force came from a spar torpedo, possibly designed by General Beauregard. Mounted to the bow, the spar held the torpedo, which terminated in a barbed lance-head. When the submarine drove toward its victim the spar's barb lodged in the timbers below the waterline. The submarine then backed off, exploding the torpedo by means of a long lanyard.

On the night of 17 February, 1864, the *H.L. Hunley* at last set out and approached the 1,934-ton screw sloop *Housatonic*. The sloop was prepared; Captain Charles Pickering had six lookouts posted, steam in the engine room was up, and crewmen were ready to slip the ship's cable at a moment's notice. At about 9:00 p.m., lookouts on the *Housatonic* spotted the *H.L. Hunley*'s two hatches above water, along with her slight wake, but this was only about 75–100 yards from the ship and too late for anything save smallarms fire to be directed against her. About three minutes after the submarine was detected, and as the sloop was getting underway, the *H.L. Hunley*'s 130-lb spar

H.L. Hunley. Confederate Navy submarine. Painting by Conrad Wise Chapman in Museum of the Confederacy. (*Naval Historical Foundation, NH 63086*)

torpedo exploded. Only five Union sailors were lost; most simply climbed into the rigging to await rescue. The unstable *H.L. Hunley* survived long enough to signal by lantern that she was returning to land, but, probably damaged in the blast, sank shortly thereafter with all hands.[37]

The Union also experimented with submarines. Among these was a one-man submarine designed by Major Edward B. Hunt of the Army Corps of Engineers. While testing his 'submarine battery' at the Brooklyn Navy Yard, he died on 2 October 1863 of carbon dioxide poisoning.[38]

Plongeur

The *H.L. Hunley* was an important step forward, but it was still a primitive craft with a highly inefficient means of propulsion. The French made the next major improvements. It was probably inevitable that France would seek some means of offsetting the advantage of its principal rival, Britain, in surface ships. In 1863 Captain Siméon Bourgeois and engineer Charles Marie Brun designed an advanced submarine, the *Plongeur*. Laid down at Rochefort in 1860 and launched in 1862, she was 139.8 feet long, 19.7 feet wide, and 9.8 feet high. She displaced 153 tons and her propeller was driven by compressed air. She was armed with a mine at the end of a 14.8 foot spar. The *Plongeur* was the largest submarine built to that time, and her slender yet solidly riveted hull was divided by watertight bulkheads. The *Plongeur* had the novel feature of a lifeboat bolted to her deck. Accessible from within the submarine by an airlock, it could be released to rise to the surface. The French Navy conducted numerous trials, both in the River Charente and at sea; but the *Plongeur*'s range was limited and she could make only 4 knots. There was also the obvious problem of tell-tale bubbles at the surface left by the compressed air.[39]

Unfortunately, the *Plongeur* lived up to her name too successfully. The problem was in maintaining stability underwater. This was supposed to be achieved by means of a hydrostatic piston and two horizontal rudders at the stern. But corrections in ballast caused her to dive rapidly to the bottom or to pop up to the surface.[40]

Other submarines

In 1875 English clergyman George William Garrett developed a submarine, one of the first to be powered by steam. By driving with a full head of steam and then extinguishing the furnaces, his *Resurgam* ('I shall rise again') could move a considerable distance. In 1889 Garrett launched a larger, 30-ton submarine, the *Resurgam II*. But these submarines were designed primarily for underwater exploration. Swedish cannon founder Thorsten Nordenfelt worked with Garrett to produce a twin-screw, steam-propelled, 64-foot-long, 60-ton submarine. Launched in 1885, the *Nordenfelt No. 1* was later sold to Greece. It could dive safely to 50 feet and was operated by a three-man crew. Nordenfelt later built and sold other submarines of this design to Turkey, Russia, and Germany, but they proved difficult to control underwater. The *Nordenfelt No. 1* is important chiefly because she was the first submarine to carry an automotive torpedo, the Whitehead. She was also armed with a Nordenfelt machine gun on her deck, probably the only reliable thing on the submarine.[41]

In 1877 Polish-born Stefan Drzewiecki constructed a small submarine. Less than 10 feet long, it was propelled by means of pedals by its single occupant. Two years later, Drzewiecki built a 19.67-foot version at St Petersburg that had a crew of five. It had the first periscope, which could be worked while the submarine was submerged. Although it had a limited range of vision, the periscope did allow a submarine to manoeuvre while underwater. The periscope, the only part of the submarine above water, was difficult to spot from an opposing ship.

Air was brought into the submarine by means of a pump connected to a tube extending above the surface of the water. Hand pumps were used to empty ballast tanks. The diving angle was adjusted by moving weights along overhead beams. Tests with this submarine proved so successful that the Russian Navy ordered 50 of them. Drzewiecki also experimented with oil engines and electric motors. His *No. 3 Submarine* of 1884 was driven by an electric motor and had a primitive periscope.[42]

In 1886 two Englishmen, Andrew Campbell and James Ash, designed a submarine. Built by the English firm of Wolseley and Lyon, and powered by two 50-hp electric batteries operating on a 100-cell storage battery, the *Nautilus* had a speed of 6–8 knots and a cruising range of 80 miles. Its limitation was its short range before recharging. Other nations became involved. Spanish Navy lieutenant Isaac Peral built a submarine to run on batteries.[43]

Gymnote

The *Jeune École* saw the submarine as a useful tool against enemy commerce as well as a defensive weapon. Admiral Hyacinthe-Laurent Théophile Aube wrote in 1879 that the days of the big armoured ship were over, and that a new navy was needed to wage war against commerce. French journalist Gabriel Charmes, who supported Aube in print, said that battleships would be replaced by many tiny craft, *la poussière navale*, mere specks of dust. Submarines delivering torpedoes seemed ideally suited to this type of war.

Admiral Aube was largely responsible for founding the French submarine service. In 1886, as French minister of marine, he revived experiments with submarines by supporting the work of engineer and designer Gustave Zédé. Dupuy de Lôme had already come up with a design, but he died in 1885 before it could be realized. Zédé took over for his friend and made some modifications to de Lôme's design. The result was an electrically-driven submarine, the *Gymnote*, 59.1 feet long, 5.9 feet in diameter, and displacing only 31 tons. Her steel hull was pointed at each end. She was powered by a 55-hp electric motor that allowed a 7-knot speed when surfaced and 5 knots when submerged. The *Gymnote*'s maximum range was 65 nautical miles on the surface and 45 submerged. Internal ballast tanks and hydroplanes facilitated submerging and surfacing; she also mounted a periscope. The *Gymnote* made her first test run on 4 September 1888.[44]

In 1893 the French Navy launched the *Zédé* at Toulon. Named for the now-deceased designer of the *Gymnote*, she too was electrically powered. Built with a bronze pressure hull, she was 159 feet long and displaced 366 tons. She had one torpedo tube with space inside the submarine to carry two additional Whitehead torpedoes. Unfortunately, the *Zédé* proved difficult to control. While she was still undergoing trials, in July 1899 the French launched another submarine, the *Morse*. She was 118 feet long and displaced 146 tons. Although showing great promise, she was soon overshadowed by another French submarine.

Narval

In 1898, following a competition announced by the minister of the navy, France laid down the *Narval* at Cherbourg. Launched in October 1899 she joined the fleet in 1900. One of the first practical submarine designs, she displaced 200 tons submerged but only

Narval, French Navy submarine. (*Naval Historical Foundation, NH 55767*)

120 tons on the surface. The *Narval* was 111.5 feet × 12.3 feet and had a double hull, the first heavier to withstand pressure underwater; the second, lighter hull provided buoyancy and improved surface seaworthiness. The space between the two was used for water ballast for diving purposes. This arrangement also equalized pressure on the thinner hull. The *Narval's* other novel feature was that she was powered by two motors on the same shaft: a steam motor for surface cruising also turned an electric motor acting as a dynamo that in turn charged storage batteries; the electric motor powered underwater operation. The *Narval* was armed with 4 × 17.7-inch torpedoes. It took about 15 minutes to shut down her steam motor.

Although France continued to build submarines it persisted in steam propulsion, and by 1912 the Royal Navy had overtaken the French in both quality and quantity of construction. France concentrated on coast defence types rather than oceangoing boats able to operate in all kinds of conditions.[45]

Holland

The first really practical submarine was invented by an Irish immigrant to the United States. John P. Holland had arrived in America in 1873 with a hatred of the English, and he hoped that his submarine would end Britain's dominance at sea and perhaps its hold on Ireland as well. Holland planned to use water ballast to submerge his vessel and horizontal rudders to make it dive. Navy Department officials were unimpressed, and so Holland went to the Fenian Brotherhood, which was dedicated to independence for Ireland. In 1876 Holland demonstrated a 30-inch model of his submarine to Fenian supporters at Coney Island, New York. They were sufficiently impressed to advance money for the project.

The *Holland I* was lozenge shaped, and 24.5 feet long and 12.5 feet in breadth, with

Holland, first US Navy submarine (SS-1), preparing for launching at Elizabeth, New Jersey, 1898. (*Naval Historical Foundation, NH 53458*)

a square turret top. She sank when launched, unoccupied, on 22 May 1878. Easily recovered by means of lines left on her, a week later she went out with Holland as the crew, compressed into a space 3 feet 8 inches long and little more than 2 feet high with his head sticking out into the sealed conning tower. The *Holland* proved successful.

Holland then constructed the *Holland II,* also funded by the Fenians. Weighing 19 tons, she was powered by a 15-hp combustion engine. Utilizing horizontal rudders while underway, she actually 'dived' beneath the surface, unlike her predecessor, which simply sank in place. The *Holland II* was equipped with a pneumatic cannon to fire a torpedo.[46]

Twice Holland entered and won US submarine design competitions. But Holland thought the Navy's specifications were unrealistic, and his steam-powered *Plunger,* built to Navy orders in 1897, was unsuccessful. Holland then decided to build a submarine to his own specifications.

During 1896–97 Holland built his sixth submarine, at Elizabeth, New Jersey. The *Holland VI,* which made her first surface run in February 1898, is usually known simply as the *Holland*. Forerunner of all modern submarines, she had an internal combustion 45-hp gasoline engine for running on the surface with hatches open and an electric motor for submerged cruising. While it was running, the gasoline engine powered a generator that recharged the batteries. The *Holland* was the first submarine to be equipped with this system, which became common on submarines for the next half century. With a length of 53 feet 10 inches and breadth of 10 feet 3 inches, the *Holland* displaced only 63.3 tons on the surface and 74 tons submerged. She had a single 18-inch torpedo tube and could carry two reload torpedoes. She was also equipped with an 8-inch pneumatic 'dynamite' gun mounted forward. The *Holland* could travel at 8 knots on the surface and 5–6 knots submerged. She carried a crew of five.

Her stability while submerged and her greater range put the *Holland* in a class by herself. The US Navy recognized the success of the design and, in April 1900, purchased the *Holland*, formally commissioning her that October. Later she was assigned hull number SS-1 as the US Navy's first submarine. In September 1900, during North Atlantic Squadron war games off Newport, Rhode Island, the *Holland* carried out mock torpedo attacks against the battleship *Kearsarge*, during which the *Kearsarge* was ruled to have been 'sunk'. A month earlier, Washington had signed a contract with the Holland Torpedo Boat Company for six additional boats. The first was launched in July 1901. Given names, they were known as the 'Adder' class.[47]

At the same time Holland was at work on his submarine, Simon Lake, his principal competitor, experimented with submarines off New York. Lake's *Argonaut First* of 1897 displaced 59 tons submerged, was 36 × 9 feet and built of 3/8-inch steel plate. A 30-hp gasoline engine drove its single propeller. The *Argonaut* had a double hull. The light outer hull was flooded on diving. Four levelling valves kept the boat on a substantially level keel when submerged. She also had intake and exhaust pipes for air while the submarine was submerged, a forerunner of the German snorkel of the Second World War. Remodelled and enlarged in 1899, her final length in 1900 was 66 feet. She had a five-man crew.

Lake then built a powerful, torpedo-armed submarine, the *Protector*, launched at Bridgeport, Connecticut, on 1 November 1902. Content with its arrangement with Holland, the US Navy was slow to act, and, before she could be accepted, Lake had sold the *Protector* to Russia. It was not until 1911 that Lake began to influence US submarine design.[48]

Lake's *Protector* submarine, sold to Russia. (*Anne S.K. Brown Military Collection, Brown University Library*)

The Diesel engine

A major problem in submarine development was solved by Rudolph Diesel's new engine. Early gasoline combustion engines emitted dangerous fumes, which never could be completely vented. With these fumes there was always the danger of an explosion. Diesel's new engine, which appeared in the 1890s, burned a fuel far less volatile than gasoline. Diesel engines also had the advantages of being cheaper to run and more efficient in fuel consumption, particularly important when space was at an absolute premium. The world's first diesel-powered submarine was the French *Aigrette* of 1904. The *A-13* was the first British submarine with a diesel engine; it was working by 1905; the United States adopted the diesel for its submarines in 1911. The *U-19*, launched in 1912, was the first German diesel-powered submarine.[49]

Originally the submarine was conceived to be most useful for picket/observation duty to provide information on enemy movements. Even when fitted with a small deck gun, the submarine on the surface was no match for anything other than an unarmed merchant ship.

The new automotive torpedo was, however, well suited to submarine use. By the First World War torpedoes powered by electric motors with stubby vanes to control their running depths could travel 7–8,000 yards at up to 36 knots and deliver a 500-lb charge of TNT. These could be loaded from inside the submarine and launched when the submarine was totally submerged.

Fitted with a periscope, powered by a diesel-electric power plant, and armed with torpedoes and 4- to 5-inch deck guns, the submarine was a weapon that could challenge the largest surface ship. The submarine's only real limitation was the length of time it could remain submerged operating on its electric engine. The maximum was only about 48 hours. Running on the surface, the submarine was vulnerable to attack.[50]

Ironically in view of what happened during 1914–18, it was the smaller naval powers that most pushed submarine development. Even those recognizing the submarine's potential as an offensive weapon against enemy warships failed to think in terms of it as a commerce destroyer. Nonetheless, one of the agenda items at the 1899 Hague Conference on arms limitation was a proposal to outlaw submarines. It was defeated.[51]

Germany entered the First World War with few submarines because Minister of Marine Admiral Alfred von Tirpitz was busy building a balanced surface fleet, centred on dreadnoughts, in order to contest Britain for world naval mastery. He saw submarines not as a means of reducing Britain's advantage in surface ships or as commerce destroyers, but primarily as defensive weapons. Germany did not order its first submarine, the *Unterseeboot 1* (*U-1*), built by Krupp, until 1906.

Tirpitz rejected a June 1914 recommendation that Germany build 222 submarines for a projected blockade of the British Isles. During the First World War, however, Germany built 332 additional submarines, almost three times the number built by Britain, the second leading submarine builder, with 128. German submarines had the best diesel engines in the world and also the best periscopes.[52]

Britain was also slow to embrace the submarine. Admiral Sir A.K. Wilson described the new weapon as 'underhand, unfair, and damned un-English'; Lord Charles Beresford dismissed it as a useless weapon, 'always in a fog'.[53] But with the French and Germans building them, the British had to enter the race. Perhaps surprisingly, given his advocacy of the dreadnought and battle-cruiser, First Sea Lord John 'Jackie' Fisher (1904–10, 1914–15) supported submarine development. The easiest way was to secure the rights to build Hollands. In December 1900 London made arrangements with the Holland Torpedo Boat Company to build five of its boats, referred to as Type Number VII, in Britain.

Soon the British had developed their own submarines. The thirteen 190-ton 'A'-class boats, launched from 1902, were more powerful than any of the Hollands. By 1904 the Royal Navy had reluctantly accepted submarines as part of its naval armament; that year it began the 'B' class, building eleven of these 287-ton boats. 'B'-class submarines continued in service into the First World War, and one of these, *B-11*, penetrated the Dardanelles to sink the

Turkish battleship *Messudieh* in December 1914.

Beginning in 1906, thirty-eight 238-ton 'C'-class submarines were launched. Two years later the British laid down the 'D' class, the first of which were completed in 1910-11. These eight boats weighed 490 tons each and were diesel powered. By 1914 the British had their 'E' class, 700-ton submarines with 4 × 18-inch torpedo tubes, capable of 16 knots on the surface and 10 knots submerged. With a range of 1,500 miles, they were the first oceangoing submarines. On the eve of the war First Lord of the Admiralty Winston Churchill was planning even more submarines and was negotiating with the Bethlehem Steel Company about building twelve larger submarines in the United States. France also

E-55, Royal Navy submarine. (*Imperial War Museum, SP2490*)

kept in the race, with twenty 70-ton 'Naïde'-class in 1904 and eighteen 398-ton 'Pluviôse'-class submarines, beginning in 1907. Curiously, neither Japan nor Russia had submarines in their navies by the time of the Russo-Japanese War.[54]

By 1914 submarine design had reached a plateau and, in fact, changed little in the course of the First World War. Naval leaders were slow to realize the submarine's offensive potential, simply because the last sinking of a ship by a submarine had occurred 50 years earlier, and no surface ship had yet to be sunk by a submarine-launched automotive torpedo. A Greek submarine, the *Delfin*, hit a Turkish cruiser with a torpedo during the First Balkan War (1912–13), but it was a dud. The admirals persisted in thinking of the submarine primarily for observation duties and mine laying. Submarines came into their own during the First World War, but their potential as offensive weapons had long been apparent.[55]

On the eve of the First World War Britain had the most submarines, 73. France had 55; the United States 38; Russia 24; and Italy 24. Germany, the great practitioner of submarine warfare during the war, had only 35 boats in 1914. Nonetheless, qualitatively, the Germans probably had the best submarines when the war came. The newest German submarines had superior range and they were more modern than those of Britain or France.[56]

The submarine phase of the First World War did not begin well for Germany. On 9 August in the North Sea the British cruiser *Birmingham* rammed and sank the *U-15*, which was on the surface for engine repair. On 5 September, however, *U-21* sank the British destroyer *Pathfinder* off the Firth of Forth, the first warship sunk by a submarine in the war. She went down with 259 men. A far more graphic illustration of the submarine's potential, however, came on 22 September when *U-9* sank an entire squadron of three old British cruisers, the *Aboukir*, *Cressy*, and *Hogue*, off the Dutch coast. The *Aboukir* was the first to be torpedoed. The captains of her two sister ships, believing she had been the victim of a mine, stopped their ships dead in the water to take aboard survivors, making them easy prey. While the loss of 1,459 seamen (837 others were rescued) and three cruisers hardly upset the naval balance, it did signal a new age in naval warfare.[57]

CHAPTER 8

THE PRE-*DREADNOUGHT* ERA, 1890–1906

The 1890s saw the dramatic rise of two new major naval powers: Germany and the United States. In part this was the result of popular sentiment in those two states created by propagandists.

Alfred Thayer Mahan (1840–1914)

The most enthusiastic and influential proponent of the big-gun battleship was American naval historian and strategic thinker Alfred Thayer Mahan. In 1884 the US Navy established the Naval War College to provide postgraduate education for naval officers. Commander Mahan joined its faculty to lecture on naval history and tactics. In 1886 he became its president, in which post he served until 1889 and again during 1892–93. Mahan was the son of Dennis Hart Mahan, a professor at the US Military Academy at West Point who had initiated the study of military theory in the United States. Alfred Mahan had graduated from the Naval Academy at Annapolis in 1859 and served in the Navy during the Civil War. In 1883 he published *The Gulf and Inland Waters* about US Navy operations during the war.

Mahan was a prolific author, but by far his most important book was the compilation of his lectures, *The Influence of Sea Power upon History, 1660–1783* (1890). This important book is at once a history of the rise of Britain as the pre-eminent naval power, a philosophical treatise on naval warfare, and a propaganda document justifying a big navy.

The fact that Mahan's illustrations were drawn chiefly from English naval history won him immediate acclaim in that country, and the governments of Germany and Japan disseminated his work. In the United States, where the book had less influence, expansionists nonetheless seized on it as justification for American imperialism.

Mahan asserted that the United States needed bases in the Caribbean to protect an isthmian canal and in the Pacific. He pleaded for his country to build a navy to compete for world trade. Sea power, according to Mahan, included not only naval strength afloat but commerce, industry, shipping, colonies, and foreign markets. He also argued that there was no instance of a great commercial power retaining its position of leadership for long without a large navy.

Mahan criticized the traditional *guerre de course* approach of American naval policy. This could not win control of the seas which, he argued, must be the object of all naval strategy. Mahan believed in the necessity of a seagoing fleet, an overbearing force that could beat down an enemy's battle line. The strength of this should be in battleships rather than cruisers or destroyers. Mahan believed in concentrating naval resources with the goal of destroying an enemy fleet.

Mahan overlooked new technology such as the torpedo and the submarine as well as speed in battleships; but despite this he was the most influential apostle of the new navalism. Mahan also raised the respectability of naval history and later served as president of the American Historical Association.

THE NAVAL RACE BETWEEN BRITAIN AND GERMANY

Mahan's writings had their most profound influence in Germany, which in the span of a generation became the world's second naval power. Even before 1888 when he became kaiser, Wilhelm II had been deeply interested in naval affairs. Afterward he became increasingly convinced of the need for a larger and more powerful German Navy. Such a fleet would support his new foreign policy of world involvement or *Weltpolitik* and provide expression to the greatness of the new Germany. It would also provide protection for Germany's growing commercial and colonial interests, and in war it would prevent Germany from being cut off from indispensable food supplies and raw materials. A powerful navy would also help Germany secure commercial and colonial advantage; it might, in fact, compel even Great Britain to make colonial concessions rather than 'risk' a naval struggle.

When the aggressive, impetuous Wilhelm became kaiser most Germans believed that because Germany was already supporting the world's largest standing army it could not hope to rank as a first-class naval power. Despite Wilhelm's desire for a more

powerful fleet, in 1895 Germany's navy stood fifth in the world, although by that time it was second in the world in foreign trade.[1]

By the mid-1890s the kaiser was joined in his demand for a large navy by many others: certain commercial interests and professors, the German Colonial League, and the Pan-German League. All wanted more warships in order that Germany could pursue a forceful policy in Europe and abroad. Also of great influence was the translation into German in 1897 of Mahan's book; the Navy Office distributed 8,000 copies of it, placing one in each warship.[2]

Alfred von Tirpitz (1849–1930)

In 1896 Wilhelm took advantage of rising sentiment for a navy to appoint as his minister of marine Alfred von Tirpitz. Certainly one of the most capable naval administrators and propagandists in modern history, Tirpitz built the German Navy almost from scratch and lived to see it destroyed. The strong-willed Tirpitz had been commander of the German Far East Squadron. He disagreed with Wilhelm's emphasis on more cruisers and destroyers and insisted it be shifted to capital ships.

Tirpitz immediately launched a great propaganda effort for a large navy. In March 1897 the Reichstag had rejected the naval building programme of his predecessor, Friedrich Hollmann, but by the early months of 1898, thanks largely to Tirpitz's enthusiastic lobbying efforts both inside and outside the Reichstag, there was a great change in public opinion, particularly in the Reichstag.

The construction bill that Tirpitz took to the Reichstag was passed overwhelmingly in April 1898. Tirpitz's bill called for the construction by 1 April 1904, of 19 battleships, 8 armoured cruisers, 12 large cruisers, and 30 light cruisers. What is more, the bill specified that the heavy ships were to be replaced automatically every 25 years, and the light cruisers every 15 years. It was to include the existing 12 battleships, 10 large and 23 light cruisers. The bill thus meant new construction of only 7 battleships, 10 large and 25 light cruisers.[3]

Tirpitz maintained that this force would be adequate in a war with France or Russia or even both these powers. Such a force would enable Germany to prevent a blockade of its coasts and keep lanes of commerce and supply open. Although this German fleet could not challenge Britain on the seas, Tirpitz argued that it would lead the British to take a more conciliatory attitude toward Germany. Bismarck had warned that the building of a German Navy would drive Britain into the arms of France, and this is precisely what happened. British volumes dealing with the origins of the First World War start with 1898. The German Foreign Office and the kaiser believed – wrongly – in the permanence of the Franco-British and Anglo-Russian rivalries.

Although Tirpitz had announced, probably for British consumption, that this projected fleet would fill Germany's requirements, already by the summer of 1899 he concluded that a new programme was necessary. Tirpitz wanted to take advantage of sentiment aroused by the Boer War, when a British warship seized a German merchant ship. In December 1899 Chancellor Chlodwig von Hohenlohe-Schillingsfürst announced in the Reichstag that Germany had to have a navy so powerful that even the strongest naval power would not dare to attack it without grave risk.

The government also had the support of the newly organized Navy League (founded 1898). Heavily financed by the great German steel interests, within a year it had a membership of more than 100,000 people and by 1914 more than a million. It also had its own newspaper, *Die Flotte* ('The Navy' or 'The Fleet'), which soon had a circulation of 750,000, and an active group of lecturers.[4]

The second navy bill, approved by the Reichstag in June 1900, called for doubling the fleet, to 38 battleships, 20 armoured cruisers, and 38 light cruisers. All were to be completed in 20 years and, in contrast to the first bill, there was no cost limit for construction. Tirpitz did not see even this as the end. He had already spoken to the kaiser of the need for 45 battleships.[5] What the two wanted was a fleet large enough to meet the British Home Fleet, at that time 32 battleships. They evidently believed that Germany would then appear as an attractive possible ally of Britain, or failing this, of France or Russia.

The ensuing naval building contest between Germany and Britain was arguably the most discussed arms race in modern history. In 1906 Germany passed a new navy law providing for construction of six dreadnoughts. Although less heavily gunned they were much tougher than their British counterparts. Tirpitz ordered that the Kiel Canal be widened to allow the new and bigger ships to pass swiftly between the Baltic and North Sea. He increased the number of shipyards and gun factories and laid down more and better battle-cruisers. In Britain, First Sea Lord Admiral Fisher introduced the 13.5-inch gun while Tirpitz raised the German heavy gun calibre from 11 to 12 inches. Tirpitz, although a late convert, also ordered long-range submarines and as early as 1912 was writing to the kaiser urging him to promote naval airship construction.

Britain's two-power naval standard

By 1889 the British government had adopted a policy of maintaining a two-power naval standard, that is a navy as powerful as the next two naval powers combined. Germany's intention to construct a powerful fleet greatly disturbed the British. As Germany progressed with its naval building programme it seemed to the British as designed largely to satisfy the ego of the kaiser, who indeed got great satisfaction from possessing and reviewing his fleet.

Other considerations entered into the German naval construction programme. Tirpitz saw the navy as the key to Germany's future. In his initial Reichstag speech on behalf of the first Navy Law he had stated that the navy had become an 'absolute necessity', an *Existenzfrage* ('question of survival') for Germany. Failure to build a great battle fleet would bring first economic and then political decline.[6] Tirpitz said that if Germany were not ready to take advantage of the expected power shifts with a mighty battle fleet she 'would sink back to the status of a poor farming country'.[7] German Foreign Minister Bernhard Bülow echoed this theme when he declared in December 1899: 'In the coming century the German people will be the hammer or the anvil.'[8] Meanwhile, Tirpitz explained doubling the fleet in 1900 as the result of an unstable international situation, specifically the Spanish-American and Boer wars.

'Risk Theory'

Tirpitz justified all this on the basis of the *Risikogedanke* ('risk theory'). This argument held that the German Navy's ultimate strength would deter any potential opponent from risking an all-out naval encounter because, even if that country should emerge victorious, it would suffer sufficient losses that it might then find itself at the mercy of a third naval power, or even a coalition.[9]

Tirpitz and the kaiser believed that the fleet would enhance Germany's value as an ally, especially with relatively minor naval powers. Tirpitz saw the greatest danger as the possibility that the British might decide to 'Copenhagen' the embryonic German naval force in its harbours, though by 1914 or 1915 this danger would be past.[10] In fact, the risk theory makes sense only if one realizes that it was a subterfuge designed to hide more far-reaching considerations that Tirpitz was unwilling to share with either the Reichstag or the public.

Other judgements guided the naval construction programme. Wilhelm had discarded Bismarck's policy of concentrating on Europe and avoiding colonial conflict. Tirpitz and Wilhelm held that this policy was wrong because it enabled Germany's neighbours to increase their economic and political influence at Germany's expense. They wanted Germany to consolidate her position in Europe while simultaneously laying the foundations for her future expansion overseas. Only a strong battle fleet would enable Germany to pursue *Weltpolitik*' and add to her colonial empire.[11]

Tirpitz believed Britain was rapidly declining as an imperial power and the spoils of its empire would fall to its strongest rivals. Thus Tirpitz's fleet was directed primarily against Great Britain. In December 1899 Tirpitz confided to the Saxon military representative in Berlin: 'For political reasons the government cannot be as specific as the Reichstag would like it to be; one cannot directly say that the naval expansion is directed primarily against England.'[12] Tirpitz said that Germany would have to prepare for an encounter with Britain or America. He apparently regarded the two powers as a single opponent, a unified economic and financial bloc standing in the way of German *Weltpolitik*, but hoped by 1920 to have a fleet that stood a good chance of winning such a contest.

189

Tirpitz believed that the existence of his battle fleet in the North Sea would exert sufficient pressure on the British to grant Germany concessions in distant parts of the world. This aggressive policy of forcing colonial expansion with a powerful battle fleet stationed off the British coast became the dominant aspect of the kaiser's naval policy. If in the future Great Britain should refuse to yield to this pressure, Tirpitz was willing to stake Germany's fate on a single decisive naval battle *(Entscheidungsschlacht)* in the North Sea.

Tirpitz's ambitious programme held the centre stage of Wilhelm's policies from 1898 until approximately 1907–08, when many of this initial calculations had been effectively countered by British adjustments. In the first place Tirpitz underestimated Britain's and over-estimated Germany's financial power. The Royal Navy not only kept pace with German construction but pulled ahead of it. Britain also ended her policy of 'splendid isolation'. After 1905 it was Germany rather than Britain that was isolated in Europe. Finally, in 1912 Britain and France agreed that the French would patrol the Mediterranean while the British guarded the English Channel and the North Sea. This allowed the Royal Navy to recall units from Gibraltar and station them in the North Sea, achieving overwhelming naval superiority vis-à-vis the German High Seas Fleet. Then too, by 1907–08 the army was again given priority in German armaments production and military strategy.

In the end the 'Tirpitz Plan' was a failure. Wilhelm II bears major responsibility for this. His admiration for, and envy of, the Royal Navy and his hatred of 'perfidious Albion', this 'hateful, mendacious, unscrupulous nation of shopkeepers,' moved him to opt for the programme.[13]

NEW NAVAL CONSTRUCTION

The advance of capital ships continued, meanwhile, away from the low freeboard turret ships that suffered the disadvantage of not being able to steam fast in a seaway. The low bows that facilitated fire from the forward turret meant that they took heavy seas on the foredeck. Designers had failed to grasp that the height of the bow determined the speed at which a ship could be driven at sea.[14]

Royal Sovereign

The 'Royal Sovereign' class of battleships embodied a number of design changes that led to them sometimes being considered the first pre-dreadnought battleships. Designed by Director of Naval Construction William White and laid down beginning in 1889, they combined fighting efficiency with greater speed. This was possible only in a barbette design with the guns carried high above the waterline for better seakeeping. White was able to take advantage of the development of nickel steel armour-plate, which meant a great savings in weight and armour thickness. The result was a powerful class of ships, completed over 1892–94, that were both handsome and practical and set the standard for most of the pre-dreadnought capital ships to follow.

One of 70 vessels ordered under the Naval Defence Act of 1889, the *Royal Sovereign* was 14,150 tons and 380 × 75 feet. Her main armament was 4 × 13.5-inch guns; her secondary armament was all in quick-firing guns: 10 × 6-inchers, 16 × 6-pounders, 12 × 3-pounders, and 7 torpedo tubes. Her twin-screw, triple-expansion engines drove her at 18 knots. Seven of this class were built, the others being the *Empress of India*, *Ramillies*, *Repulse*, *Resolution*, *Revenge*, and *Royal Oak*. Of these ships only the *Revenge* saw service in the First World War, as a bombarding ship. Renamed *Redoubtable* in 1915, she was broken up in 1919.[15]

Royal Sovereign, Royal Navy battleship. (*Royal Naval Museum, 1891*)

The Board of Admiralty agreed with White's arguments in favour of larger capital ships, but Prime Minister William Gladstone's last Liberal government (1892–94) was reluctant to increase naval expenditures. However, both France and Russia – now linked together in military alliance – had embarked on ambitious naval expansion programmes. As a consequence the Sea Lords, the naval members of the Board of Admiralty, threatened to resign as a body and Gladstone gave way.

Majestic

The new programme, to be spread over five years, included nine 'Majestic'-class battleships. The best battleships of the 1890s, they set the pattern for capital ship design until the *Dreadnought* of 1906.

Ultimately an unprecedented 29 ships of virtually the same type were built. Completed in 1895 and weighing 16,060 tons, the *Majestic* was larger than any of her predecessors. The other ships in this class were *Caesar, Hannibal, Illustrious, Jupiter, Magnificent, Mars*, and *Prince George*. These ships were 421 × 75 feet and could make 17 knots from their twin-screw, triple-expansion engines. Their main battery was 4 × 12-inch guns. Their secondary armament was 12 × 6-inch quick-firing guns, 16 × 6-pounders, 12 × 3-pounders, and five torpedo tubes. Improved armour and a new wire-wound 12-inch gun allowed considerable savings in weight and better protection.[16]

The British also built other large battleship classes in this period: five 'Canopus'-class

HMS *Majestic.* (*Royal Naval Museum, 1987/477 (14)*)

Implacable, Royal Navy battleship. (*Royal Naval Museum*)

Brandenburg, German battleship. (*Imperial War Museum, Q22317*)

(1896–1902), three 'Formidable'-class (1896–1902), five 'London'-class (1899–1904), and six 'Duncan'-class (1900–04). The 'Canopus'-class battleships were 12,950 tons each and 390 × 74 feet. They mounted 4 × 12-inch and 12 × 6-inch guns along with 12 × 12-pounders. The 'Formidables' were slightly larger: 15,000 tons and 400 × 75 feet. The 'Londons' were the same size and carried the same armament, with the exception of 18 rather than 12 × 12-pounders. The 'Duncans' were slightly lighter at 14,000 tons and 400 × 75 feet, but had the same main armament.

The only real change was in the last large class of British pre-dreadnoughts, the eight 'King Edward VII'-class battleships, built during 1903–07. Displacing 16,350 tons, they were 425 × 78 feet and mounted 4 × 12-inch, 4 × 9.2-inch, and 10 × 6-inch guns as well as 14 × 12-pounders. During this period the British also built some smaller battleships for colonial service. In all, between 1890 and 1905 Great Britain built 47 first class and five second class battleships.[17]

The Kaiser Friedrich III

The Germans countered the British construction with their strong 'Kaiser Friedrich III'-class ships. The first, of this line, the *Kaiser Friedrich III*, was laid down in 1895 and completed in 1898. All vessels in this class were named for German emperors: the *Kaiser Friedrich III, Kaiser Barbarossa, Kaiser Wilhelm der Grosse, Kaiser Wilhelm II*, and *Kaiser der Grosse*. These 11,599-ton vessels were driven by their triple-screw, triple-expansion engines at 17 knots. Armament consisted of 4 × 238-mm (9.4-inch) guns, 18 × 152-mm (6-inch) guns, and 12 × 86.3-mm (3.4-inch) guns. The ships were protected by a 12-inch armour belt and they had 10-inch armour on the main turrets and 6-inch protection on secondary turrets and casemates.[18]

Benedetto Brin

Brin of Italy also designed another large battleship, which on completion was named for him. The *Benedetto Brin* of 1905 and her sister ship the *Regina Margherita*, were 13,215 tons and 449.5 feet × 78 feet 3 inches. They had an armament of 4 × 304-mm (12-inch) guns, 4 × 203-mm (8-inch) guns, and 12 × 152-mm (6-inch) guns. Brin sacrificed armour for speed. The ships had only 6-inch side armour, 3-inch deck armour, and 8-inch turret armour, but they had a top speed of 20.3 knots.[19]

FRENCH BATTLESHIPS

At the end of the 1880s France abandoned the ideas of the *Jeune École*. The second leading naval power until Germany decided to challenge Britain for naval supremacy, in 1889 France laid down the *Brennus* of 11,000 tons and 3 × 13.4-inch guns, the first of its pre-dreadnoughts. Completed in 1896 she was a revolutionary ship for the French. She had a main armament on the centreline in two turrets (a twin turret forward and a single aft), no ram, and an upper belt of 4.7-inch armour above the main belt. Five battleships of similar design were laid down during 1890–92: the *Jauréguiberry, Charles Martel, Carnot, Bouvet,* and *Masséna*. Begun in response to the British *Royal Sovereigns,* these were characterized by a lozenge arrangement for their main batteries and a pronounced tumble-home in high, relatively unprotected

Brennus, French Navy battleship. Photograph *c.* 1894. (*Naval Historical Foundation, NH 82700*)

Bouvet, French Navy battleship. (*Naval Historical Foundation, NH 64442*)

Gaulois, French Navy battleship. (*Musée de la Marine, PH 36931*)

hulls. These were similar ships but each was built by a different engineer, working from the same specifications. They were around 12,000 tons and had 18 knots speed. They carried a main battery of 2 × 12-inch guns and 2 × 10.8-inch guns (the latter mounted in sponsons that protruded from each side of the hull), as well as 8 × 5.5-inchers. In the three 'Charlemagne'-class ships (*Charlemagne*, *St Louis*, and *Gaulois*), laid down in 1894–96 and completed in 1899–1900, the French returned to the standard configuration of twin turrets fore and aft.[20]

RUSSIAN BATTLESHIPS

Russia began building pre-dreadnought battleships in 1892, with three of 11,000 tons each that mounted a main armament of 4 × 12-inch guns: the *Petropavlovsk*, *Poltava* and *Sevastopol*. Russia's largest pre-dreadnoughts were the four 13,500 ton 'Borodino'-class vessels: *Borodino*, *Imperator Alexander III*, *Orel* and *Kniaz Suvarov*. Commissioned during 1903–04, they were 397 × 76.2 feet. Designed to displace 13,500 tons, they were in fact heavier due to design changes during construction. This meant that when loaded they rode two feet lower in the water than intended, which, given their narrow armour belt, left their waterlines unprotected. They each mounted 4 × 12-inch guns in twin turrets, 12 × 6-inch quick-firing guns in twin turrets, three on each side; and 10 × 3-inch quick-firers to protect against torpedo boat attack. During this period France built 18 pre-dreadnoughts and Russia built 20 such ships.[21]

NEW US NAVY

Concurrent with the rise of Germany as a major naval power the US Navy underwent a renaissance. Following the Civil War, Congress refused to provide funds for modern warships and, between 1866 and 1883, the US Navy went from second in the world, with some 700 ships mounting 5,000 guns, to the 12th-ranked naval power, with only 52 vessels in commission mounting fewer than 500 obsolete guns. This resulted in part from budgetary constraints, but part of it was also a reactionary attitude within the Navy itself. In 1875 a British journalist wrote, 'There never was such a hapless, broken down, tattered, forlorn apology for a Navy as that possessed by the United States.'[22]

The Civil War fleet rotted out at the naval yards. By 1880 the Navy was inferior to every major European power and even to that of Chile. Congress halted plans to break up the ironclads and reconstruct the ships entirely of iron. Most were simply laid up, to be kept available against foreign attack, and some remained on the navy list into the twentieth century. Only a few ships were in condition for normal cruising, and these were the pre-war wooden vessels mounting smoothbore guns.

Virginius affair (1873)

Part of the impetus for the rebirth of the US Navy came from the *Virginius* Affair. A small iron side-wheel steamer that had been built in Scotland in 1864 as a Confederate blockade runner during the Civil War, in 1873 the *Virginius*, under a dubious US registry, was smuggling arms to rebels against Spain in Cuba. On 30 October 1873, a Spanish gunboat seized the *Virginius*, then laden with war matériel and recruits for the rebels. The Spanish governor at Santiago declared her a pirate vessel, and the authorities executed her captain, Joseph Fry, an 1841 graduate of the US Naval Academy who had fought for the South in the Civil War, along with

52 passengers and crew. The same fate undoubtedly would have befallen 155 other men aboard her had not the HMS *Niobe* rushed to Cuba from Jamaica. Her captain, Sir Lambton Loraine, demanded that the executions be halted. With the *Niobe* cleared for action, the Spanish complied; the remaining prisoners were finally transported to New York.

The ensuing diplomatic crisis forced the US Navy to mobilize for possible war with Spain, but it took three months to assemble its collection of ancient vessels at Key West under Admiral David Dixon Porter in an attempt to bluff down the Spanish in Cuba, just 90 miles away. This fiasco provided acute embarrassment for the United States and amusement to the Europeans. Although the dispute was finally settled by diplomacy – Spain agreed to pay $80,000 in compensation – the *Virginius* Affair pointed out the total inadequacy of the US Navy.

The growth of the US Navy was also related to US imperialism, basically a drive for Pacific bases to support American trade, and to US interest in building an Isthmian canal. Both owed much to the stimulus of the US Naval Institute (created in 1871), the Naval War College, and the writings of Mahan.[23]

The modern US Navy dates from 3 March 1883, when Congress authorized the construction of three modern cruisers, the *Atlanta, Boston,* and *Chicago,* along with the gunboat *Dolphin,* the so-called 'ABCD' ships. From 1885 to 1899 Congress also authorized 30 new warships of different classes, aggregating nearly 100,000 tons.

Congress authorized the first modern US battleship, the *Texas,* in 1886. During 1890–1896 four classes of battleships of 10,000–11,000 tons each were designed; and, in 1900–02 two large classes of 14,000–16,000 tons were planned. As of 1904 the United States had 12 battleships in service, a like number under construction and another authorized. Eight large armoured cruisers were also under construction.[24]

Texas

The United States had no experience in building modern battleships and difficulties in obtaining material delayed completion of the *Texas*. Laid down in 1889 and completed in 1895, she was of British design and was obsolete before she was completed. She weighed only 6,650 tons, was 308 feet 10 inches × 64 feet 1 inch, and was armed with a main battery of 2 × 12-inch main guns. Her secondary battery contained 6 × 6-inch guns, 12 × 6-pounders, 6 × 1-pounders, and 4 × 37-mm guns. She also had 4 × 14-inch torpedo tubes. She had only a 118-foot long armour belt; 12 inches in depth, it extended 2 feet above and 4.5 feet below the waterline. Powered by vertical triple-expansion engines on twin screws, the *Texas* could make 17 knots.[25]

Maine

In 1890 the Navy proposed a total redesign of the *Texas* in which the two heavy 12-inch guns were mounted in separate turrets and the redoubt eliminated, but new Secretary of the Navy Benjamin Tracy ordered that the heavy redoubt be retained. The result was the *Maine,* at that point the largest ship ever built in a US Navy yard. Commissioned in 1895, she was designated a 'second-class battleship', but at 6,315 tons and with a main battery of 10-inch guns she really belonged in the category of armoured cruiser. Fated to be sunk at Havana, the *Maine* carried a 12-inch thick belt of armour that extended three feet above and four feet below the waterline, and she was armed with 4 × 10-inch and 6 × 6-inch guns.

Maine, US Navy battleship/armoured cruiser. (*Naval Historical Foundation, NH 48620*)

Massachusetts, US Navy battleship (BB-2), off New York City during the victory review, August 1898. (*Naval Historical Foundation, NH 46423*)

Iowa, US Navy battleship (BB-4), photographed in 1898. (*Naval Historical Foundation, NH 61212*)

She also had 7 × 6-pounders and 4 × 1-pounder guns, 4 machine guns, and 6 × 18-inch torpedo tubes. The Maine had a speed of 17 knots.[26]

Indiana

The earliest modern first class battleships in the US Navy were the three ships of the 'Indiana' class: *Indiana, Massachusetts,* and *Oregon.* Authorized in 1891 the *Indiana* was completed four years later. At 350 feet 11 inches × 69 feet 3 inches, these ships had almost double the displacement of the *Texas.* Each displaced 10,225 tons and had a speed of 15 knots. The 'Indiana'-class ships had belts of 18-inch armour. They were described as coast defence battleships and had a low freeboard. Elegant ships in their while hulls and buff upperworks, they had two tall funnels, two masts, and two turrets,

one each fore and aft. They carried a decidely mixed armament of 4 × 13-inch guns in two turrets and 8 × 8-inch guns in barbettes. Their secondary battery consisted of 4 × 6-inch guns as well as 20 × 6-pounders, 6 × 1-pounders, and four machine guns (in tops). Each also had six torpedo tubes.

The 'Indiana' was followed by two more battleship classes: the 'Iowa' (1897) and the 'Kearsarge' (1898). The *Iowa*, the most recently designed of the battleships that participated in the war with Spain, displaced 11,410 tons, considerably more than the *Indiana*. But thanks to recent improvements in manufacture, the thickness of her armour belt was reduced to only 14 inches. Her armament was mixed for fighting at different ranges. She had a main battery of 4 × 12-inch guns and 4 ×

8-inch guns. Her secondary battery consisted of 14 × 5-inch guns, 20 × 6-pounders, 19 × 1-pounders, and 2 × 6-mm machine guns. Her design speed was 16 knots. The *Kearsarge*, the only battleship not named for a state, and her sister ship *Kentucky* displaced 11,540 tons. Their main battery was 4 × 13-inch and 4 × 8-inch guns. The secondary battery consisted of 14 × 5-inch guns, 20 × 6-pounders, 19 × 1-pounders, and 2 × 6-mm machine guns. They also had 4 × 18-inch torpedo tubes. Design speed was 16 knots.[27]

Other US battleships followed in succession: the 1898 'Alabama'-class also mounted 4 × 13-inch guns. It included the

Illinois and *Wisconsin*, 375 feet 4 inches × 72 feet 3 inches, with a displacement of 11,565 tons. In 1901 three 'Ohio'-class ships were completed: the *Ohio*, *Maine*, and *Missouri*. They were 393 feet 11 inches × 72 feet 3 inches and displaced 12,846 tons. They reverted back to a main battery of 4 × 12-inch guns but with a secondary battery of 16 × 6-inch guns, 6 × 3-inch guns, and 8 × 3-pounders. Each had 2 × 18-inch submerged torpedo tubes. In 1904 five other battleships appeared in the 'Virginia'-class: the *Virginia*, *New Jersey*, *Georgia*, *Nebraska*, and *Rhode Island*. They were 441 feet 3 inches × 76 feet 3 inches, displaced 14,943 tons, and had a main battery of 4 × 12-inch

Kearsarge, US Navy battleship (BB-5), in drydock at Puget Sound Navy Yard, 1902. (*Naval Historical Foundation, NH 60250*)

Virginia, US Navy battleship (BB-13), photographed with one cage mast and one military mast. (*Naval Historical Foundation, NH 90776*)

and 8 × 8-inch guns. Then came *Louisiana* and *Connecticut*. In 1905–06 four more were added: the *Kansas, Vermont, Minnesota*, and *New Hampshire*.[28]

JAPANESE BATTLESHIPS

In 1893 Japan ordered two battleships from Britain, similar to the 'Royal Sovereign' class. In 1896 it ordered four comparable to the *Majestic*. These six ships were the core of the Japanese Navy that won the 1904–05 Russo-Japanese War.

The period beginning in 1890 and ending in 1906 with the launch of the *Dreadnought* was one of the most intense in capital-ship construction history. The irony of this is that these pre-dreadnoughts were all rendered obsolete in 1906. Most participated in the First World War only in secondary roles.

CRUISERS

In the early 1890s there was a reaction in Britain against increases in naval expenditures, that is bigger ships. In naval circles many believed that the bigger guns were driving the need for larger ships. There was considerable support for more moderate sized and armed vessels instead of a few very large capital ships.

In a letter to the Board of Admiralty Director of Naval Construction Sir William White stated the reasons for more numerous, smaller ships but then argued against them. Proponents of smaller ships pointed out that the largest ships had considerable unarmoured areas subject to destruction by high explosive shells of moderate size from quick-firing guns, and that even a modest roll at sea would expose unarmoured portions of the ship's side, which could allow shells to penetrate the ship's vitals. Given this, they believed that it was not necessary for ships to have guns larger than 9.2- or 10-inches, and that few of these need be carried. The bulk of a ship's armament should be in quick-firing 6-inch or smaller guns. Because armour was so limited in its protection, it should be done away with or at the least made moderate in thickness and extent.

For the same money that produced a few large capital ships many smaller vessels might be had. A larger number of smaller ships armed with quick-firing guns would be able to defeat a smaller number of giant ships with the largest guns. Larger numbers of ships would also be useful in protecting the coasts, and squadrons might easily be dispatched without seriously crippling the force: 'In short, increase in numbers is held to favour both the power of *concentration* and *distribution* according as the necessity of the moment may dictate; so that there is an elasticity in the employment of a force not attainable with a few large ships representing the same capital expenditure.'[29]

White then went on to demolish this argument by pointing out that the largest ships could more easily maintain speed at sea and were far more stable gun platforms. They were less likely than smaller warships to be put out of action by a single blow, whether it be from a shell, ram, or torpedo. Also with their powerful guns on one ship and under one direction they could produce a concentration of fire that could easily destroy the smaller vessels. Small ships could not carry the heaviest guns in protected positions, and destruction of the unarmoured portions of a ship would be accomplished more easily by the larger guns in association with the quick-firing smaller pieces. White also argued that concerted attacks by smaller vessels were unlikely. A few larger ships might more easily concentrate their fire than a crowd of smaller warships.[30]

Armoured cruisers had dominated production in the 1880s, but because of the belief that side armour offered little protection from plunging shells, second class or protected cruisers predominated in 1890s construction. With the development of new steel armour at the turn of the century there was a switch back to armoured cruisers.

Cruisers played key roles in the wars of this period. Japanese cruisers defeated a Chinese force, including older battleships, in the 1894 Battle of the Yalu during the Sino-Japanese War. And a US cruiser force won the naval battle of Manila Bay.

British cruisers

With their worldwide commitments the British built a variety of cruiser types. By 1890 the Royal Navy had divided its cruisers into three categories based on size: first, second, and third class. The smallest first-class cruisers were the nine 7,350-ton 'Edgar'-class protected cruisers of 1890. They were 360 × 60 feet and mounted 2 × 9.2-inch, 10 × 6-inch, and 12 × 6-pounder guns. The *Ariadne* of 1898 weighed 11,000 tons, was 435 × 69 feet, and was capable of 20 knots. She was armed with 16 × 6-inch guns, 14 × 12-pounders, and 2 × 18-inch torpedo tubes. She had 12-inch armour on her conning tower, 6-inch armour on the gun casemates, and a 4-inch armoured deck. Britain had held back from building big, heavily armed cruisers, but with France building cruisers such as the *Dupuy de Lôme* as a threat for commerce raiding, Britain responded with six armoured 'Cressy'-class ships. Laid down in 1898–99, these 12,000-ton cruisers were 440 × 69.5 feet, and each carried 2 × 9.2-inch guns as compared with the French 7.6-inch, along with 12 × 6-inch guns and 13 × 12-pounders. The largest British first class cruisers were the three 14,600-ton 'Minotaur'-class laid down in 1905. They were 490 × 74.5 feet and mounted 4 × 9.2-inch, 10 × 7.5-inch, and 14 × 12-pounder guns.

Second-class cruisers ranged in size from 3,000 to 5,000 tons and usually mounted a main battery of 6-inch guns. The four 'Mersey'-class cruisers of the mid-1880s were 4,050 tons and were 300 × 46 feet. They mounted 2 × 8-inch guns, 10 × 6-inch, and 3 × 6-pounders. All second-class cruisers were 'protected' in that they had armoured decks and but little or no vertical armour. Generally the armoured deck varied in thickness between four and six inches. The largest single class of second-class cruisers built during this period were the 21 'Apollo'-class, completed beginning in 1891. These 3,400-ton ships were 300 × 44 feet and mounted 2 × 6-inch guns, 6 × 4.7-inch, and 8 × 6-pounders.

The final category was that of third-class cruisers. These included vessels of 2,000 to 3,000 tons. Most were known as 'scout' cruisers. They carried 4-inch guns and had no armour. The largest of these were eleven 2,135-ton 'Pelorus'-class ships of 300 × 36.5 feet. Commissioned during 1896–1901, each mounted 8 × 4-inch guns and 8 × 3-pounders.[31]

German cruisers

In 1896 Germany laid down the armoured cruiser *Fürst Bismarck*. Completed the next year, she weighed 10,700 tons and made 19 knots. She was armed with 4 × 9.4-inch and 12 × 6-inch guns, 10 × 15-pounders, and a number of smaller guns as well as 5 × 17.7-inch torpedo tubes. The *Bismarck* had an 8-inch armour belt amidships that tapered to 4 inches at the ends, 8 inches on her barbette, turrets, and conning tower, and 4 inches of protection for the smaller guns. *Scharnhorst* and *Gneisenau* were easily the most famous of Germany's armoured cruisers. Laid down in 1904, they were completed two years later. At 11,600 tons and 449 feet 9 inches × 71 feet they mounted a main armament of 8 × 8.2-inch guns. Secondary armament included 6 × 6-inch guns and 20 × 24-pounders. In 1899 Germany laid down five smaller, 6,390-ton 'Victoria Louise'-class protected cruisers. Completed during 1901–02 they displaced 9,050 tons and were 394 × 65 feet. They mounted 4 × 8.21-inch guns as their main armament. Their secondary armament included 10 × 6-inch, 10 × 15.5-pounders, and 10 × 1-pounders. Their armored belt was only 4 inches. In 1897 Germany laid down ten 'Gazelle'-class light cruisers. These 3,030-ton ships had a main armament of 10 × 4-inch guns. Other German light cruiser classes followed into the First World War.[32]

French and Italian cruisers

France built 22 armoured cruisers in this period, most of 9,000- to 13,000-tons, with a priority on speed. In 1905–06 France laid down her largest armoured cruisers. Completed two years later, the 14,100-ton *Edgar Quinet* and *Waldeck Rousseau* were 515 feet × 70 feet 8 inches. These six-stackers had a main armament of 14 × 6.6-inch guns. The *Dupuy de Lôme* was an important design of protected cruiser. Completed in 1893, she weighed 6,400 tons and was capable of 22 knots. Armed with 2 × 7.6-inch and 6 × 6.4-inch guns, 4 × 9-pounders, and 4 × 18-inch torpedo tubes, she had both a protected deck and a 4.25-inch belt of armour amidships and on the conning tower and 4-inch armour on her gun turrets and bases. Italy built six armoured cruisers at the turn of the century. These were considered some of the best armed and protected ships of their day for a small displacement. Two 'San Giorgio'-class ships, laid down in 1905 and completed in 1908, each mounted 4 × 10-inch and 8 × 7.5-inch guns, in addition to smaller guns and torpedo tubes.[33]

US cruisers

The US Navy, with a view toward coast defence, emphasized greater armour in its cruisers. The size of the ships increased dramatically and individual tonnage almost doubled. Between 1890 and 1903 the US Navy built 20 armoured/first class cruisers.

In 1888 Congress authorized construction of the *New York* (for illustration, *see* page 154, renamed the *Rochester* in 1917). Completed two years later, this advanced design ship turned out to be one of the most seaworthy ever built for the US Navy. She displaced 8,150 tons and was 384 feet × 64 feet 10 inches. Her hull was divided into 184 watertight compartments, with 11 more such compartments in her double bottom. The *New York* initially mounted a main battery of 2 × 8-inch guns; she also carried 10 × 5-inch rapid-fire guns, 6 × 6-pounders, and 8 × 1-pounder rapid-fire guns, 4 × 37-mm revolving cannon, and six torpedo tubes.[34]

The *New York* was followed by the *Brooklyn*, completed in 1896. This 9,125-ton cruiser, 402 feet 7.5 inches × 64 feet 8.5 inches, mounted 8 × 8-inch guns. Her secondary armament included 12 × 5-inchers and 12 × 6-pounders as well as 4 × 18-inch torpedo tubes. In 1899 Congress authorized three new armoured cruisers, the *Pennsylvania*, *West Virginia*, and *California*. In 1900 three additional vessels of this class were also

authorized: *Colorado*, *Maryland*, and *South Dakota*. These ships were of slightly differing sizes but approximated to 504 × 70 feet. They displaced 13,680 tons and mounted 4 × 8-inch guns in their main armament. Secondary armament included 14 × 6-inch rapid fire guns and 2 × 18-inch torpedo tubes. In 1902 Congress authorized the three-ship 'Tennessee'-class armoured cruisers. The powerful *Tennessee*, *North Carolina*, and *Montana* were 504.5 × 72 feet 10.5 inches, displaced 14,500 tons, and were armed with a main battery of 4 × 10-inch guns. Their secondary armament included 16 × 6-inch rapid-fire guns and 4 × 21-inch torpedo tubes.[35]

Among US protected cruisers was the large 5,865-ton *Olympia* (for illustration, *see* page 155. Laid down in 1891 she was completed four years later. Built as a commerce raider, the *Olympia* earned fame as Admiral George Dewey's flagship in the Battle of Manila Bay. She was 340 × 53 feet and her initial main battery was 4 × 8-inch guns. Later she was rearmed with 10 × 5-inch guns. In 1888 Congress authorized five smaller 'Cincinnati'-class cruisers, and in 1900 the Navy laid down six 'Denver'-class cruisers. At 3,200 tons and 292 × 44 feet they were completed during 1901–03 and mounted 8 × 5-inch guns as their main armament.[36]

Other cruisers

Russia built few armoured and protected cruisers, but she did have the largest armoured cruiser: the 15,190-ton *Rurik*. Mounting 4 × 10-inch and 8 × 8-inch guns, the *Rurik* was lost in the Battle of Ulsan during the Russo-Japanese War. Japan had only a few armoured and protected cruisers.[37]

As the naval building race between Britain and Germany intensified in the first years of the twentieth century, the size, armament, and protection of armoured

Surcouf, French cruiser, 1892. (*Imperial War Museum, Q22307*)

Szigetvar, Austrian protected cruiser, 1901. (*Imperial War Museum, Q22228*)

cruisers all increased. The German armoured cruisers *Prinz Adalbert*, *Friedrich Karl*, *Roon*, and *Yorck*, laid down during 1900–02 and completed during 1903–04, were 9,050 tons. They had a main armament of 4 × 8.2-inch guns and a secondary armament that included 10 × 6-inch guns.

Armoured cruisers had two chief functions: as commerce raiders and, conversely, as commerce raider destroyers; and to serve as scouts for the battle fleet. In the latter capacity they had to be fast enough to escape from the big guns of the battleships, yet strong enough to deal with light cruisers and destroyers. Light cruisers were supposedly fast enough to escape from armoured cruisers and to be able to act as scouts, yet powerful enough to deal with enemy destroyers.[38]

THE TORPEDO BOAT DESTROYER

During this time period great improvements were made both in the range and destructiveness of the Whitehead torpedo. This and construction of large numbers of high-speed torpedo boats to deliver the torpedoes prompted the development of a larger but similar vessel, the 'torpedo-boat destroyer'. The first attempt at a counter to the torpedo boat was the Royal Navy 'torpedo ram' *Polyphemus* of 1887. The chief problem with the *Polyphemus* was that she was slower than the torpedo boats she was supposed to ram!

Swift

Initially the counter torpedo boats were simply larger and faster torpedo boats, mounting guns as well as torpedoes. In 1885 a leading British ship builder, J. Samuel White, built and sold to the Admiralty a boat of his own design. The *Swift* (renamed by the Admiralty, *Torpedo Boat No. 81*) was 125 tons and 157 × 17.5 feet. Although

somewhat slower than the torpedo boats, her greater beam allowed her to carry more armament; she mounted six quick-firing 3-pounders and three torpedo tubes.

The *Swift* inspired similar types of 'torpedo boat catchers'. The Royal Navy itself now designed four 'Rattlesnake'-class 'torpedo gunboats'. These were the *Rattlesnake* (1886), *Grasshopper* (1887), *Sandfly* (1887), and *Spider* (1887). They displaced 550 tons and were 200 × 23 feet. Each mounted a 4-inch quick-firing gun, 6 × 3-pounders, and 4 torpedo tubes. In 1887 trials were held involving the *Rattlesnake* and torpedo boats. These were not encouraging; the *Rattlesnake* was only 2 knots faster, hardly enough to be decisive. Although in 1889 the Admiralty ordered 13 torpedo gunboats of an improved design, they too proved unsuccessful.[39]

Meanwhile France and Russia had become allies. With both building large numbers of torpedo boats, Britain had to do something. Because the Royal Navy had not been able to build a satisfactory vessel, the Admiralty decided to entrust this to the private firms building the torpedo boats. In June 1892 the Navy contracted for four vessels: two each with Thornycroft and Yarrow. The only conditions were that they have 27-knot speed and a powerful armament. That August the term 'torpedo boat destroyer' appeared in official correspondence for the first time.

Havock

HMS *Havock*, completed in October 1893, was the first modern torpedo boat destroyer. She weighed 275 tons, was 180 × 18.5 feet, and was capable of nearly 27 knots. She behaved well in a seaway, had good manoeuvrability, and in the 1894 fleet manoeuvres, 'caught' two torpedo boats. She also 'caught' and circled around one of the 'Swift'-class torpedo boat 'catchers'. The *Havock*'s sister ship the *Hornet* was fitted with

Havock, 1893, Royal Navy torpedo boat destroyer. (*Royal Naval Museum, 5234*)

Hornet, Royal Navy destroyer. (*Naval Historical Foundation, NH 60590*)

Daring, Royal Navy destroyer. (*Naval Historical Foundation, NH 61114*)

Lightning, Royal Navy destroyer, 1895. (*Naval Historical Foundation, NH 59901*)

the new water-tube boiler instead of the *Havock*'s locomotive-boiler, and could travel at up to 27.3 knots, which made her the fastest ship in the world. At such speeds the new torpedo boat destroyers were indeed a match for the torpedo boats. Both the *Havock* and the *Hornet* were armed with a 12-pounder and 3 × 6-pounder guns as well as 3 × 18-inch torpedo tubes; both were sold out of the Navy before the First World War.

Seal, Royal Navy destroyer. (*Imperial War Museum, Q21742*)

During 1893–95 the Royal Navy ordered some 33 destroyers of this type, all capable of 27-knot speed and later designated Class 'A' and 'B'. They were followed by 43 Class 'C' and 'D' destroyers built through 1900, all capable of 30 knots. Each was armed with a 12-pounder, 5 × 6-pounders, and 2 × 18-inch torpedo tubes. Typical of British destroyers at the end of the pre-dreadnought era were the 34 'River'-class (later designated 'E'-class) destroyers. Known as good sea boats and averaging 550 tons and 225 × 23.5 feet, they were armed with 4 × 12-pounders and 2 × 18-inch torpedo tubes.[40]

French destroyers

High speed and the ability to inflict significant damage were the hallmarks of both the torpedo boat and torpedo boat destroyer. Each new design registered improvements. The French Navy followed the British lead and turned to a private torpedo boat designer, Jacques-Augustin Normand. He came up with three designs. The one selected was for a 300-ton *torpelleur d'escadre* ('squadron torpedo boat'); later such a ship was called simply *contre-torpilleur*. At 189 × 21 feet the 'Durandal'-class were about the size of the *Havock*. The French *torpilleur de haute mer* ('sea-going torpedo boat') mounted 2 × 3-pounders and two torpedo tubes. Over the next decade the French built 55 destroyers of this successful type. The *Forban* of 1895 achieved 31 knots. This was accomplished with a reciprocating engine; speeds with the turbine engine were

Durandal, French Navy contre-torpilleur. (*Naval Historical Foundation, NH 64459*)

higher. Generally speaking the British led this race, laying down vessels that were both larger and faster than those built by the French.[41]

Larger torpedo boats/destroyers could accompany and provide perimeter protection for the battleships. The first of these light ships were subject to hull strain, excessive vibration, wet conditions, and excessive rolling while at sea. They were thus difficult ships for their crews. Some of this was mitigated in later designs that altered the superstructure and weight displacement.

Turbina

During Queen Victoria's Diamond Jubilee in 1897, the greatest of all Victorian naval reviews, a novel new craft made its appearance. This was the yacht *Turbina*, powered by the steam turbine engine developed by the firm of Parsons. In the steam-turbine engine, steam heated by means of a water-pipe boiler was passed through a series of nozzles. Gaining velocity, it was then directed onto a series of blades on the periphery of a rotor. The velocity of the steam passed along these blades, turning the rotor and powering the propellers.

The revolutionary steam-turbine engine was both more reliable and faster than the reciprocating engine it replaced, which tended to shake itself to pieces. It also avoided design and protection problems resulting from the growing height of the reciprocal engine's large pistons. As the *Turbina* was faster than either the torpedo boats or torpedo boat destroyers in the review, the Admiralty ordered a turbine-powered destroyer.[42]

Viper

HMS *Viper*, launched in 1899, incorporated both the design changes above as well as the new turbine engine. This 440-ton destroyer was 210 × 21 feet. Armed with one 12-pounder and 5 × 6-pounder guns, and two torpedo tubes, she was also the first naval vessel powered by the steam-turbine engine. This drove her at a maximum speed of 37 knots and she was able to sustain 34 knots for more than three hours; this made her the fastest ship in the fleet. The *Viper* suffered an untimely end, being wrecked in 1901.[43]

Destroyers of other nations

Beginning in 1886 Germany built ten large 'division boats' or flotilla leader torpedo boats. The last six of these, in the 400-ton range, were considered destroyers. In 1896 Germany began construction of larger, high-speed destroyers. Japan purchased some British-built destroyers for the Russo-Japanese War and built her own, beginning with the 375-ton 'Harusame'-class of 1902. During this period Russia built 59 destroyers and Italy 12. By the start of the dreadnought era, although the destroyer had replaced the torpedo boat in most navies, it still had limited seagoing capabilities.[44]

Beginning in 1896 the US Navy built four ships officially classified as torpedo boats but generally held to be the forerunners of the first US destroyers. The *Farragut*, 279 tons, 214 × 21 feet, and armed with 4 × 6-pounders, had 30-knot speed. Although the United States employed torpedo boats during the war with Spain, they achieved little. Indeed, their employment on patrol

Viper, Royal Navy destroyer. (*Royal Naval Museum, 5134*)

Princeton, US Navy patrol boat (PB-2). One of four 'Annapolis'-class vessels built during 1896–8, she was 204 feet × 36 feet × 12 feet and weighed 1,000 tons. She was armed with 4 × 4-inch guns and 4 × 6-pounders, and 2 × 1-pounders. (*Naval Historical Foundation, NH 59451*)

Ericsson, US Navy torpedo boat (TB-2), 1897. (*Naval Historical Foundation, NH 54064*)

Bainbridge, US Navy destroyer, photographed in 1901. (*Naval Historical Foundation, NH 69702*)

duties revealed their shortcomings in seaworthiness.

Beginning in 1899 the US Navy ordered 15 true destroyers, most of them four-stackers. Part of the impetus for this was the Spanish success in bringing three new destroyers across the Atlantic during the war. In 1898 Congress authorized 'sixteen torpedo boat destroyers of about four hundred tons displacement'. The *Bainbridge* (DD-1), completed in 1902, began the US Navy numbering system for destroyers; the last US destroyer was DD-997, the 'Spruance'-class *Hayler*, in 1983.[45]

The eight 'Bainbridge'-class destroyers were designed for 28 knots. They were 420 tons, 245 × 23 feet, and mounted 2 × 3-inch guns as their main armament, along with 4 × 6-pounders and 2 × 18-inch torpedo tubes. The 'Bainbridge'-class ships incorporated the important design change of raised forecastles. Abandoning the characteristic torpedo boat bow of rounded shape forward ending in the deck – the so-called turtleback bow – made it easier to handle rough seas. Five of the 'Bainbridge'-class destroyers spent most of their service life in the Philippines; two others were in Panama. By the First World War, the two 'Lawrence'-, two 'Hull'-, three 'Truxtun'-, and five 'Bainbridge'-class destroyers, all unofficially known as 'tinclads', were no longer capable of fleet service and had been reclassified as coast torpedo vessels.[46]

STEEL ARMOUR

For some years armour – behind guns in the race for supremacy – had grown increasingly thicker. The first armour protection was 4-inch wrought-iron plates bolted to the ship's wooden hull. The next step was rolled-iron armour on double layers of wood, the whole supported by iron girders and an inner iron plate. In 1870 came sandwich iron, layers of rolled-iron plates alternating with wood, and inner layers of sheet iron. Compound armour appeared in 1877; it consisted of steel-clad wrought-iron plates. But improved armour-piercing projectiles of tremendous striking energy could penetrate test plates of 24-inch wrought-iron armour, the thickness on the battleship *Inflexible*.[47]

The new process of steel manufacture, introduced in warship construction in the mid-1870s, now expanded to armour. This enabled ship constructors to build thinner yet tougher armour-plating. At the end of the 1880s the French Schneider works added some 3–4 per cent nickel to its steel armour plates; this reduced the tendency to crack. In 1890 American H.A. Harvey improved on this process by introducing what became known as Harvey plate. It was nickel steel alloy armour, 'face hardened' by a carbonizing process. This raised the carbon content of the outer inch or so of the armour from 0.02 per cent to over 1 per cent. It was the best armour in the world. In 1895 Krupp engineers in Germany introduced KC or Krupp-Cemented Plate steel. It involved heating the plate to 2000°F. and playing coal gas across its face. The heat broke up the gas and deposited carbon on the face, which was then ingested into the armour to form a hard skin. This process took some three weeks to complete, but the result was stronger than Harvey steel. Chromium and manganese were also added

to nickel steel, both increasing the hardness of the face of the armour and the toughness and elasticity of its back; all major navies of the world adopted it. Harvey, Krupp, Armstrong in Britain, and Creusot in France all experimented with combinations of nickel, carbon, chromium, and manganese in their steel to produce ever more effective rolled armour-plate that also yielded savings in weight and thickness.[48]

ARMOUR-PIERCING SHELLS

In the race between guns and armour, naval ordnance experts simultaneously developed armour-piercing projectiles as the answer to armoured warships. In 1881 Hadfield of Sheffield began manufacturing cast-steel projectiles. In 1885 that firm patented a 'Compound Armour Piercing Shell'. As with compound armour, this combined a hardened steel point and a resilient body; a completely hardened shell would shatter on impact. Other types of hardened shells followed, including one of chrome steel. But most broke up on contact with the new armour.[49]

In 1878, Captain English of the Royal Engineers discovered, while testing shells and armour at Woolwich Arsenal, the idea of capping the tip of the projectile. A number of shells had broken up when fired against steel plate; then, by accident, a 2.5-inch iron plate was left in front of a steel armour plate. A 9-inch Palliser shell passed through the iron plate and penetrated 13 inches into the steel-faced plate. English then proposed making a shot with a wrought-iron cap of approximately the thickness of the plate the shell had passed through. When this was done and the shell was fired, it went entirely through the compound armour. Strangely, nothing was done to exploit this discovery and it was left to the Russian Admiral S.O. Makarov to reinvent the capped projectile in 1890.

The cap received the full shock of the initial impact and distributed it over the length of the shell; it also lengthened the time in which the shock was distributed to the shell; and it acted as a support for the point at the beginning of penetration, softening the plate slightly so as to give the point a better opportunity for penetration. The US Navy came up with the Johnson capped shell. The French improved on this in their 1896 Holtzer cap. In spite of evidence of the success of the capped shell the Royal Navy resisted adopting it until 1905.[50]

Explosive fillers

Until the early 1890s armour-piercing (AP) projectiles were inert. The use of an explosive filler in the Palliser shells was soon abandoned. AP shells were fired at such high velocities that there was real danger of the powder filler exploding when the shell was fired. The AP projectile reverted to solid shot only, as it had been in the American Civil War, effecting its damage by kinetic energy only.

In 1895, however, the Wheeling-Sterling Company of America introduced a 'Semi-Armour-Piercing' shell. It had a fuse and small explosive equal to only about 5 per cent of the shell's weight. The idea was for the shell to pass through the target armour and then explode. In 1903 the Firth-Stirling Company produced its 'Rendable' shell. With a bursting charge of 2.5 per cent and ability to pass through its own calibre in steel armour, it was soon adopted by the Royal Navy. Trinitrotoluene (TNT) and other new explosive fillers reduced the possibility of the charge exploding when the shell was fired; they also increased the shell's explosive effect.[51]

CHANGES IN ORDNANCE DESIGN

This was also a period of great change in ordnance design. As noted above, the Royal Navy 'Majestic'-class battleships utilized a new wire-wound 12-inch gun. Manufactured in stages, the main, inner barrel was bound with layers of steel wire, the number of layers depending on the size and type of gun. The barrel was then encased in steel outer tubes. Wire-wound guns were much stronger than earlier designs.[52]

Dynamite gun

Among the more remarkable naval ordnance experiments in this period was the so-called 'dynamite gun', which hurled its projectile by compressed air. In 1882 D.M. Mefford in the United States patented a compressed-air gun 'for discharging projectiles filled with dynamite or other detonating powders'. The idea was to provide a less jarring initial shock for the projectile to enable it to have a dynamite filler. In 1884 Mefford demonstrated a 2-inch calibre gun made from brass tubing. It fired a 5-lb solid shot for half a mile, where it penetrated 26 inches into a concrete target. Mefford believed some redesign of the gun was necessary, but before he could do so, G.H. Reynolds patented a design more or less after Mefford's but sufficiently different to avoid patent infringement. US Army lieutenant E.L. Zalinski, present at the Mefford trial, now resigned from the service and teamed up with Reynolds to form the Pneumatic Dynamite Gun Company.

Eventually the company produced a 15-inch calibre smoothbore gun that fired a variety of dynamite-filled projectiles, from 12-inch, 966 lbs to 8-inch, 298 lbs. The smaller projectiles had wooden sleeves to bring them up to the gun calibre. The projectiles also had fins to aid in stability in flight. In 1890 the US government purchased a number of these guns for coast defence purposes, and the Navy fitted three aboard the *Vesuvius*. They were at a fixed angle on the fore deck and were

Vesuvius, US Navy 'dynamite cruiser' (note compressed-air guns forward). (*Naval Historical Foundation, NH 69214*)

aimed by turning the ship. Range was regulated by the amount of air pressure on the shell. The chief problem lay in all the necessary compressing equipment, which left little room for anything else aboard the ship.

The only use of this weapon in battle came during the Spanish-American War, when the 'dynamite cruiser' *Vesuvius* shelled Morro Castle in Cuba, but without significant effect. The dynamite gun's chief failing was its relatively short range. Advances in slower burning gunpowder that produced longer pressure on the projectile quickly brought its eclipse.[53]

Other innovations

The threat of underwater attack during fog or at night caused concern in all navies and led to the compartmentalization of ship hulls and double-bottomed hulls for greater security. The loss of the Chilean ironclad *Blanco Encalada* to a Whitehead torpedo on 23 April 1891, intensified the search for better quick-firing guns to protect against torpedo boat attack. Although she was armed with 6 × 6-pounder quick-firing Hotchkiss guns capable of firing 25–30 rounds a minute, the *Blanco Encalada* had been successfully attacked by two torpedo boats.[54]

Before this period, work had already begun, particularly in the British and American navies, on improving long-range fire control. Technological advances included optical range-finders and telescopic gun sights. In 1905 both the Russian and Japanese navies fought the Battle of Tsushima with identical British-built Barr and Stroud optical range-finders. These allowed them to fight at 5,000-yards range, which in a few years would be considered almost point-blank. New gun carriages also appeared, incorporating hydraulic recoil control.[55]

CHAPTER 9

THE *DREADNOUGHT* ERA, 1906–14

Mahan's theory that the big gun always wins seemed borne out in the 1905 Battle of Tsushima, the only example of a decisive fleet engagement between modern battleships in history. The battleships that fought at Tsushima on 27 May 1905 were about to be obsolete, however. Even before that battle, improvements in torpedoes had led navies to experiment with longer gun ranges. In 1899 the Royal Navy had initiated firing at up to 6,000 yards, approximately the limit at Tsushima. Its experiments revealed that the most effective way of firing at such long range was in salvo, that is a number of guns firing together. Covering a small area with shells greatly increased the possibility of a hit; and if the guns were correctly sighted the shells straddled their target.

In 1903–04 the British carried out gunnery experiments with the battleships *Venerable* and *Victorious*. Leading experts such as Royal Marine captain Edward Harding argued that better methods of directing and controlling gunfire, and the flatter trajectory of the 12-inch heavy gun and improvements in its rate of fire, had doomed the 6-inch quick-firing gun as a major weapon for capital ships. Future engagements would simply be beyond its effective range. Battleships and heavy cruisers should rely on a main armament solely of 12-inch guns.[1]

During this period British naval superiority was threatened by heavy outlays for new warships by France and Russia, and by Germany's construction of a powerful battle fleet. To keep pace Britain dramatically increased its own spending on construction. The budget figure for 1904 was more than twice that of 1889, and by 1904 Britain had reached financial crisis. That October Admiral John A. Fisher, who had made known his willingness to economize, was appointed First Sea Lord.[2]

FISHER'S NAVAL REVOLUTION

A visionary and radical innovator but irascible and outrageous, 'Jackie' Fisher was famous for his 'three R's: Ruthless, Relentless, Remorseless'.[3] Under his domination the leisurely ways of the old Royal Navy disappeared. Supported by enthusiastic young reformers, Fisher radically transformed the Royal Navy and brought it into the new era.

Fiscal pressures alone might have led Fisher to seek a radical alternative to the steady expansion of Britain's battle fleet and her armoured cruiser squadrons. But there were other reasons for him to consider such a course. Fisher saw the submarine as a serious threat to troop transports and to the relatively slow formations of battleships. New and more effective armour-piercing

Dreadnought, Royal Navy super battleship. (*Royal Naval Museum, 1990/180 (15)*)

shells were another threat, even to the largest warships. Fisher's answer was new and more heavily gunned armoured cruisers, what in effect became the new battle-cruiser class. Fast and manoeuvrable, they could operate in flotillas and respond quickly to any threat. Their high speed minimized the threat of torpedo attack. Convinced of the fiscal and operational need for such a change, Fisher immediately advocated replacement of the battleship and armoured cruiser by the new battle-cruiser, while at the same time urging additional spending on and development of submarines to go after soft targets such as troop ships and thus eliminate the threat of invasion. It is somewhat ironic that Fisher's name is forever linked to the construction of a new super battleship. According to historian Jon Sumida, Fisher not only opposed the *Dreadnought*'s construction but fought unsuccessfully to halt construction of additional ships of this type.[4]

Dreadnought

The new super battleship *Dreadnought* was the Admiralty's answer to Tirpitz's massive increase in German battleship strength. This all-big-gun capital ship revolutionized ship design and made obsolete every other battleship in the world, including those of Britain itself. Up to this time all battleships had mixed armaments to deal with opponents at varying ranges. The Japanese *Mikasa*, completed in Britain in 1902 and rated at the time by the editor of *Jane's Fighting Ships* as the biggest and most powerful vessel in the world, had 4 × 12-inch guns in two turrets, but also 14 × 6-inch and 20 × 3-inch guns to deal with torpedo boats. These would enable her to fight at close, intermediate, and long range.[5]

But the Battle of Tsushima confirmed the belief of many experts that mixed battery battleships were less efficient than those with a single calibre broadsides. Although quick-firing smaller guns had exacted a toll in the later close-range fighting, it was the 12-inch guns fired at long range that were the true ship destroyers and had decided the battle's outcome. One battleship mounting ten 12-inch guns would be the mathematical equivalent of 2.5 *Mikasa*s. With central gunnery control and presenting less of a target, she might even be the equivalent of four or five.

It appeared not to be in Britain's interest to introduce the all-big-gun ship and throw aside the advantages of her vast existing fleet. But Britain had little choice. Other powers were already contemplating such a ship. In the 1903 edition of *Jane's Fighting Ships* Italian Naval Architect Colonel Vittorio Cuniberti had written an article

entitled: 'An Ideal Battleship for the British Navy.' In it he had called for a ship with, 'very high speed – superior to that of any existing battleship afloat . . . with medium calibres abolished – so effectively protected as to be able to disregard entirely all the subsidiary armament of an enemy, and armed only with twelve pieces of 12-inch'.[6]

Soon Cuniberti was working on such a ship. In the United States Commander H. C. Poundstone attracted the attention of President Theodore Roosevelt with a 1901 paper touting the advantages of an all big-gun ship. The idea was also discussed by navy gunnery experts in the US Naval Institute *Proceedings*. With the Bureau of Construction supporting the idea, in March

Mikasa, Japanese battleship, shown following restoration as a Japanese national monument in 1960. (*Naval Historical Foundation, NH 44621*)

1905 the US Congress authorized building two such ships, the *South Carolina* and *Michigan*. Russia, Germany, and Japan were also considering such a vessel.[7]

In March 1905 the Board of Admiralty approved plans for both a new battleship and a new armoured cruiser with all-big gun armament. One of Fisher's favourite expressions was *totus porcus* (whole hog), and he went furiously at building the new ship. The design called for a ship of 18,000 tons with 10 × 12-inch guns mounted in five turrets. All materials were collected in advance, some scavenged from other ships then building, and nothing was allowed to delay her construction.

The new super battleship was laid down at Portsmouth on 2 October 1905. Completed with astonishing speed on 2 October 1906, she displaced 17,900 tons and was 490 (527 overall) × 82 feet. She was the first all-big gun, turbine-powered fast battleship. Her new lighter and more durable turbines drove the *Dreadnought* at 21 knots, 2 knots faster than her nearest competitor. Her 10 × 12-inch guns could all be centrally controlled and aimed at a single target. She also had 27 × 12-pounders and some smaller guns to deal with the threat of torpedo boats; and she mounted 5 × 18-inch torpedo tubes (four in broadside and one in her stern). Twelve of the 12-pounder guns were mounted on the superstructure, two were on the top of each turret, and two were on the quarterdeck. She had 11-inch steel plate below the waterline and an 8-inch belt above it. Bow and stern were protected with 6- and 4-inch armour respectively.[8]

The *Dreadnought* was not without her critics. Among them was A. T. Mahan. He claimed that Tsushima had been decided by the smaller 6- and 9-inch guns, with their 'rain of fire'. Indeed, thanks to Tsushima, a secondary battery of smaller guns returned to succeeding dreadnoughts.[9]

In the short run, construction of a brand new super ship enabled Britain to reduce her own naval construction and realize some financial savings. But such advantage was short-lived. Other powers built their own dreadnoughts, but Britain relied on its technological lead to provide more years of naval superiority, and on its greater ship-building resources to keep ahead. Indeed it was not until 1910 that most of Britain's competitors had completed their own super battleships, and by that time the Royal Navy was already working on a new generation of dreadnoughts.

The Royal Navy followed the *Dreadnought* with two three-ship classes: the 'Bellerophon' and 'St Vincent', beginning in 1906 and 1908 respectively. Although slightly larger – the *Bellerophon* was 18,600 tons and 490 (526 total) × 82.5 feet, and the *St Vincent* was 19,250 tons and 500 (536) × 84 feet – they were essentially the same design as the *Dreadnought*, although the 27 × 12-pounders were replaced with 16 × 4-inch guns on the 'Bellerophon' class and 20 of the same size on the 'St Vincents'. The *Bellerophon* was also the first with anti-torpedo bulkheads.

In 1908 another German naval law accelerated the retirement of old warships and authorized construction of four dreadnoughts yearly from 1908 to 1911 and two yearly from 1912 to 1917. When in 1908 the British attempted to reach some naval agreement with Germany, Wilhelm II indignantly declared that he would fight before he accepted dictation from a foreign government. In consequence Great Britain was thrown into what was known as the 'naval panic of 1909', when she accelerated her dreadnought construction. That year the *Neptune* was laid down; larger than her predecessors at 19,900 tons and 510 × 85 feet, she copied the American innovation of superfiring turrets.[10]

Super dreadnoughts

During the dreadnought and battle-cruiser construction race the British managed to keep well ahead. One of Fisher's maxims was, 'Build few and build fast, each one better than the last.'[11] By the end of 1911 the Royal Navy had in service 10 dreadnoughts of five continuously improved classes and four battle-cruisers of two classes. A second generation, known as 'super dreadnoughts', was also under construction. Completed in 1910–11, the four 'Orion' class 22,200-ton super dreadnoughts mounted 10×13.5-inch and 16×4-inch guns. Four 'King George V'-class ships (*King George V, Centurion, Ajax,* and *Audacious*) followed during 1911-13. At 23,000 tons they had the same armament as the 'Orion's. The last class of super dreadnoughts completed before the First World War was the four-ship Iron Duke-class ships – *Iron Duke, Benbow, Emperor of India,* and *Marlborough* – completed during 1912–13. Displacing 25,000 tons, they mounted 10×13.5 inch and 12×6-inch guns. There were also two sequestered super dreadnoughts: the 23,000-ton *Erin* (ex-*Reshadieh*, built for Turkey), laid down in 1911 and mounting 10×13.5-inch guns; and the *Canada* (ex-*Almirante Latorre*, built for Chile), of 28,000 tons with 10×14-inch guns.[12]

The largest super dreadnoughts before the First World War, although they did not actually join the fleet until 1915, were the five Royal Navy super dreadnoughts of the 'Queen Elizabeth' class of 1912–13: the *Queen Elizabeth, Warspite, Valiant, Barham,*

Queen Elizabeth, Royal Navy super dreadnought. (*Royal Naval Museum, 1985/64 (4)*)

and *Malaya*. Displacing 27,500 tons, they were 600 (645 overall) × 90.5 feet and capable of 24-knot speed. Originally to mount 13.5-inch guns, but because the Japanese and Americans were moving to larger guns they mounted 8 × 15-inchers in two superfiring turrets fore and aft. They also carried 12 × 6-inch guns as well as 2 × 3-inch anti-aircraft guns, 4 × 3-pounders, five machine guns, and 4 × 21-inch broadside torpedo tubes. They were protected by a belt of 13-inch armour and had 25-knot speed. The 'Queen Elizabeth'-class ships were also the first battleships to run on oil rather than coal.[13]

The German response

As the Admiralty had hoped, the *Dreadnought* upset German plans. Not only had the Germans already laid the keels for a number of mixed-armament battleships, but the new, larger dreadnought-type ships would require the Kiel Canal to be widened, an expensive undertaking. Germany's response to the *Dreadnought* did not come until the summer of 1907, when it laid down the *Nassau*. Completed in 1908, she was the first of four of her class, which included *Westfallen*, *Posen*, and *Rheinland*. These 18,900-ton ships mounted 12 × 11-inch guns along with 12 × 150-mm (5.9-inch) guns. But only two of the turrets were on the centre line as opposed to three for the *Dreadnought*, so the broadside firepower of the British ship was considerably greater. In 1908 Germany laid down four 22,400-ton 'Helgoland'-class ships (*Helgoland*, *Thüringen*, *Ostfriesland*, and *Oldenburg*) of 22,800 tons displacement and completed during 1909–10. They mounted 12 × 12-inch guns as well as 14 × 5.9-inch.

Kaiser

In 1909–10 the Germans laid down a new class of dreadnought. Completed in 1911, the *Kaiser* was the first of a new type of dreadnought that would eventually develop into the *Bismarck* and *Tirpitz* of the Second World War. The Germans built five of this class, completed during 1911–12: the *Kaiser*, *Friedrich der Grosse*, *Kaiserin*, *König Albert I*, and *Prinzregent Luitpold*. They were 24,700 tons and 564 × 95.25 feet. Their engines developed 31,000 hp, driving the ships at 23.5 knots. They had a 14-inch armour belt and their main armament was 10 × 12-inch guns, mounted two each in one turret forward and two aft, and in two diagonally offset wing turrets. Secondary armament consisted of 14 × 5.9-inch guns.

The 'Kaiser'-class ships were followed by four 25,390-ton 'König'-class: *König*, *Kron Prinz*, *Grosser Kurfürst*, and *Markgraf*. Completed in 1913, they displaced 25,500 tons and had 10 × 12-inch guns along with 14 × 5.9-inch, 12 × 24-pounders, 4 × 14-pounder anti-aircraft guns, and four broadside torpedo tubes.[14]

Although British and German dreadnoughts were approximately the same in displacement tonnage the British dreadnoughts mounted larger guns and the ships themselves were somewhat larger in size. German dreadnoughts were also slower reciprocating-engine ships. The weight difference is explained in additional features of survivability that the Germans built into their ships, something in which they excelled. The Germans designed their capital ships chiefly for service in the North Sea, and so did not have to build with the need to accommodate crews at sea for prolonged periods; when in port German crews were generally housed ashore. Tirpitz was able to use this savings in weight and space for armour and improved compartmentalization. The Germans paid great attention to having their ships survive a hit below the waterline, and toward that end their ships were divided by many watertight bulkheads. As Tirpitz put it,

The whole part of the ship below the waterline was designed to provide for failure to localize the effects of the explosion or for several hits being made . . . endless labour was expended upon details such as the pumping system or the possibility of speedily counteracting a list by flooding corresponding compartments.[15]

The German answer to the 'Queen Elizabeth'-class came late in the First World War in two ships: the *Baden* and *Bayern*. Displacing 28,000 tons each, they were 623 feet 4 inches × 90 feet 9 inches and had 22-knot speed. Each mounted a main battery of 8 × 15-inch centre line guns. Two of the turrets were superfiring. Their secondary batteries included 16 × 5.9-inch guns as well as anti-aircraft protection and torpedo tubes.[16]

US dreadnoughts

Parallel to the *Dreadnought*, but independent of her, were the first US dreadnoughts. Actually authorized in March 1905 before the *Dreadnought*, the *South Carolina* and the *Michigan* were completed in 1908, well after the British ship. Their proponents, including President Theodore Roosevelt, stressed the advantages of a single size battery in homogeneity of ammunition supply and ability to move men from disengaged guns to replace wounded crews elsewhere. The 'South Carolinas' introduced the superfiring (superimposed) main battery in battleship design; their second and third turrets were higher than the first and fourth and could fire over them. This provided a better protected broadside on about 3,000 tons less displacement than her British counterpart. Chief Constructor Washington Capps saw the primary objective of battleships as broadsides fire and the individual ship as an element of a larger fleet; fleet action was synonymous with broadsides fire. This led Capps to the superfiring main battery, which became the international standard. Capps held that all main battery guns must be located on the centerline if they were to fire in broadsides. Superfiring was essential to conserve length and volume, and, since Congress had mandated only 16,000-ton ships, the 'South Carolinas' were little bigger than their predecessor, *Connecticut*. But this meant their armament was less than the *Dreadnought*, 8 × 12-inch guns plus a secondary armament that included 14 × 3-inch guns. These first two American dreadnoughts, while slow at 19 knots, were nonetheless well-designed ships.[17]

Other US dreadnoughts soon followed. In fact, after Britain and Germany, the United States built the most dreadnoughts. The tonnage limit was lifted with the next class. The 'Delaware's (*Delaware* and *North Dakota*) laid down in 1907, weighed 20,000 tons and were 510 × 85.25 feet. In 1909 the 'Utah'-class (*Utah* and *Florida*) was laid down. Completed a year later, these 21,812-ton ships were 510 × 86.25 feet. They mounted 10 × 12-inch and 12 × 5-inch guns. Size grew substantially with the 'Arkansas' class (*Arkansas* and *Wyoming*). Laid down in 1910 and completed a year later, they displaced 26,000 tons each, were 554 × 93.25 feet in size, and mounted 12 × 12-inch and 16 × 5-inch guns. In 1911 the United States laid down its first super dreadnoughts, the two 'Texas'-class ships. The first US dreadnoughts to carry 14-inch guns, the *Texas* and *New York* were 565 × 95.25 feet and displaced 27,000 tons. They mounted 10 × 14-inch and 16 × 5-inch guns. The *Texas*, now serving as a Texas state memorial, is the only example of a World War I dreadnought surviving.

Two 'Nevada'-class super dreadnoughts (*Nevada* and *Oklahoma*) completed in 1914, were 27,500 tons and 575 × 95.25 feet.

Armed with 10 × 14-inch and 12 × 5-inch guns, they had a speed of 21 knots. Their number one and number four turrets had three guns each; numbers two and three – the two superimposed turrets – had two guns each. These ships also incorporated 'all or nothing armour', that is, heavy armour protection in the armour belt, turrets and their trunks, conning tower, and little elsewhere. This system was soon adopted by many other countries.

The last pre-war US super dreadnoughts were two 'Pennsylvania'-class ships. The *Pennsylvania* and *Arizona* were considerably larger than their predecessors – 31,400 tons and 600 × 97 feet. They carried 12 × 14-inch guns, three to a turret, as well as 14 × 5-inch guns. The United States laid down five other super dreadnoughts during the First World War.[18]

France

Other countries also built dreadnoughts. For many years the second largest naval power, France had to shift attention to meet the threat posed by the German Army on land, but in 1907 it laid down six 'Danton'-class battleships, sometimes called 'semi-dreadnoughts' (also *cuirassés d'escadre*). All were completed in 1909. They were the *Danton, Mirabeau, Diderot, Condorcet, Verginaud,* and *Voltaire.* At 18,400 tons they were 475.75 × 84.75 feet. They had some more modern features but retained the pre-dreadnought armament mix of 4 × 12-inch and 12 × 9.4-inch guns, and smaller guns and torpedoes. The first French dreadnoughts were laid down only in 1910 and completed in 1911–12. These were the four 23,120-ton 'Courbet'-class ships: the *Courbet, Jean Bart, Paris,* and *France.* They mounted 12 × 12-inch guns and 22 × 5.5-inch. In 1912 three 23,000-ton 'Bretagne'-class ships were laid down, the *Bretagne, Lorraine,* and *Provence.* All completed the

next year, they had 10 × 13.4-inch guns along with 22 × 5.5-inch. Five 'Normandie'-class dreadnoughts, laid down in 1913–14, were never completed.[19]

Other nations

Russia was more strained financially than the other major powers. It had to rebuild its navy after the disastrous Russo-Japanese War of 1904–05 and to maintain a large army. Russia was also carrying out major industrial expansion. In 1909 it laid down four 23,400-ton 'Gangut'-class battleships. Carrying 10 × 12-inch guns, these ships were quite fast at 23 knots.[20]

In 1909 Italy laid down the 19,500-ton *Dante Aligheri* with 12 × 12-inch guns. Completed the next year and weighing 20,500 tons, she was the first capital ship to mount her main guns three to a turret. She was followed in 1910 by three 'Conte di Cavour'-class ships of 22,000 tons, and in 1912 by two 'Andrea Doria'-class dreadnoughts. The *Andrea Doria* and the *Caio Duilio* were completed in 1913. They had an unusual turret arrangement: numbers one and five turrets had three guns each. Superimposed numbers two and four turrets had two guns each. The third turret, with three guns, was located amidships.

Beginning in 1907 Austria-Hungary laid down three 24,500-ton 'Radetsky'-class pre-dreadnoughts with only 4 × 12-inch guns. Not until 1910 did it lay down its first dreadnoughts, the four 20,000-ton 'Tegetthoff'-class ships with 12 × 12-inch guns.[21]

Japan's first dreadnought was the 21,420-ton, 500 feet × 84 feet 2 inch *Settsu.* Laid down in 1909, she was completed two years later. She mounted 12 × 12-inch guns as well as a secondary armament of 10 × 6-inchers. The main battery guns were in an unusual arrangement of two guns each in six turrets:

'Danton'-class, French dreadnought. (*Imperial War Museum, Q22267*)

Jean Bart, French dreadnought, September 1913. (*US Naval Institute*)

two fore and aft and two each amidships to port and starboard.

In 1912–13 Japan laid down two super dreadnoughts: the *Fu-so* (1914) and *Yamashiro* (1915). They displaced 30,600 tons, were 630 × 94 feet and carried a main, centre line armament of 12 × 14-inch guns and a secondary armament that included 16 × 6-inchers. On their trials they reached speeds of nearly 25 knots. Japan built other battleships during the First World War and, in 1919, it was the first nation to have battleships mounting 16-inch guns, the 'Nagato' class.[22]

Other nations also built battleships during this period. For a time Argentina, Brazil, and Chile carried on an arms race that included purchase of capital ships abroad. Britain sequestered both Chilean and Turkish dreadnoughts on the eve of the First World War. The Scandinavian states also built smaller coastal battleships.

THE BATTLE-CRUISER

Fisher, as has been noted, regarded the *Dreadnought* as an 'Old Testament' ship.[23] His chief interest was in a new class of heavy cruisers that incorporated the dreadnought principles of higher speed, greater armament, and bigger size. The new ships had battleship armament on a high-speed cruiser hull. For Fisher speed and firepower were everything. He reasoned that this new ship type, known first as the battleship cruiser and then as the battle cruiser, would be able to use her superior speed to keep a range sufficient to avoid enemy torpedoes and gunfire, while at the same time relying on larger guns and enhanced gunnery equipment to hit her opponent before she could be struck in return.[24]

Invincible

The first three British battle-cruisers, the *Invincible*, *Inflexible*, and *Indomitable*, were authorized in 1905 and completed in 1907. Displacing 17,250 tons and 550 feet (567 feet overall) × 78 feet 8.5 inches, the *Invincible* had a main battery of 8 × 12-inch guns. The turrets forward and aft were on the centre line. The other two turrets were offset: number two turret was to port and number three was to starboard. The secondary battery included 12 × 4-inch guns.[25]

New turbines of unprecedented power allowed the battle-cruisers to sustain speeds of up to 27 knots. The *Invincible* was misnamed. She blew up early in the 1916 Battle of Jutland. With her 8 × 12-inch guns, the *Invincible* had only two less guns than the *Dreadnought*. The standard armoured cruiser had 12 × 8-inch guns, whereas the new battle-cruiser had just the reverse. But an 8-inch shell weighed only 250 lbs, whereas a 12-inch shell weighed 886 lbs and was fired at greater range. The battle-cruisers could also outrun the 22–23-knot armoured cruisers. Again it was the principle of what the battle-cruiser could not destroy she could outrun. The proof of the superiority of the new design was shown in the Battle of the Falkland Islands in December 1914.

The flaw in the design was the sacrifice for speed of armour protection to resist battleship shells. Whereas the *Dreadnought* had an 11-inch armour belt, the 'Invincible's had only 6 inches. The battle-cruiser had battleship guns but could not stand against them; but because of their guns the tendency was to place the battle-cruisers, as at Jutland, in a pitched fleet engagement against battleships.

British battle-cruisers also suffered from serious design flaws: the lack of sufficient armour on the top of the turrets and poor fire control. These shortcomings became all too apparent at Jutland. Fisher had understood the vulnerability of the battle-cruiser, but he believed that their long-range heavy firepower and high speed and mobility would enable them to destroy their opponents first.[26]

In 1909 Fisher supported the demand by the Conservative Party for six new British capital ships to meet the threat posed by new German construction; ultimately the Liberals increased this to eight new capital ships. Fisher wanted this construction all in battle-cruisers. With the four then built or building, this would give a total of 10, two more than the eight dreadnoughts ordered thus far. Fisher believed that battle-cruisers could best deal with the threat posed both by new German battleships and French armoured cruisers. But following the 1904 *Entente Cordiale* France was an ally, and the Russian threat was erased in the Battle of Tsushima. This left only Germany, and she had few armoured cruisers. The Admiralty decided, therefore, to press ahead with more dreadnoughts and build only a few

'Invincibles' as a fast squadron. It insisted that six of the eight new capital ships be dreadnoughts, in effect killing Fisher's plan to shift the balance of Royal Navy capital ships to battle-cruisers.[27]

In 1909 three smaller battle-cruisers were begun: the *Indefatigable*, *New Zealand*, and *Australia*. These 18,800-ton ships had virtually the same battery as the 'Invincibles': 8 × 12-inch guns in the main battery and 10 × 4-inch guns in the secondary battery. The 'Indefatigables' had an unusual turret arrangement. Numbers one and four were in standard position fore and aft. Number two turret was to port amidships, and number three was to starboard but with its guns across deck and facing to port for broadsides fire but with limited traverse.[28]

The equivalents of the super dreadnoughts among the battle-cruisers were the 'Lion'-class ships. Laid down in 1909, the *Lion* (1910) and the *Princess Royal*

Lion, Royal Navy super battle cruiser, 1903. (*Imperial War Museum, SP510*)

Achilles, Royal Navy armoured cruiser. (*Imperial War Museum, Q20910*)

(1911) displaced 26,350 tons and were 660 (700 total) × 88.5 feet. They mounted 8 × 13.5-inch guns in four centre-line turrets: two forward (number two was superimposed), number three amidships, and number four aft. Their secondary armament included 16 × 4-inch guns. Two other British super dreadnoughts were the *Queen Mary* (1912) of 27,500 tons with 8 × 13.5-inch and 16 × 4-inch guns and the *Tiger* (1913) at 28,500 tons, with the same main armament. These two ships also carried a heavier, 9-inch armour belt. Other British battle cruisers were laid down during the First World War.[29]

Fisher resigned in 1910. The next year Winston Churchill, an ally of Fisher, became First Lord of the Admiralty (in October, after Britain went to war, Churchill engineered Fisher's return as First Sea Lord). Just before the war, in a secret move, Churchill shifted some money from new battleship construction to submarines. The Admiralty believed that if Germany assumed the British were concentrating on dreadnoughts it would continue with its own, which might then fall prey in the North Sea to large numbers of improved British submarines.[30]

Clearly the intention was to use the battle-cruisers to destroy enemy armoured cruisers, either in a fleet action or as raiders. This first premise was best demonstrated during the 8 December 1914, Battle of the Falklands when the *Invincible* and *Inflexible* used their superior speed to overtake the German armoured cruisers *Scharnhorst* and *Gneisenau* and then employed their longer-range guns to destroy the German ships.[31]

German battle-cruisers

As with the *Dreadnought*, the German response to the *Invincible* was delayed. The first German battle-cruiser was the *Von der Tann*, laid down in 1907 and completed in 1909. She displaced 19,400 tons, was 561 × 85 feet, and mounted 8 × 11-inch guns as main armament as well as 10 × 6-inch guns and 16 × 24-pounders, and 4 × 18-inch torpedo tubes.[32]

In 1909 Germany laid down two 'Moltke'-class battle-cruisers, the *Moltke* (1910) and the *Goeben* (1911). Displacing 23,000 tons and 610 feet × 96 feet 9 inches in size, these ships were armed with 10 × 11-inch guns as well as 12 × 6-inch, 12 × 24-pounders, and 4 × 20-inch torpedo tubes. The *Goeben* was one of the most famous ships of the First World War. In August 1914 she was the fastest ship in the Mediterranean. Supposedly turned over to Turkey and renamed the *Yavuz Sultan Selim*, she retained her entire German crew. Without the *Goeben* at Constantinople and her later activities in the Black Sea, Turkey might not have entered the war on the German side.[33]

In 1911 Germany laid down the *Seydlitz*. Completed the next year, she was 25,000 tons and 656 feet × 93 feet 4 inches. She mounted 10 × 11-inch guns. Her secondary battery included 12 × 6-inchers and a like number of 24-pounders. The *Seydlitz* also had an 11-inch armour belt. In 1912 Germany introduced the 12-inch gun in its 'Derflinger'-class battle-cruisers: *Derflinger* (1913), *Lützow* (1913), and *Hindenburg* (1914). These 28,000-ton ships mounted 8 × 12-inch guns as their main armament. Secondary armament was the same as the *Seydlitz*.[34]

German battle-cruisers carried smaller guns but had a number of advantages including heavier armour protection. The 'Moltke'-class ships, for example, had 10-inch belt armour versus only 6 inches on the Invincibles. The German ships also had better range-finding equipment, superior fire-control, and improved compartmentalization. The German Navy also had better shells. British armour-piercing shells did not penetrate well and tended to break up on contact. The only real weakness in the German battle-cruisers was that their bow sections were not as well compartmentalized as those of the rest of the ships.

Japanese battle-cruisers

Only three navies – Britain, Germany, and Japan – built battle-cruisers. Japan's decision in 1905 to build two heavy 'Tsukuba'-class, 13,800-ton, 450 × 75 foot, armoured cruisers, each mounting 4 × 12-inchers guns, 12 × 4.75-inch and 2 × 14-pounders, with a rated speed of 22 knots, prompted design changes in the initial British battle-cruisers. In 1905 Japan laid down two 'Ibuki'-class battle-cruisers and in 1911 four 27,500 'Kongo' class: *Kongo* (1912), *Hi-Yei* (1912), *Haruna* (1913), and *Kirishima* (1913). They mounted 8 × 14-inch guns and 16 × 6-inchers.[35]

In 1916 the United States announced plans to build six battle-cruisers, but these were not begun until 1920 and then they fell victim to the Washington Treaty of 1922. Only two were completed, but as the aircraft carriers *Lexington* and *Saratoga*. In the 1930s there would be a revival of battle-cruisers; the United States built the *Alaska* and *Guam*, finished in 1944; Germany built the *Scharnhorst* and *Gneisenau*; and France built the *Dunkerque* and *Strasbourg*.

Cruisers

The appearance of the battle-cruiser with its heavier, long-range guns and higher speed made the old armoured/first-class cruiser obsolete. No longer capable of standing in the main battle line, armoured cruisers

Tsukuba, Japanese cruiser. (*Imperial War Museum, Q33423*)

suffered grievously in the First World War battles such as the Falklands, the Dogger Bank, and Jutland. Some nations retarded or suspended cruiser construction; the United States and France halted it altogether. Russia laid down 10 small cruisers in 1913 but completed only two of them during the war. During 1909–12 Japan completed four smaller cruisers in the 4,100–5,000-ton range; the largest mounted 8×6-inch guns as its main battery.[36]

Fisher opposed cruiser construction, believing that battle-cruisers had rendered the armoured/first-class cruisers obsolete, and that those tasks previously assigned to second-, and third-class/light cruisers could be handled by the large 1,825-ton, 345 feet $\times$ 34 feet 2 inch 'Swift'-class destroyer flotilla leaders, with their 4×4-inch guns. The Admiralty did not agree and, following

Fisher's departure as First Sea Lord, the Royal Navy resumed cruiser construction.

Before the First World War the Royal Navy built a large number of light cruisers: five 'Bristol'-class, four 'Weymouth'-class, six 'Chatham'-class, seven 'Boadicea'-class, and eight 'Arethusa'-class. The first three classes were 4,800–5,440 tons and 430 feet. The 'Bristol's carried only 2×6-inch and 10×4-inch guns; the 'Weymouth's and 'Chatham's mounted a main armament of eight or nine 6-inch guns. The 'Boadicea'-class scout cruisers were only 3,300 tons, 385 $\times$ 41 feet, and mounted 10×4-inch guns. The 'Arethusa'-class scout cruisers were 410 $\times$ 39 feet and 3,500 tons. They mounted $3 \times$ 6-inch and 4×4-inch guns.[37]

In January 1913 the Royal Navy redesignated its cruiser classification system. All first-class and armoured cruisers were

Gneisenau, German armoured cruiser. (*Imperial War Museum, Q22307*)

henceforth known simply as cruisers, and all second-, and third-class cruisers were known as light cruisers. Other countries also adopted this commonsense system, which continued through the 1950s.[38]

Germany also built cruisers, although not nearly as many as Britain. *Scharnhorst* and *Gneisnau*, both completed in 1906, displaced 11,600 tons, were armed with 8 × 8.2-inch and 6 × 6-inch guns, and were well protected by 6-inch Krupp armour. The largest armoured cruiser was the 15,000-ton *Blücher* of 1908. Armed with 12 × 8.2-inch and 8 × 6-inch guns she was capable of 25 knots. In the 24 January 1915, Battle of the Dogger Bank, nevertheless, the *Blücher* was slower than the German battle-cruisers and took an incredible pounding by British 13.5-inch and 12-inch shells before she finally succumbed to torpedoes. The *Blücher* was

evidence of the German ability to build strong ships; before sinking, she took perhaps 70 shell hits and 7 torpedoes. Of her complement of 1,026 men, 792 were lost. Germany also completed eight light cruisers during 1906–14. These were of 3,470–4,900 tons each; the largest mounted a main battery of 7 × 5.9-inch guns.[39]

Italian naval architect Colonel Cuniberti designed the 'Vittorio Emanuele' class of four armoured cruisers. Almost small battleships, they displaced 12,000 tons, had 21-knot speed, and an armament of 2 × 12-inch and 12 × 8-inch guns, and a 10-inch armoured belt. Cuniberti saved weight by a steel girder-like construction and employing asbestos instead of wood in interior fittings.

Light cruisers contributed to the fleet in the role of scouts. On detached service they could act as commerce raiders. The typical

Blücher, German armoured cruiser. (*Imperial War Museum, Q22315*)

light cruiser of the period just before the First World War was armed with 6- to 3-inch guns, protected only by an armoured deck, and capable of 24- to 26-knot speed. The US Navy 'Chester'-class (*Chester, Birmingham,* and *Salem*) represented this type. All were completed in 1907, were 423 × 47 feet, weighed 3,750 tons, and were turbine powered and coal fuelled. The four-stack cruisers were capable of 25-knot speed, were armed with 4 × 5-inch and 2 × 3-inch guns, and had 2-inch armour. The 'Chester'-class scout cruisers also began the cruiser numbering system in the US Navy. They were designated CS-1 through 3. This system continued through to the *Newport News*, CA-148, in 1949.[40]

The German light cruiser *Emden*, which won notoriety as a commerce raider at the beginning of the First World War, was a powerful ship in her class. Officially known as a 'small protected cruiser' she was 450' × 43.5 feet and displaced 4,200 tons. Armed with 10 × 4.1-inch rapid-fire guns, she had a top speed of 25 knots.[41]

DESTROYERS

By the dreadnought era the destroyer with its guns and torpedoes had entirely replaced the torpedo boat for fleet service. Destroyers became larger and more stable, copying the raised forecastles of the US 'Bainbridge'-class. This change enabled destroyers to operate more effectively with the battle fleet in rough seas. To get maximum value from destroyers, they operated in flotillas. The British had 20 destroyers in each flotilla, divided into five divisions; German flotillas usually had 12 vessels. Destroyer advocates hoped to use two flotillas in tandem. These would use their superior speed to work into position to launch torpedo attacks across the line of advance of an enemy fleet at some 2,000 yards. This would most likely cause the enemy ships to turn away, only to encounter torpedoes launched by the second flotilla on the other quarter.[42]

Defensively, destroyer flotillas provided defence against enemy destroyers and submarines. The turbine engine dramatically increased destroyer speed. By the First World War, 1,000-ton destroyers, armed with new, large heater torpedoes could make 30–35-knots.

Admiral Fisher believed that large destroyers could replace light cruisers. After he became first sea lord the Royal Navy laid down 12 large (up to 1,000 ton) 'Tribal' class (later 'F' class) 'oceangoing destroyers'. Completed by 1909, these were up to 280 × 26 feet and were armed with 2 × 4-inch guns and 2 × 18-inch torpedo tubes. Also completed in 1907 was the oil-fired 1,825-ton destroyer flotilla leader (usually known simply as 'destroyer leader') *Swift*. Capable of up to 39 knots and 345 × 34 feet 2 inches in size, she was armed with 4 × 4 inch guns and 2 × 18-inch torpedo tubes.

'G' to 'L' classes soon followed. In just these classes and three Greek and three Turkish sequestered ships, the Royal Navy added 95 destroyers to the fleet before the war. Eighteen 'M' class destroyers began to enter service at the beginning of the war. The largest of these, the *Mansfield*, weighed 1,057 tons, was 271 × 27 feet, and had a design speed of 35 knots. She was armed with 3 × 4-inch guns, 1 × 2-pounder anti-aircraft guns, and 4 × 21-inch torpedo tubes.[43]

German destroyers

Generally speaking, British destroyers had heavier guns but carried smaller torpedoes than their German counterparts. This was because the primary task of German destroyers, known as *grosse torpedoboote* ('large torpedo boats'), was to attack enemy capital ships. These were some 550–650 tons in displacement and were armed with up to 3 × 3.4-inch guns and 6 × 19.7-inch torpedo tubes.[44]

Other destroyers

The French built mostly smaller destroyers for coastal protection; in fact they were initially known as *torpilleurs de défence mobile* ('mobile

defence torpedo boats'). The *Téméraire* was typical of French destroyers on the eve of the war. Built for Argentina but sequestered after the start of the war, she weighed 950 tons, was 284.5 × 28 feet 3 inches, and was armed with 4 × 4-inch guns and 4 × 18-inch torpedo tubes. She was capable of 32 knots.

Italy also built smaller destroyers, although it also built some larger destroyer leader types. Russia built few destroyers, but had the largest of its day, the 1,200-ton, 336' × 31 feet 2 inches *Novik* of 1912. Armed with 4 × 4-inch guns and 8 × 18-inch torpedo tubes, she could make 36 knots. During the First World War she was used as a mine layer. The Japanese also built some large oceangoing destroyers.

Beginning in 1909 the US Navy launched five 700-ton 'Flusser'-class destroyers. They were followed by 21 'Drayton'-class ships. These were 742 tons, 289' × 26 feet 2 inches, and mounted 5 × 3-inch guns and 6 × 18-inch torpedo tubes. Both these classes were known as 'Flivvers', slang for a cheap automobile. Six 'Cushing' class followed during 1912–14, along with eight 'Aylwin' class in 1913. The latter were unofficially known as 'thousand tonners,' the first US Navy destroyers of that displacement. The *Aylwin* displaced 1,036 tons, was some 300' × 30 feet 4 inches in size, mounted 4 × 4-inch guns and 8 × 18-inch torpedo tubes, and could make 29-plus knots. During the First World War, the United States laid down 285 flush-deck, 'four-pipers' (for their four smokestacks), beginning with six 'Caldwell'-class ships.[45]

COAL TO OIL

One of the chief innovations at sea in this period was the change from coal to oil. Coal was bulky and extremely dirty; it also took a long time to refuel and was a fire hazard. Indeed, the USS *Maine* may have been lost to a fire in one of her coal bunkers that 'cooked off' a magazine. During recoaling, virtually everything halted aboard ship as all hands took part in the refuelling process. The chief advantage of oil was that much more of it could be carried, but refueling was also greatly simplified. Large hoses were all that were necessary, and with oil it was also possible to refuel while underway.

In 1909 the Royal Navy decided that future destroyers should burn oil exclusively. Soon all ships were oil-fired, including the 'Queen Elizabeth's of 1912, the first battleships so fuelled.[46] Britain had no oil itself, and this gave it a special geopolitical interest in the Persian Gulf.

NAVAL GUNNERY

A handful of officers also pushed through a revolution in naval gunnery. Until the early 1890s the chief method of pointing a naval gun was the simple tangent sight. In 1892 the Royal Navy had adopted the new Barr & Stroud range-finder device, which had two mirrors set 4.5 feet apart. The Japanese Navy adopted it the next year and the US Navy soon thereafter. Later longer-base instruments were much more accurate, but this was nonetheless a significant step forward. For the first time, gunners could obtain something like an accurate range to their targets. In the mid-1890s Zeiss in Germany developed an improved stereoscopic range-finder for naval use.[47]

A number of individuals were pushing for changes in aiming and fire-control. The United States had Rear Admiral Bradley Fiske and Captain William Sims. Fiske produced an electric range-finder as early as 1889; two years later he patented a naval telescopic sight. Mounted on a sleeve around the gun barrel, the sight did not recoil when the gun was fired. Fiske may also have been the first person to attempt to control a ship's gunfire from aloft, when he was stationed in the foremast of the USS

Petrel at the Battle of Manila Bay in 1899. Later he wrote, 'Ninety percent of the art of naval gunnery seems to me to be the art of merely shooting to the correct distance.'[48]

The most important figure in the dramatic change in naval gunnery practice was Royal Navy captain Percy Scott, 'the pocket Hercules'. Scott had been trained on HMS *Excellent* and later commanded this gunnery school. In 1898, while commanding the *Scylla* in the Mediterranean, Scott invented a technique of continuous aiming. In the Mediterranean Fleet annual firing competition the average for the ships participating was only 30 per cent hits, but the *Scylla* scored a staggering 80 per cent. Scott also introduced salvo firing.[49]

The 1905 Battle of Tsushima seemed to confirm the sentiment that the big gun was the key at sea and that only the largest shells could inflict crippling damage on a ship's superstructure. Increasing attention was paid to gunnery practice and methods, therefore, and in the decade after Tsushima naval gunnery was transformed. Longer base length range-finders were adopted, capable of accurate range measurement out to 10,000 yards. Early analogue computer systems were also developed to help solve the considerable problem of calculating the precise location of the target ship when the shells arrived.

The Royal Navy turned down a privately developed fire-control computer system, in effect an early analogue computer, designed by Arthur Pollen, a civilian, in favour of an inferior, less-sophisticated system developed by Admiral Sir Frederic Dreyer. There is disagreement over whether the Pollen system would have improved Royal Navy gunnery sufficiently to have made a difference during the First World War. One scholar has argued that accurate very long-range fire was simply beyond the technology of the time.[50]

Then in 1905 Scott perfected a system of 'director firing'. Taking advantage of new electrical circuitry, he came up with a system that, in normal circumstances, concentrated control of all the big guns in the hands of one man, the 'director' or first gunnery officer. Along with his enlisted assistants, the director was located in a 'director tower' high in the foremast. From this observation platform with its master sight, cables ran to a central transmitting station, which produced firing data for the director, and to the individual turrets. This gave the director control over laying and firing all the main guns, eliminating individual gunlayers having to make their own calculations of range and bearing. In emergency circumstances or if the director tower were out of action, individual turrets could still fire on their own.

The Admiralty long resisted this change but, in November 1912, the super dreadnought *Thunderer*, fitted for director firing, achieved a hit ratio six times that of her sister ship, *Orion*, which employed the older independent method. This result could not be ignored, but the Admiralty moved so slowly with the change that, on the outbreak of the First World War, only a third of Royal Navy dreadnoughts were fitted with director towers. Nonetheless, by that war capital ships could engage their opponents at ranges out to five miles or more, double that of the Battle of Tsushima less than a decade before.

Elevation in ship guns reflected this change. Those ships constructed before the fire-control revolution had gun mounts capable of only modest elevation. In the Royal Navy gun elevation was 13.5 degrees until 1909, when in new ships it became 15 degrees. In 1911 it became 20 and in 1915 it was increased to 30 degrees.[51]

By 1912, with assistance from instruments to plot range changes (the dumaresqs or trigometric slide rule developed in 1902 by Royal Navy lieutenant John S. Dumaresq), Vickers range clocks to determine changes of range rate, and new Barr & Stroud range-finders, British capital ships could conduct firing practice out to 14,000 yards. The next year British battle-cruisers, joined by the new 13.5-inch gunned 'Lion' class of 'super battle-cruisers', experimented with 12,000-yard fire under tactical conditions of high speed and sharp turns. If ships during the First World War scored about the same number of hits as the US Navy had registered at Manila Bay and Santiago, it was in considerably more difficult circumstances and at up to ten times the range.[52]

TACTICS

Submarines, modern torpedoes, and more effective mines all led to significant change in the manoeuvring of surface fleets, particularly in closing an enemy's coasts. In December 1912 the Admiralty predicted that, 'The enemy's submarine, in conjunction with the destroyer, has made an efficient blockade impossible'.[53]

Although this referred to close blockades, and the British were still able to carry out an extremely effective blockade of Germany's coasts during the First World War, clearly battle fleets had to be handled with much more circumspection than in the past. This is reflected in the attitude of Home Fleet commander Sir John Jellicoe in the First World War. In October 1914 and again in April 1915 he had submitted this to the Admiralty: 'If, for instance, the enemy battle fleet were to turn away from an advancing fleet, I should assume that the intention was to lead us over mines and submarines, and should decline to be so drawn.' This policy had been approved by the Sea Lords and by Churchill as First Sea Lord.[54] It would cost the Royal Navy the opportunity for a decisive victory in the 1916 Battle of Jutland, but pressing the attack in these circumstances could also bring disaster; as Churchill put it after the battle, Jellicoe, 'was the only man on either side who could lose the war in an afternoon'.[55]

Eugene Ely flying his Curtiss Hudson Flyer off the USS *Birmingham* (CS-2), 14 November 1910. USS *Roe* (DD-24) serves as plane guard. (*Naval Historical Foundation, NH 1385*)

Eugene Ely landing his Curtiss Pusher on the USS *Pennsylvania* (CA-4), 18 January 1911. (*Naval Historical Foundation, NH 1385*)

236

MILITARY AVIATION

Locating the enemy battle fleet now became more important than ever. Submarines were useful for this purpose but so too was aviation. The United States was the first country to experiment with military aviation. In 1903 the brothers Wilbur and Orville Wright achieved the first manned powered flight. Five years later they built a 'military flier' for the US Army Signal Corps. The US Navy also experimented with aviation. On 14 November 1910, Eugene Ely flew a plane from an inclined platform mounted on the scout cruiser *Birmingham* off the Virginia Capes. On 11 January 1911, Ely landed a pusher biplane, fitted with special arresting hooks, on the old armoured cruiser *Pennsylvania*, fitted as an aviation platform.[56]

The German Zeppelin airship had great naval potential as a means to locate an enemy battle fleet, but the German Navy was initially reluctant to employ it. Nonetheless, by 1914 Germany had some 20 Zeppelins supporting both its army and navy.[57]

The first British experiments with a heavier-than-air ship were unsuccessful, although Churchill was a strong supporter of the Royal Naval Air Service, and after 1911 it expanded rapidly. In June 1914, with 91 aircraft and 7 non-rigid airships, it was the largest naval air arm in the world. Subsequently the Royal Navy put into service the world's first aircraft carrier and the Royal Naval Air Service developed all the techniques that were to prove so effective in the Second World War.

Some nations also converted existing ships into seaplane tenders: the French *Foudre* in March 1912, the British cruiser *Hermes* in May 1913, and the Japanese former merchantman renamed *Wakamiya*, in November 1913. The Royal Hellenic Navy was the first navy to use an airplane in combat when one of its seaplanes dropped four small bombs, all of which missed their target, on Turkish warships in the Dardanelles during the Second Balkan War (1913).[58]

COMMUNICATIONS

The potential of radio in ship-to-ship communication was limited for a long time. In 1914 flag hoists and signal lamps were far faster as a means of communication. These took two or three minutes to carry out; because of time lost in handling, wireless transmissions could take 10–15 minutes. Radio traffic could also be intercepted, which explains why Rear Admiral Zinovi Petrovitch Rozhdestvenski was reluctant to employ his shipboard radios at Tsushima in 1905. Indeed German radio traffic immediately preceding the Battle of Jutland alerted the British that a major German sortie was underway.

Radio traffic also could be used to deceive the enemy, as in October 1914 when Vice Admiral Count Maximilian von Spee deliberately restricted radio use to give the false impression that his force consisted of only one cruiser. This helped decoy Rear Admiral Sir Christopher Cradock's much weaker squadron into a trap off Cape Coronel. Communications intelligence became a key factor in the war at sea. 'Room 40', the Admiralty operation to intercept and break German codes, was hugely successful during the First World War, in large part because of windfalls in obtaining German codebooks.[59]

Despite all of the changes then underway in naval warfare, in 1914 the gun-armed capital ship was still the supreme arbiter at sea. Its guns still outranged torpedoes, and screens of light cruisers and destroyers could help shield the battle fleet against enemy torpedo boat attack. Despite this, the new threats led to the movements of capital ships being much more circumscribed than before. Battle fleets had become more important as fleets-in-being than as instruments of decisive victory.

CHAPTER 10

NAVAL WARFARE IN THE LATE 19TH AND EARLY 20TH CENTURIES

Many of the wars of the period immediately preceding the First World War sprang from imperialistic ambitions. During these conflicts there were important naval battles and a number of the wars were decided by sea power. First were a series of conflicts in Latin America.

WAR OF THE PACIFIC (1879–84)

During 1864–66 Peru and Spain were at war. Spanish warships bombarded Valparaíso and later attacked Callao, but Spain could not defeat Peru and the war ended in US mediation. The net effect, however, was that Chile, Peru's rival, built up its own navy. In 1879 the War of the Pacific broke out between Chile, Peru, and Bolivia. It was fought for control of the guano–producing provinces of Tacna, Arica, and Tarapacá, which belonged to Peru, and of Atacama, which belonged to Bolivia, and was that country's only outlet to the coast. Chilean companies engaging in the exploitation of nitrate were so heavily taxed by Bolivia and Peru that Chile declared war in February 1879.

Peru had 10 ships in its navy, but they were somewhat older than those of its adversary. In 1864 Peru had acquired two ships building in France for the Confederacy, the *Georgia* and the *Texas*, which in the Peruvian Navy were known as the *Union* and the *America* respectively. The *America* was lost to a tidal wave in 1868 but the *Union* remained. She weighed 1,827 tons, had a speed of 12 knots, and mounted 12 × 70-pounder Armstrong muzzle-loading rifles. Peru also had two ironclads built in Britain: the *Independencia*, a broadsides ironclad resembling the US Navy *New Ironsides* and an ironclad turret ram, the *Huascar*. The *Independencia* mounted 2 × 150-pounders, 12 × 70-pounder Armstrong rifles, and possibly 4 × 30-pounders. The *Huascar* weighed 2,030 tons and was capable of 13 knots. She mounted in her turret 2 × 10-inch 300-pounder Armstrong rifles. She also had 2 × 40-pounders and a 12-pounder. Peru also had the *Atahualpa* (1864) and *Manco Capac* (1865), each mounting 2 × 15-inch Dahlgren guns.

With 11 ships the Chilean Navy was approximately the same size as that of Peru, but Chile had a decided advantage in that its two most powerful warships were a decade newer. These were the ironclad battleships *Almirante Cochrane* (1874) and her sister ship *Blanco Encalada* (1875). Designed by Edward Reed and purchased from Britain, they were each 210 × 45 feet, weighed 3,560 tons, and were armed with six 9-inch Armstrong muzzle-loading rifles, three or four smaller guns, and one or two Nordenfeldt machine guns.

Battle of Angamos (8 October 1879)

The naval part of the war was over quickly. A Chilean naval expedition quickly seized Antofagasta, which gave Chile access to her nitrate deposits, and Chilean forces occupied the nearby area; Chile then imposed a coastal blockade. Captain Miguel Grau of the *Huascar* then harassed Chilean warships off Iquique, bringing out the entire Chilean Navy against him.

On 8 October 1879, five Chilean warships commanded by Patricio Lynch, including the *Blanco Encalada* and *Almirante Cochrane*, caught up with and engaged the *Huascar* off Point Angamos, Chile. The ensuing hour and a half engagement was fought at close range and the rifled guns on the Chilean ships exacted a considerable toll. The *Huascar*'s turret was disabled, her steering was shot away, and a third of her crew of 193 became casualties. Captain Grau and the four other officers who succeeded him in command were all killed. The *Huascar* surrendered, and Chile had command of the sea.

In January 1880 Chilean naval forces blockaded Arica and Callao; the Peruvians responded with both mines and ineffective torpedoes. Although several Chilean land thrusts were repulsed, Chilean troops landed by sea near Callao and marched inland, occupying the Peruvian capital of Lima in December 1880. The war finally ended in October 1883 with Chile securing permanent possession of both Antofagasta and Arica, and Bolivia cut off from access to the sea.[1]

In January 1891 civil war broke out in Chile between the party of President Balmaceda and the Congress. Two new torpedo gunboats purchased in Europe arrived in the midst of the war and fell into the hands of the Balmacedists. As the Congressists controlled the navy, the Balmacedists welcomed the two vessels: the *Almirante Condell* and *Almirante Lynch*. Twin-screwed, they were capable of 18–19 knots. Armed with small guns and machine guns, they also had 5 × 14-inch Whitehead torpedoes and powerful searchlights to locate their prey at night.

The torpedo boats now sought out the Congressist ships, and at 4:00 a.m. on 23 April they found the *Blanco Encalada* at the port of Caldero. The *Almirante Condell* launched three torpedoes, all of which missed; but in the attack the *Blanco Encalada* concentrated her fire on the *Almirante Condell*. This allowed the *Almirante Lynch* to approach and fire two torpedoes while stationary. These had a charge of 56 lbs of gun cotton. One of them hit the *Blanco Encalada* amidships and exploded. There was no time to close the watertight doors and, within five minutes, the ironclad had gone down, taking with her 182 men; 102 were saved. The *Blanco Encalada* was the first battleship sunk by a modern torpedo.[2]

THE SINO-JAPANESE WAR (1894–5)

Naval fighting had also erupted in Asia. Unlike China, Japanese leaders recognized the need for their nation to Westernize, at least to the extent of acquiring advanced Western military arts. At first this was for the purpose of preventing their country from falling under the control of a Western power; but, by the closing decade of the century Japanese leaders were ready to embark upon their own imperial expansion. They were especially desirous of securing Korea, a tributary kingdom of China just across Tsushima Strait from Japan. As a result of Japanese interference in Korean affairs, war between China and Japan began in 1894. On 20 July Japan seized control of the Korean government. Then on 25 July

Battle of the Yalu River, Haiyang, 17 September 1894, from a drawing by Nishimura. (*Anne S.K. Brown Military Collection, Brown University Library*)

Japanese Admiral Tsuboi Kozo attacked a Chinese troop convoy bringing reinforcements to Korea, sinking one transport and severely damaging its naval escorts. At the same time fighting began on land. On 1 August both sides declared war.

The Sino-Japanese War of 1894–95 quickly revealed that unarmoured wooden ships were no match for the new warships. China's military was antiquated, while Japan's was modern. Both sides now rushed reinforcements to Korea by sea, although neither attempted to interfere with the other's resupply effort. Chinese Admiral Ting Ju-ch'ang had two newer ironclad battleships: the *Ting Yuen* and *Chen Yuen*. He also had four light cruisers and six torpedo boats. These escorted six transports carrying 4,500 men and 80 guns to the Yalu River. Simultaneously, Japanese Admiral Ito Yuko

disembarked troops some 100 miles farther down the Korean coast, after which he sailed north to locate Ting's squadron.

Battle of the Yalu River or Haiyang (17 September 1894)

At 11:00 a.m. on 17 September 1894, Ito's larger force came on Ting's ships between the mouth of the Yalu River and Haiyang Island. The Japanese had the advantage of newer and faster ships. Ito flew his flag in the 4,277-ton *Matsushima*. Close by were two sister ships, the *Itsukushima* and *Hasidake*. In all, Ito had four heavy cruisers, four light cruisers, and six torpedo boats. He enjoyed a considerable advantage in larger (over 5-inch), quick-firing guns, and Japanese gunnery and ship handling were superior to those of the Chinese. The Chinese cruiser *Tsi Yuen* was quickly hit, whereupon she tried to run to Port Arthur, followed by the *Kwang Chia*. The Japanese quick-firing guns soon riddled the unprotected Chinese ships, setting their exposed wooden areas ablaze. In the battle the Chinese lost four or five ships. Although only one of his own ships was seriously damaged, Ito feared the two larger Chinese battleships and did not press his advantage; as a result, during the night the remaining Chinese vessels escaped to Port Arthur.[3]

In March 1895 the Japanese took both Port Arthur and Wei-hai-wei, fortified harbours guarding access to Peking. China then sued for peace and, in the Japanese-dictated Treaty of Shimonoseki, ceded to Japan the Island of Formosa (Taiwan) and the Liaotung peninsula in southern Manchuria. China also had to pay an indemnity of $150,000,000 and to recognize Korea as an independent kingdom, clearly a step toward its absorption by Japan.

Japan's acquisition of a foothold on the Asian mainland was particularly distasteful to Russian leaders. If Japan had Korea it would control both sides of the Tsushima Strait, the southern outlet of the Sea of Japan upon which Vladivostok was located. Should Japan also secure Port Arthur and the Liaotung peninsula, Russia would be prevented from obtaining a warm-water port in that region.

Russian leaders were determined to force Japan to withdraw from the Asian mainland, and they turned to France and Germany for support. France, which had only recently secured Russia as an ally, supported the Russian request for joint intervention in the Far East, as did Kaiser Wilhelm II. He hoped to weaken the Franco-Russian alliance by causing Russia to become so deeply involved in the Far East that it would be unable to play an aggressive role in the West.

Soon after the conclusion of the Treaty of Shimonoseki, Russia, France, and Germany in a joint note 'advised' Japan to refrain from annexing any part of the Chinese mainland. Japan then gave up claim to territory on the Asian mainland and in return received from China an additional indemnity.

SPANISH-AMERICAN WAR (1898)

Meanwhile the United States went to war with Spain, its first war with a foreign power since Mexico in 1846. In 1897 a Republican Congress enacted the Dingley Tariff. It was so high that the Republicans sought an issue to divert popular attention. Cuba provided this. Partly as a result of economic dislocation caused by the tariff's increase in duties on imported sugar, Cuba soon flared up in revolt against Spain.

Spain's efforts to suppress the rebellion were unsuccessful and aroused American ire. There was actually great savagery on both sides, but the 'Yellow Press' led Americans to believe that the Spaniards were committing all the atrocities. American sympathy was stirred by the plight of insurgents in concentration camps instituted under Spanish General Veleriano Weyler y Nicolau to curb guerrilla activities. The struggle in Cuba threatened to go on indefinitely as 150,000 Spanish troops were unable to subdue an estimated 40,000 rebels. In October 1897 a new Spanish premier proposed to abandon the concentration policy, recalled Weyler, and promised Cuba a measure of home rule.

Then on 15 February 1898, the USS *Maine* blew up in Havana harbour, killing 266 of 354 men on board. Sending the *Maine* to Havana was itself a provocative act, much resented by Spain. Ostensibly this was to protect US interests in Cuba, but Washington's real reason was to pressure Spain to change its policies.

On 28 March a naval court of inquiry determined the cause to be an external explosion by a submarine mine. In 1910 Congress authorized moving the *Maine* out to sea and resinking her. Engineers then constructed the world's largest cofferdam before refloating her. The investigation of the wreck resulted in a finding similar to the first, although the inquiry concluded that the principal explosions came from the ship's magazines and not the mine. In the 1970s Admiral Hyman Rickover and his staff, citing stress studies of metal in underwater explosions, concluded that spontaneous combustion of bituminous coal in one of the ship's bunkers had set off ammunition in an adjacent magazine.[4]

Probably the cause of the explosion will never be proven, but even if it had been an external mine that sunk the ship it is difficult to conceive what interest Spain might have had in doing this, and easy to imagine that Cuban rebels had planned it in order to involve the United States in war with Spain. The sinking of the *Maine* was probably decisive in bringing about the Spanish-American War. It produced a clamour in the Yellow Press for war ('Remember the Maine; to Hell with Spain').

President William McKinley did not want war but decided in favour of it for political reasons. On 25 April 1898, Congress declared war on Spain. Americans entered upon it with no consideration of the heavy responsibilities it would bring.

On paper Spain was a formidable enemy. It had more armoured cruisers and torpedo craft than did the United States, and worries that Spain might attack US Atlantic ports led to some Civil War-vintage monitors being hastily put into service. The Spanish Navy, however, was neglected, ill-armed, and largely untrained. The US Navy, a creation of the last 15 years, was new and efficient. The war was in fact decided by two naval battles off Cuba and the Philippines.

The Battle of Manila Bay (1 May 1898)

Commodore George Dewey's US Asiatic Squadron was in Chinese waters when he received news of the outbreak of hostilities via cablegram to Hong Kong. Dewey's squadron consisted of the protected cruisers *Olympia* (his flagship), *Baltimore*, *Boston*, and *Raleigh*; two gunboats, the *Concord* and *Petrel*; and the *McCulloch*, a revenue cutter that was pressed into service; two colliers also accompanied the squadron. On 27 April the ships departed China waters. On the night of 30 April, ignoring the threat of mines, they entered Manila Bay, running the Boca Grande Channel, reportedly mined, without major incident.

The Spanish had some 40 naval vessels in and around Manila, but most of these were small gunboats. Spanish Admiral Patricio Montojo y Pasarón's squadron consisted of two large cruisers, the *Reina Cristina* and *Castilla* (the latter of wood), and four small cruisers (each less than 1,200 tons and none with more than four 4.7 guns in her main battery). The Spanish ships were greatly inferior in armament to the American squadron. Montojo originally had his ships at Subic Bay but the water there was over 120 feet deep and its defences were unready. Reportedly, he decided that if his ships were to be sunk he would prefer it to be in shallower water. He returned them to Manila Bay.

To help offset his weakness in firepower Montojo anchored his ships off the fortified naval yard of Cavite, in order that they might be supported by land batteries. The next morning, 1 May, only a week after the declaration of war, Dewey's ships reached Manila and were met by wildly inaccurate fire from the shore batteries there. His ships advanced to within 2.5 miles of the Spanish line before, at 5:40 a.m., Dewey turned to his flag captain and said, 'You may fire when you are ready, Gridley.'

The ships of the American squadron closed to about 3,000 yards and ran parallel back and forth along the Spanish line, pounding it with their guns. The cruisers' 8-inch main battery guns, hurling 150-lb shells, exacted the most damage. The Spanish ships and shore batteries responded but failed to inflict significant damage. Dewey then called a halt to assess damage and the status of ammunition stocks, and at the same time he ordered breakfast served to the crews. At 11:16 the American ships stood in again to complete their work. Within little more than an hour the American ships had sunk the remaining Spanish vessel firing at them and had secured the surrender of the naval station at Cavite. Dewey then sent a message to the Spanish commander at Manila that if the shore batteries did not cease fire he would shell and destroy the city. The city's guns immediately fell silent. In the ships and at Cavite the Spanish lost 381 dead and wounded; the Americans had but six men wounded. Rarely was a victory more cheaply obtained.[5]

Dewey then took Cavite and blockaded the City of Manila while awaiting troops to take it. On 30 June General Wesley Merritt and 10,000 men arrived. On 13 August Merritt's troops, assisted by naval gunfire from Dewey's squadron and Filipino guerrillas under Emilio Aguinaldo, attacked Manila. After a short, nominal defence, the city surrendered.

After only 10 weeks the United States had wrested an empire from Spain, and it was control of the ocean that did it. The Philippines were secured to provide a bargaining chip to get Spain to conclude peace.

Fighting in Cuba

The US Army was almost completely unprepared for the war, and the American triumph on land in Cuba was largely from superior numbers. The wiser policy, as Mahan and others urged, would have been to blockade Cuba, preventing Spain from reinforcing the island. Army commander Major General Nelson Miles wanted a period of training and then an invasion, but public opinion demanded an immediate assault. The result was near-chaos. Finally, during 22–25 June Major General William Shafter's V Corps of nearly 17,000 troops landed unopposed at Daiquiri. Spanish commander Arsenio Linares failed to concentrate his 200,000 men on the island against the American threat. Badly outnumbered before Santiago, on 1 July the Spanish suffered defeat at San Juan and El Caney. These two American victories sealed the fate of Santiago.

Battle of Santiago Bay (3 July 1898)

At the end of April, Spanish Admiral Pascual Cervera had left the Cape Verde Islands with four modern cruisers, the flagship *María Teresa*, *Vizcaya*, *Cristobal Colón*, and the *Oquendo*; torpedo destroyers *Plutón* and *Furor*; and three destroyers. Americans along the coast were terrified of an imminent descent by the Spanish squadron. An erroneous sighting of the Spanish ships off New England even led the Navy Department to send two cruisers and other vessels to look for them. Cervera, however, was headed for Cuba.

US Atlantic Fleet commander Rear Admiral William T. Sampson first looked for Cervera at Puerto Rico but, not finding him there, had steamed to Cuba in hopes of intercepting the Spanish ships at sea. Cervera was presumed to be carrying supplies for the garrison on Cuba. His ships were not carrying supplies and were, in fact, themselves desperately short of coal and in acute need of maintenance. On 19 May Cervera slipped into the port of Santiago de Cuba.

On 1 June Sampson instituted a blockade with his five battleships, two armoured cruisers, and several smaller vessels. His force included Commodore Winfield Scott Schley's 'Flying Squadron' formed at Hampton Roads to protect the Atlantic coast from Cervera.

On 3 June, in a daring attempt, eight US Navy volunteers tried unsuccessfully to block Cervera's ships in the harbour by sinking the collier *Merrimack* at its mouth; she overshot the mark, going down too slowly when only two of the ten demolition charges exploded. On 6 July the Americans began bombarding the Spanish works and inner harbour. Several of the Spanish ships were hit and some coastal defence guns were knocked out.

The American land force was now in desperate straits, its numbers rapidly diminishing from disease. While the Americans were trying to decide how the Navy might best assist the Army in bringing about a Spanish capitulation, the Spanish themselves solved the problem. On 1 July Cervera had been ordered to re-embark his crews and, on the first opportunity, attempt to break out. Early on the morning of 3 July plumes of smoke indicated to American lookouts that Cervera's ships were getting up steam. Led by the *María Teresa*, his ships then exited the harbour one at a time, at intervals of 10 minutes and 600 yards. Commodore Schley's *Brooklyn* and eight other blockading ships quickly converged on the harbour entrance. Captain Robley Evans of the *Iowa* hoped either to ram or torpedo the *María Theresa*, but before he could do so, the *Iowa* managed to score hits with both shells from her forward 12-inch turret. The Spanish ships were simply overwhelmed by superior US firepower. Engulfed in flames, they tried to make the shore, and the Americans turned to the work of rescue. In the Battle of Santiago Bay the Spanish lost 323 killed and another 151 wounded. The US lost only one killed and another injured. As Captain Evans put it, 'God and the gunners had had their day.'[6] Santiago formally surrendered on 17 July.

Later there was a bitter public controversy as Commodore Schley feuded with Sampson over who was responsible for the victory. Schley claimed that Sampson, aboard the flagship *New York* and headed for a conference with General Shafter, was out of sight when the battle began. Who was in charge and the manoeuvres of individual ships certainly made no difference whatsoever in the outcome of the battle, but the controversy damaged the reputations of both men and denied them the satisfaction they deserved for their achievement.[7]

On 25 July Major General Miles landed on Puerto Rico with 5,000 men. In a well-planned, well-executed operation, they had almost eliminated Spanish resistance by the end of hostilities on 13 August.

Spain asked for terms of peace and McKinley dictated them on 30 July. These were immediate evacuation and definite relinquishment of Cuba, cession of the island of Puerto Rico and an island in the Marianas chain (Guam), and US occupation of the city, harbour, and bay of Manila. Spain signed a preliminary peace to that effect on 12 August.

Formal peace negotiations began at Paris on 1 October 1898. The only serious dispute to be resolved was the disposition of the Philippines. If they had been contented under Spanish rule, there would have been no question of annexing the islands; but an insurrection was already underway in the Philippines when the war began, and when the Americans captured Manila on 13 August, the Insurrectos organized a republic. The obvious thing to do was to turn the Philippines over to the Filipinos. McKinley hesitated.

Manila had one of the finest harbours in all the Pacific and hence was appealing as a naval base. An expansionist fervour was now sweeping the US, and the Hawaiian Islands had been annexed in July. Imperialism and German interest in the Philippines induced McKinley to keep the islands.

Spain was persuaded to part with the archipelago for $20 million, and its cession was included in the 10 December 1898, Treaty of Paris that formally ended the war. Acquisition of the Philippines affected America's future far more than any other settlement following the war. Cuba was made independent (although later had to grant to the United States use of the Guantanamo naval base), Puerto Rico was gradually advanced to Commonwealth status, but the Philippines made the United States a power in the Far East, involved her in Asian power politics, and made eventual war with Japan probable. Annexing the Philippines was thus a major turning point in American history.

In 1899 Germany purchased from Spain the remainder of her Pacific empire: the Marianas (except Guam) and the Caroline Islands. During the First World War Japan easily captured these and the Marshalls from Germany; and in the Second World War the United States had to fight for them at heavy cost.

The great success of the US Navy in the war fuelled sentiment for more ships. By 1917 the United States had the third largest navy in the world. It had also become a world power.

RUSSO-JAPANESE WAR (1904–5)

At the same time that the United States was defeating Spain, Japan and Russia were moving toward confrontation over Manchuria. In the 1890s Russia temporarily set aside her ambitions in the Balkans to seek a warm-water port in the Far East by obtaining outright, or securing influence over, the Chinese territories of Manchuria and Korea. These would provide excellent ports to supplement Vladivostok, closed by ice for part of each year. Control of Manchuria would also enable Russia to build across that province a shorter and more direct rail line to Vladivostok.

Following the Sino-Japanese War, Russia had posed as the defender of Chinese territorial integrity to advance its own position in China, including a 25-year lease on about 500 square miles of territory that contained part of the land surrendered by Japan in 1895. The Japanese were furious at this and at Russia's sending troops into Manchuria during the 1900–1 Boxer Rebellion.

Tsar Nicholas II and most of his advisors were determined to hold Manchuria and even had visions of adding Korea, which the Japanese since 1895 had considered part of their special sphere. For a time, however, Japanese statesmen were divided on the policy to pursue. Some argued that Japan might better come to a compromise agreement with Russia. Others held that war against Russia was inevitable and that Japan should seek to secure an anti-Russian alliance with Great Britain. The latter won out, and in 1902 Japan and Great Britain concluded an alliance.

In 1903 Japan attempted to reach an agreement with Russia, but Tokyo demanded that Russia first withdraw all her troops from Manchuria. Japanese leaders suggested that they might be willing to recognize Russia's ascendancy in the greater part of that province if Russia would recognize Japan's right of intervention in Korea and be allowed to build a railway from Korea into Manchuria to connect with the Chinese Eastern Railway. When Russia delayed both her response and a commitment, Tokyo broke off diplomatic relations. Apparently Nicholas II and most of his advisors wanted war, but they were certain Japan would never dare to instigate it.

The Japanese decided not to wait for Russia's convenience, and prepared a pre-emptive strike to secure control of the seas. On 6 February 1904 Vice Admiral Togo Heihachiro's Combined Fleet, consisting of two main fleets and a supply train including gunboats, merchant cruisers, and auxiliaries, departed for Port Arthur. At the same time, Vice Admiral Uryu Sotokichi left with four cruisers for Chemulpo (now Inchon), Korea.

Uryu's force consisted of the second-class protected cruiser *Naniwa*, second-class cruisers *Takachiho* and *Niitaka*, and first-class cruiser *Asama*. Built in Britain in 1899, the *Asama* and her sister ship *Tokiwa* were armoured with a steel belt and mounted 4 × 8-inch and 14 × 6-inch quick-firing guns, all of which could be fired electrically.

Outside the harbour Uryu met three transports loaded with 3,000 troops, horses, and equipment of the Army's 12th Division. On the following day they were joined by the protected cruiser *Akashi* and two flotillas of torpedo boats. In the early afternoon of 8 February Uryu's squadron arrived at Chumelpo, joining the armoured cruiser *Chiyoda*, which had been keeping under surveillance three Russian ships there: the first-class protected cruiser *Varyag*, gunboat *Koreetz*, and transport *Sungari*.

The *Koreetz* had put to sea with dispatches and mail for Port Arthur, only to encounter the Japanese ships. Realizing that their presence could have only one meaning, the *Koreetz*'s commanding officer ordered her to return to her anchorage. The opening shots of the war actually occurred about 2:15 p.m. There is some confusion about which side actually fired first; the Japanese said the *Koreetz* first fired its one gun at them; in any

case Uryu's torpedo boats soon attacked the *Koreetz*, but their Whitehead torpedoes missed.

That evening as the Russian sailors watched from their ships, Japanese troops, protected by the warships, began disembarking from their transports. This continued until the next morning, when some of them set off to capture the Korean capital of Seoul. Uryu then sent an ultimatum demanding that the Russian ships depart by noon or be attacked at 4:00 p.m. He also sent letters to the captains of foreign warships in the harbour, informing them of the beginning of hostilities between Japan and Russia and his ultimatum to the Russians. Uryu urged them to depart as well, warning that if they chose to remain, it would be at their own risk.

Captains of the British, French, and American ships all protested Uryu's intention to attack inside the three-mile limit and Japan's violation of Korean neutrality. The Russians, meanwhile, decided that honour dictated that they fight. The *Varyag* was the only ship capable of battle. Built in the United States a few years before, she mounted 12 × 6-inch guns. She was, however, only partly armoured; her hull was completely unprotected and only thin shields protected her guns.

The *Varyag* and then the *Koreetz* exited the harbor. At 11:45 the *Asama* opened fire and the *Varyag* replied. The completely one-sided battle was over in only an hour. Although the *Varyag*'s gunners fired more than 1,000 shells and claimed a number of hits, most of the shells failed to explode. The Japanese concentrated on the *Varyag*, which was soon a wreck; the *Koreetz* was set on fire. Both ships managed to make it back into the harbour. Uryu was debating his next move but was spared the decision of attacking and risking an international incident when the Russians scuttled their ships. In the battle the Japanese claimed they suffered no casualties and no damage to their ships.[8]

Japanese attack on Port Arthur (8 February 1904)

In the Pacific, aside from the warships at Chemulpo, the Russians had at Vladivostok four first class cruisers, the *Rossiya*, *Rurik*, *Gromoboi*, and *Bogatuir* as well as 17 torpedo boats. But their most powerful ships – seven battleships and four cruisers – were at Port Arthur. Since the Japanese had cut the cable between Port Arthur and Korea early on the 7th, the Russians did not know of the attack on Chemulpo.

Togo flew his flag in the *Mikasa*. Completed in Britain in 1902, she weighed 15,179 tons, was 432 × 76 feet 3 inches, and was capable of 18 knots. The *Mikasa* mounted 4 × 12-inch guns and had 14 × 6-inch rapid-fire guns. On public display today, she is the only surviving battleship of her period. The *Mikasa*, her three sister ships, and six armoured cruisers had been built in Britain, Germany, and France, just in time for the outbreak of the war.[9]

About midnight on 8–9 February 1904, Togo launched the main Japanese effort, against Port Arthur. Unwilling to risk his battleships without first knowing the situation there, Togo sent in his destroyers in a surprise torpedo attack. Just returned to Port Arthur after a period at sea, the Russian squadron was outside the harbour. In the attack two Russian battleships, the *Retvizan* and *Tsarevitch*, and the cruiser *Pallada* were all hit and badly damaged. The *Pallada* grounded near the harbour and both battleships, attempting to make it to the dockyards, grounded in the channel.

Near noon the next day Togo brought up six battleships, five armoured cruisers, and four protected cruisers to shell the shore batteries, town, and Russian ships from long range. The Russian ships, now anchored next to the forts, and some shore batteries returned fire. Only one Russian ship, the unprotected cruiser *Novik*, ventured out. Hit by a shell amidships she retreated, but not before firing a torpedo in the direction of the Japanese ships. Most of the Japanese vessels were hit by Russian shells, and Togo reluctantly ordered the Combined Fleet to withdraw after about an hour's fire.

Four Russian ships, the *Novik*, *Askold*, *Diana*, and *Bayan*, were damaged in the exchange, but all eventually returned to duty, as did the three ships badly damaged in the torpedo attack. While Togo announced that his fighting strength was unimpaired, in fact, considerable damage had been done to the battleships *Mikasa*, *Fuji*, *Hatsuse*, and *Shikishima* and the armoured cruiser *Iwate*, among others. In personnel losses the Japanese suffered 132 casualties and the Russians 150. Togo had gambled on the success of the torpedo attack, not daring to risk his battleships in the first assault.[10]

There were no pangs of conscience in Tokyo over the surprise attacks, and not until 10 February did Japan formally declare war. The struggle to decide which power would dominate the Far East was on. To the casual observer the war appeared to be a mismatch, but appearances were deceiving. Although Russia was vastly superior in resources and manpower, she was seriously handicapped at the outset of the war by being unable to bring her full strength to bear. The conflict was distant from the heart of Russia and the bulk of its troops and supplies would have to be shipped 5,500 miles over the single-track trans-Siberian railway, and a gap in the line at Lake Baikal complicated her logistical problems. The Russian Navy was divided into three main squadrons: Baltic, Black Sea, and Pacific, and it was difficult to concentrate those resources speedily. Furthermore, the Russian troops lacked enthusiasm for the war, the purpose of which they either did not understand or did not approve. In fact the war never received the whole-hearted support of the Russian people. Also the twin evils of inefficiency and corruption, which had so often undermined Russian armies in the past, again appeared. Finally, it was Russia's misfortune to have a supreme command lacking initiative and strategic ability.

Japan, on the other hand, had a highly disciplined, efficient, and enthusiastic army and navy. It was well trained, ably led, and was loyally supported by the populace at home. Furthermore Japan was in proximity to the seat of hostilities and, if it could secure control of the sea, it could in fact place its forces in the field with a minimum of difficulty. The absolute necessity of controlling the sea is why Japan had launched the attack on Port Arthur before declaring war; without control of the sea it could not win the war.

The Japanese were frustrated at their inability to destroy the Russian naval forces at Port Arthur in their initial attack, and in order to safeguard the lines of communication to Korea, they were obliged to keep up the pressure and adopt attrition tactics against the Russian squadron there. Meanwhile, on 8 March energetic Russian Vice Admiral S. Ossipovitch Makarov arrived at Port Arthur to take command. He initiated a series of sorties to harass the Japanese cruisers, while at the same time avoiding contact with Togo's battleships. Both sides also laid mine fields, but Makarov was killed, and the battleship *Petropavlovsk* lost when she ran over a Japanese minefield. In all, the Russians lost one battleship and the Japanese two battleships to mines off Port Arthur. Eventually Japanese troops cut off Port

Arthur from the land side and drove the tsar's forces back to the north.

On 23 June, his damaged ships repaired, Admiral Vilgelm Vitgeft, Makarov's successor, sortied. Togo, his strength weakened to four battleships and a reduced cruiser force, prepared to meet the Russians, but Vitgeft returned to Port Arthur.

Battle of the Yellow Sea (10 August 1904)

Following the first Japanese land assault on Port Arthur, on 7–8 August Tsar Nicholas II ordered Vitgeft to break free and steam to Vladivostok. Vitgeft was determined to take the whole squadron, not just his strongest and fastest ships. On 10 August 1904, flying his flag in the *Tsarevitch*, he came out with six battleships, three protected cruisers, eight destroyers, and a hospital ship. Many of the Russian vessels were shipping water from damage received from the daily shelling by Japanese shore batteries.

By mid-afternoon Togo had closed on the Russians with the *Mikasa* and three other battleships, 5 armoured cruisers, 8 protected cruisers, 17 destroyers, and 29 torpedo boats. Togo had not expected the entire Russian fleet, but he had no choice but to give battle. Superior Japanese gunnery, the heavier weight of metal thrown by the more modern Japanese battleships, and Togo's omnipresent good luck decided the outcome. The Japanese ships were hit hard in return; the *Mikasa* took 12-inch shells from the Russian battleship *Poltava* and Togo was lucky to survive the battle.

With darkness approaching, it looked as if Vitgeft might escape. Then at 5:45 p.m., about 90 minutes into the battle, two Japanese 12-inch shells found the Russian flagship *Tsarevich*; they killed Vitgeft and put the battleship out of control and the Russian line into complete confusion. These two lucky hits decided the battle. The Russian squadron now scattered.

Opening shot being fired by the Japanese squadron in the Battle of the Yellow Sea, 10 August 1904. (*US Naval Institute*)

No Russian ship had been destroyed or taken in the battle. Five battleships, a cruiser, and three destroyers regained Port Arthur. The *Tsarevich*, subsequently hit by at least fifteen 12-inch shells, managed to reach Kiaochou and was interned there, as were three destroyers; the cruiser *Diana* was interned at Saigon, and the cruiser *Askold* and a destroyer at Shanghai. The cruiser *Novik* steamed on until her boilers burst. Her crew did not want to be interned and decided to fight to the last. Cornered near Sakhalin Island on 31 August by two Japanese cruisers, she succumbed to more than 20 shells.

Battle of Ulsan (14 August 1904)

News of the battle of the Yellow Sea reached Vladivostok on the afternoon of 11 August,

but not until the 13th did the cruisers *Rossiya*, *Gromoboi*, and *Rurik*, commanded by Rear Admiral von Essen, go to the assistance of the Port Arthur Squadron. On 14 August they ran into Admiral Kamimura Hikonojo's four armoured cruisers in the Korea Strait. The Japanese sank the *Rurik* and, although the other two Russian ships were able to regain Vladivostok, Japan now had complete control of the sea.[11]

Actions on land

In the autumn Japanese Field Marshal Oyama Iwao defeated the main Russian army under General Alexei Kuropatkin in the great Battle of Liaoyang (25 August–3 September) and again at Shao-Ho (5–17 October). On 2 January 1905, Port Arthur,

'Borodino'-class, Russian Navy battleship. (*Anne S.K. Brown Military Collection, Brown University Library*)

blockaded by land and sea and its defenders starving, surrendered. The remaining ships there had been destroyed the previous month by Japanese siege howitzers. During 26–27 January, another battle occurred at Sandepu. The Russians, reinforced to 300,000 men, took the offensive to crush Oyama's 220,000 Japanese. The Russians were close to a victory that could have changed the entire war, but Kuropatkin did not press the attack and it ended in stalemate. In the great Battle of Mukden (21 February–10 March) each side had about 310,000 men engaged. The defeated Russians lost 100,000 men, the Japanese 70,000. Now Russia's fate appeared to hang on one last-ditch naval effort.

Baltic Fleet

In the summer of 1904, the Baltic Fleet, now renamed the Second Pacific Squadron, readied for a long voyage.[12] By the time the fleet sailed for the Far East it was clear that it would have to meet the full strength of the Japanese Fleet alone and that there would be no Pacific bases to which it could sail save Vladivostok. Rear Admiral Zinovi

Petrovitch Rozhdestvenski, who initially argued that Japanese naval strength was overrated, had command.

On 15 October 1904, the 36 warships of the squadron left their bases bound for the other side of the world. Pride of the squadron were the four new 13,500 ton 'Borodino'-class battleships: *Borodino, Imperator Alexander III, Orel* (flagship), and *Kniaz Suvarov*. Commissioned during 1903–04, each had a main armament of 4 × 12-inch guns. The ships were so new, however, that many problems had not been worked out before they had to sail.[13]

Over the next seven months the Russian ships steamed half way around the world. The trip went badly from the start. On 21 October, in the North Sea off the Dogger Bank, jittery Russian crews shelled their own cruiser *Aurora* and the British fishing fleet from Hull, mistaking them for Japanese torpedo boats. The trawler *Crane* was sunk and seven fishermen killed. The Dogger Bank Incident almost brought war with Britain.

After the fleet made it around France and Portugal, the less seaworthy older battleships, three cruisers, and the destroyers all proceeded eastward through the Mediterranean and Suez Canal, while the main detachment continued south around Africa. Britain refused to provide coal and so this was obtained from German colliers of the Hamburg-Amerika Line at various points along the route. The lack of coaling stations led Rozhdestvenski to order his ships to take on double their ordinary capacity by putting it in every possible space. Unfortunately for the Russians, the strain of coaling in Africa's heat and the state of the ships precluded training and gunnery practice.

It was an extraordinary progression, closely followed by the world's Press. Reunited at Madagascar, the fleet's progress was delayed by problems of coaling the vessels and repairs. Finally in mid-March 1905 the fleet started across the Indian Ocean, refuelling five times at sea, an incredible, unprecedented feat. Rozhdestvenski hoped to get to Vladivostok without battle, but when the captain of the *Imperator Alexander III* reported she was short of coal, the fleet made one last stop at Cam Ranh Bay in French Indo-China, where efforts were made to prepare for battle and where the last additions to the fleet arrived: an 1891 ironclad, an even older armoured cruiser, and three small 5,000-ton coast defence ships, all referred to by Rozhdestvenski as 'self-sinkers'. He now realized there was little hope of avoiding battle with the Japanese. At the time of the Russian defeat at Mukden, Rozhdestvenski's ships were slowly making their way northward through the South China Sea and up the Chinese coast.

An increasing sense of despair prevailed in the Russian fleet, its crews realizing that an incompetent government had sent them on a mad venture. Absent at sea for eight months from their Baltic bases and having steamed halfway around the world, they were destined to meet in its home waters Togo's efficient, proven, modern Japanese fleet.[14]

Battle of Tsushima (27 May 1905)

Rozhdestvenski did what he could. He sent most of his auxiliary vessels to anchor at the mouth of the Yangtse River and timed his advance through the Tsushima Straits to be at night. He sent two cruisers toward the east coast of Japan in an effort to persuade his adversary that the entire fleet would follow them. Again, Togo's luck held; he gambled that Rozhdestvenski would choose the most direct route to Vladivstok by means of the Tsushima Straits.

On the night of 26–27 May Japanese picket ships sighted the Russian fleet in the straits and Togo's ships immediately left their bases, dumping coal as they went in order to increase their speed. Togo relied on radio messages to keep him informed of the location of the Russians, and Tsushima was the first naval battle in which the radio was used in action. The Japanese employed it freely; the Russians had radios but feared they would give away too much; during most of the action they relied on signal flags.

The firepower of the two fleets was slightly to the Russian advantage, but the Russian crews were considerably inferior to the Japanese in gunnery. The total Russian fleet consisted of eight battleships, eight cruisers, nine destroyers, and several smaller vessels.

Togo had cut off Vladivostok from both egress and entrance. The Japanese had sown 715 mines over a 35-mile area at the entrance of Peter the Great Bay. Still, if by some outside chance the Russians could win the impending engagement and gain control of the sea, they would cut off the Japanese forces in Manchuria and be able to bombard Japanese coastal cities and towns. Japan would have to withdraw from the war.

Many factors favoured Togo. He had had ample time to prepare, and his ships had been overhauled and repaired. He had added three new destroyers as well as the *Ryeshitelni*, captured at Cheefoo and renamed the *Akatsuki*. Togo had 4 battleships, 8 cruisers, 21 destroyers, and 60 torpedo boats. The Japanese ships had the important advantage of speed; they were, on the average, about 50 per cent faster than the Russian vessels, even the newest of which were fouled from the long voyage. Togo's men were fresh and eager, battle-tested, sailing in their own waters, and led by highly skilled officers. These reasons alone were sufficient to tip the balance in favour of the Japanese.

On the afternoon of the 27th, trailed by Japanese cruisers, the Second Pacific Squadron sailed past Tsushima Island. When the Russian ships came out of some fog at 1:19 p.m., Togo on the *Mikasa* to the north-east at last sighted his prey. The Russian ships were steaming in two columns. Rozhdestvenski had his flag in the *Kniaz Suvarov*, the first ship in the starboard colmun.

The Russians assumed that Togo would turn south and bridge the gap, allowing his battleships to fire on the weaker Russian divisions, but this would have left the Russsian ships headed toward Vladivostok, with the Japanese moving in the opposite direction. Instead, Togo made a daring move, a 270-degree turn in succession to the north-east in order to cut the Russian ships off from Vladivostok. Relying on the superior speed of his vessels, Togo sought the advantages of the sun and wind. The turn brought the Japanese ships onto a course parallel to that of the Russians; with their superior speed they would turn east and cross the Russian 'T' at leisure.

This manoeuvre carried grave risks, because during the long turn Togo exposed his ships in succession to the full broadside weight of fire from the Russian fleet. Within seconds of the *Mikasa* beginning her turn the *Suvarov* opened fire at a range of about 6,400 yards. Other Russian ships followed suit, but the Russian gunnery was poor and there were few direct hits.

After four of the 12 ships in the Japanese line had turned, Togo ordered his ships to return fire; as the two fleets formed into two converging lines both blazed away at each other. The Japanese, with their 15-knot speed, easily overhauled the Russians, steaming at only 9 knots. Rozhdestvenski then altered course slightly to port, reducing the range. The early Russian fire rapidly deteriorated as the Japanese closed the range. Minutes later the *Suvorov*, on fire, turned to starboard.

The battle was very disjointed, with the Japanese never seeing the Russian fleet as a whole. Russian fire damaged three Japanese ships, hit many others, and forced the cruiser *Asama* out of the battle line. But the *Suvarov* was burning badly and another battleship, the *Oslyabya*, had been holed in her side. The Japanese now concentrated their fire on the two crippled battleships, and their superior mobility and gunnery gradually told.

By nightfall the Japanese victory was nearly complete. Wounded in the battle, Rozhdestvenski yielded command to Rear Admiral Nichlas Nebogatov of the third division. That night Togo sent in his 58 destroyers and torpedo boats to finish off those Russian vessels not already sunk or escaped. Isolated fighting continued throughout the night, and by the next day the Japanese had sunk, captured, or disabled eight Russian battleships. Of 12 Russian ships in the battle line, eight were sunk, including three of the new battleships, and the other four had been captured. Of the cruisers, four were sunk and one scuttled; three, including the *Aurora*, limped into Manila and were interned; another, the

Almaz, made it to Vladivostok. Among the cruisers sunk was the 8,524-ton *Admiral Nakhimov*, which is thought to have carried substantial sums in gold, silver, and platinum to finance the war in the Far East. Of the destroyers, four were sunk, one captured, one interned at Shanghai, and two reached Vladivostok. Three special service ships were sunk, one was interned at Shanghai, and one reached Madagascar.

Togo's losses were minuscule: three torpedo boats sunk. Although other ships suffered damage, all were serviceable. In personnel losses the Russians had 4,830 men killed or drowned and just under 7,000 taken prisoner. Japanese personnel losses were 110 killed and 590 wounded.[15]

In just one day Russia ceased to be a major power in the Pacific and in the world. Fifty years would pass before she regained status at sea. Contrarily, the battle made Japan the premier military power of the Far East. It also gave the Japanese the belief that wars could be turned on one big battle.

Togo's victory at Tsushima led to Russian capitulation on land. Both Kaiser Wilhelm II and US President Theodore Roosevelt had urged peace upon the belligerents. Although Russia, with her vast resources and manpower, might possibly have sent new armies to continue the struggle in the Far East, popular discontent and the October 1905 Revolution at home alarmed the tsar's ministers, and they were therefore willing to consider peace proposals. On the other hand, its military efforts had nearly bankrupted Japan and its leaders were quite ready to halt military operations.

On Roosevelt's invitation a peace conference opened at Portsmouth, New Hampshire. Sergius Witte ably represented Russia at the conference and succeeded in saving his country from the worst consequences of the defeat. The Treaty of Portsmouth (5 September 1905) transferred

Russia's cessions in southern Manchuria to Japan, converting that area into a Japanese sphere of influence. Russia also recognized Japan's preponderant interest in Korea and her right to control and 'protect' the Korean government. In addition it surrendered to Japan the southern half of Sakhalin Island, which Japan had occupied during the war. The treaty, favourable as it was to Japan, was not popular there. Japanese leaders had not obtained the indemnity they wanted while they had carefully concealed from the Japanese people the fact that the country was close to bankruptcy.

In terms of naval lessons learned, the war seemed to indicate that torpedoes were not the decisive weapon claimed by their protagonists. The fighting around Port Arthur and at Tsushima had been decided by main battery guns as well as medium-range quick-firing guns. Tsushima seemed to validate Mahan's theory that the big gun was always decisive, but it also showed the importance of speed in an engagement.

Ironically, Tsushima was also the only major, decisive fleet action in the history of the steel battleship. Only the gun had counted. In the future, underwater or aerial weapons, at first tactical auxiliary weapons, would come to exercise a dominant influence.

ITALO-TURKISH (TRIPOLITAN) WAR, 1911–12

In September 1911 Italy went to war against Turkey in order to secure Libya, in North Africa. Naval power was critical to the war's outcome. On 29 September Italy bombarded Preveza in Epirus, sinking several Turkish torpedo boats. Then, during 3–5 October, Italian naval units bombarded the Libyan capital of Tripoli. Turkish forces evacuated the city as Italian troops landed to secure it. On 4 October another Italian naval force took Tobruk, also in Libya, and over the next week the navy carried out other landings. Although the Italians held the coastal area of Libya, Turkish propaganda inflamed the population and the Italians dared not move into the interior.

The war dragged on and, in mid-April 1912, Italian naval units demonstrated off the Dardanelles. Turkey then closed the straits and prepared for an invasion, but the Italians withdrew. A month later the Italian Navy occupied Rhodes and the Dodecanese Islands. From July to October the Italian Army went on the offensive in Libya and won victories over the outnumbered Turkish forces. Finally, with war in the Balkans looming, Turkey concluded peace. In the 15 October Treaty of Ouchy, Turkey ceded to Italy its North African territory of Libya, Rhodes, and the Dodecanese Islands.

ROAD TO THE FIRST WORLD WAR

During the first decade of the twentieth century there were efforts to reduce friction between Germany and Britain caused by the naval building contest between the two powers. In 1909 Bernard von Bülow, who had played an aggressive international role, resigned as German chancellor. Theobald von Bethmann-Hollweg followed, and he was anxious to improve relations between Germany and Britain. Because he believed that friction between the two powers was largely a result of the naval race, Bethmann took up with London the possibility of an agreement. He proposed that each country retard naval construction in the hope of winning public support to the idea of fewer ships. But he also declared that this would have to be accompanied by a political agreement, whereby Britain promised not to attack Germany and to remain neutral if Germany were attacked by a third power.

The British Foreign Office doubted the sincerity of the proposals and in any case saw this as a German effort to prise Britain away from France and Russia and the Triple Entente alliance.

After the Second Moroccan crisis of 1911 German imperialists argued that their government had been weak in the face of British threats and demanded the navy be further increased. A sort of Anglophobia spread through Germany in 1911 and 1912, and many Germans came to believe Britain was Germany's worst enemy. The theme of General Friedrich von Bernhardi's popular 1912 book, *Deutschland und der nächste Krieg* ('Germany and the Next War'), was world power by the sword, or decline.[16]

Early in 1912 Kaiser Wilhelm announced to the Reichstag that a supplementary naval bill would be introduced. By this time certain businessmen in both Germany and Britain had decided that an effort should be made to bring about an Anglo-German understanding. Germany appeared willing to talk and invited British Foreign Secretary Earl Grey to confer, but London sent British War Minister Lord Haldane instead. As a result of conversations between Haldane and the Kaiser, Wilhelm agreed to retard construction of recently proposed ships. But again Bethmann sought to link the naval understanding with a political agreement. He proposed that the two countries promise not to join any combination of powers directed against the other and that each remain neutral in case the other were forced into war.

Both in Germany and Britain there were those who desired that the Haldane mission fail. In Germany Tirpitz and his followers opposed any change in Germany's naval programme, while in Britain there was great reluctance to accept the political formula suggested by Bethmann lest it antagonize Russia and France. In the end nothing tangible came of the Haldane mission.

Germany's Third Supplementary Naval Law (*Novelle*) of May 1912 created a new squadron that would include three dreadnoughts and which brought the total projected strength of the German fleet to 41 battleships, 20 large cruisers, and 40 small cruisers. Thereafter Germany slowed her naval construction slightly. Unfortunately for Germany, Wilhelm had, without actually having built a navy big enough to challenge Britain, succeeded in thoroughly alarming the British people and pushing that nation firmly to the side of France and Russia (the Triple Entente). In 1904 Britain concluded the Entente Cordiale with France and, three years later, reached an understanding with Russia. For Britain, an island dependent on imported food and raw materials for half its annual supply, control of the seas was a matter of national existence, and a fleet was a necessity, while for Germany it was indeed a 'luxury.'

In the end Germany's naval building programme was a colossal blunder. It not only drove Britain away from possible alliance, but it was little used as an instrument of war. With the exception of submarines, the German High Seas Fleet remained in port during most of the First World War, venturing out in full strength only once, on the occasion of the Battle of Jutland in 1916. Thus Germany's naval building programme provides a useful lesson in defence prioritizing. If the resources Germany expended on its navy had gone into the army, it would have won the First World War.

Naval balance in 1914

In 1914 on the eve of war Germany had the world's second largest navy. In capital ships alone the Imperial German Navy had 15 dreadnoughts, 5 battle-cruisers, and 20 pre-dreadnoughts. She also had 56 cruisers (36 pre-dreadnought and 20 modern) and 154 destroyers (52 pre-dreadnought and 102 modern).[17]

Austria-Hungary in 1914 had a powerful force in the Adriatic Sea, consisting of three dreadnought battleships, three 'Radetzky'-class semi-dreadnoughts, and six pre-dreadnoughts. The Dual Monarchy had 14 cruisers (11 pre-dreadnought and 3 modern). It had only 26 destroyers, although 19 of these were modern. Naval construction on the eve of the war was claiming 20 per cent of Austro-Hungarian defence spending and, much to the dismay of Chief of the General Staff General Franz Conrad von Hötzendorf, it siphoned off scarce resources from the army.[18]

Located predominantly in the Mediterranean, the French Navy had 4 dreadnoughts, 6 'Danton'-class semi-dreadnoughts, and 21 pre-dreadnought battleships. The French also had 36 cruisers, all of them pre-dreadnought era. France had many more destroyers, 84, but 53 of these were the older types.

Russia also had a powerful navy. It was, however, divided by geography into separate forces in the Baltic, the Black Sea, and the Far East. In 1914 the Russian Navy had 4 dreadnoughts and 11 pre-dreadnoughts. Russia also had 19 cruisers, only one of which was modern. She had 105 destroyers, but only 10 of these were modern, including one destroyer leader. Japan had 2 dreadnoughts, 6 battle-cruisers, and 8 pre-dreadnought battleships. Japan also had 19 older cruisers and 6 modern types; and she had 50 destroyers, 35 of which were modern.

Britain had, by European standards, a very small professional army; her military strength was in her navy. With 22 dreadnoughts, 9 battle-cruisers, and 41 pre-dreadnought battleships, it was by far the world's largest. In capital ships alone Britain outnumbered Germany about two to one.

The imbalance was even greater in smaller ships. In cruisers Britain had 94 pre-dreadnought era and 30 modern. Britain had many more destroyers than any other country – 107 pre-dreadnought and 121 modern, including three destroyer leaders. The Royal Navy, assisted by the navies of France, Russia, and Japan, gave the Allies of the First World War domination at sea. Britain also had the world's largest merchant marine. At 19 million tons it was half the world's total.[19]

In terms of quality British ships were generally faster and had heavier and longer-range guns than their German counterparts. They were not, however, steady gun platforms, the consequence of insufficient beam – itself the result of small docks dating from Victorian times that restricted the width of ships that could be built in them. German ships were beamier, and hence better gun platforms. The German ships were also better protected, both in terms of armour above and below the waterline, and their greater beam allowed more compartmentalization.

The British had an excellent system of director control for firing the main guns, but on the outbreak of the war only eight British capital ships had this innovation. The Germans had excellent stereoscopic rangefinders to aid in firing, while the British had turned down the privately developed Pollen system. British shells were also inferior to those of the Germans. British cannon powder was also less stable than that used by the Germans, and the Royal Navy ammunition hoists were not protected from the flash of an explosion in the turret, a problem compounded by the practice of leaving magazine doors open during battle in order to increase the rate of fire. These failings, coupled with insufficient turret armour, would be revealed in the Battle of Jutland. Also, German torpedoes and mines were superior to those of Britain.[20]

Crushing British naval and maritime superiority, however, overrode any disadvantages in individual ships. Royal Navy strength not only secured for the Allies their own extensive overseas resources but enabled them to utilize the industrial production of the world's neutral countries, especially the United States. Britain's naval strength also allowed it to blockade Germany by sea. This operation denied the Central Powers (Germany, Austria–Hungary and Turkey) the resources they needed to win the war and was a vital factor in their defeat. It did violate the 1909 Declaration of London, which accorded neutrals the right to trade with belligerent states, but Britain took the position that modern war rested on the strength of entire societies and included as contraband all foodstuffs intended for German consumption.[21]

To win the First World War the Central Powers needed either a short war or to knock out one of their two principal land opponents. Providing France and Russia could survive the initial German and Austro-Hungarian land offensives and remain in the war, Allied naval superiority would make it possible for the Allies to triumph.

Events had come full circle. In the 130 years since the beginning of the Wars of the French Revolution and Napoléon, naval technology had undergone the greatest period of change in history. Wooden ships powered by the wind and carrying iron muzzle-loading cannon had given place to steel warships driven by steam turbines, carrying vastly more powerful, accurate, long-range guns. Mines had appeared and submarines and naval aviation were poised to make their mark. Yet, in 1914 as in 1793, the task facing the Royal Navy was the same: that of seeking to prevent a single power from controlling the European continent.

NOTES

1. THE STATE OF NAVAL WARFARE AT THE END OF THE 18TH CENTURY

1. J.J. Colledge, *Ships of the Royal Navy* (Annapolis, MD, Naval Institute Press, 1987), Vol. I: p. 368. Both the HMS *Victory* and the frigate USS *Constitution* (launched in 1797) remain commissioned vessels in their respective navies.

2. D.K. Brown, *Before the Ironclad. Development of Ship Design, Propulsion and Armament in the Royal Navy, 1815–60* (London, Conway Maritime Press, 1990), pp. 11–14.

3. See Robert Gardiner, *The Heavy Frigate: Eighteen-Pounder Frigates: Volume I, 1778–1800* (London, Conway Maritime Press, 1994); Jean Boudriot, 'L'évolution de la frégate dans la marine française, 1600–1850', in D. Howse, *Five Hundred Years of Nautical Science, 1400–1900* (London, National Maritime Museum, 1981), pp. 229–40; Spencer C. Tucker, *Arming the Fleet. U. S. Navy Ordnance in the Muzzle-loading Era* (Annapolis, MD, Naval Institute Press, 1989), pp. 102–3.

4. *The Great Admirals. Command at Sea, 1587–1945* ed. Jack Sweetman (Annapolis, MD, Naval Institute Press, 1997), p. 132.

5. *Flagship Portsmouth* (Portsmouth, England, Flagship Portsmouth Trust, 1997), p. 20.

6. Brian Lavery, *Nelson's Navy: The Ships, Men and Organisation, 1793–1815* (London, Conway Maritime Press, 1989), p. 43; L. Denoix and J.-N. Muracciole, 'Historique de l'Artillerie de la Marine des ses Origines à 1870,' *Mémorial de l'Artillerie française*, Volume XXXVIII, no. 3 (1964), p. 346. On the ship of the line see Jean Boudriot's superb study, *Le Vaisseau de 74 Canons*, (4 vols; Grenoble: Editions des Quatres Seigneurs, 1973–1977); also Brian Lavery, *The Ship of the Line* (2 vols; London: Conway Maritime Press, 1983–84), Vol. I.

7. John D. Harbron, *Trafalgar and the Spanish Navy* (London, Conway Marine Press, 1988), p. 170.

8. Tucker, *Arming the Fleet*, pp. 6–8.

9. Spencer C. Tucker, 'The Navy Discovers Shore Bombardment', *Naval History*, Vol. VIII, no. 5 (October 1994), p. 30.

10. Tucker, *Arming the Fleet*, p. 2.

11. Ibid., pp. 6–8.

12. Ibid., pp. 8–10.

13. Adrian B. Caruana, *The History of English Sea Ordnance, 1523–1875. Volume II: The Age of the System, 1715–1815* (Ashley Lodge, Rotherfield, East Sussex, Jean Boudriot Publications, 1997), pp. 255–67.

14. C. Derrick, *Rise & Progress of the Royal Navy* (London, 1806), in Caruana, *The History of English Sea Ordnance*, Vol. II, pp. 273–4.

15. The most thorough treatment of the carronade is in Adrian B. Caruana, *The History of English Sea Ordnance*, Vol. II, pp. 161–214. See also Spencer C. Tucker, 'The Carronade', *Nautical Research Journal*, Vol. XXXXII, no. 1 (March 1997), pp. 15–23.

16. Caruana, *English Sea Ordnance*, Vol. II, p. 280.

17. On the French carronade see Jean Boudriot, 'L'Artillerie de Mer de la Marine Française, 1674–1856: B – Bouches – à Feu à Boulets Explosifs', *Neptunia*, Vol. LXXXXIV, pp. 1–7.

18. For French sea ordnance of the period see Denoix and Muracciole, 'Historique de

l'Artillerie de la Marine des ses Origines à 1870', *Mémorial de l'Artillerie française*, XXXVIII, nos. 2 and 3 (1964), pp. 271–359; pp. 526–602.

19. Peter Padfield, *Guns at Sea* (New York, St Martin's Press, 1974), pp. 111–16.

20. Ian Hogg and John Batchelor, *Naval Gun* (Poole, Dorset, Blandford Press, 1978), pp. 35–6; Tucker, *Arming the Fleet*, pp. 32–3.

21. *Fleet Battle and Blockade. The French Revolutionary War, 1793–97*, ed. Robert Gardiner (London, Chatham Publishing, 1996), p. 35.

22. For details of crew composition aboard the *Constitution* see Tyrone G. Martin, *A Most Fortunate Ship. A Narrative History of Old Ironsides* rev. edn (Annapolis, MD, Naval Institute Press, 1997), pp. 70–4.

23. Lavery, *Nelson's Navy*, pp. 297–298; Padfield, *Guns at Sea*, pp. 138–43.

24. Spencer C. Tucker and Frank T. Reuter, *Injured Honor: The Chesapeake-Leopard Affair, June 22, 1807* (Annapolis, MD, Naval Institute Press, 1996), pp. 194–6.

25. Brian Tunstall, *Naval Warfare in the Age of Sail: The Evolution of Fighting Tactics, 1650–1815*, ed. Nicholas Tracy; (London, Conway Maritime Press, 1990), p. 2.

26. Tunstall, *Naval Warfare in the Age of Sail*, p. 1.

27. Quoted in Padfield, *Guns at Sea*, p. 121.

28. See Jean Boudriot, *John Paul Jones and the Bonhomme Richard*, tr. David H. Roberts; (Annapolis, MD, Naval Institute Press, 1987).

29. Sweetman, *Great Admirals*, p. 140.

30. Keegan, *The Price of Admiralty*, p. 45.

31. Tunstall, *Naval Warfare in the Age of Sail*, p. 7.

32. Sweetman, *The Great Admirals*, pp. 138–9.

33. William James, *The Naval History of Great Britain, 1793–1820, From the Declaration of War by France in 1793 to the Accession of George IV* (6 vols, London, Richard Bentley, 1859), Vol. VI: p. 289; Vol. II: pp. 440–4. Also C. Northcote Parkinson, *Britannia Rules: the Classic Age of Naval History, 1793–1815* (London, Weidenfeld and

Nicolson, 1977; reprint Stroud, Alan Sutton, 1994), p. 168.

34. Gardiner, *Fleet Battle and Blockade*, pp. 42–3.

35. See Nathan Miller, *Sea of Glory. The Continental Navy Fights for Independence, 1775–1783* (New York, David McKay, 1974), pp. 456–95; Harold A. Larrabee, *Decision at the Chesapeake* (London, William Kimber, 1965).

36. Sweetman, *The Great Admirals*, p. 147.

37. Ibid., pp. 148–9.

38. Tunstall, *Naval Warfare in the Age of Sail*, pp. 1–2, 264; see also Julian S. Corbett, *Fighting Instructions, 1530–1816* (London, Naval Records Society, 1905), pp. 213–59.

2. THE WARS OF THE FRENCH REVOLUTION AND NAPOLÉON

1. Denoix and Muracciole, 'Historique de l'Artillerie de la Marine des ses Origines à 1870', *Mémorial de l'Artillerie française*, Vol. XXXVIII, no. 3 (1964), p. 346.

2. Caruana, *English Sea Ordnance*, Vol. II, p. 276.

3. Denoix and Muracciole, 'Historique de l'Artillerie de la Marine', p. 346.

4. William James, *Naval History of Great Britain* (London, 1826), Vol. I, p. 26.

5. David Howarth, *Trafalgar: The Nelson Touch* (New York, Atheneum, 1969), p. 23.

6. The table is from Robert Fulton, *Torpedo War and Submarine Explosions* (New York, 1810), p. 48, and is reprinted in Otto von Pivka, *Navies of the Napoleonic Era* (New York, Hippocrene Books, 1980), p. 30. Figures on numbers of ships vary widely and any effort to bring about agreement is an exercise in futility. For example, Brian Lavery gives the French Navy figure for 1792 as 241 vessels of all types, including 83 ships-of-the-line and 77 frigates. Brian Lavery, *Nelson's Navy: The Ships, Men and Organisation, 1793–1815* (London, Conway Maritime Press, 1989), p. 279.

7. Gardiner, *Fleet Battle and Blockade*, p. 10; for the effects of the Revolution on the French Navy see W.S. Cormack, *Revolution and*

Political Conflict in the French Navy, 1789–1794
(Cambridge, 1995).

8. Quoted in Gardiner, *Fleet Battle and Blockade*,
p. 16.

9. Lavery, *Nelson's Navy*, pp. 78–94; Von Pivka,
Navies of the Napoleonic Era, pp. 29–33.

10. Fleet sizes vary. William James, who was
prone to exaggerate the strength of Britain's
opponents, gives a total of 85 French ships-
of-the-line in 1793. Gardiner, *Fleet Battle and
Blockade*, p. 9.

11. Quoted in William S. Cormack, *Revolution
and Political Conflict in the French Navy*
(Cambridge, 1995), p. 219.

12. Gardiner, *Fleet Battle and Blockade*, pp. 86–9,
pp. 94–7, pp. 103–5; figures on the losses at
Toulon are from James, *The Naval History of
Great Britain*, Vol. I, pp. 84–91; see also John
Barrow, *Life and Correspondence of Admiral Sir
William Sidney Smith, G.C.B.* (2 vols, London,
Richard Bentley, 1848), Vol. I, pp. 153–57.

13. R.R. Palmer, *Twelve Who Ruled. The Year of
Terror in the French Revolution* (Princeton, NJ,
Princeton University Press, 1941), pp. 203–9.

14. William Laird Clowes, *The Royal Navy.
A History from the Earliest Times to 1900*
(London, Sampson Low, Marston & Co.,
1849), IV: 479.

15. Palmer, *Twelve Who Ruled*, pp. 342–9; Gardiner,
Fleet Battle and Blockade, pp. 27–33, pp. 38–41.
See also Oliver Warner, *The Glorious First of
June* (New York, Macmillan, 1961).

16. Gardiner, *Fleet Battle and Blockade*, pp. 58–69,
pp. 77–81; the best account of operations
there during 1793–97 is Michael Duffy,
*Soldiers, Sugar and Seapower: The British
Expeditions to the West Indies and the War
against Revolutionary France* (Oxford, 1987).

17. Gardiner, *Fleet Battle and Blockade*, pp. 70–1.

18. Ibid., p. 16.

19. Ibid., p. 138.

20. Richard Hough, *Nelson, A Biography*
(London, Park Lane Press, 1980), pp. 56–67;
Brian Tunstall, *Naval Warfare in the Age of
Sail: The Evolution of Fighting Tactics*,

1650–1815 ed. Nicholas Tracy (London,
Conway Maritime Press, 1990), pp. 216–19;
Gardiner, *Fleet Battle and Blockade*, pp. 121–7.

21. See Gardiner, *Fleet Battle and Blockade*,
pp. 165–7. For a comprehensive study of the
mutinies see James Dugan, *The Great Mutiny*
(New York, G.P Putnam's Sons, 1965). For
conditions in the fleet see Michael Lewis, *The
Navy in Transition, 1814–1864: A Social History*
(London, Hodder and Stoughton, 1965).

22. Tunstall, *Naval Warfare in the Age of Sail*,
pp. 219–24; Gardiner, *Fleet Battle and
Blockade*, pp. 173–9.

23. David Walder, *Nelson* (New York, Dial Press,
1978), p. 275.

24. Hough, *Nelson: A Biography*, pp. 77–92;
Tunstall, *Naval Warfare in he Age of Sail*,
pp. 224–7; for the best full-length study see
Brian Lavery, *Nelson and the Nile: The Naval
War Against Bonaparte, 1798* (London,
Chatham Publishing, 1998); Jean Meyer and
Martine Acerra, *Histoire de la Marine Française
des origines à nos jours* (Rennes, Éditions
Ouest-France, 1994), p. 163.

25. Barrow, *Admiral Sir William Sidney Smith*,
Vol. I, pp. 268–9.

26. See Dudley Pope, *The Great Gamble: Nelson at
Copenhagen* (New York, Simon & Schuster,
1972), pp. 411, 512, 530; Hough, *Nelson*,
pp. 118–31.

27. On the battle see Alan Schom, *Trafalgar.
Countdown to Battle, 1803–1805* (Oxford and
New York, Oxford University Press, 1990),
pp. 229–36, 282–4.

28. Tunstall, *Naval Warfare in the Age of Sail*,
pp. 249–50; Hough, *Nelson*, pp. 152–60.

29. Schom, *Trafalgar*, p. 315.

30. Hough, *Nelson*, pp. 160–81. Parliament did
vote a special award so that each captain
received £3,362 and no seaman less than £6
10s. On the battle see David Howarth,
Trafalgar. The Nelson Touch (New York,
Atheneum, 1969); Dudley Pope, *Decision at
Trafalgar* (Philadelphia, J. B. Lippincott,
1959); Schom, *Trafalgar*.

31. Schom, *Trafalgar*, pp. 355–6.

32. E.H. Jenkins, *A History of the French Navy. From its Beginnings to the Present Day* (Annapolis, MD, Naval Institute Press, 1973), p. 264.

33. Schom, *Trafalgar*, p. 362.

34. Denoix and Muracciole, 'Historique de l'Artillerie de la Marine des ses Origines à 1870', *Mémorial de l'Artillerie française*, XXXVIII, no. 3 (1964), p. 346.

35. Tunstall, *Naval Warfare in the Age of Sail*, p. 259.

36. Richard Woodman, *The Victory of Seapower. Winning the Napoleonic War, 1806–1814* (London, Chatham, 1998), pp. 20–4. On the Buenos Aires campaign, see I. Fletcher, *The Waters of Oblivion: the British Invasion of the Rio de la Plata, 1806–1807* (Turnbridge Wells, Spellmont, 1991) and J.D. Granger, *The Royal Navy in the River Plate, 1806–1807* (Brookfield, VT, Ashgate Publishing, 1996).

37. Woodman, *The Victory of Seapower*, pp. 144–6. See also R.C. Gwilliam, 'The Dardanelles expeditions of 1807' (unpublished MA thesis, University of Liverpool, 1955).

38. Otto von Pivka, *Navies of the Napoleonic Era*, pp. 111–14. See also A.N. Ryan, 'The Causes of the British Attack upon Copenhagen in 1807', *English Historical Review*, Vol. LXVIII (1953), pp. 7–55; and, same author, 'The Navy at Copenhagen in 1807', *Mariner's Mirror*, Vol. XXXIX (1953), pp. 201–10.

39. Leo Gershoy, *The French Revolution and Napoleon* (Englewood Cliffs, NJ, Prentice-Hall, 1964), pp. 420–50; also G.J. Marcus, *The Age of Nelson: The Royal Navy in the Age of its Greatest Power and Glory, 1793–1815* (New York, The Viking Press, 1971), pp. 295–330.

40. Denoix and Muracciole, 'Historique de l'Artillerie de la Marine des ses Origines à 1870', *Mémorial de l'Artillerie française*, Vol. XXXVIII, no. 3 (1964), p. 346.

41. See Gordon C. Bond, *The Grad Expedition, The British Invasion of Holland in 1809* (Athens, GA, University of Georgia Press, 1979). British order of battle is on pp. 167–72.

42. See Tucker and Reuter, *Injured Honor*.

43. On the causes of the war see Reginald Horsman, *The Causes of the War of 1812* (Cranbury, NJ, A.S. Barnes, 1962). Also Donald R. Hickey, *The War of 1812, A Forgotten Conflict* (Urbana and Chicago, IL, University of Chicago Press, 1989), pp. 5–51.

44. On the gunboat programme see, Spencer C. Tucker, *The Jeffersonian Gunboat Navy* (Columbia, SC, University of South Carolina Press, 1993).

45. Hugh Francis Pullen, *The Shannon and the Chesapeake* (Toronto: McClelland and Stewart, 1970), pp. 41–2, 52–63; Tucker, *Arming the Fleet*, pp. 25–6, p. 48.

46. David Curtis Skaggs and Gerard T. Altoff, *Signal Victory. The Lake Erie Campaign, 1812–1813* (Annapolis, MD, Naval Institute Press, 1997), p. 148.

47. Two classics on the naval aspect of the War of 1812 are: Alfred Thayer Mahan, *Sea Power in Its Relations to the War of 1812*, 2 vols, (Boston, Little Brown, 1918); and Theodore Roosevelt, *The Naval War of 1812* (New York, G.P. Putnam's Sons, 1882). See also an excellent book: Robert Gardiner, ed., *The Naval War of 1812* (London, Chatham Publishing, 1998).

48. James, *Naval History of Great Britain*, Vol. V, pp. 390–3.

49. J.W. Norie, *Naval Gazeteer, Biographer and Chronologist* (1827), p. 534, in Lavery, *Nelson's Navy*, p. 317; see also James, *The Naval History of Britain*, appendices at end of each volume, and von Pivka, *Navies of the Napoleonic Era*, pp. 217–65.

50. See Donald E. Worcester, *Sea Power and Chilean Independence* (Gainesville, Florida, University of Florida Press, 1962).

51. William James, *The Naval History of Great Britain*, Vol. VI, pp. 358–80; Len Ortzen, *Guns at Sea. The World's Great Naval Battles* (London, Cox & Wyman, 1976), pp. 77–82;

Meyer and Acerra, *Histoire de la Marine Française*, pp. 203–6.

3. THE REVOLUTION IN SHIPS, ARMAMENT AND PROPULSION, 1815–65

1. Andrew D. Lambert, B*attleships in Transition: the Creation of the Steam Battlefleet, 1815–1860* (London: Conway Maritime Press, 1984), p. 13; Brown, *Before the Ironclad*, pp. 17–19, 31–4, 36–7.

2. Lambert, *Battleships in Transition*, p. 15; Brown, *Before the Ironclad*, p. 32; Colledge, *Ships of the Royal Navy*, pp. 69, 293.

3. Tom Perlmutter, *War Machines, Sea* (Np, Octopus Books, nd), pp. 56–8; Frederick L. Robertson, *The Evolution of Naval Armament* (London, Harold T. Storey, 1968), p. 225.

4. Brown, *Before the Ironclad*, pp. 44–5.

5. R. Ernest Dupuy and Trevor N. Dupuy, *The Harper Encyclopedia of Military History* 4th ed. (New York) HarperCollins, 1993), p. 12.

6. Charles O. Paullin, *Paullin's History of Naval Administration, 1775–1911* (Annapolis, MD, US Naval Institute, 1968), p. 179.

7. Frank M. Bennett, *The Monitor and the Navy under Steam* (Boston: Houghton, Mifflin, 1900), pp. 12–17.

8. Tucker, *Arming the Fleet*, pp. 170–1; Samuel Eliot Morison, *Old Bruin: Commodore Matthew Calbraith Perry* (Boston, Little, Brown, 1967), pp. 127–9.

9. Spencer C. Tucker, *Raphael Semmes and the Alabama* (Abilene, Texas, McWhiney Foundation Press, 1998), pp. 40–1.

10. Brown, *Before the Ironclad*, p. 47; Colledge, *Ships of the Royal Navy*, pp. 87, 201, 227.

11. Brown, *Before the Ironclad*, p. 57.

12. Ibid., pp. 48–50.

13. Ibid., p. 50; Colledge, *Ships of the Royal Navy*, p. 88; George, *History of Warships*, p. 62; Gardner W. Allen, *Our Navy and the West Indian Pirates* (Salem, MS, Essex Institute, 1929), pp. 41–2; Sweetman, *Great Admirals*, p. 242.

14. Andrew D. Lambert, ed., *Steam, Steel, and Shellfire: the Steam Warship, 1815–1905* (London, Conway Maritime Press, 1992), p. 17. Lambert gives her armament as two long 32-pounders and four carronades.

15. Brown, *Before the Ironclad*, pp. 53–5.

16. Ibid., pp. 61–72; Lambert, *Steam, Steel, and Shellfire*, p. 23; Colledge, *Ships of the Royal Navy*, pp. 98, 103, 153, 345.

17. Lambert, *Steam, Steel, and Shellfire*, pp. 18–19; *Musée de la Marine* (Paris, Association des Amis du Musée de la Marine, nd), p. 43.

18. George, *History of Warships*, p. 62.

19. Bennett, *The Monitor and the Navy under Steam*, pp. 22, 43; Paul H. Silverstone, *Warships of the Civil War Navies* (Annapolis, MD, Naval Institute Press, 1989), pp. 21–2.

20. Lambert, *Steam, Steel, and Shellfire*, pp. 27–8.

21. Brown, *Before the Ironclad*, pp. 102–7, Lambert, *Steam, Steel, and Shellfire*, pp. 31–3.

22. Brown, *Before the Ironclad*, pp. 100–1.

23. Spencer C. Tucker, 'U.S. Navy Steam Sloop *Princeton*,' *The American Neptune* (Spring 1989), pp. 96–113.

24. Colledge, *Ships of the Royal Navy*, p. 283; George, *History of Warships*, p. 64.

25. Brown, *Before the Ironclad*, p. 110–14.

26. Ibid., 122–4.

27. Lambert, *Battleships in Transition*, p. 111.

28. *Musée de la Marine*, p. 47. Brown gives her claimed speed as 12.1 Knots. Brown, *Before the Ironclad*, p. 129.

29. Brown, *Before the Ironclad*, pp. 127–8.

30. Andrew Lambert, *Warrior. The World's First Ironclad Then and Now* (London, Conway Maritime Press, 1987), p. 10; Lambert, *Battleships in Transition*, p. 111; Lambert, *Steam, Steel, and Shellfire*, p. 41.

31. Lambert, *Steam, Steel, and Shellfire*, pp. 36–7; Sweetman, *Great Admirals*, p. 243.

32. Brown, *Before the Ironclad*, p. 161.

33. Donald L. Canney, *The Old Steam Navy. Volume One: Frigates, Sloops, and Gunboats, 1815–1885* (Annapolis, MD, Naval Institute Press, 1990), pp. 45–8.

34. Ibid., pp. 48–58.

35. Canney, *Frigates Sloops, and Gunboats*, pp. 61–89.

36. Quoted in Sweetman, *Great Admirals*, p. 244.

37. Lambert, *Steam, Steel, and Shellfire*, p. 47–8; George, *History of Warships*, p. 67.

38. Brown, *Before the Ironclad*, p. 75–80.

39. Spencer C. Tucker, 'The Stevens Battery', *The American Neptune*, LI, No. 1 (Winter 1991), pp. 12–21.

40. Bradley A. Rodgers, *Guardian of the Great Lakes. The U.S. Paddle Frigate Michigan* (Ann Arbor, MI, University of Michigan Press, 1996).

41. Brown, *Before the Ironclad*, pp. 80–8; Lambert, *Warrior*, p. 11; Baxter, *The Introduction of the Ironclad Warship*, p. 34.

42. Darrieus and Quéguiner, *Historique de la Marine française*, p. 54; Brown, *Before the Ironclad*, p. 156.

43. Peter Padfield, *Guns at Sea* (New York, St Martin's Press, 1974), pp. 165, 168; James Phinney Baxter III, *The Introduction of the Ironclad Warship* (New York, Archon Books, 1968), pp. 81–6; Lambert, *Steam, Steel, and Shellfire*, p. 52.

44. Baxter, *The Introduction of the Ironclad Warship*, pp. 86–7; Brown, *Before the Ironclad*, pp. 156–7.

45. Baxter, *The Introduction of the Ironclad Warship*, p. 110; Lambert, *Warrior*, p. 12. Lambert gives her battery as 34 x 6.4–inch rifled muzzle-loaders. Ibid., p. 22; *Musée de la Marine*, p. 47.

46. Steve Crawford, *Battleships and Carriers* (London, Brown Packaging Books Ltd., 1999), p. 220; Robertson, *The Evolution of Naval Armament*, p. 272.

47. Baxter, *Introduction of the Ironclad Warship*, p. 111; Crawford, *Battleships and Carriers*, p. 81.

48. Padfield, *Guns at Sea*, p. 168.

49. Colledge, *Ships of the Royal Navy*, pp. 227, 250; Lambert, *Warrior*, pp. 12–13, 23.

50. Lambert, *Warrior*, pp. 7, 12–13, 20–1, 27, 28, 32. The restored *Warrior* is now at Portsmouth.

51. Lambert, *Warrior*, p. 22.

52. Baxter, *Introduction of the Ironclad Warship*, pp. 156–60; Colledge, *Ships of the Royal Navy*, 21.

53. Robertson, *The Evolution of Naval Armament*, p. 272; Colledge, *Ships of the Royal Navy*, pp. 229–30; Baxter, *Introduction of the Ironclad Warship*, pp. 179, 204.

54. George M. Brooke, Jr., *John M. Brooke, Naval Scientist and Educator* (Charlottesville, VA, University Press of Virginia, 1980), pp. 236–51.

55. Silverstone, *Warships of the Civil War Navies*, pp. 158–9.

56. Ibid., p. 151.

57. Ibid., p. 16.

58. Ibid., p. 4. See James Tertius deKay, *Monitor; The Story of the Legendary Civil War Ironclad and the Man Whose Invention Changed the Course of History* (New York, Walker, 1997).

59. William H. Roberts, *USS New Ironsides in the Civil War* (Annapolis, MD, Naval Institute Press, 1999), pp. 9–17.

60. Silverstone, *Warships of the Civil War Navies*, pp. 4–10.

61. Ibid., p. 12.

62. Ibid., p. 3.

63. Roberts, *USS New Ironsides in the Civil War*, pp. 75, 108–11.

64. Crawford, *Battleships and Carriers*, p. 70.

4. DRAMATIC CHANGES IN NAVAL ORDNANCE

1. Frederick Leslie Robertson, *The Evolution of Naval Armament* (London, Constable, 1984), pp. 55, 136, 162–3; Dupuy and Dupuy, *Harper Encyclopedia of Military History*, p. 763.

2. Tucker, *Arming the Fleet*, pp. 177–80.

3. On this see William Gilkerson, *Boarders Away. With Steel – Edged Weapons & Polearms* (Lincoln, RI, Andrew Mowbray, 1991) and *Boarders Away II. Firearms in the Age of Fighting Sail* (Lincoln, RI, Andrew Mowbray, 1993).

4. Tucker, *Arming the Fleet*, pp. 177–8.

5. Thomas F. Simmons, *Ideas as to the Effect of Heavy Ordnance Directed Against and Applied by Ships of War, Particularly with Reference to the*

Use of Hollow Shot and Loaded Shells (London, P. Pickney, 1837), p. 2.

6. Tucker, *Arming the Fleet*, pp. 178–80.

7. Brown, *Before the Ironclad*, p. 132.

8. Lambert, *Battleships in Transition*, pp. 15–16.

9. Howard Douglas, *A Treatise on Naval Gunnery* 3rd ed. (London, John Murray, 1851), pp. 216–18.

10. Tucker, *Arming the Fleet*, pp. 186–7; Douglas, *A Treatise on Naval Gunnery*, pp. 208–12.

11. See Spencer C. Tucker, 'The Dahlgren Boat Howitzer', *Naval History* Vol. VI, no. 3 (Fall 1992), pp. 50–4.

12. On Dahlgren see Robert J. Schneller, Jr., *Quest for Glory. A Biography of Rear Admiral John A. Dahlgren* (Annapolis, MD, Naval Institute Press, 1996). The best source for the Dahlgren guns, however, is Edwin Olmstead, Wayne Stark, and Spencer Tucker, *The Big Guns. Civil War Siege, Seacoast and Naval Cannon* (Alexandria Bay, NY, and Bloomfield, Ont., Canada, Museum Restoration Service, 1997), pp. 83–110. See also Tucker, *Arming the Fleet*, pp. 198–225.

13. M. Dahlgren, *Memoirs of John A. Dahlgren*, p. 226.

14. Testimony of Captain James Alden, in Congress, *Report of the Joint Committee*, p. 170.

15. Lambert, *Steam, Steel, and Shellfire*, p. 158; Tucker, *Arming the Fleet*, pp. 176–82; Madeleine Vinton Dahlgren, *Memoir of John A. Dahlgren* (New York, Charles I. Webster, 1891), p. 87.

16. Barrow, *Life and Correspondence of Admiral Smith*, Vol. I: p. 299.

17. Tucker, *Arming the Fleet*, pp. 187–90.

18. Robertson, *The Evolution of Naval Armament*, pp. 112–24.

19. Quoted in H. Garbett, *Naval Gunnery: A Description and History of the Fighting Equipment of a Man of War* (London, G. Bell, 1897), pp. 32–3.

20. Hogg and Batchelor, *Naval Gun*, p. 67; Douglas, *Naval Gunnery*, pp. 248–54.

21. Tucker, *Arming the Fleet*, pp. 225–26.

22. US Congress Joint Committee on the Conduct of the War, 'Heavy Ordnance', in *Report of the Joint Committee on the Conduct of the War at the Second Session, Thirty–Eighth Congress* (Washington, GPO, 1906), p. 30.

23. Spencer C. Tucker, 'The Explosion of the 'Peacemaker' aboard Sloop Princeton', *New Interpretations in Naval History: Selected Papers from the Eighth Naval History Symposium* (Annapolis, MD, Naval Institute Press, 1989), pp. 175–89.

24. Hogg and Batchelor, *Naval Gun*, pp. 67–8; Padfield, *Guns at Sea*, p. 172; Sandler, *The Emergence of the Modern Capital Ship*, pp. 102–3.

25. Hogg and Batchelor, *Naval Gun*, p. 68; US Congress, *Report of the Joint Committee on the Conduct of the War*, p. 89.

26. Tucker, *Arming the Fleet*, pp. 233–6.

27. Ibid., pp. 228–33.

28. On Brooke see George M. Brooke, Jr. *John M. Brooke, Naval Scientist and Educator* (Charlottesville, VA, University Press of Virginia, 1980). On his ordnance see Olmstead, Stark, and Tucker, *The Big Guns*, pp. 125–34.

29. George, *History of Warships*, p. 76.

30. Commander James H. Ward, *Elementary Instruction in Naval Ordnance and Gunnery*, rev. ed. (New York, D. Van Nostrand, 1861), p. 149.

31. Edward Simpson, *A Treatise on Naval Ordnance and Gunnery* 2nd ed., revised (New York: D. Van Nostrand, 1862), p. 418.

32. M. Dahlgren, *Memoir of John A. Dahlgren*, p. 301.

33. Douglas, *A Treatise on Naval Gunnery*, p. 302

34. M. Dahlgren, *Memoir of John A. Dahlgren*, p. 226.

35. Hogg and Batchelor, *Naval Gun*, p. 73.

5. THE TECHNOLOGICAL REVOLUTION IN PRACTICE

1. K. Jack Bauer, *Surfboats and Horse Marines. U.S. Naval Operations in the Mexican War, 1846–1848* (Annapolis, MD, Naval Institute

Press, 1969), p. 22. This is still the standard work on the naval aspects of the war.

2. Duncan Haws and Alex A. Hurst, *The Maritime History of the World* (Brighton, Sussex, Teredo Books, 1985), Vol. II, pp. 34–5; Brown, *Before the Ironclad*, pp. 137–8.

3. A.J. Barker, *The War Against Russia, 1854–1856* (New York, Holt, Rinehart and Winston, 1970), p. 13.

4. Brown, *Before the Ironclad*, p. 137.

5. Barker, *The War Against Russia*, p. 46.

6. Ibid., pp. 269–70; Haws and Hurst, *Maritime History of the World*, Vol. II, p. 35.

7. Brown, *Before the Ironclad*, pp. 152–3.

8. Barker, *The War Against Russia*, pp. 270–4; Haws and Hurst, *Maritime History of the World*, Vol. II, pp. 35–6; Brown, *Before the Ironclad* suggests the bombardment of Svaeborg was much more punishing to the Russians. See pp. 155–6.

9. Winfried Baumgart, *The Peace of Paris, 1856* (tr. Ann P. Saab; London and Santa Barbara, CA, ABC–Clio, 1981), pp. 164–68.

10. Stephen R. Wise, *Lifeline of the Confederacy. Blockade Running during the Civil War* (Columbia, SC, University of South Carolina Press, 1988), p. 24; Baumgart, *The Peace of Paris, 1856*, p. 165.

11. For statistical information on both Union and Confederate warships see Silverstone, *Warships of the Civil War Navies*.

12. Wise, *Lifeline of the Confederacy*, pp. 50–2.

13. Raimondo Luraghi, 'Background', in *The Confederate Navy: The Ships, Men and Organization, 1861–65*, ed. William N. Still, Jr (London, Conway Maritime Press, 1997), p. 19.

14. Philip Van Doren Stern, *The Confederate Navy. A Pictorial History* (Garden City, NY, Doubleday, 1962), p. 62.

15. Wise, *Lifeline of the Confederacy*, p. 226.

16. On Confederate commerce raiding see William M. Robinson, Jr, *The Confederate Privateers* (New Haven, CT, Yale University Press, 1928); Chester G. Hearn, *Gray Raiders of the Sea* (London and Baton Rouge, LA, Louisiana State University Press, 1992);

Murray Morgan, *Confederate Raider in the North Pacific: The Saga of the C.S.S. Shenandoah, 1864–65* (Pullman, WA: Washington State University Press, 1995); Frank L. Owsley, Jr., *The C.S.S. Florida; Her Building and Operations* rev. ed. (London and Tuscaloosa: University of Alabama Press, 1987); Spencer C. Tucker, *Raphael Semmes and the Alabama*; and Raphael Semmes, *Memoirs of Service Afloat* (reprint; Secaucus, NJ, The Blue and Grey Press, 1987).

17. Fran M. Bennett, *The Monitor and the Navy Under Steam* (New York: Houghton Mifflin, 1900), p. 184.

18. George W. Dalzell, *The Flight from the Flag: The Continuing Effect of the Civil War upon the American Carrying Trade* (Chapel Hill, NC, University of North Carolina Press, 1940), pp. 237–62.

19. Benjamin F. Cooling, *Forts Henry and Donelson; The Key to the Confederate Heartland* (Knoxville, TN, The University of Tennessee Press, 1987), pp. 101–9.

20. Ibid., pp. 147–60.

21. On this campaign see Cooling, *Forts Henry and Donelson* and Spencer C. Tucker, *Admiral Andrew Hill Foote* (Annapolis, MD, Naval Institute Press, 2000).

22. Olmstead, Stark, and Tucker, *The Big Guns*, pp. 11–13. On the siege of Island No. 10 see Larry J. Daniel and Lynn N. Bock, *Island No. 10. Struggle for the Mississippi Valley* (London and Tuscaloosa, University of Alabama Press, 1996).

23. John D. Milligan, *Gunboats Down the Mississippi* (Annapolis, MD: Naval Institute Press, 1965), pp. 64–7.

24. Jay Slagle, *Ironclad Captain. Seth Ledyard Phelps and the U.S. Navy, 1841–1864* (London and Kent, OH, Kent State University Press, 1996), pp. 225, 230, 232.

25. Milligan, *Gunboats Down the Mississippi*, pp. 68–77.

26. James P. Duffy, *Lincoln's Admiral; the Civil War Campaigns of David Farragut* (New York: John Wiley and Sons, 1987), pp. 59–111.

27. On the two ships and the battle see deKay, *Monitor*, and Gene A. Smith, *Iron and Heavy Guns; Duel Between the Monitor and Merrimack* (Abilene, Texas, McWhiney Foundation Press, 1998).

28. Charles Oscar Paullin, *Paullin's history of Naval Administration, 1775–1911* (Annapolis, MD, Naval Institute Press, 1968), p. 280.

29. Silverstone, *Warships of the Civil War Navies*, pp. 200–209; on Confederate ironclads see William N. Still, Jr, *Iron Afloat. The Story of the Confederate Armorclads* (Nashville, TN, Vanderbilt University Press, 1971).

30. Still, *Iron Afloat*, pp. 62–78.

31. Duffy, *Lincoln's Admiral*, p. 218.

32. *Civil War Naval Chronology*, Vol. III, p. 95.

33. At the time this was printed, the editors were unaware of the outcome of the battle, Richmond *Whig* (8 April 1863), quoted in *Civil War Naval Chronology*, Vol. III, p. 59.

34. Welles to Hoppin, 8 October 1873, Hoppin, *Life of Admiral Foote*, p. 395; Du Pont to his wife; 26 May 1863, *Du Pont Letters*, p. 137.

35. *Civil War Naval Chronology, 1861–1865*, Vol. VI, pp. 218–19; Philip Van Doren Stern, *The Confederate Navy, A Pictorial History*, pp. 175–6.

36. Semmes, *Memoirs of Service Afloat*, p. 762; Frank M. Bennett in *The Monitor and the Navy Under Steam* takes exception.

37. Semmes, *Memoirs*, pp. 759–62; US, Navy Dept, *Official Records of the Union and Confederate Navies in the War of the Rebellion Series 1*, vol. 3: 758; Dalzell, *Flight From the Flag*, p. 163.

38. Ibid., pp. 258–9.

39. Semmes, *Memoirs*, p. 757; Stern, *The Confederate Navy*, p. 194.

40. Dalzell, *The Flight from the Flag*, p. 160; Bennett, *The Monitor and the Navy Under Steam*, p. 187; Porter, *Naval History of the Civil War*, pp. 653–4.

41. Sinclair, *Two Years*, p. 281.

42. Still, *Iron Afloat*, pp. 207–11; Duffy, *Lincoln's Admiral*, pp. 219–53.

43. Still, *Iron Afloat*, pp. 157–65.

44. *Civil War Naval Chronology, 1861–1865*, Vol. IV, pp. 124–6.

45. Dalzell, *Flight from the Flag*, pp. 231–6.

46. Paullin, *Paullin's History of Naval Administration*, p. 313.

47. Helmut Pemsel, 'William von Tegetthoff, Admiral of the Unexpected', in Sweetman, *Great Admirals*, pp. 286–91; Jack Greene and Alessandro Massignani, *Ironclads at War. The Origin and Development of the Ironclad Warship, 1865–1891* (Consholocken, PA, Combined Publishing, 1998), pp. 228–41; Sandler, *The Emergence of the Modern Capital Ship*, pp. 133–40.

48. Indeed, Lissa counted for so little that historian Geoffrey Wawro's only mention of it in his book *The Austro-Prussian War; Austria's War with Prussia and Italy in 1866* (Cambridge, Cambridge University Press, 1999) is a passing reference to 'Tegetthoff – the victor of Lissa'.

49. Greene and Massignani, *Ironclads at War*, pp. 244–5.

50. Henri Darrieus and Jean Quéguiner, *Historique de la Marine française (1815–1918)* (Saint–Malo, L'Ancre de Marine, 1997), p. 70.

6. THE PERIOD OF EXPERIMENTATION, 1865–90

1. Padfield, *The Battleship Era*, p. 46.

2. Arthur Hawkey, *Black Night off Finisterre. The Tragic Tale of an Early British Ironclad* (Annapolis, MD, The Naval Institute Press, 1999), pp. 24–5.

3. Padfield, *Guns at Sea*, 1818; Peter Padfield, *The Battleship Era* (New York, David McKay, 1972), pp. 44–5; Oscar Parkes, *British Battleships: Warrior 1860 to Vanguard 1950: A History of Design, Construction, and Armament* (Hamden, Conn, Archon Books, 1971), pp. 44–5.

4. Hawkey, *Black Night off Finisterre*, p. 28.

5. Ibid., p. 40.

6. Lambert, *Steam, Steel, and Shellfire*, p. 79; Colledge, *Ships of the Royal Navy*, p. 273.

7. Silverstone, *Warships of the Civil War Navies*, p. 6.

8. George, *History of Warships*, p. 71.

9. Stanley Sandler, *The Emergence of the Modern Capital Ship* (Newark, DE, University of Delaware Press, 1979), pp. 25–6; Robertson, *The Evolution of Naval Armament*, p. 272.

10. Richard Hough, *Fighting Ships* (New York, G. P. Putnam's Sons, 1969), p. 231.

11. Crawford, *Battleships and Carriers*, p. 284.

12. Padfield, *The Battleship Era*, pp. 48–9; Colledge, *Ships of the Royal Navy*, pp. 231, 297.

13. Padfield, *Battleship Era*, pp. 48–9.

14. Sandler, *The Emergence of the Modern Capital Ship*, p. 20.

15. Hawkey, *Black Night off Finisterre*, p. 138.

16. Lambert, *Steel, Steam, and Shellfire*, pp. 79–80; Colledge, *Ships of the Royal Navy*, p. 72; for an excellent short summary of the *Captain*, see Sandler, *The Emergence of the Modern Capital Ship*, pp. 204–33.

17. Hawkey, *Black Night off Finisterre*, pp. 173–4.

18. Robertson, *The Evolution of Naval Armament*, p. 282.

19. Perlmutter, *War Machines Sea*, pp. 74–6; Hawkey, *Black Night off Finisterre*, pp. 73–4; Padfield, *Battleship Era*, p. 53.

20. Padfield, *Guns at Sea*, pp. 204–5.

21. Perlmutter, *War Machines Sea*, pp. 74–6; Steve Crawford, *Battleships and Carriers* (New York, Barnes and Noble, 1999), p. 95; Colledge, *Ships of the Royal Navy*, pp. 106, 349.

22. Hawkey, *Black Night off Finisterre*, p. 175; Robertson, *Evolution of Naval Armament*, p. 284.

23. Crawford, *Battleships and Carriers*, pp. 102, 113; Hough, *Fighting Ships*, 2, pp. 31–2.

24. Lambert, *Steam, Steel, and Shellfire*, pp. 86–7; Crawford, *Battleships and Carriers*, p. 184.

25. Lambert, *Steam, Steel, and Shellfire*, pp. 86, 96; Colledge, *Ships of the Royal Navy*, pp. 24–5.

26. Ropp, *The Development of a Modern Navy*, p. 92.

27. Ibid., pp. 92–4.

28. Crawford, *Battleships and Carriers*, p. 128; Ropp, *The Development of a Modern Fleet*, pp. 95–6.

29. Crawford, *Battleships and Carriers*, p. 190.

30. George, *History of Warships*, p. 74; Crawford, *Battleships and Carriers*, p. 71.

31. Dimensions are from Colledge, *Ships of the Royal Navy*, p. 353; the rest is from Hawkey, *Black Night off Finisterre*, pp. 175–6.

32. Sandler, *The Emergence of the Modern Capital Ship*, p. 72; George, *History of Warships*, p. 74.

33. Robertson, *Evolution of Naval Armament*, p. 290.

34. Quoted in Ropp, *Development of a Modern Navy*, p. 19.

35. Ibid., p. 20.

36. Ibid., p. 21.

37. Jenkins, *A History of the French Navy*, p. 307.

38. George, *History of Warships*, p. 112; Silverstone, *Warships of the Civil War Navies*, p. 32; Colledge, *Ships of the Royal Navy*, p. 178.

39. George, *History of Warships*, p. 112; Colledge, *Ships of the Royal Navy*, p. 315.

40. George, *History of Warships*, p. 113; Colledge, *Ships of the Royal Navy*, pp. 177, 199.

41. George, *History of Warships*, pp. 112–13; Colledge, *Ships of the Royal Navy*, p. 250; Lambert, *Steam, Steel, and Shellfire*, pp. 105–10.

42. Lambert, *Steam, Steel, and Shellfire*, pp. 89–90; George, *History of Warships*, p. 75; Colledge, *Ships of the Royal Navy*, pp. 181, 226.

43. Perlmutter, *War Machines Sea*, pp. 84–5.

44. George, *History of Warships*, p. 75.

45. Hogg and Batchelor, *Naval Gun*, pp. 75–6.

46. Ibid., p. 76; Lambert, *Steam, Steel, and Shellfire*, p. 98.

47. Robertson, *Evolution of Naval Armament*, pp. 208–9, 291; George, *History of Warships*, pp. 75–6; Lambert, *Steam, Steel, and Shellfire*, p. 98.

48. Padfield, *Guns at Sea*, pp. 175, 194, 197; Ropp, *The Development of a Modern Navy*, p. 94.

49. Lambert, *Steam, Steel, and Shellfire*, p. 162; Ropp, *Development of a Modern Navy*, p. 96.

50. Tucker, *Arming the Fleet*, p. 23; Hogg and Batchelor, *Naval Gun*, p. 78.

51. Padfield, *Guns at Sea*, pp. 194–5.

52. Hogg and Batchelor, *Naval Gun*, p. 912.

53. Ibid., pp. 94–5; Lambert, *Steam, Steel, and Shellfire*, p. 164.

54. Lambert, *Steam, Steel, and Shellfire*, p. 164; Brodie, *Sea Power in the Machine Age*, p. 225; Hogg and Batchelor, *Naval Gun*, pp. 94, 97, 100.

7. MINES, TORPEDOES, TORPEDO BOATS AND SUBMARINES

1. R.B. Bradford, *History of Torpedo Warfare* (Newport, RI, U.S. Torpedo Station, 1882), p. 3.
2. Nathan Miller, *Sea of Glory; The Continental Navy Fights for Independence, 1775–1783* (New York, David McKay, 1974), p. 164; Philip K. Lundeberg, *Samuel Colt's Submarine Battery. The Secret and the Enigma* (Washington, DC, Smithsonian Institution Press, 1974), pp. 2–3; Gregory K. Hartman with Scott C. Truver, *Weapons that Wait. Mine Warfare in the U.S. Navy* (Annapolis, MD, Naval Institute Press, 1991), pp. 17–19; Alex Roland, *Underwater Warfare in the Age of Sail* (Bloomington, IN, and London, Indiana University Press, 1978), p. 83.
3. Schom, *Trafalgar*, p. 87.
4. Wallace S. Hutcheon, Jr, *Robert Fulton, Pioneer of Undersea Warfare* (Annapolis, MD, Naval Institute Press, 1981), pp. 62–92. The quote is on page 87.
5. Hartman and Truver, *Weapons that Wait*, pp. 28–9.
6. Roland, *Underwater Warfare in the Age of Sail*, p. 121.
7. Lundeberg, *Samuel Colt's Submarine Battery*, p. 3; Hartman and Truver, *Weapons that Wait*, pp. 27–8; Roland, *Underwater Warfare in the Age of Sail*, pp. 129–30.
8. What remained of the *Cairo* was raised in 1965. Today it is exhibited at the Vicksburg battlefield site.
9. *Civil War Chronology*, Vol. V, p. 16.
10. Ibid., Vol. IV, p. 56.
11. Bradford, *History of Torpedo Warfare*, pp. 46–7; for a list of Union ships destroyed see Milton F. Perry, *Infernal Machines: The Story of Confederate Submarine and Mine Warfare* (Baton Rouge, LA: Louisiana State University Press, 1965), pp. 199–201.

12. Edwyn Gray, *The Devil's Device. Robert Whitehead and the History of the Torpedo* rev. ed. (Annapolis, MD, Naval Institute Press, 1991), pp. 75–7.
13. Perlmutter, *War Machines Sea*, pp. 77–8.
14. Hartman and Truver, *Weapons that Wait*, pp. 38–40.
15. Ibid., p. 43.
16. See Spencer C. Tucker, *The Great War, 1914–18* (London, UCL Press, 1998), pp. 77–86.
17. Tamara Moser Melia, *'Damn the Torpedoes'. A Short History of U.S. Naval Mine Countermeasures, 1777–1991* (Annapolis, MD, Department of the Navy, Naval Historical Center, 1991), p. 33.
18. *Musée de la Marine*, p. 56.
19. Gray, *The Devil's Device*, p. 58.
20. Drew Middleton, *Submarine. The Ultimate Naval Weapon – Its Past, Present & Future* (New York, Playboy Press, 1976), p. 25; Anthony Preston, *Destroyers* (London, Bison Books, 1977), p. 6; Gray claims that the Austrian government, strapped by its effort in the 1866 war against Prussia and Italy, declined to buy the exclusive rights to the invention. Gray, *The Devil's Device*, p. 58.
21. Haws and Hurst, *The Maritime History of the World*, Vol. II, p. 55.
22. Perlmutter, *War Machines Sea*, pp. 78–80.
23. Eric Grove, *Big Fleet Actions: Tsushima, Jutland, Philippine Sea* (London: Arms and Armour Press, 1995), p. 49.
24. Haws and Hurst, *Maritime History of the World*, Vol. II, p. 62.
25. Jenkins, *A History of the French Navy*, p. 306.
26. Colledge, *Ships of the Royal Navy*, pp. 338, 367; Permutter, *War Machines Sea*, p. 82; Preston, *Destroyers*, p. 6.
27. Anthony Preston, *Destroyers* (Englewood Cliffs, NJ, Prentice–Hall, 1977), p. 9.
28. Theodore Ropp, *The Development of a Modern Navy. French Naval Policy, 1871–1904* ed. Stephen S. Roberts (Annapolis, MD, Naval Institute Press, 1987), p. 236.
29. Lambert, *Steam, Steel, and Shellfire*, p. 92; George, *History of Warships*, p. 135; Colledge, *Ships of the Royal Navy*, p. 268, 284, 336.

30. Middleton, *Submarine*, p. 5.
31. Roland, *Underwater Warfare in the Age of Sail*, pp. 69–82; Miller, *Sea of Glory*, pp. 159–64.
32. Hutcheson, *Robert Fulton*, pp. 31–49.
33. Ibid., p. 49.
34. Ibid., pp. 49–53.
35. Roland, *Underwater Warfare in the Age of Sail*, p. 121.
36. Lambert, *Steam, Steel, and Shellfire*, pp. 148–9.
37. *Civil War Chronology*, Vol. III, pp. 34, 125–6, 128, 134; Vol. VI, p. 5; Ragan, *Union and Confederate Submarine Warfare*, pp. 113–203. The *H.L. Hunley* has been located and plans are underway to raise her.
38. Ragan, *Union and Submarine Warfare in the Civil War*, pp. 132–3.
39. *Musée de la Marine*, p. 52.
40. Jenkins, *A History of the French Navy*, p. 299.
41. Richard Compton-Hall, *Submarine boats, the beginnings of underwater warfare* (London, Conway Maritime Press, 1983), pp. 46–53, 63–71; Middleton, *Submarine*, pp. 22, 25–6.
42. Haws and Hurst, *Maritime History of the World*, Vol. II, p. 60, Perlmutter, *War Machines Sea*, p. 89; George, *History of Warships*, p. 156.
43. Perlmutter, *War Machines Sea*, p. 92; Middleton, *Submarine*, p. 23; George, *History of Warships*, p. 156, claims Pearl's submarine was the first to run on batteries.
44. Compton-Hall, *Submarine boats*, p. 87; *Musée de la Marine*, p. 53.
45. *Musée de la Marine*, p. 53; Compton-Hall, Submarine boats, pp. 89–90.
46. Middleton, Submarine, 24; Compton-Hall, *Submarine boats*, p. 43.
47. Compton-Hall, *Submarine boats*, pp. 95–100, 114; Tom McGoonan, 'The Navy's First Submarine USS *Holland*', *Nautical Research Journal* (Vol. 44, no. 3, September 1999) pp. 131–3.
48. Ibid., pp. 103–9.
49. George, *History of Warships*, p. 158; Compton-Hall, *Submarine boats*, pp. 167–79.
50. Perlmutter, *War Machines Sea*, pp. 92–4.
51. George, *History of Warships*, p. 157.
52. Holger H. Herwig, *'Luxury' Fleet. The Imperial German Navy, 1888–1918* (London, George Allen & Unwin, 1980), p. 218; George, *History of Warships*, p. 159; Middleton, *Submarine*, pp. 30–2.
53. Hough, *Fighting Ships*, pp. 245–6.
54. Compton-Hall, *Submarine boats*, p. 26–7; pp. 112–25, 150; George, *History of Warships*, pp. 157–8.
55. Sweetman, *Great Admirals*, p. 355.
56. Paul G. Halpern, *A Naval History of World War I* (Annapolis, MD, Naval Institute Press, 1994), p. 8; George, *History of Warships*, p. 159.
57. For discussion of early submarines see Gardinier, *Steam, Steel & Shellfire*, pp. 147–57; Randal Gray with Christopher Argyle, *Chronicle of the First World War, Vol. I: 1914–1916* (Oxford and New York, Facts on File, 1990), pp. 19, 33, 41.

8. THE PRE-*DREADNOUGHT* ERA, 1890–1906

1. Holger Herwig, *'Luxury' Fleet. The Imperial German Navy, 1888–1918* (London, George Allen & Unwin, 1980), p. 350.
2. Ibid., p. 40.
3. Ibid., pp. 38, 42.
4. Ibid., p. 40.
5. Ibid., p. 42.
6. Peter Padfield, *The Great Naval Race. Anglo-German Naval Rivalry, 1900–1914* (New York, David McKay, 1974), p. 82.
7. Herwig, *'Luxury' Fleet*, p. 35.
8. Ibid., p. 19.
9. Padfield, *Great Naval Race*, p. 93; Herwig, *'Luxury' Fleet*, p. 36.
10. Herwig, *'Luxury' Fleet*, p. 37.
11. Ibid., pp. 38–9.
12. Ibid., p. 37.
13. Ibid., pp. 38–9.
14. Hawkey, *Black Night off Finisterre*, p. 177.
15. Crawford, *Battleships and Carriers*, p. 274; characteristics and armament is from Hawkey, *Black Night off Finisterre*, p. 178.

16. Hawkey, *Black Night off Finisterre*, p. 180; characteristics are from Crawford, *Battleships and Carriers*, p. 222.

17. George, *History of Warships*, pp. 89–90; Colledge, *Ships of the Royal Navy*, pp. 72, 115, 139, 192, 207.

18. Crawford, *Battleships and Carriers*, p. 197.

19. Ibid., p. 48.

20. Ropp, *Development of a Modern Navy*, pp. 222–3; Lambert, *Steam, Steel, Shellfire*, pp. 118–19.

21. Lambert, *Steam, Steel, and Shellfire*, p. 120; Eric Grove, *Big Fleet Actions: Tsushima, Jutland, Philippine Sea* (London, Arms and Armour, 1995), pp. 11–14.

22. Ivan Musicant, *U.S. Armored Cruisers, a Design and Operational History* (Annapolis, MD, Naval Institute Press, 1985), p. 3; Canney, *Frigates, Sloops, and Gunboats*, p. 145.

23. Musicant, *U.S. Armored Cruisers*, p. 7; Robert G. Albion, 'George M. Robeson', in Paolo E. Coletta, ed. *American Secretaries of the Navy* (Annapolis, MD, Naval Institute Press, 1980), Vol. I, pp. 372–7.

24. Norman Friedman, *U.S. Battleships, An Illustrated Design History* (Annapolis, MD, Naval Institute Press, 1985), p. 17.

25. Crawford, *Battleships and Carriers*, p. 290; Friedman, *U.S. Battleships*, pp. 424–5.

26. Friedman, *U.S. Battleships*, pp. 21, 424.

27. Ibid., pp. 426–7.

28. Ibid., p. 428.

29. Hawkey, *Black Night off Finisterre*, pp. 178–9.

30. Ibid., p. 179–80.

31. George, *History of Warships*, pp. 113–14; Colledge, *Ships of the Royal Navy*, pp. 35, 119, 227, 230, 259.

32. George, *History of Warships*, p. 114; *Jane's Fighting Ships of World War I*, pp. 111–12; Hough, *Fighting Ships*, p. 252.

33. George, *History of Warships*, pp. 114–15; Hough, *Fighting Ships*, p. 252; *Jane's Fighting Ships of World War I*, pp. 188, 209.

34. Musicant, *U.S. Armored Cruisers*, pp. 15–43.

35. Ibid., pp. 45–210.

36. *Jane's Fighting Ships of World War I*, pp. 139–41; George, *Fighting Warships*, p. 115.

37. George, *History of Warships*, p. 115.

38. Hough, *Fighting Ships*, pp. 251–2, 254; Colledge, *Ships of the Royal Navy*, pp. 37, 95; *Jane's Fighting Ships of World War I*, pp. 111–12.

39. Preston, *Destroyers*, pp. 8–9; Colledge, *Ships of the Royal Navy*, pp. 268, 284, 336.

40. Preston, *Destroyers*, p. 11; Perlmutter, *War Machines Sea*, pp. 84–6; *Jane's Fighting Ships of World War I*, p. 76.

41. Preston, *Destroyers*, p. 12; Ropp, *Development of a Modern Navy*, p. 284; *Jane's Fighting Ships of World War I*, p. 196.

42. Preston, *Destroyers*, p. 13; Sweetman, *Great Admirals*, p. 349.

43. Hough, *Fighting Ships*, p. 239; Colledge, *Ships of the Royal Navy*, p. 371; Perlmutter, *War Machines Sea*, p. 86; *Jane's Fighting Ships of World War I*, p. 197.

44. George, *History of Warships*, p. 136.

45. William Schofield, *Destroyers – 60 Years* (New York, Bonanza Books, 1962), p. 24; Friedman, *U.S. Destroyers*, pp. 428, 455.

46. *Jane's Fighting Ships of World War I*, p. 148; Norman Friedman, *U.S. Destroyers, An Illustrated Design History* (Annapolis, MD, Naval Institute Press, 1982), p. 19.

47. George, *History of Warships*, p. 75.

48. Padfield, *The Battleship Era*, pp. 148–9.

49. Hogg and Batchelor, *Naval Gun*, p. 101.

50. Ibid., pp. 103–4.

51. Ibid., p. 104.

52. Hawkey, *Black Night off Finisterre*, p. 186.

53. Hogg and Batchelor, *Naval Gun*, pp. 104–5.

54. Greene and Massignani, *Ironclads at War*, p. 221.

55. Sweetman, *Great Admirals*, p. 302.

9. THE *DREADNOUGHT* ERA, 1906–14

1. Grove, *Big Fleet Actions*, p. 47.

2. For a brief summary of the Fisher programme, see John Sumida, 'Fisher's

Naval Revolution', *Naval History*, Vol. X, no. 4 (August 1996), pp. 20–6.

3. Compton-Hall, *Submarine boats*, pp. 18–19.

4. Ibid., pp. 21–2. On Fisher's advocacy of submarine construction, see Compton-Hall, *Submarine boats*, pp. 22–7.

5. Noel F. Busch, *The Emperor's Sword. Japan vs. Russia in the Battle of Tsushima* (New York, Funk & Wagnalls, 1969), x.

6. George, *History of Warships*, p. 91.

7. David K. Brown, ed., *The Eclipse of the Big Gun. The Warship, 1906–45* (London, Conway Maritime Press, 1992), p. 15.

8. Ibid.; *Jane's Fighting Ships of World War I*, p. 41; Oscar Parkes, *British Battleships Warrior (1860) to Vanguard (1950): A History of Design, Construction, and Armament* (London, Seeley Service, 1970), p. 477.

9. George, *History of Warships*, p. 92.

10. Colledge, *Ships of the Royal Navy*, pp. 51, 239, 303.

11. Hough, *Fighting Ships*, p. 269.

12. *Jane's Fighting Ships of World War I*, pp. 35–9.

13. Ibid., p. 35.

14. *Jane's Fighting Ships of World War I*, pp. 105–6; Crawford, *Battleships and Carriers*, p. 196.

15. Alfred von Tirpitz, *My Memoirs* (London, 1919), quoted in Hough, *Fighting Ships*, p. 270.

16. *Jane's Fighting Ships of World War I*, p. 104.

17. Friedman, *U.S. Battleships*, pp. 51–7.

18. Ibid., p. 93. *Jane's Fighting Ships of World War I*, pp. 133–5.

19. *Jane's Fighting Ships of World War I*, pp. 183–4.

20. Most writers list these as battleships, which I have done here; *Jane's Fighting Ships of World War I*, however, lists them as battle-cruisers. See p. 235.

21. *Jane's Fighting Ships of World War I*, pp. 206–07.

22. Hough, *Fighting Ships*, p. 272; *Jane's Fighting Ships of World War I*, pp. 164–5.

23. Grove, *Big Fleet Actions*, p. 48.

24. Sumida, 'Fisher's Naval Revolution,' p. 25.

25. *Jane's Fighting Ships of World War I*, p. 45; Colledge, *Ships of the Royal Navy*, p. 181.

26. Brown, ed., *The Eclipse of the Big Gun*, p. 15–17; *Jane's Fighting Ships of World War I*, p. 45; Sumida, 'Fisher's Naval Revolution', p. 24.

27. Sumida, 'Fisher's Naval Revolution', p. 24.

28. *Jane's Fighting Ships of World War I*, p. 44.

29. Ibid., pp. 43–4.

30. Sumida, 'Fisher's Naval Revolution', p. 24.

31. Randall J. Metscher, 'Falklands, Battle of', in Spencer C. Tucker, ed., *The European Powers in the First World War* (New York: Garland, 1996), pp. 246–7.

32. *Jane's Fighting Ships of World War I*, p. 108.

33. Ibid., p. 108; on the *Goeben*, see Dan van der Vat, *The Ship that Changed the World. The Escape of the Goeben to the Dardanelles in 1914* (Bethesda, MD, Adler and Adler, 1986).

34. *Jane's Fighting Ships of World War I*, pp. 107–8.

35. Brown, ed., *Eclipse of the Big Gun*, p. 21; *Jane's Fighting Ships of World War I*, pp. 165–7.

36. George, *History of Warships*, p. 16; *Jane's Fighting Ships of World War I*, p. 170.

37. Hough, *Fighting Ships*, pp. 252–4; *Jane's Fighting Ships of World War I*, pp. 59–62.

38. George, *History of Warships*, p. 114.

39. Malcolm Muir, Jr., 'Dogger Bank, Battle of', *The European Powers in the First World War*, pp. 220–1; *Jane's Fighting Ships of World War I*, pp. 110, 114.

40. George, *History of Warships* 115; Hough, *Fighting Ships*, pp. 245–55; *Jane's Fighting Ships of World War I*, pp. 61, 113, 141.

41. Hough, *Fighting Ships*, pp. 254–5; *Jane's Fighting Ships of World War I*, pp. 61, 113.

42. Preston, *Destroyers*, p. 17.

43. *Jane's Fighting Ships of World War I*, pp. 72–6.

44. Ibid., pp. 117–18.

45. Hough, *Fighting Ships*, p. 241; George, *History of Warships*, pp. 137–9; *Jane's Fighting Ships of World War I*, pp. 146–8, 194–7, 240.

46. Ibid., p. 8.

47. Hogg and Batchelor, *Naval Gun*, p. 108.

48. Padfield, *Guns at Sea*, pp. 211–12, 218, 220.

49. Hogg and Batchelor, *Naval Gun*, p. 110; Padfield, *Guns at Sea*, pp. 211–18.

50. Robert L. O'Connell, *Sacred Vessels: The Cult*

of the Battleship and the Rise of the U.S Navy (New York, Oxford University Press, 1991), pp. 118–19.

51. Brodie, *Seapower in the Machine Age*, pp. 231–2; Padfield, *Guns at Sea*, pp. 245– 54.

52. Scott, *Big Fleet Actions*, pp. 49–50; Sweetman, *Great Admirals*, pp. 352–4; Brown, *The Eclipse of the Big Gun*, p. 14.

53. A. Marder, *From the Dreadnought to Scapa Flow*, (Oxford, 1962), Vol. I, p. 334; quoted in Grove, *Big Fleet Actions*, p. 50.

54. Commander John Irving, *The Smoke Screen of Jutland* (New York, 1967), p. 143.

55. Winston S. Churchill, *The World Crisis* (6 vols; New York, 1923–31), Vol. II, p. 106.

56. Theodore Roscoe, *On the Seas and in the Skies. A History of the U.S. Navy's Air Power* (New York, 1970), pp. 27–31; Ivan Musicant, *U.S. Armored Cruisers, A Design and Operational History* (Annapolis, MD, Naval Institute Press, 1985), p. 126.

57. Richard R. Muller, 'Zeppelins', in *The European Powers in the First World War, An Encyclopedia*, pp. 765–7.

58. Grove, *Big Fleet Actions*, p. 51; Sweetman, *Great Admirals*, p. 357.

59. Sweetman, *Great Admirals*, pp. 300–1.

10. NAVAL WARFARE IN THE LATE 19TH AND EARLY 20TH CENTURIES

1. Greene and Massignani, *Ironclads at War*, pp. 269–318; Sandler, *The Emergence of the Modern Capital Ship*, p. 94.

2. Greene and Massignani, *Ironclads at War*, pp. 319–21.

3. Figures on ships involved and lost vary widely according to the source. Dupuy and Dupuy. *The Harper Encyclopedia of Military History*, p. 947; Anthony Bruce and William Cogar, *An Encyclopedia of Naval History* (New York, Facts on File, 1998), p. 408; Haws and Hurst, *The Maritime History of the World*, Vol. II, p. 72.

4. On this see Hyman G. Rickover, *How the Battleship Maine Was Destroyed* (Washington, DC, US Government Printing Office, 1976). Also see Michael Blow, *A Ship to Remember. The Maine and the Spanish American War* (New York, William Morrow, 1992).

5. G.J.A. O'Toole, *The Spanish War. An American Epic, 1898* (New York, W. W. Norton, 1984), pp. 181–9.

6. Ibid., pp. 209–16, 235–7, 328–8; Musicant, *U.S. Armored Cruisers*, pp. 34–7.

7. O'Toole, *The Spanish War*, p. 232.

8. Denis and Peggy Warner, *The Tide at Sunrise. A History of the Russo-Japanese War, 1904–1905* (New York, Charterhouse, 1974), pp. 187– 95.

9. Crawford, *Battleships and Carriers*, p. 226; Noel F. Busch, *The Emperor's Sword. Japan vs Russia in the Battle of Tsushima* (New York, Funk & Wagnalls, 1969), pp. x–xi.

10. Warners, *The Tide at Sunrise*, pp. 188, 196–203.

11. Ibid., pp. 324–36.

12. On this see Richard Hough, *The Fleet That Had To Die* (New York, Viking, 1958)

13. Grove, *Big Fleet Actions*, pp. 11–14.

14. Grove, *Big Fleet Actions*, pp. 11–12.

15. Warners, *The Tide At Sunrise*, pp. 402–26; 494–519. See also, Busch, *The Emperor's Sword*.

16. General Friedrich von Bernhardi, *Germany and the Next War*, trans. Allen H. Powles (New York, 1914), p. 152.

17. Naval strength figures are from George, *History of Warships*, pp. 99, 118, 139.

18. Samuel R. Williamson, Jr, *Austria-Hungary and the Origins of the First World War* (London, Macmillan, 1991), p. 51.

19. Richard Hough, *The Great War at Sea* (London, Oxford University Press, 1983), p. 55.

20. Paul G. Halpern, *A Naval History of World War I* (Annapolis, MD: Naval Institute Press, 1994), p. 9.

21. Eugene L. Rasor, 'Blockade, Naval of Germany', *European Powers*, pp. 134–5.

SELECTIVE BIBLIOGRAPHY

BOOKS

Ballard, G.A. *The Fighting Ship from 1860 to 1890*. London, The Society for Nautical Research, 1970.

Bennett, Frank M. *The Monitor and the Navy under Steam*, Boston, Houghton Mifflin, 1900.

Boudriot, Jean, *The History of the French Frigate, 1650–1850*, tr. David Roberts, Rotherfield, East Sussex, J. Boudriot, 1993.

——. *John Paul Jones and the Bonhomme Richard*. tr. David H. Roberts. Annapolis, MD, Naval Institute Press, 1987.

——. *Le Vaisseau de 74 Canons*. 4 vols, Grenoble, Editions des Quatres Seigneurs, 1973–77.

Bradford, R.B., *History of Torpedo Warfare*. Newport, RI: U.S. Torpedo Station, 1882.

Brodie, Bernard, *Sea Power in the Machine Age*, Princeton, NJ, Princeton University Press, 1941.

Brown, David K., *Before the Ironclad: the Development of Ship Design, Propulsion, and Armament in the Royal Navy, 1815–1860*, London, Conway Maritime Press, 1990.

——.*Paddle Warships: the Earliest Steam Powered Fighting Ships, 1815–1850*, London, Conway Maritime Press, 1993.

——, ed., *The Eclipse of the Big Gun. The Warship, 1906–45*. London, Conway Maritime Press, 1992.

——. *Warrior to Dreadnought: Warship Development, 1860–1905*, Annapolis, Naval Institute Press, 1997.

Burt, R.A., *French Battleships, 1876–1946*, London, Arms and Armour, 1990.

Busk, Hans, *The Navies of the World. Their Present State and Future Capabilities*, London, Routledge, Warnes, and Routledge, 1859.

Canney, Donald L., *The Old Steam Navy: Frigates, Sloops, and Gunboats, 1815–1885*, Annapolis, MD, Naval Institute Press, 1990.

——. *The Old Steam Navy: Ironclads, 1842–1885*, Annapolis, MD, Naval Institute Press, 1993.

Caruana, Adrian B., *The History of English Sea Ordnance, 1523–1875. Volume II: The Age of the System, 1715–1815*, Ashley Lodge, Rotherfield, East Sussex, Jean Boudriot Publications, 1997.

Clarke, B., *The Applicability of Steam to the Purposes of Naval Warfare Considered*, London, 1831.

Chapelle, Howard I., *The American Sailing Navy. The Ships and Their Development*, New York, W.W. Norton, 1949.

Colledge, J.J., *Ships of the Royal Navy. The Complete Record of all Fighting Ships of the Royal Navy from the Fifteenth Century to the Present*, Annapolis, MD, Naval Institute Press, 1987.

Compton-Hall, Richard, *Submarine Boats, The Beginnings of Underwater Warfare*, London, Conway Maritime Press, 1983.

Corbett, Julian S., *Fighting Instructions, 1530–1816*, London, Navy Records Society, 1905.

Crawford, Steve, *Battleships and Carriers*, London, Brown Packaging Books Ltd., 1999.

Dahlgren, John A., *Shells and Shell Guns*, Philadelphia, King and Baird, 1856.

Darrieus, Hernri and Jean Quéguiner, *Historique de la Marine française (1815–1918)*, Saint-Malo, L'Ancre de Marine, 1997.

Douglas, Lieut. General Sir Howard, *A Treatise on Naval Gunnery* 5th ed., rev., London, John Murray, 1860.

Dupuy, Trevor N., Curt Johnson, and David L. Bongard, *The Harper Encyclopedia of Military Biography*, Edison, NJ, Castle Books, 1995.

Eardley-Wilmot, S., *The Development of Navies during the Last Half Century*, London, Seeley and Co., 1892.

Evans, David C., *Kaigun: Strategy, Tactics, and Technology in the Imperial Japanese Navy, 1887–1941*, Annapolis, Naval Institute Press, 1997.

Friedman, Norman, *U.S. Battleships, An Illustrated Design History*, Annapolis, MD, Naval Institute Press, 1985.

——. *U.S. Destroyers, An Illustrated Design History*, Annapolis, MD, Naval Institute Press, 1982.

Gardiner, Robert, ed., *Conway's All the World's Fighting Ships, 1860–1905*, London, Conway Maritime Press, 1979.

——, ed., *Fleet Battle and Blockade: The French Revolutionary Wars, 1793–1797*, London, Chatham Publishing, 1996.

——, ed., *The Naval War of 1812*, London, Chatham Publishing, 1998.

——, ed., *The Line of Battle: the Sailing Warship, 1650–1840*, London, Conway Maritime Press, 1994.

George, James L., *History of Warships: From Ancient Times to the Twenty-First Century*, Annapolis, Naval Institute Press, 1998.

Goodwin, Peter, *The Construction and Fitting of the English Man of War, 1650–1850*, Annapolis, Naval Institute Press, 1987.

Greene, Jack and Alessandro Massignani. *Ironclads at War. The Origin and Development of the Armored Warship, 1854–1891*, Conshohocken, PA, Combined Publishing, 1998.

Groner, Erich, *German Warships, 1815–1945*, Annapolis, Naval Institute Press, 1990.

Harbron, John D., *Trafalgar and the Spanish Navy*, London, Conway Marine Press, 1988.

Harding, Richard, *Seapower and Naval Warfare, 1650–1830*, London, University College London Press, 1999.

Hartmann, Gregory K. with Scott C. Truver, *Weapons that Wait. Mine Warfare in the U.S. Navy*, Annapolis, Naval Institute Press, 1991.

Herwig, Holger H., *'Luxury' Fleet. The Imperial German Navy, 1888–1918*, London, George Allen & Unwin, 1980.

Hogg, Ian and John Batchelor, *Naval Gun*, Poole, Dorset, Blandford Press, 1978.

Honsinger, Vernon C., *History of Warships, 1860–1942*, Newport News, VA., Mariner's Museum, 1959.

Hough, Richard, *Fighting Ships*, London: George Rainbird, 1969.

Hovgaard, William, *A Modern History of Warships, Comprising a Discussion of Present Standpoint and Recent War Experiences, for the use of Students of Naval Construction, NavalConstructors, Naval Officers, and Others Interested in Naval Matters*, New York, Spon and Chamberlain, 1920.

Howarth, David, *Trafalgar. The Nelson Touch*, New York, Atheneum, 1969.

Howse, Derek, *Five Hundred Years of Nautical Science, 1400–1900*, London, National Maritime Museum, 1981

James, William, *The Naval History of Great Britain, 1793–1820,*
From the Declaration of War By France in 1793 to the Accession of George IV, 6 vols., London, Richard Bentley, 1859.

Jane's Fighting Ships of World War I, London, Jane's Publishing Co., 1919.

Jenkins, E.H., *A History of the French Navy. From its Beginnings to the Present Day*, Annapolis, MD, Naval Institute Press, 1973.

Keegan, John, *The Price of Admiralty. The Evolution of Naval Warfare*, New York, Viking, 1989.

Kennedy, Paul M., *The Rise and Fall of British Naval Mastery*, London, Allen Lane, 1976.

——. *The Rise of the Anglo-German Antagonism, 1860–1914*, London, Allen & Unwin, 1980.

King, J. W., *The Warships and the Navies of the World, 1880*. Reprint. Annapolis, MD, Naval Institute Press, 1982.

Lambert, Andrew D., *Battleships in Transition: the Creation of the Steam Battlefleet, 1815–1860*, London, Conway Maritime Press, 1984.

——. *The Crimean War: British Grand Strategy, 1853–1856*, Manchester, Manchester University Press, 1990.

——. *The Last Sailing Battlefleet: Maintaining Naval Mastery, 1815–1850*, London, Conway Maritime Press, 1991.

——. ed., *Steam, Steel, and Shellfire: the Steam Warship, 1815–1905*, London,Conway Maritime Press, 1992.

——. *Warrior. The World's First Ironclad, Then and Now*, Annapolis, MD, Naval Institute Press, 1987.

Lavery, Brian, *The Arming and Fitting of English Ships of War, 1600–1815*, Annapolis, MD, Naval Institute Press, 1987.

——. *The Line of Battle: The Sailing Warship, 1650–1840*, Annapolis, MD, Naval Institute Press, 1992.

——. *Nelson's Navy: The Ships, Men and Organisation, 1793–1815*, London, Conway Maritime Press, 1989.

——. *The Ship of the Line.* 2 vols, London, Conway Maritime Press, 1983–84.

Longridge, C. Nepean, *The Anatomy of Nelson's Ships*, Hemel Hempstead, Herts, Model and Allied Publications, 1955.

Lyon, David, *Steam, Steel, and Torpedoes. The Warship in the 19th Century*, London, Her Majesty' Stationery Office, 1980.

Mahan, Alfred Thayer, *The Influence of Sea Power upon the French Revolution and Empire, 1793–1812*, Boston, MA, Little, Brown and Co., 1890.

Marder, Arthur J., *The Anatomy of British Seapower: A History of British Naval Policy in the Pre-Dreadnought Era, 1880–1905*, New York, Octagon, 1940.

——. *From 'Dreadnought' to Scapa Flow: The Royal Navy in the Fisher Era, 1904–1919.* 5 vols, London, Oxford University Press, 1961–1970.

Marshall, Ian, *Armored Ships: the Ships, their Settings, and the Ascendency that they Sustained for Eighty Years*, Charlottesville, VA., Howell Press, 1993.

Meyer, Jean and Martine Acerra, *Histoire de la Marine Françaisedes origines à nos jours*, Rennes, Éditions Ouest-France, 1994.

Morriss, Roger, *Cockburn and the British Navy in Transition.Admiral Sir George Cockburn, 1772–1853*, Columbia, SC, University of South Carolina Press and Exeter, UK, University of Exeter Press, 1998.

Musicant, Ivan, *U.S. Armored Cruisers, A Design and Operational History*, Annapolis, MD, Naval Institute Press, 1985.

Olmstead, Edwin, Wayne Stark, and Spencer Tucker, *The Big Guns. Civil War Siege, Seacoast and Naval Cannon*, Alexandria Bay, NY and Bloomfield, Ont., Canada, Museum Restoration Service, 1997.

Ortzen, Len, *Fighting Ships in the Age of Steam*, London, A. Barker, 1978.

——. *Guns at Sea. The World's Great Naval Battles*, London, Weidenfeld and Nicolson, 1976.

Padfield, Peter, *The Battleship Era*, New York, David McKay, 1972.

——. *The Great Naval Race. Anglo-German Naval Rivalry, 1900–1914*, New York, David McKay, 1974.

——. *Guns at Sea*, New York, St Martin's Press, 1974.

Parkes, Oscar, *British Battleships: Warrior (1860) to Vanguard (1950): A History of Design, Construction, and Armament*, London, Steeley Service, 1970.

Parkinson, C. Northcote, *Britannia Rules: the Classic Age of Naval History, 1793–1815*, London, Weidenfeld and Nicolson, 1977; reprint Gloucestershire, Alan Sutton, 1994.

Pivka, Otto von, *Navies of the Napoleonic Era*, New York, Hippocrene Books, 1980.

Pope, D., *Decision at Trafalgar*, Philadelphia, J. B. Lippincott, 1959.

Preston, Anthony, *Destroyers*, London, Bison Books, 1977.

Rapp, Theodore, *The Development of a Modern Navy. French Naval Policy, 1871–1904*, Annapolis, MD, Naval Institute Press, 1987.

Rasor, Eugene L., *British Naval History Since 1815. A Guide to the Literature*, New York, Garland, 1990.

Rippon, P.M., *The Evolution of Engineering in the Royal Navy*, Turnbridge Wells, Kent, Spellmount Ltd., 1989.

Roberts, Stephen S., *The Introduction of Steam Technology in the French Navy, 1818–1852*, Chicago, University of Chicago Press, 1976.

Roberts, William H., *USS New Ironsides in the Civil War*, Annapolis, MD, Naval Institute Press, 1999.

Robertson, Frederick Leslie, *The Evolution of Naval Armament*, London, Constable, 1984.

Robinson, S. S. and Mary L., *A History of Naval Tactics, 1530 to 1930*, Annapolis, MD, Naval Institute Press, 1942.

Roland, Alex, *Underwater Warfare in the Age of Sail*, Bloomington, IN and London, Indiana University Press, 1978.

Ropp, Theodore, *The Development of a Modern Navy. French Naval Policy, 1871–1904*, ed. Stephen S. Roberts, Annapolis, MD, Naval Institute Press, 1987.

Sandler, Stanley, *The Emergence of the Modern Capital Ship*, Newark, DE, University of Delaware Press, 1979.

Schom, Alan, *Trafalgar. Countdown to a Battle, 1803–1805*, New York, Oxford University Press, 1990.

Silverstone, Paul H., *Warships of the Civil War Navies*, Annapolis, MD, Naval Institute Press, 1989.

Simmons, Thomas F., *Ideas as to the Effect of Heavy Ordnance Directed Against and Applied by Ships of War, Particularly with Reference to the Use of Hollow Shot and Loaded Shells. London*, P. Pickney, 1837.

Sumida, Jon Tetsuro, *In Defense of Naval Supremecy: Finance, Technology, and British Naval Policy, 1889–1914*, Boston, Unwin Hyman, 1989.

——. *The Pollen Papers: The Privately Circulated Works of Arthur Hungerford Pollen, 1901–1916*, Navy Records Society, London, Allen & Unwin, 1984.

Sweetman, Jack, ed. *The Great Admirals. Command at Sea, 1587–1945*, Annapolis, MD, Naval Institute Press, 1997.

Tomblin, Barbara B., *From Sail to Steam: the Development of Steam Technology in the United States Navy*, Rutgers, NJ, University of New Jersey Press, 1988.

Tucker, Spencer C., *Arming the Fleet. U.S. Navy Ordnance in the Muzzle-Loading Era*, Annapolis, Naval Institute Press, 1989.

——. and Frank T. Reuter, *Injured Honor: The Chesapeake-Leopard Affair, June 22, 1807*, Annapolis, MD, Naval Institute Press, 1996.

Tunstall, Brian, *Naval Warfare in the Age of Sail: The Evolution of Fighting Tactics, 1650–1815*, ed. Nicholas Tracy, London, Conway Maritime Press, 1990.

US Navy Department, Naval History Division, *Civil War Naval Chronology, 1861–1865*, Washington, DC, Government Printing Office, 1971.

Winton, John, *Warrior: the First and the Last* London, Maritime Books, 1987.

ARTICLES

Boudriot, Jean, 'L'Artillerie de Mer de la Marine Française, 1674–1856' *Neptunia*, Vols. LXXXIX–LXXXXV.

Denoix, L. and J.-N. Muracciole, 'Historique de l'Artillerie de la Marine des ses Origines à 1870,' *Mémorial de l'Artillerie française*, Vol. XXXVIII, nos. 2 and 3 (1964), pp. 271–359; 526–602.

Sandler, Stanley 'A Navy in Decay: Some Strategic Technological Results of Disarmament, 1865–69 in the U.S. Navy', *Military Affairs*, Vol. XXXV, no. 4 (December 1971), pp. 138–42.

Tucker, Spencer C., 'The Carronade', *Nautical Research Journal*, Vol. XXXII, no. 1 (March 1997), pp. 15–23.

——. 'The Explosion of the 'Peacemaker' aboard Sloop Princeton', *New Interpretations in Naval History: Selected Papers from the Eighth Naval History Symposium*, Annapolis, MD, Naval Institute Press, 1989. pp. 175–189.

——. 'The Stevens Battery', *The American Neptune* Vol. LI, no. 1 (Winter 1991), pp. 12–21.

——. 'U.S. Navy Steam Sloop *Princeton*', *The American Neptune*, Vol. XLIX (Spring 1989), pp. 96–113.

INDEX

Figures in **bold** denote illustrations

INDEX